Thomas Leland

The history of remarkable events in the kingdom of Ireland

Vol. 2

Thomas Leland

The history of remarkable events in the kingdom of Ireland
Vol. 2

ISBN/EAN: 9783337273422

Printed in Europe, USA, Canada, Australia, Japan

Cover: Foto ©ninafisch / pixelio.de

More available books at **www.hansebooks.com**

THE HISTORY

OF

REMARKABLE EVENTS

IN THE

KINGDOM OF IRELAND.

EXHIBITING THE VERY

EXTRAORDINARY TRANSACTIONS

OF

WENTWORTH Earl of Strafford; CHARLES the Firſt; OLIVER CROMWELL the Great; CHARLES the Second; JAMES the Second; BUTLER Earl of Ormond; King WILLIAM the Glorious Deliverer; and GEORGE WALKER, the Military Clergyman, and Governor of London Derry, who victoriouſly defended that City for 105 Days againſt a very large Army, and finally forced them to raiſe the Siege.

By *THOMAS LELAND*, D. D.

Senior Fellow of Trinity College, and Prebendary of St. Patrick's Dublin.

IN TWO VOLUMES.

VOLUME THE SECOND.

LONDON:

Printed for JAMES THUCYDIDES in the Strand.

M.DCC.LXXXI.

THE HISTORY OF IRELAND

FROM THE

INVASION OF HENRY II.

BOOK VI. CHAP. I.

State of Ireland on the departure of the marquis of Ormond.—Preston defeated at Dungan-hall.—Owen O'Nial called to the defence of Lienster.—Progress of lord Inchiquin.—Battle of Knocknoness.—General assembly at Kilkenny.—Intemperance of the nuncio.—Agents chosen for Rome and France.—Their instructions.—Answer of the queen and prince to the Irish agents.—Irish treat about a cessation with lord Inchiquin.—He revolts to the royalists.—The nuncio opposes the cessation.—It is concluded.—Excommunication pronounced on those who should support it.—Appeal against the excommunication.—O'Nial and the nuncio declare war against the supreme council.---The nuncio driven to Galway.—O'Nial treats with Jones.—Successes of Monk.—Antrim unites with O'Nial.—Their ill success.—Return of the agents from France.—The nuncio admonished to depart from the kingdom.—Arrival of the marquis of Ormond.—He commences a treaty of peace with the confederates.—Clamours of the clergy.—Treaty interrupted, renewed, and concluded.—Appointment of COMMISSIONERS OF TRUST.—*Charles executed.—His son proclaimed in Ireland.—Consternation and flight of the nuncio.—Various parties* and interests in Ireland.---Ormond practises with O'Nial, with Coote, and with Jones, but in vain. ---Difficulties and distresses of the marquis.---The king purposes to repair to Ireland.---Ormond takes the field.---Jones embarrassed.---O'Nial treats with Monk.---Preston's officers corrupted.---Ormond advances to Dublin.---Inchiquin marches to Drogheda.---His successes.---Coote relieved in Derry.---Succours arrive in Dublin.---Alarming intelligence. ---Lord Inchiquin detached to Munster.---Battle of Rathmines.---Effects of Ormond's defeat.---He conceives new hopes from a junction with Owen O'Nial. ---He relieves Drogheda.---Arrival of Oliver Cromwell.---Storm and massacre of Drogheda.---Progress of the parliamentarians in Ulster.---Ormond urges the king to repair to Ireland.---The design prevented.---Wexford strengthened.---Betrayed to Cromwell.---Ross surrendered.--Siege of Duncannon raised.---Ormond reinforced.---He resolves to engage Cromwell, who invests Waterford.---Perverseness of the citizens.---Their garrison reinforced.---Cromwell raises the siege.---Ormond prevented from attacking his rear.---The Munster garrisons revolt to Cromwell.---Consequence of this event.---The cities refuse to admit Ormond's garrisons.---Obstinacy and insolence of the citizens of Waterford. ---Ormond's forces dispersed.---His conduct maligned.---Assembly of bishops.---Their declaration.---County-agents at Kilkenny, alarmed at the approach of Cromwell.---He retires.---Again returns to Kilkenny, which is surrendered.---He marches to Clonmel.---Brave defence of Hugh O'Nial.---Attempt to relieve Clonmel,---defeated by lord Broghill.---Resolution of a bishop of Ross.---Clonmel surrendered.---Cromwell embarks for England.

IRELAND

IRELAND, on the departure of the marquis of Ormond[a], seemed reduced to its ancient state of anarchy and distraction[b]. Harrassed by different armies, different factions, various pretenders to power and authority, wasted by war[c], oppressed by poverty, the nation seemed ready to sink under its complicated miseries. In the capital colonel Michael Jones was appointed governour by the parliament, and commander of their forces in Leinster. The inhabitants, who had been habituated to the state and decorum of Ormond and his court, were shocked at the vulgar manners of this republican and his unpolished train, and provoked at his severity and reserve. Some weak attempts to restore discipline, only served to irritate a famished soldiery. They plundered the inhabitants; they insulted their officers; and Jones who could not supply their necessities, found it necessary to connive at their outrage. Three different armies of catholics were quatered in different stations. Owen O'Nial, and his barbarous followers, were equally enemies to the king and to the ruling powers of England; they professed an entire devotion to the pope and his nuncio. The army of Preston, and that of Munster, seemed at length convinced of the errour and obstinacy of their party, wished for the return of Ormond, and were inveterate enemies to the parliamentarians. The Scots of Ulster were offended at the late proceedings of England, and averse to the present government. In Munster, Lord Inchiquin was incensed at some attempts to remove him from his command, during the time that Lord Lisle resided in this province, with the insignificant title of the parliament's

[a] A. D. 1647. Carte. [b] Orm. Vol. II. [c] Borlase.

parliament's chief governour. On the same principle which had seduced him from the service of the king, he was now disposed to abandon his present masters. Such was the disunion both of catholics and protestants. And from this state of confusion we are now to deduce the affairs of Ireland, to the last conflict of its parties, and the complete and final reduction of the kingdom under the dominion of the crown of England.

Lord Digby, who still continued to reside near Dublin, was indefatigable in practising against the parliamentarians, and to affect the return of Ormond. His dependence was on the catholic armies of Munster and Leinster; and with their leaders he concerted his designs. The Munster army was now entrusted to the command of lord Taafe, with the consent of Muskerry, that he might have leisure to attend the supreme council, and support the interests of their party in this assembly. That of Preston was composed of seven thousand foot, and one thousand horse, ready for action; and, with this force, he advanced into the English quarters. Naas, and some other inconsiderable places, he soon reduced, and had the honour of repelling Jones in two skirmishes[d]. By investing Trim, he again called out this general; and, by the advice of Lord Digby, resolved to seize the advantage of his absence from the capital. The garrison was weak; many of the inhabitants disaffected to the parliament. By a forced march, Preston advanced towards Dublin, in full hope of suddenly surprizing it. Jones pursued with equal alacrity; and, at a place called Dungan-hill, the armies came to an engagement. The English general had been reinforced by some northern troops, so that

that his numbers were nearly equal to those of Preston. They rushed upon the enemy with an impetuous valour and enthusiastic hatred of the Irish; and, though they fought without regard to orders, or any settled scheme of attack, they soon gained a complete and bloody victory. As Jones could not improve this advantage from the want of provisions, he returned to Dublin, possessed of the enemy's arms, cannon, and baggage, with a number of prisoners, several of distinguished rank and consequence; while Preston fled to Carlow with his horse, and there collected the shattered remains of his infantry.

The nuncio, and his creatures, dreaded that this general, if possessed of Dublin, would resign it to Ormond, and invite the prince of Wales into Ireland, to the utter confusion of all their fantastical projects. They received the intelligence of his defeat with joy; and insisted on the necessity of recaling O'Nial from some petty hostilities which he carried on in Connaught, and entrusting him with the defence of Lienster. Preston had the mortification of receiving an order from the supreme council, to resign most of his remaining forces to his rivale. O'Nial derided the general who could be forced to an engagement against his will, and cautiously avoiding this errour, eluded every attempt of Jones to meet him in the field, although his depredations were extended even to the walls of Dublin.

The preservation of the Munster army commanded by lord Taafe, became now of greater consequence; and the general seemed determined against exposing it to any wanton hazard. Lord Inchiquin was obliged to act with vigour against the Irish, as well

e Carte, Orm. Vol. II. p. 5.

well to supply the necessities of his men, as to allay the suspicions of the ruling powers in England. He over-ran some counties, took several forts, and invested Cahir, an ancient castle, environed by two branches of the river Sure, strongly fortified, and difficult of access. No sooner had some of the outworks been gained, when the castle, which, in the reign of Elizabeth, had sustained the assaults of the earl of Essex and his whole army, for a considerable time, was, in a few hours, surrendered to lord Inchiquin. Thus, was a way opened for his famished troops to range freely over the fertile county of Tipperary. Without any opposition from Taafe, he continued his victorious progress, and advanced against the city of Cashel. The inhabitants fled to their cathedral church, seated on a rock well fortified, and provided with a strong garrison. Inchiquin proposed to leave them unmolested, on condition that they would advance him three thousand pounds, and a month's pay for his army. But, as this proposal was rashly rejected, he took the place by storm, with considerable slaughter both of the citizens and soldiery. Here he gained a prodigious booty; yet still insufficiently provided for continuing in the field, on the approach of winter he dispersed his army into garrisons.

In storming the rock of Cashel^f, about twenty ecclesiastics had fallen in the indiscriminate slaughter, an incident shocking to the nuncio, who inveighed against this sacrilegious cruelty, and clamoured for revenge. He imputed the inactivity of Taafe to some secret concert between this lord, Muskerry, and Inchiquin. To this traiterous desertion of the catholic cause he ascribed all the calamities of the faithful,
the

f Carte, Orm. Vol. II. p. 7.

the innocent blood shed before the holy altars, and every outrage and enormity of the heretical army. His whole party were on fire, and so violent and so popular were their clamours, that lord Taafe was obliged to take the field in November. Inchiquin collected his forces, and encountered him at a place called Knocknoness. The left wing of the Irish, commanded by lord Taafe, was quickly broken, nor could he stop the flight though he killed several of the fugitives with his own hand. On the right, an officer of the family of Mac-Donnel, famed in the Irish wars, and known by the name of Kolkitto, or the left-handed, commanded a gallant body of Highlanders, supported by two regiments of horse. After one discharge of musketry, the Highlanders, according to their custom, fell sword in hand upon the enemy, broke, pursued, slaughtered them, and seized their cannon and carriages. On the return of Inchiquin to the assistance of his left wing, they were abandoned by the cavalry, and by the fall of Kolkitto left without a commander g. Yet still they obstinately stood their ground, until seven hundred of their number were slaughtered; when the remains of this brave body laid down their arms, and accepted quarter. Thus was the victory of Inchiquin complete; more than three thousand Irish, the flower of their Munster army, were cut to pieces; six thousand arms, all their baggage and artillery, their general's tent and cabinet, thirty-eight colours and standards fell into the hands of the victor.

THESE repeated calamities had their full impression on the more temperate of the confederates. Several resolved to contend no longer with the pride and violence of the nuncio, and the outrages of
O'Nial

g Borlase.

O'Nial, but to abandon a cause so desperate, and a country so miserably wasted by war, and threatened with the extremity of famine. Lord Muskerry prevailed on them, with difficulty, to make one attempt more to give their country peace, and thus to avert its impending ruin. For this purpose, it was in the first place necessary to gain their party a superiority in the general assembly now summoned to Kilkenny, and they laboured so vigourously, and so successfully for this point, that the nuncio soon discovered the design of subverting his power, and resolved to counteract it. He had recommended eleven persons to Rome, to be made bishops. He prevailed on the supreme council, formed of his own creatures, to summon these ecclesiastics by writ to the assembly. The lawyers objected, that their bulls were not yet arrived, that they were not consecrated, nor invested with their temporalties. The nuncio, at first, threatened to consecrate them himself; but as the safer and more expeditious method, ordered them to take their seats directly. The assembly was intimidated, and acquiesced; and the nuncio, of consequence, grew more insolent. Ulster had usually sent sixty-three members to the genaral-assembly; nine only now attended from this province; he insisted, that as the war had prevented a full election, these nine should be allowed sixty-three voices, but the opposite party proved strong enough to reject this extravagant demand.

IN despite of all the opposition of Rinunccini[h], the assembly now declared almost unanimously for peace; and, for this purpose, resolved to send agents to the queen and prince in France, the only persons with whom they could commence a treaty. The nuncio

[h] Carte, Vol. II. p. 17.

ashamed of their superstitious fears. In his former sentence of excommunication, he had been supported by a considerable number of bishops; now only by four. The pretence for the first was, that no provision had been made for religion in the articles of peace. In the present treaty there were express provisions for the interests of the clergy, and the freedom of the catholic worship; and these seemed so favourable, that eight prelates retracted the protest formerly signed against the cessation, and recommended pacific measures to the nuncio. The supreme council ventured to appeal in form against his censures, in which they were supported by two archbishops, twelve bishops, all the secular clergy of their dioceses, by all the Jesuits and Carmelites, many of the Augustinians and Dominicans, above five hundred Franciscans, the most exemplary and intelligent of all those legions of ecclesiastics which overspread the nation.

Though the power of the nuncio was thus evidently on the decline, yet still he was supported by no inconsiderable party[r]. Those of the clergy who expected preferment from his favour, those of the laity who looked for the restoration of their paternal lands by the expulsion of the English and Scots, they who were oppressed by debts, and they who only subsisted by public commotions, all declared for desperate measures, and crowded to the standard of Owen O'Nial; who, though sworn to obey the orders of the confederates, yet acted as if the nuncio had absolved him from his oath, and solemnly denounced war against the supreme council and their adherents. Taafe, Preston, and Clanricarde, took vigourous measures for opposing him[s]. Their armies

[r] Belling Vindiciæ, cap. 12.   [s] Carte, Orm. Vol. II. p. 35.

mies were so formed, that the officers, to a man, despised the censures of the nuncio. Though it was in their power to have seized him and O'Nial as they lay at Maryborough, yet they industriously avoided all violent measures. They contented themselves with desiring that the nuncio should not trouble them with any letters or orders, as they were determined to obey those only of the supreme council; and a considerable force was detached to Kilkenny to support the authority of this assembly.

WAR being thus declared between the different parties of the confederates, O'Nial contrived to make a truce with the Ulster Scots, in order to be more at leisure to prosecute his operations. He collected his forces from Connaught and Ulster; but the nuncio had now no money to supply them. Their ravages were universally detested, and they soon found themselves unable to contend with the army of Preston, reinforced by some troops of Inchiquin and Taafe. Athlone, which had for some time been possessed by the nuncio's partizans, was besieged by Preston and the marquis of Clanricarde, reduced before O'Nial could arrive to its relief, and the nuncio driven from this city to Galway. Here he endeavoured to convene a synod of the clergy, in order to confirm his censures by their sanction. Clanricarde, by order of the supreme council, prevented them from assembling, invested the city, and obliged the inhabitants to proclaim the cessation, to pay a considerable sum of money, and utterly to renounce the nuncio and his adherents.

THIS prelate, still undismayed, issued his comminations in his own name, and by his own authority, since he could not collect the clergy, and declared those who favoured or adhered to the cessation to be guilty of mortal sin. Yet, notwithstanding these ridiculous censures of all those who presumed to treat with the heretics, his favourite, Owen O'Nial was permitted to make overtures of accommodation to Jones at Dublin, the inveterate enemy of the king, the confederates, and Roman Catholic religion. Jones had not been inattentive to the distractions of the Irish, but could not venture to take advantage of them, as he suspected the fidelity of his garrison, and was persuaded that numbers of his officers only waited for the arrival of Ormond to declare in favour of the king. To quiet his apprehensions, he boldly seized the most suspected, sent some to England, imprisoned others in the castle of Dublin, while Monk, to whom the parliament had entrusted the command of Ulster, made a bold irruption into this province, surprised Carricfergus, seized Monroe, and sent him prisoner to England, easily reduced Belfast and Colerain, and stationed his garrisons on the frontiers, to restrain the incursions of the Irish. Owen O'Nial, who, in effect, declared against the marquis of Ormond, was received with open arms by these triumphant independents. Jones readily consented to an accommodation with him, and permitted him to march unmolested through Leinster, in prosecution of his designs against the common enemy. Disappointed in his attempt to relieve Athlone, Owen now formed a bold design to surprize Kilkenny, and at once to seize the whole supreme council.

In this city, the capital of the Irish quarters, and chief seat of their government, there were not wanting a number of busy spirits, impatient for innovation, and zealous for the interest of the nuncio and O'Nial,

O'Nial, those champions of the church t. Of these, one Paul King, an ecclesiastic, engaged to form a party, and betray Kilkenny to O'Nial. No season could be more favourable to such design. The marquis of Antrim had lately returned from France, with all his hopes of being advanced to the government of Ireland utterly confounded. Provoked at this disappointment, he joined the party who opposed the cessation, and gave O'Nial the most magnificent assurances of support, by his interest in Ulster. This conjunction served to encrease the consequence of Owen, and to animate his partizans. On the other hand, the forces of his adversaries were dispersed. But the slow and cautious procedure of this general was not calculated for an enterprize of alacrity. The design on Kilkenny was discovered, and Inchiquin had already arrived to the assistance of the supreme council, when his forces were ravaging the country at some miles distance from this city.

O'Nial could now but continue his depredations, while Inchiquin and part of Preston's army advanced close upon him. Unable to contend with their united numbers, he craftily proposed an accommodation to lord Inchiquin, offering to leave Munster unmolested, provided that his operations in the other provinces were not opposed. Instead of accepting this proposition, Inchiquin endeavoured to force him to an engagement; but the wary Northern eluded all his attempts, and after some inconsiderable operations and successes gained on each side, at length found it necessary to retreat to Ulster.

Nor was the marquis of Antrim more successful in his attempts to oppose the cessation u. He had led

t Belling Vindiciæ, cap. 14.　u Carte, Orm. Vol. II. p. 42.

led a party of Scottish Highlanders into Ireland, reinforced them by some Irish partizans at Wexford, and seemed to grow to some degree of consequence and power, when his party was suddenly attacked by a detachment of the confederate forces, and defeated, with the slaughter of his brave Highlanders. The nuncio, dismayed at this accident, fled to O'Nial; but the vanity of Antrim was not abated; he addressed himself to Jones, he boasted his power in the Northern province, and promised the most important services against the Irish. Jones agreed to support him; O'Nial consented to serve under him; but his sanguine hopes and ostentatious engagements only served, as usual, to expose him to disgrace. His insignificance was soon discovered, and the command, rashly conferred upon him, was resumed by O'Nial.

In the mean time, a general assembly was convened at Kilkenny, composed almost entirely of those who wished for peace[x], and condemned the excesses of the nuncio. Muskerry and Browne arrived from France, and assured them, that the marquis of Ormond was speedily to follow, and to cooperate with them in restoring the public tranquillity. Encouraged by this intelligence, they proceeded with unusual vigour and resolution. They formally approved and ratified the cessation made by the supreme council. Provoked at the outrages of Owen O'Nial, and affecting the utmost horrour at his transactions with Jones, equally repugnant to loyalty and religion, they declared him a traitor by proclamation. Scarcely did they discover more tenderness to the nuncio. They renewed the appeal to Rome against his sentence of excommunication; and when Rinuccini contrived to have their messenger to the pope

[x] Belling Vindiciæ. Borlase.

pope secured, and his papers seized, this new outrage only served to enflame their resentments. All the catholics of Ireland, and particularly those of Galway, where his influence was greatest, were forbidden, under the severest penalties, to hold any intercourse or correspondence with him; at the same time he received a letter signed by the prolocutor of the assembly, exhorting him to depart from a kingdom so long harrassed by his factious turbulence, and to prepare his defence against those articles of accusation which the assembly had drawn up, and intended to exhibit to the pope, whose instructions he had neglected, and whose authority he had so notoriously disgraced.

Such was the situation of affairs, when the marquis of Ormond embarked y, at the repeated instances of lord Inchiquin, arrived at Cork, and was received with the respect due to a chief governour. The object of his enterprize was to unite the protestant and popish royalists, which in the present desperate situation of the king, seemed to be the only expedient left for averting his ruin. It was in the first place, necessary, to conciliate the Munster army commanded by Inchiquin. As he had been disappointed in his expectations from France, and the small sums of money he had been enabled to procure, were totally exhausted, he was obliged to recur to artifice and evasion to conceal his poverty; lavished his promises of an immediate supply; and particularly assured them, that the prince would send that part of the navy, which had revolted to him, to some port of Munster, to assist them with large quantites of corn, and to enrich the soldiery by continual prizes. These promises he enforced by

---

y Carte, Orm. Vol. II. p. 39.

by a declaration, addressed to all the protestants of Munster [z]. In the usual stile of such addresses, he apologized for his late surrender of Dublin; professed that in obedience to his majesty's commands, founded on observation of that integrity which the protestant army of this province had manifested, he was now returned for recovery of the king's rights; that he was resolved at the hazard of his life to oppose all rebels; and, particularly, to suppress the independent party: that all engaged in this cause should be treated with equal favour, and without any invidious distinction; and that his utmost diligence should be exerted to provide for their subsistence, and preservation from those hardships they had formerly experienced.

For the present, the army appeared satisfied; and the marquis was in the next place to treat with the general assembly at Kilkenny [a]. His authority as lord lieutenant, still subsisted, but his commission for concluding a peace with the confederates had determined upon the treaty made in the year sixteen hundred and forty-six. The queen and prince, indeed, had given him powers to treat; but, in a transaction which demanded the utmost caution and delicacy, he required immediate instructions from the king. Charles was, at this time, engaged in the treaty of Newport. Among his other concessions to the parliament commissioners, he agreed, that an act should pass, rescinding all cessations and treaties with the Irish, and investing the houses with a full power of prosecuting the war in Ireland. He instantly notified this incident to his lieutenant, at the same time directing him to take no notice of any of his public commands, during his present state of restraint,

[z] Cox, Append. No. xlii. [a] Carte, ut supra.

restraint, but to obey those of the queen. "Be not startled," said he, "at my great concessions concerning Ireland, for they will come to nothing." It is not here necessary to enter into a discussion of this conduct of the king, or to consider how far it may be defended by the nature of his negociations at Newport, in which the concessions on his part were but conditional, and to be valid only on the final conclusion of the whole treaty. Let it be sufficient to observe, that Ormond had now an additional authority, to satisfy the scruples of those who might object to the sufficiency of his powers from the queen and prince.

In full expectation of receiving such authority, he had notified to the general assembly, that, agreeably to their petition presented at Saint Germains, he was sent with power to conclude a peace, and that as little time might be lost as possible, he would expect their commissioners at his house at Carrick, about fourteen miles distant from Kilkenny. Their commissioners were appointed, to the utter mortification of the nuncio and his party. In the agonies of their expiring power, these ecclesiastics exclaimed outrageously against the impiety of betraying the holy church, and all her rights, and precipitating the conclusion of a pernicious treaty, without even waiting the return of their emissaries from Rome, who were daily expected with vast sums of money to support the catholic cause. Nor were such clamours without their effect. The assembly were the more careful to shew their attachment to the church. A bishop was appointed one of their commissioners; and he was admitted by the lord lieutenant, contrary to his former sentiments. Their demands relative to religion were extensive and explicit, and for twenty

nuncio dreaded such a deputation, as the first step to recalling Ormond, and inviting the prince of Wales to Ireland. He vehemently opposed it; he pressed the assembly to address themselves to Rome, and to implore the protection of the pope: and so far were his instances successful, that it was resolved to send deputations to Rome and Madrid, as well as to France; that those to Rome should depart first, and that the agents destined to France should there await their answer. The choice of these agents was a point of delicate discussion. The opposers of the nuncio laboured to have such persons nominated as were likely to obstruct their measures, if continued in the assembly. By their management, the popish bishop of Ferns, and Nicholas Plunket, two zealous enemies to peace, were appointed to repair to Rome. But when they proceeded to nominate Mac Mahon of Clogher to go to France, in conjunction with lord Muskerry and Geoffry Browne [i], this active partizan of the nuncio saw through their design, and positively and haughtily refused to obey the order of the assembly. This insult raised a considerable ferment; but so effectually was Mac Mahon supported by the nuncio, that it was soon found necessary to substitute the marquis of Antrim in his place.

The instructions to be given to these agents was a point in which the nuncio was particularly interested. He and his clergy had, in the fulness of their pride and folly, subscribed a declaration, that they never would consent that either the queen or prince should be invited into Ireland, until the pope's articles relative to religion were secured [k]; that any but a Roman catholic should ever be appointed chief governour; that the forts and armies of the confederates

[i] Carte, Orm, Vol. II. p. 19.   [k] Ibid. p. 18.

rates should ever be delivered to heretics, or that any peace should be concluded, which might lessen the present state and public exercise of their religion. They now contended, that the instructions of the agents destined to France, should be submitted to their inspection, and modelled agreeably to their declaration. The opposite party suffered these zealous churchmen to amuse themselves with framing the instructions, and inserting all their extravagant demands, as Muskerry and Browne had privately agreed to neglect them, and not to insist upon demands which had been already rejected, which must ever be rejected, or which tended to the subjection of their country to a foreign power, now the avowed design of the clergy and the old Irish*.

As the session of the assembly drew towards a conclusion, each party was solicitous about the choice of members of the supreme council. After some debates it was agreed, that the council should be formed equally of both parties. Lord Muskerry artfully suggested, that as the public affairs might call away several members from their attendance, it was necessary to appoint some supernumeraries to supply

---

* It was particularly avowed in a tract written by an Irish Jesuit, printed about this time, and privately dispersed through the nation. The positions of the author were, that the kings of England never had any right to Ireland; that supposing they once had, they had forfeited it by turning heretics, and neglecting the conditions of pope Adrian's grant; that the old Irish natives might by force of arms recover the lands and goods taken from their ancestors by usurpers of English and other foreign extraction, that they should kill not only all the protestants, but all the Roman Catholics of Ireland who supported the crown of England; and that they should chuse an Irish native for their king, and throw off at once the yoke both of heretics and foreigners.—The priest in whose custody this book was seized escaped punishment by the interest of the nuncio, who laboured to save the book from censure. But, to his utter mortification, it was condemned by the supreme council, and ordered to be burnt at Kilkenny by the common hangman. Carte, Orm. Vol. II. p. 17.

supply their places. His propofal was haftily embraced; and, among thefe occafional counfellors, he contrived to introduce forty eight of his own partizans, to the utter confufion of the nuncio.

In the mean time, the agents proceeded in their voyage to France, arrived at Saint Germains, and were gracioufly received by the queen and prince [l]. Notwithftanding her majefty's partiality to the marquis of Antrim, fhe foon learned that her attention was to be given principally to lord Mufkerry and Geoffry Browne, as men of more real confequence and power. She conferred with them in private; they produced fecret inftructions, figned by Prefton and lord Taafe, whereby they were directed to affure her of the unfhaken loyalty of their party, and their unalterable adherence to the king's caufe, in defpite of thofe who laboured to introduce a foreign jurifdiction into Ireland; to entreat the countenance and affiftance of her majefty and the prince; and to propofe, as the meafure moft effectual for fupporting the royal authority, that the prince fhould come over with arms and money, condefcend to the requefts of moderate and well affected fubjects, and take them under his command. Having thus executed their private commiffion, they attended Antrim to a public audience, and prefented the propofitions dictated by the clergy, as the mere form and ceremonial of their office.

In thefe tranfactions the queen found an able and ufeful affiftant in the marquis of Ormond [m]. On his departure from Ireland, this lord had been permitted to prefent himfelf before the king at Hampton-Court, and was received with the affection due to his fervices:

---

l Carte, Orm. Vol. II. p. 20.   m Ibid. p. 11.

services. When he tendered his commission for the lieutenancy of Ireland to the king, lamenting that it had succeeded so unhappily, Charles refused to receive it, and generously replied, that the marquis alone should use it hereafter, and, he trusted, with better success. The king consulted him with the utmost confidence, and when the jealousies of the army forced the marquis to return to London, directed him to confer with the Scotch commissioners, and concert measures for engaging Scotland and Ireland in his service. The retreat of Charles to the Isle of Wight retarded his secret negociations but could not damp his zeal. The committee of Derby-house were alarmed; they required him to engage not to take any measures disserviceable to the parliament; they sought pretexts for seizing him: he was assured that a warrant had issued for this purpose, and instantly resolved to escape to France, whither he was soon followed by his eldest son, lord Ossory.

By advice of the marquis, the queen and prince returned a general and gracious answer to the Irish agents[n]. They gently condemned the violation of the late peace, but expressed their satisfaction that the confederates seemed at length to discern their true interest. They observed, that the agents were not yet ready to propose their particular desires with respect to religion, nor empowered to conclude finally on other points of moment, which might require particular discussion and alteration. In these circumstances, they were assured, that the queen and prince would take the only part that could be reasonably expected; that a person should be speedily sent into Ireland, duly authorised to receive full and particular propositions from the confederates,
and

[n] Carte, Orm. Vol. II. p. 26.

and to grant them every grace confiftent with juftice and the honour and intereft of his majefty.

The earl of Glamorgan had been for fome time in Paris, foliciting the lieutenancy of Ireland, with recommendations from Rinunccini to cardinal Mazarine. The marquis of Antrim indulged himfelf with fanguine hopes, that he fhould be advanced to this ftation by the favour of the queen. But Mufkerry and Browne were privately affured, that the perfon intended for the government of Ireland was no other than the marquis of Ormond; and that he was fpeedily to be fent with fuch aids as could be procured from France. Next to the prince, who declared againft an adventure into Ireland while the nuncio continued in the kingdom, no perfon was more acceptable than Ormond to thefe agents and their party. They took their leave with perfect fatisfaction in their fuccefs, and returned to circulate the pleafing intelligence.

During thefe negociations in France, the fupreme council was deeply impreffed with the prefent dangerous fituation of the catholic confederacy [n]. Two fucceffive defeats had almoft totally deftroyed their armies. Their refources were exhaufted, their adherents, impatient of diftrefs, grew querulous and mutinous. Their declining caufe was every day deferted by numbers, who purchafed protection from the parliamentarians by grievous compofitions. Their enemies were powerful in every province, and prevented only by the feverity of winter from falling on them with irrefiftable violence. With fome of them it feemed abfolutely neceffary to effect a ceffation. Even the nuncio himfelf recommended a truce

[n] Belling Vindiciæ, cap. 7.

truce either with the Scots of Ulster, or with lord Inchiquin, the more formidable enemy, that the confederates might be thus enabled to march securely to Dublin and exterminate the odious sectaries.

Lord Inchiquin was prepared to meet their wishes[o]. Immediately after his victory at Knocknoness, he had given some sign of disaffection to the parliament[p], by a bold remonstrance against their neglect of his forces, and the distresses to which he had been abandoned. And though he continued his operations against the Irish, and even threatened Kilkenny with a siege, yet he held a secret correspondence with the marquis of Ormond, and projected schemes for recalling him to Ireland, and uniting with him against the governour of Dublin and his party. Lord Broghill, second to Inchiquin in command, had conceived some displeasure against this lord. Ormond contrived to reconcile them, and to engage Broghill in their design. An emissary was dispatched to the confederates to treat about a cessation. Taafe and Preston bound themselves by a solemn oath, to support the king's rights and to obey his lord lieutenant. Inchiquin entered into the same engagements. The Scots of Ulster gave assurances of uniting with Ormond, not only against Owen O'Nial and all the Irish who continued in their disobedience to the crown, but against the independent party of England and Ireland. Thus was a powerful union successfully concerted in favour of the royal cause, when some English officers of Munster attached to the independent party, suspecting the design of their general, formed a scheme for defeating it, by seizing Cork and Youghall. They were discovered and imprisoned. But this incident obliged
lord

[o] A. D. 1648. [p] Borlase.

lord Inchiquin publicly to avow his revolt, before the necessary measures were sufficiently secured; and particularly before the cessation with the Irish was concluded; a point of the utmost moment, as it was to prepare the way for a powerful conjunction of the confederates with the protestant royalists.

But in this point, embarrassments and delays were now experienced[q]. The nuncio had but a few weeks since earnestly recommended a cessation. Equally an enemy both to the royal and popular party, he indulged his imagination with projects of detaching Ireland entirely from the English government, in whatever form, and by whatever powers it was administered. Transported by his visions of a pope supreme monarch of Ireland, and a stately hierarchy to execute his government, he turned his eyes from the calamities of the nation with a steady insensibility; and, from the moment that Inchiquin declared for the king, exclaimed loudly against any cessation with this lord. The supreme council repeatedly endeavoured to obviate his wild objections. The nuncio, as usual, recurred to the clergy. A number of bishops assembled at his house, and protested against the cessation. The council was provoked and astonished at this extravagance; yet, not entirely superiour to the fear of excommunication, hesitated and delayed. Clanricarde, Taafe, and Preston, laboured to confirm them in the resolution of giving some relief to their distracted country. The supernumerary members of the supreme council supported the sentiments of these leaders; the provincial assemblies of Leinster and Munster appeared at Kilkenny, and loudly urged the necessity of a cessation. The nuncio, and his clergy, while they raved of the church and its rights, of

opposing

[q] Carte, Orm. Vol. II. p. 31.

opposing heretics, of avenging the slaughter of their holy brethren, and the pollution of their altars at Cashel, could propose no reasonable scheme for carrying on the war. It was, therefore, resolved, after various debates and conferences, that the cessation should be concluded, with the clause of mutual assistance against all those who should oppose it by hostilities.

THE nuncio was enraged even to a degree of phrenzy, He fled secretly from Kilkenny, and cast himself into the arms of his favourite, O'Nial, whom he conjured to march without delay against the profane betrayers of the church. The council respectfully entreated him to return, and to confer temperately on public affairs. He disclaimed all connection with them, unless the generals of their Lienster and Munster armies were displaced, provisions and quarters assigned to the forces of O'Nial, and the whole conduct of peace and war submitted absolutely to the clergy. He caused their protest against the cessation to be affixed on the doors of the cathedral in Kilkenny; and, when this was contemptuously torn down, his sentence of excommunication was thundered against all those who contrived or favoured the cessation, and an interdict denounced on all places in which it should be accepted or maintained.

RINUNCCINI, in the blindness of his persumption, conceived that these severities must have the same force and effect with the censures published on the peace of forty-six. But times and circumstances were changed. By fulminating his spiritual terrours upon many trivial occasions, he had rendered them contemptible. Men were gradually rouled by his violences from a state of stupid submission, and grew

ashamed

ty days became the subject of perpetual conferences.

THE commissioners who attended at Carrick were so limited in their instructions [b], and so much time was wasted in reporting their proceedings to the assembly, receiving their further directions, returning to the marquis, and renewing their conferences, that the assembly invited Ormond to repair to his own castle at Kilkenny, where he might reside with honour and security, and carry on the treaty with expedition. He accepted the invitation. He was met at some distance from the city by the whole body of the assembly, nobility, clergy, and gentry, conducted with the utmost pomp, received by the magistrates in their formalities, lodged in his castle, and surrounded by his own guards, with all the honour due to his station, and every expression of reverence and affection. But, while Ormond was here engaged in negociation, a dangerous spirit of mutiny in the army of lord Inchiquin required his presence in Cork. These forces, confounded at the success of the independent party, and disappointed in their expectations of money, grew discontented and clamourous [c]. Some of their officers thought it necessary to make their peace in time with the ruling power of England. Propositions were sent to parliament, in which it was pretended that Inchiquin himself concurred; they complained of dangerous concessions meditated by Ormond in favour of the Irish; they talked of joining with Jones at Dublin, or forcing their way to the quarters of Owen O'Nial. The treaty was thus necessarily suspended. The general assembly consented to continue their session while the marquis was called away to the assistance

[b] Borlase. [c] Carte, Orm. Vol. II. p. 44.

of lord Inchiquin. A meffenger from the prince landed opportunely at Cork, with affurances, that the fleet was fpeedily to arrive with ammunition and provifions; that the duke of York was immediately to fail, and that the prince of Wales was foon to follow. This flattering intelligence, together with the vigilance of Inchiquin, and the addrefs of Ormond, foon quieted the commotions of the army. Some officers were imprifoned, others difplaced, and the forces fo modelled as to enfure their future quiet and attachment. And thus was the marquis of Ormond enabled to return to Kilkenny, and refume his negociations.

A copy of his letter to the fupreme council, notifying his arrival in Ireland d, and his powers of concluding a peace, had by this time been procured by Jones, tranfmitted to England, and fent by the parliament to their commiffioners in the Ifle of Wight. Charles was required to difavow this proceeding; and, by a public letter to the marquis, he commanded him to defift from any further treaty with the Irifh. But he had already contrived to convey a private anfwer to the application made by Ormond for his immediate inftructions. He repeated his direction that he fhould obey the queen's commands, and proceed in the courfe he was purfuing. He, therefore, proceeded without fcruple.

During the interval of his abfence at Cork, the Irifh agents arrived from Rome, laden with reliques and benedictions, but without fupplies of any kind. The pope pleaded the diftreffes of the holy fee, which prevented him from advancing any money to the Irifh; nor would he exprefs his fenfe of the conditions

d Borlafe.

ditions fit to be demanded in matters of religion, but left them to pursue the dictates of their own judgment. This disappointment served to confirm the moderate part of the confederates in their dispositions to peace. Yet still the various passions, prejudices, and interests which prevailed in the general assembly, embarrassed the progress of the treaty, and obliged Ormond to remonstrate warmly against the extravagance of their demands, and the danger of their delay[e]. But, what was of still greater effect, the remonstrance of the army to the parliament of England, requiring that the king should be brought to justice, was about this time received by lord Inchiquin, and sent to Kilkenny. Its effect in Ireland was sudden and powerful. All complaints in the protestant army were silenced; the confederates, stricken with a violent impression of the king's situation, and possibly of their own danger, at once acceded to the terms proposed by Ormond. The treaty was concluded, the peace proclaimed; and even the clergy, however disappointed in some of their extravagant demands, expressed their satisfaction, and by declarations, and circular letters, recommended the strict observance of this peace.

WITH respect to civil affairs, the articles were generally copied from those of the year forty-six. In religion the concessions of the marquis of Ormond were such as had been formerly rejected with firmness, and such as had been abhorred by the general body of protestants[f]. All the penal statutes were to be repealed, and the catholics left to the free and secure exercise of their religion. They were not, indeed, expressly allowed their ecclesiastical jurisdiction, nor the grant of churches and church-livings; nor

[e] Carte, Orm. Vol II, p. 49.   [f] Cox, Append. No. xlii.

nor were they expressly restrained in these points [g]. On the contrary, they were secured in the possession of such churches as they now held, until the king's pleasure should be freely and authentically declared. And that greater precision was not used, and more extensive concessions granted in these articles, was imputed entirely to the limited powers of the lieutenant. What was equally odious, and appeared highly dangerous, the marquis consented to divest himself of the full power inherent in his office, in order to allay the fears of those who were conscious of their former perfidy and guilt, and dreaded that the articles of the present treaty might not be observed. Twelve commissioners were named by the general assembly, and styled COMMISSIONERS OF TRUST [h]. They were to take care that the articles of peace should be duly performed, until they should be ratified in a full and peaceable convention of parliament. They were to be joint sharers with the lord lieutenant in his authority; so that he could neither levy soldiers raise money, nor even erect garrisons, without the approbation of the major part of these commissioners.

ORMOND, sensible that such concessions must prove highly offensive to the zealous protestants, instantly published a declaration to explain and justify his treaty [i]. He professed, that his care for the protestant religion, and the interests of the crown had been continued through his whole conduct, to the conclusion of the peace; for this he appealed to the articles, which, as he alledged, amounted to no more than some moderate indulgence to the confederates, together with some things necessary to their present security, until an act of oblivion should be
passed

[g] Belling. Vind. cap. 17. p. 74. [h] Clarendon. Hist. of the Irish Reb. [i] Carte, Orm. Vol. II. p. 32.

passed in parliament. He observed, that he had made no accommodation with those who had any share in the barbarities committed in the beginning of the rebellion; that he had not condescended to any articles, until the treaty between the king and parliament had been broken off, and the army proclaimed their horrid design against the king's life."
" This," said he, " we mention not to invalidate any
" of the concessions made unto his people; but, on
" the contrary, to render them in every point the
" more sacred and inviolable, by how much the ne-
" cessity on his majesty's part for granting them is
" greater, and the submission on their part to his
" majesty's authority, in such his great necessity,
" more opportune and seasonable; as also, to call
" the world, (and whomsoever either any peace
" at all with the Irish, or the terms of this peace
" may be distasteful unto) to testify hereafter, that
" as the full benefit thereof cannot without great
" injustice, and somewhat of ingratitude (if we may
" so speak in the case of his majesty) with reference
" to this last act of theirs, be denied unto them;---so
" any blame thereof, ought to be laid on those alone
" who have imposed the said necessity, the saddest
" to which any king was ever reduced."

But whatever hopes the marquis conceived from his liberal concessions to the Irish; whether he still flattered himself with expectations of leading a powerful army of royalists to the king's rescue; whether he fancied that the prosecutors of this unhappy prince might be terrified from their present purpose, by the apprehensions of a powerful invasion from Ireland; it was now too late to serve his royal master. Charles was brought to his trial; and, before

fore the intelligence of the Irish treaty arrived at London, he had already received the fatal stroke.

The news of this catastrophe was received by the marquis of Ormond at Youghal[k], as he returned from visiting prince Rupert; who, to the great consolation of the royalists, had arrived at Kinsale with the fleet so long expected. He instantly proclaimed the prince of Wales king, and caused the like proclamation to be made in all places subject to his authority. Such was the detestation expressed by the Irish at the execution of Charles, that the nuncio at once concluded the whole party would submit to the lord lieutenant[l]. He had for some time continued in Ireland, notwithstanding his disgraces, in hopes that some favourable incident might draw the nation into his measures. His hopes were now desperate; he resolved to retire from a country, which he had so long distracted by his senseless ambition; he embarked privately; and, from France, still continued to enflame the Irish clergy by his letters, until he was recalled to Rome.

The marquis of Ormond[m], who was confirmed in his government by the new king, and whose attachment to the royal cause was fixed and invariable, had now a variety of enemies and difficulties to encounter[n]. The capital was in possession of the parliament; and Jones, their governour, expected powerful reinforcements. Sir Charles Coote maintained Derry for the parliament. The British forces of Ulster professed an abhorrence of the king's death; but their abhorrence of the Irish was equally violent. They disdained any connection with the confederates or their supreme council, and neither acceded to the peace, nor acknowledged the authority

[k] Borlase. [l] Carte, Orm. Vol. II. p. 56. [m] Borlase. [n] A. D. 1649.

thority of the Lord lieutenant. Owen O'Nial leader of a formidable Irish army, still declared in favour of the nuncio's measures, and bad defiance to the royal party. Some of these various enemies were, if possible, to be reconciled. Ormond first applied to O'Nial, who consented to a treaty. But the commissioners of trust, who hated and dreaded him, refused to allow him such a number of forces as he demanded on an accommodation. The treaty was thus broken off. The marquis next addressed himself to Coote. Coote returned only vague and general professions, although he had formerly declared against taking any part with those who should change the government, or injure the person or posterity of the king. He endeavoured, in the last place to practise with Jones. Jones declared his firm resolution of adhering to his principles and party, and supporting the English interest. To his pathetic representations of the king's injuries and sufferings, he coldly answered that Ormond must blame himself for the death of this unhappy prince! for, by his arrival and transactions in Ireland, while the treaty of Newport was depending, he had impressed the minds of men with a firm persuasion of the king's total insincerity, and determined them to desperate measures. It scarcely served to allay the mortification arising from these repeated disappointments, and the distresses of the marquis, that the British forces of Ulster declared for the king, and blocked up Sir Charles Coote in Derry.

ORMOND was now to collect an army from men of different nations, religions, interests, and passions[o]; to unite those who for eight years had waged bitter war against each other with every circumstance

[o] Carte, Orm. Vol. II. p. 60.

stance of barbarous animosity and revenge. He had few officers on whose affection and abilities he could rely; was utterly ignorant of the circumstances of the confederate party, their stores, magazines, artillery, lists, and quarters of their men, the state of their garrisons, and dispositions of the commanders in their several forts and cities. They had engaged for an army of fifteen thousand foot, and two thousand five hundred horse. But the provinces could not maintain this number; and those whom they dismissed found a ready entertainment from O'Nial. The leaders contended with each other for military honours and commands, and perplexed the lord lieutenant by their rivalships and competitions. The marquis of Clanricarde soon perceived his distress; and with a disinterested zeal for the royal service, resigned his post of lieutenant-general, to assist him in contenting the various claimants. The commissioners of trust, attentive only to their private interests, took little care to provide magazines or money. They had, indeed, applotted sixty thousand pounds upon the kingdom; but, when the marquis was to take the field, no part of the applotment was collected. He applied, in person, to several cities and incorporate towns. These, like so many petty republics, obeyed no orders of the general assembly, but directed all contributions by their own acts, and granted or denied them, as they deemed most suitable to their own convenience. At Waterford, he procured seven thousand pounds, by mortgaging the king's rents and customs; five thousand were promised by Limerick; Galway engaged for the same sum. The securities were reluctantly accepted, and the money slowly paid.

Some assistance he expected from the fleet under the

the command of prince Rupert[p], though this fleet was not directly subject to his orders; but Rupert, whether he envied the glory which Ormond might acquire from reducing Ireland to the king's obedience, or from whatever other mean and factious motive, studied from the first to disconcert the lieutenant. He had desired one thousand landmen to man his fleet; and, no sooner were they granted, when his partiality to the Irish encouraged them to sedition. Contrary to the articles of peace, they were allowed to celebrate their mass in the sea-ports: and, spirited up by the attendants of the prince, they insulted the protestants, and raised such commotions, as all the diligence and prudence of lord Inchiquin were scarcely sufficient to allay. Rupert himself held a correspondence with Antrim, O'Nial, and other discontented Irish. Encouragement was given in his name to all who were willing to serve the king in " an opposite way to the present government." Thus was a turbulent spirit excited in Connaught, which Clanricarde with difficulty repressed; schemes were formed for raising forces in the South; Ormond discovered these practices, and Rupert was ashamed to avow them. As the marquis now meditated the design of investing Dublin, the prince was intreated to block up the harbour with his fleet. Jones must have thus been speedily reduced to extremity; but, a service so easy and so essential to the king's interest, prince Rupert unaccountably declined. With the same obstinacy he refused to favour the blockade of Derry and to cut off the supplies expected by Sir Charles Coote; nor would he furnish Ormond with the money which the king had directed him to pay to his lieutenant for the public service.

[p] Carte, Orm, Vol, II, p. 65.

IN this complicated diſtreſs, Ormond earneſtly urged that the king himſelf ſhould repair to Ireland[q]. The power of the commiſſioners of truſt would be thus diſſolved; the loyaliſts enlivened; every man would preſs forward to diſtinguiſh himſelf in the ſervice of his ſovereign; moſt of the forces of Jones would deſert; Owen O'Nial would be reconciled to government. He had already aſſured the king of his ſubmiſſion immediately on his arrival, on the terms of being included in the act of oblivion, allowed liberty of conſcience, employed in his Majeſty's army, and advanced to the dignity of an earl. The king himſelf ſeemed perfectly convinced of the propriety of this adventure: when the Scottiſh commiſſioners attended him at the Hague, he referred them to his arrival in Ireland for an anſwer to their imperious propoſitions. His heavy baggage and inferiour ſervants were embarked, and actually landed. But three months were waſted in a vain expectation of aſſiſtance from the ſtates; more time loſt at Saint Germains; and, though the king ſtill adhered to his reſolution; and proceeded to the Iſle of Jerſy, yet the time of action was already arrived, and Ormond obliged to take the field.

THE reduction of Dublin was now the great object of his enterprizes[r]. To gain this city, was, in effect, to gain the whole kingdom. He flattered himſelf that it would alſo produce an inſurrection in England; that numbers who deteſted the king's death would be encouraged to declare themſelves; and was particularly aſſured that many London merchants only waited until Dublin ſhould be in the hands of the royaliſts, to tranſport themſelves and their effects amounting to an immenſe value, and carry

[q] Carte. Orm. Vol. II. p. 62.   [r] Ibid. p. 69.

carry on their commerce in Ireland. For an attempt of such consequence, Ormond was miserably provided: he had no magazines, no money; the forces on which he was to depend grew mutinous by their distresses; and the Irish, in particular, were unused to discipline, impatient of restraint, without zeal for the cause in which they were engaged, and only to be bribed to their duty; proud of being found necessary to the king's service; filled with their own imaginary consequence, and insolent to their fellow-soldiers. About two thousand of the Munster army, which Ormond contrived to collect in the month of May, were employed under the earl of Castlehaven to reduce those places in Leinster which were still possessed by the forces of Owen O'Nial; and though they struggled with extreme difficulties, yet they performed this service. Sir George Monroe, whom the king had commissioned to command in Ulster, was detached into Connaught to make a diversion in favour of the forces employed against Coote; and, having in conjunction with Clanricarde, reduced the parliamentarian garrisons in the West, marched to the support of the army which lay before Derry. In the mean time, the lord lieutenant mustered six thousand foot, and two thousand horse, near Carlow, and, by the help of some money borrowed from private persons, put this body in motion. He reduced Kildare, and other places held by the enemy; but the necessities of his army were a fatal impediment to his progress: so that when Jones had marched to some distance from the capital, and Ormond had the fairest opportunity of egaging him to advantage, he was forced to keep his station westward of the Liffey, and to suffer the governour to retire unmolested.

Nor was Jones without his difficulties and diſtreſſes. A great part of his garriſon was diſaffected, held a ſecret correſpondence with Ormond, and impatiently expected his approach. His proviſions were exhauſted; nor were his forces ſufficient to meet the enemy in the field, even if no ſuſpicions were entertained of their fidelity. But as prince Rupert obſtinately and repeatedly refuſed to block up the harbour of Dublin, he ſoon gained ſome reinforcements and ſome proviſions from England. Nor did he want addreſs and induſtry to find reſources in Ireland. Owen O'Nial, whoſe overtures had been diſdainfully rejected by the confederates, commenced a treaty with the parliamentarian leaders, which Jones found it highly expedient to encourage. Owen was now encamped in the county of Monaghan, with his rear to Dundalk, Newry, Carlingford, and other places poſſeſſed by Monk[ſ]. Their mutual intereſt produced a ceſſation between theſe two commanders. The Iriſh general even declared his readineſs to form a permanent accommodation with the ruling powers of England; offered his propoſitions, and was amuſed with frequent conferences. To Jones he promiſed, that he would find full employment for the marquis of Ormond, if he was furniſhed with money and ammunition; and of theſe he was readily aſſured. At the ſame time, the governour of Dublin found means of practiſing with the officers who ſerved under Preſton[t], and ſo wrought on theſe, and their general, that they formed a baſe deſign upon the life of Ormond, which was either timely diſcovered, or which they had not the hardineſs to execute.

In

[ſ] Belling. Vind, cap. 19.   [t] Carte, Orm. Vol. II. p. 71—78.

In the midst of these dangers and difficulties, Ormond was reinforced by two thousand of lord Inchiquin's foot; and, having received some supplies of money, by the industry of Castlehaven and Taafe, proceeded in his expedition. At Naas, it was resolved, in a council of war, to advance against Dublin. He marched to Castle-knock, within cannon shot of the gates, in hopes of raising some commotion within the walls; but, after some inconsiderable skirmishes, found it necessary to encamp at Finglas, within two miles of the city. Here he received intelligence, that Jones had detached most part of his horse to Drogheda, a motion, which, by cutting off his provisions, must reduce his army to extreme distress. Lord Inchiquin was instantly sent in pursuit of them with a strong body of cavalry, surprised, and routed the party, laid siege to Drogheda, and soon obliged this city to surrender. Having intelligence of a body of horse and foot employed to escort some ammunition furnished by the parliamentarians to Owen O'Nial, he attacked and routed the horse, cut the infantry to pieces, invested Dundalk, which Monk, was forced, by his own soldiers, to surrender; and, having reduced some less considerable garrisons, returned triumphantly to the camp at Finglas.

On the return of Inchiquin, the army was found to consist of seven thousand foot, and four thousand horse, a force insufficient to form the siege of an extensive and populous city, defended by a numerous garrison. It was resolved, however, to encompass Dublin on all sides; and while lord Dillon of Costello was left on the North with two thousand five hundred men, Ormond, with the rest of the army, crossed

crossed the Liffey, and encamped at Rathmines, proposing to extend his works to the East, so as to command the entrance of the river. Some disagreeable advices served to damp the joy arising from the late successes of lord Inchiquin. In the northeren province, the British troops who had invested Derry, from their aversion to the independent party, began to suspect that their leaders, regardless of the ends of the covenant, really intended to restore the king without conditions, and to re-establish the hated order of bishops. Possessed with these fears, they refused obedience to their general, lord Montgomery of Ardes, renounced the cause and adherents of an uncovenanted king, deserted in great numbers, and dispersed. Sir Charles Coote seized the advantage of this dissension; and, addressing himself to Owen O'Nial, engaged him by a large sum of money to march to his relief. Lord Ardes was too much weakened to await his approach; and, therefore, raised the siege of Derry, at the time when Coote was reduced to extreme distress. What was still more alarming to the army before Dublin, three English officers, Reynolds, Hunks, and Venables, arrived at this city with two thousand foot and six hundred horse, a considerable sum of money, and various necessaries for the garrison, at the time when Ormond was on his march to Rathmines. By the very ships which brought these succours, intelligence was conveyed to Ormond and Inchiquin, that Dublin was now thought to be sufficiently defended; that Cromwell lay at Bristol with a great army, and that he designed to land in Munster.

In this province many were devoted to the ruling power of England; the royal garrisons were weak; and Cromwell, it was justly supposed, would be perfectly

fectly informed of their condition. By reducing Munster, he would become master of the best ports of the kingdom, he would cut off the provisions of the army, so that, if Dublin were reduced, they must be still distressed; and should they fail in their present attempt, their cause must be utterly desperate. It was, therefore, resolved without hesitation, that lord Inchiquin should march to the South with three regiments of horse to strengthen the garrisons, and by his presence, to confirm the people in their attachment to the royal cause. At the same time, it was determined to continue the blockade of Dublin, as it must prove a dangerous discouragement to their party, should the present enterprize be abandoned. Yet, as their diminished numbers required greater caution, it was the opinion of a council of war, that the marquis (when the enemy's party was first driven from Rathfarnham, a service easily effected) should remove from Rathmines to a securer quarter, at a place called Drumnagh, whence he might hold an uninterrupted communication with the party stationed on the North side of the river.

A motion, which had the air of a retreat, was utterly intolerable to many officers, who had more confidence than skill[u]. They represented the reduction of Dublin as a work of less difficulty than was pretended; they observed, that the enemy's horse subsisted only by the convenience of some meadows near the walls on the south-side of the river; that to deprive them of this pasture, and thus, in a few days, to starve their horse, nothing more was necessary than to possess the adjoining castle, called Baggatrath, which might be sufficiently fortified in one night. Hence might the works be advanced securely to

[u] Carte, Orm. Vol. II, p. 79——81.

to the river, so as to cut off the garrison from farther succours, and provoke them to compel their officers to relieve their intolerable distress by a surrender of the city.

An overture so plausible was approved by the council of war; nor did Ormond venture, by his own authority, to forbid an enterprize of gallantry, which, in the opinion of his principal officers, was practicable and promising. At the close of day, an officer of the name of Purcell was detached with fifteen hundred foot to Baggatrath, while the rest of the forces were drawn up in battalia to support him against any interruption from the town. Although the castle lay but about a mile distant from the camp, yet the whole night was wasted in traversing the adjacent country, before Purcell could gain his place of destination and commence his works. The treachery of the guides alone could have occasioned this delay; and one Reily, an ecclesiastic, who had carried on a correspondence between Jones and O'Nial, afterwards claimed the merit of betraying the royal army. Ormond had been all night employed either in the field, or in his tent. In the morning, he found Baggatrath not so strong, nor his works so far advanced as he expected. Parties of the enemy were discovered lying between this castle and the strand. It was evident that Jones would hazard an engagement; and, as the whole army must now be drawn out, it seemed not more dangerous to support their party, in their works, than to cover their retreat. Ormond having made the necessary dispositions, in full expectation of a sally, retired to his tent to take some repose, but was quickly roused by repeated vollies; and, scarcely had he ridden one hundred yards,

when

when he found the party of Purcell driven from their works; Sir William Vaughan, another of his officers, routed and flain; his horfe flying, and his whole right wing completely broken. When he had, in vain, endeavoured to correct this diforder, he forced his way to the left; but here the troops at once caught the panic, and fled, without firing on the enemy. Thofe ftationed on the other fide of the river, inftead of endeavouring to recover the victory from an enemy in confufion, and folely intent on plunder, confulted only their prefent fecurity, and caft themfelves into Trim and Drogheda; while the marquis retired to Kilkenny with fome fhattered remains of his army. Fifteen hundred private foldiers, and three hundred officers, were made prifoners; about fix hundred flain; many of thefe, to the difgrace of the conquerours, when they had accepted quarter and laid down their arms.

Such was the event of this enterprize againft Dublin, an event naturally to be expected from a general controuled in his authority, an army weak and unprovided, compofed of difcordant parts; the officers faithlefs, negligent, and ignorant, countenanced in their difobedience by the commiffioners of truft; the men undifciplined, unufed to danger, indifferent to the fervice, and fecure of an afylum among their Irifh affociates, when, on the firft alarm of an enemy, they fhould abandon their leaders. The lofs of fuch men was not fo confiderable as that of arms and ordnance. And the ftill more important effects of this difafter, were the dejection of the friends, and exultation of the enemies of the royal caufe, the diminution of that reverence which had generally been paid to Ormond, and the fears, jealoufies, and complaints induftrioufly propagated by the enemies of the late peace; who imputed the misfortune of the confederates entirely to the marquis[x], and tranfmitted the intelligence of his defeat to Rome with the utmoft joy and triumph.

* ORMOND, himfelf, was not difpirited by this accident. Owen O'Nial had grown difgufted with his new friends, the independents [y]. They had rejected his overtures in England; they had formally condemned the treaties made with him by Monk and Coote; thus they offended his pride, and convinced him of the neceffity of confulting his fecurity by other meafures. He renewed his treaty with the marquis of Ormond; the marquis was folicitous to gain him; the commiffioners of truft were rendered more tractable by misfortune; the treaty was carried on with fome appearance of fuccefs; and, it was expected, that O'Nial would foon join the king's lieutenant with fix thoufand well appointed foot, and five hundred horfe. The profpect of fuch a reinforcement infpired Ormond with hopes of fuccefsfully renewing his attempt on Dublin, (efpecially if any accident fhould detain the fupplies expected from England) and even of reducing the whole kingdom. To confirm him in his hopes of better fortune, when about a week after the battle of Rathmines, he advanced only with three hundred horfe to Drogheda, which, as he expected, was invefted by Jones, this governour was fo alarmed, that he raifed the fiege precipitately, and retired to Dublin.

BUT

---

* Soon after his defeat, the marquis wrote to Jones, defiring that he would fend a lift of the prifoners he had taken. In the pride of his fuccefs, the republican governour returned the following laconic anfwer.

" My Lord,

" SINCE I routed your army, I cannot have the happinefs to know where you are, that I may wait upon you MICHAEL JONES.

[x] Carte Orm, Vol. II. p. 82. [y] Borlafe.

But, the time was now come, when the ruling powers of England were ready to demonstrate, that if they had so long appeared insensible to the distresses of Ireland, it arose from necessity, from their still more important concerns in England, from their attention to a momentous cause, which engaged all their faculties, and all their resources. From the moment that their triumph over the royal power was completed, the necessity of reducing Ireland was seriously and sincerely weighed, and motions made in parliament for a powerful army to be sent into this kingdom, for the chastisement of popish rebels, and the relief of their protestant brethren. The opposite interests of the presbyterian and independent parties for some time suspended the design. The first contended for entrusting the Irish expedition to the command of Sir William Waller; the latter were for employing Lambert. The divisions between the parliament and the army raised new obstacles. The revolt of Wales, insurrections, preparations of the Scots to invade England, banished all thoughts of an Irish expedition; and had not the confederates of Ireland been obstinately hardened in their infatuation, had they formed a real and a timely union under the marquis of Ormond, they must have soon expelled every partizan of the English parliament from their country. But a dreadful chastisement was reserved for their pride and bigotry. The progress of Ormond again awakened the parliament to a lively sense of the danger of their cause in Ireland. Waller was no longer considered as a general proper to be employed in this country; Lambert was secretly supplanted by a more powerful competitor. Cromwell was persuaded, that the conduct of an Irish war was not unworthy of his own abilities, and

might

might add to his power and confequence. He contrived, by his intrigues to be chofen lord lieutenant of Ireland, by an unanimous vote of parliament.

The preparations for his expedition [y], the fuppreffion of the levellers, who faw through the defign of tranfporting them into Ireland, and oppofed it by violence, the reluctance of many others to ferve in Ireland, where their countrymen had hitherto been abandoned to diftrefs and famine, and fome difficulties in procuring fhips, occafioned confiderable delays. It began to be queftioned whether Cromwell would at all embark. But his armament was at length completed [z]; the late change of affairs, by the action of Rathmines, or the accidents of wind and weather, diverted him from his purpofe of invading the fouthern province; he fteered his courfe to Dublin; and, on the fifteenth day of Auguft, landed with eight thoufand foot, four thoufand horfe, twenty thoufand pounds in money, a formidable train of artillery, and all other neceffaries of war.

In Dublin, he exercifed his new authority [a]; regulated all civil and military affairs, offered indemnity and protection to all thofe who would fubmit to the parliament, an offer readily embraced by many of the bittereft adverfaries to the peace and Ormond; and, having committed the care of the city to a new governour, Sir Theophilus Jones, took the field with ten thoufand chofen men. Ormond, who was now reduced to act on the defenfive, rightly judged that Cromwell would make his firft attempt on Drogheda, a frontier town, the moft expofed, and of greateft confequence for opening a communication with the northern province. He infpected and repaired

Carte Orm. Vol. II. p. 83. z Ludlow. a Carte Orm. Vol. II. p. 84.

paired the fortifications of this city; committed it to the government of Sir Arthur Afton, a catholic officer, diftinguifhed by his gallantry. His garrifon was augmented to two thoufand foot, and three hundred horfe, all chofen men, encouraged by the prefence of many officers of reputation, and furnifhed with a full proportion of ammunition and provifions. Such difpofitions were deemed fufficient for the fecurity of Drogheda; and, while Ormond retired in expectation of being reinforced by lord Inchiquin, he indulged his hopes that the numbers of the enemy would be fpeedily diminifhed by their unfuccefsful affault, and by the inconveniences and feverities of a fiege.

But Cromwell was poffeffed with that intrepidity and vigour which quickly diffipated thefe expectations. Difdaining all regular approaches and formal operations of a fiege, he fummoned the governour to furrender; and, on his refufal, thundered againft the walls for two days, until he had made a fufficient breach. The affault was given, and his men twice repulfed. In the third attempt led by Cromwell himfelf, the town was gained. Quarter had been promifed to all thofe who fhould lay down their arms; a promife obferved until all refiftance was at an end. But the moment that the city was completely reduced, Cromwell, with an infernal calmnefs and deliberation, refolved by one effectual execution to terrify the whole Irifh party. He iffued his fatal orders, that the garrifon fhould be put to the fword. His foldiers, many of them with reluctance, butchered their prifoners. The governour, and all his gallant officers, betrayed to flaughter by the cowardice of fome of their troops, were maffacred without mercy. For five days this hideous

ous execution was continued with every circumstance of horrour. A number of ecclesiastics was found within the walls [b]; and Cromwell, as if immediately commissioned to execute divine vengeance on these ministers of idolatry, ordered his soldiers to plunge their weapons into the helpless wretches. Some few of the garrison contrived to escape in disguise. Thirty persons only remained unslaughtered by an enemy glutted and oppressed by carnage; and these were instantly transported as slaves to Barbadoes.

This execrable policy had the intended effect [c]. The garrisons of Trim and Dundalk, in their consternation, neglected the orders of the marquis of Ormond to burn these towns, and demolish the fortifications; so that they were immediately possessed by the enemy. Venables was detached into the province of Ulster. He soon reduced Carlinford: Newry was surrendered: in marching against Lisburne, he was attacked, and exposed to some danger, but fortunately extricated himself, and was received into the town without resistance. Belfast was surrendered upon articles, in four days after his approach; Colerain was betrayed to Sir Charles Coote, who drove Sir George Monroe from the counties of Downe and Antrim, and reduced the whole country except the castle of Carricfergus.

During this rapid progress, the marquis of Ormond, in all the mortification of a discomfited general, kept himself retired, at the head of fifteen hundred foot, and seven hundred horse, most of them new raised levies, and many of suspected faith. He, indeed, expected to be reinforced both by lord Inchiquin

[b] Borlase, Carte, ut supra.

iquin and lord Ardes; but he had neither money nor provisions. In the absence of the commissioners of trust, he issued his own warrants for raising both. The commissioners, with unabated insolence, complained of this procedure as an infringement of the articles of peace, and talked of treating with the enemy. The only measure now to be pursued was, that of putting the confederate forces into garrisons; and, as winter was approaching, to prosecute their levies, and discipline their men. But the consent of the commissioners was necessary for forming any new garrisons, and appointing any governours; and these men had neither power nor credit with the cities most likely to be attacked, either to force or persuade them to admit garrisons. Wexford, Waterford, and Limerick, peremptorily declared that they would neither obey orders, nor receive soldiers.

In this distressed and embarrassed condition, Ormond saw no means of preventing the utter ruin of the king's interests, but his presence in Ireland. While the event of his design on Dublin was uncertain, he had recommended that the king should suspend his purpose of appearing in this kingdom. Charles seemed still disposed to share the common danger with his Irish subjects. His emissary was sent to Ormond to learn his opinion of the propriety of such an adventure, and to present the marquis with the ensigns of the order of the Garter. Ormond returned a melancholy account of the weakness dejection, and confusion of the royalists[d]; yet still recommended that his majesty should repair to Ireland, as the only measure for preserving any remains of interest and authority in this kingdom. If the progress of the enemy should be thus stopped, it would prove their ruin; to oppose them under such disadvan-

[d] Carte, ut supra, p. 86.

disadvantages, would be honourable to the king, whatever the event might be; and the security of his residence, and the conveniences of a retreat, might still be as great in Ireland as in Jersey. While the embarkation of Cromwell was preparing, Blake was ordered to keep prince Rupert's squadron blocked up in the harbour of Kinsale; when the forces were once landed, the English admiral retired; this squadon, therefore, was destined to attend the king, and convoy him from Jersey, and Ormond exerted all his efforts to furnish the ships with seamen and provisions. But Charles, by this time, listened to new counsels; accepted the propositions of the Scottish commissioners, and chose rather to attempt the recovery of his dominions by hypocrisy and perjury in Scotland, than by any gallant enterprize in Ireland.

In the mean time, Cromwell with his usual vigour[e], resolved to seize the advantage of the consternation and dissensions of his enemies, and to proceed in his operations notwithstanding the advanced season of the year. He had his correspondencies in Munster, his secret partizans in the cities and forts possessed by the Irish, and now marched with nine thousand men through the county of Wicklow, while his fleet attended the motions of this army; and the country people assured of protection, and made to believe that they should enjoy the liberty of their religion, crowded to his camp with provisions, for which they immediately received the full value. As he advanced, the forts and towns of inferiour note were at once surrendered; and, on the first day of October, he sat down before Wexford. The citizens had hitherto neglected all

means

[e] Carte, ut supra, p. 88.

means of defence, and obstinately refused to admit any troops. In their present terrour, which was artfully enflamed by those who held intelligence with Cromwell, they first proposed to open their gates to the enemy; at the urgent instances of the marquis of Ormond, they at length deigned to accept of succours; yet, with a fanaticism not peculiar to popery, they continued in their extremity to reject the assistance of heretics, and demanded a garrison composed entirely of the faithful. Ormond was by this time considerably strengthened; he, therefore, contrived to throw fifteen hundred catholic troops into Wexford; and, at the requisition of the magistrate, five hundred more. Having thus provided for the security of the city, he retired with the remains of his army, and arrived securely at Ross, though an attempt had been made to intercept him by a party under the command of Michael Jones.

But all the provisions made for the defence of Wexford, could not secure it from secret treachery f. One Stafford, governour of the castle, had been suspected by Ormond; but as he had the merit of being a catholic, the commissioners of trust would not consent to remove him. No sooner had Cromwell's batteries began to play, when this man admitted his soldiers into the castle upon conditions. The citizens were suddenly confounded at sight of his colours waving on the battlements, and their own cannon pointed against the town. In the first tumult of terrour and consternation, they sent commissioners to treat with the enemy; but the townsmen were impatient of delay; the soldiers ran tumultuously from the walls; every man consulted only his own safety, and thus were all destroyed. The ene-

f Carte, ut supra. p. 92——98.

my gained the city without farther resistance, and proceeded to put all to the sword who were found in arms, with an execution as horribly deliberate as that of Drogheda. Hence Cromwell proceeded to lay siege to Rofs, a town situated on the river Barrow, and more considerable for navigation than that of Wexford. At the same time he detached a strong party under the command of Ireton, to invest Duncannon. Such was the general consternation, occasioned by the progress and severities of Cromwell, that the citizens of Waterford, though nearly interested in the defence of this fort, refused to supply it with provisions, and seemed ready to submit on the first appearance of an enemy; while the commissioners of trust, seated at Kilkenny in all the futile pomp of authority, began to tremble for their security, and were scarcely restrained from flying to some place more inaccessible to the parliamentarians. To confirm these terrours, the town of Rofs was immediately surrendered upon articles.

The fort of Duncannon made a more honourable resistance: and so considerably had the victorious army been reduced by the severity of the season, in a country at this time unfriendly to English constitutions, that a reinforcement of fifteen hundred men was sent from Dublin, and had been some time expected by Cromwell. Lord Inchiquin was informed of the march of these forces; and, with consent of Ormond and the commissioners of trust, resolved to intercept them. In this attempt he was foiled and defeated. Yet Wogan, the officer who commanded in Duncannon, continued to make a brave defence[g]. By the assistance and encouragement of lord Castlehaven, he made a sally with such vigour and

---

[g] Castlehaven's Memoirs.

and success, that the enemy at once raised the siege, not without some confusion. On retiring to their main body, they found the general transporting his troops to the county of Kilkenny, by a bridge of boats constructed on the Barrow, a device utterly strange and astonishing to the rude Irish [h]. Ormond, who had concluded his accommodation with Owen O'Nial, and already received part of his forces, made some preparations for disputing the passage of the river; but Cromwell, superiour in vigilance and expedition, as well as numbers, had already transported his army, and obliged the marquis to retire gradually to the city of Kilkenny [i]. Here he found the rest of the northern Irish forces ready to receive his commands. The presence of their favourite general was still wanting; for O'Nial now laboured under a grievous malady, which soon after put a period to his life [*]. So powerful a reinforcement, however, encouraged Ormond to the design of meeting the enemy in the field.

He represented to his soldiers the necessity of fighting, in order to enlarge their quarters, and the glory of making one brave effort for their country, instead of perishing ignobly by famine. He demanded an explicit declaration of their sentiments: they declared unanimously for battle: he issued from Kilkenny in search of the enemy; but Cromwell, who had advanced within five miles of the city, and reduced the fort of Knocktopher, passed suddenly with all his army over the Sure, and marched to invest Waterford. This city, with the usual obstinacy

[h] Borlase. [i] Carte, ut supra.
[*] The Irish did him the honour frequently paid to great personages, of discovering something extraordinary in his sickness and death. They were ascribed to poison conveyed by a fatal present of a pair of russet boots.

nacy of popish corporations, had disdainfully rejected the assistance of lord Castlehaven, who was sent with some troops to provide for their security, as well as that of the neighbouring fort of passage, over-against Duncannon. But the approach of a bloody enemy rendered them more tractable. While Inchiquin was detached to recover Carrick, which Cromwell had surprised in his march, Ormond hastened to the defence of Waterford. The citizens accepted a reinforcement of fifteen hundred Ulster troops, under their commander Ferral, all immaculate in the faith, without any mixture of heretical depravity; and the marquis was on the point of returning to Carrick, in full confidence that his forces were already masters of the town, when he received intelligence that they had failed in their attempt, and retired to Clonmel. With the few troops he had left, he sought the same place, by an indirect and tedious march, through a country filled with terrour; the inhabitants collecting their wretched effects, abandoning their habitations; peasants, citizens, women, children, all flying different ways, to find some shelter from the English army.

This consternation was encreased by the reduction of Passage-fortk. The citizens of Waterford now declared, that unless they were instantly supplied with additional troops and provisions, they could make no resistance. Though the commissioners of trust sat in useless state at Kilkenny, without contributing to the public service, or concurring in any measures for relieving the distresses of the soldiery, yet Ormond contrived to march once more to Waterford, and to strengthen the garrison with a new reinforcement. He had the gratification of discovering

k Carte, ut sup. p. 99———104.

ing the enemy in some terrour at his approach, and raising the siege with evident marks of confusion. But when he proposed to fall on the rear of an army wasted by fatigue and sickness, and mortified by their present disappointment, the insolence of the citizens revived; they now considered his soldiers as an useless and oppressive burden, and refused to supply boats for ferrying them over the river, until the opportunity of annoying the enemy was lost.

THE marquis, on his return to Clonmel, found himself involved in new vexations and disappointments. Antrim was detected in labouring to corrupt his soldiers, and secretly to enflame that spirit of insolence and disobedience which had already been discovered in the corporate towns. He had forged articles of agreement between Michael Jones and Inchiquin, whereby this lord engaged to betray the royalists. The forgery was detected and confessed. What was still more afflicting, several designs formed in Munster against the king's cause, though hitherto defeated by Inchiquin, were now on the point of final success [1]. Cromwell, before his departure from London, had learned that lord Broghill intended to repair to the king and attend him into Ireland. He surprised this lord by a visit; informed him, that his designs were no secret to the council of state; terrified him with the prospect of immediate imprisonment; promised, that if he would engage in the service of the common-wealth, no disagreeable oaths should be imposed on him; that he should draw his sword only against the Irish, and be invested with an honourable command. Broghill readily complied, arrived in Ireland about the end of October, raised a troop for the service of Cromwell, and

[1] Memoirs of lord Orrery.

and practised secretly and successfully with the Munster protestants. These men soon repented of their unnatural conjunction with the confederate Irish; and those among them who had not already determined to forsake their present service, were easily seduced. In a moment all the chief garrisons of Munster declared for Cromwell; who thus, having first reduced Dungarvan, found commodious quarters for his harrassed and distempered forces, without conducting them by a tedious march to Dublin.

This sudden defection, in a juncture so critical, when the distresses of Cromwell, from the severity of the season, the sickness of his army, and scarcity of provisions, had raised men's spirits, and inspired them with favourable hopes, dissolved the whole frame of the royal party, and extinguished all remains of confidence between the English and Irish, who were originally united by the principal of obedience and submission to their leaders, not incorporated by inclination and affection. Ormond was now obliged to give his troops some respite. He represented to the commissioners of trust the necessity of quartering them in the cities, from whence they might be readily collected in the spring. But, except Kilkenny and Clonmel, none of these cities could be persuaded to admit them. The magistrates of Waterford even refused his few troops a passage through their city to succour Ferral, who had failed in his attempt to recover the fort of passage, and was seen flying in disorder; so that half the party was cut to pieces before he could appear, and deter the enemy from their pursuit. He proposed to renew the attack of this fort, if his forces were but permitted to take their quarters under the walls in huts,

huts, where they should not be burdensome to the city, but depend on the country for subsistence; but this proposal was rejected, and so insolent were these burghers, so obedient to the clergy, and so infected by the malicious suggestions of their faction, that it was proposed in their council to seize the person of the lord lieutenant, and fall on all his adherents. The proposal, indeed, was rejected, but without any reprehension.

The only part now left for Ormond, was to dismiss his forces to seek shelter and subsistence where-ever they were most likely to procure them. Those of Connaught retired to their own province: lord Dillon disposed his men in Meath, and the neighbourhood of Athlone; lord Inchiquin, with that part of the Munster army which had not yet deserted, gained the county of Clare. Daniel O'Nial, who, as a native of Ulster, and nephew to Owen, was acceptable to the northern Irish, and, as a protestant, unexceptionable to the Scots, was sent with two thousand men to assist lord Ardes and Sir George Monroe in the recovery of those places lately lost in the counties of Down and Antrim. After a tedious march, he found these commanders routed by Sir Charles Coote, Carricfergus surrendered, and the whole northern province in the hands of the parliamentarians, except Charlemont and Enniskillen.

To what hath been already observed of that insolence and bigotry which appeared in several of the cities, it seems scarcely necessary to add, that they were under the dominion of the most turbulent and refractory of the Irish ecclesiastics[m]. The consequence of such men revived with the public misfortunes,

---

[m] Carte, Orm. Vol. II. p. 105.

tunes. These, with an ignorant and vulgar malignity, they imputed to the misconduct of their governours, and laboured to infuse their illiberal prejudices into the minds of all those who listened to their insinuations. They were assisted by the marquis of Antrim, who still aspired to the station of chief governour, and was indefaticable in his endeavours to render Ormond odious to the people, and obnoxious to the king. A general discontent, suspicions, jealousies, murmurs, were the natural consequence of such practices. And the clergy now affected a solicitude to allay those disorders, which they themselves had excited. About twenty of their bishops assembled voluntarily at Clonmacnoise, on the banks of the Shannon, to deliberate on the state of the nation. The whole Irish party was anxious for the event of this self-appointed council, and looked for nothing less important than a violent protestation against the government of Ormond. Happily the temper of one of their bishops, Heber Mac Mahon, the Romish prelate of Clogher, disappointed these expectations. From the time of the accommodation between Ormond and Owen O'Nial, in which Mac-Mahon had been instrumental, the marquis frequently conversed with him on public affairs, and inspired him with an high opinion of his talents for government, and his zeal for the interests of Ireland. With these sentiments he entered the assembly of his brethren, where he had the consequence naturally derived from superiour abilities. He silenced the factious, he encouraged the moderate, he defeated all the secret practices of Antrim; and, at length, with difficulty, prevailed on the prelates to declare, by a formal instrument, that no security for life, fortune, or religion, could be expected from Cromwell, to express their detestation of all odious distinctions

tinctions and animosities between the old Irish, English, and Scottish royalists, and their resolution of punishing all the clergy who should be found to encourage them.

But these declarations did not operate on the public disorders with any considerable effect. What the factious clergy could not venture to declare in full assembly, was secretly whispered and propagated. A people, irratated by the galling burden of contribution and assessment, provoked by disappointment, and weary of a declining cause, readily listened to those who taught them to ascribe the effects of their own perfidy and disobedience to the misconduct of the king's governour. Some of their clergy, more particularly devoted to the nuncio and his principles [n], did not scruple to insinuate, that if their countrymen must accept of an heretical administration, they might as well submit to Cromwell as to Ormond; and some were said to have even offered public prayers for the success of the republican general [o]. The marquis, conscious of his own rectitude and zeal, was provoked at such ingratitude. He desired the king's permission to retire from Ireland; the king consented that he should withdraw himself when the necessity became unavoidable [p]. But, as his treaty with the Scots was to produce a diversion in England, which might have an happy effect upon his Irish interests, the lieutenant was still to struggle with his difficulties. He addressed himself to the commissioners of trust. He demanded the reason of those dissatisfactions, by which the people had been seduced from their obedience, and abandoned all thoughts of union and defence. The commissioners recommended, that the several counties should be directed to send agents to Kilkenny,

[n] Belling. Vind. cap. 24.   [o] Borlase.   [p] Carte, ut sup.

reprefent their grievances, and to propofe means for their relief; an expedient fuggefted by thofe who were fecret enemies to Ormond, and calculated to enflame, rather than to fupprefs, fedition. Should the marquis oppofe it, he muft be reproached with a confcioufnefs of guilt, and a reluctance to hear, or to relieve the people. The agents were fuffered to affemble. They menaced, they clamoured, they fpread their flanders, but when they attempted to form a remonftrance, they could find no grievances to compofe it. In the midft of their futile deliberations, they were alarmed at the approach of Cromwell q; fled to Ennis, and there found it equally difficult to frame their remonftrance.

CROMWELL had advanced in a dreary feafon, not prepared for a regular fiege, but relying on the promifes of an officer called Tickle, that he would betray the city of Kilkenny into his hands. The plot was difcovered, and the agent executed. Ormond, at the head of a little troop, compofed of his friends and domeftics, fo animated the citizens, and difplayed fuch an appearance of defence, that the enemy retired; and the cuftody of the city and adjacent country was entrufted to lord Caftlehaven, with a body of twelve hundred men. But the fate of Kilkenny was but fufpended. Cromwell, fenfible that his prefence muft fpeedily be demanded in England, and that the Irifh, who wanted provifions, muft be particularly diftreffed by an early campaign, took the field about the end of February. Fatigue and ficknefs had confiderably diminifhed his Englifh forces. But the revolt of the Munfter garrifons furnifhed him with foldiers inured to the climate, and habituated to the feverities of an Irifh war. One part of his army he entrufted to Ireton; and each

com-

q Borlafe.

mander reduced several places in his march. They met at Callen, which was instantly taken. At Gouran they received an additional reinforcement, commanded by colonel Hewson, now governour of Dublin; and thus they were enabled to invest Kilkenny with a considerable army.

A PLAGUE, by which most parts of Ireland had been infested [r], raged particularly in this city, obliged Castlehaven to retire, and reduced the garrison to about four hundred and fifty. With this body Sir Walter Butler made a brave defence, and repelled the assaults of the besiegers with such spirit and success, that Cromwell, despairing to gain the town with that expedition which his affairs required, began to meditate a retreat [s], when the mayor and citizens invited him to stay, and promised to receive him into their town. His assaults were renewed, and again repelled. But a weak and sickly garrison, every moment in danger of being betrayed, was soon obliged to capitulate. They surrendered the city and castle upon honourable terms; and were applauded by Cromwell for their defence.

FROM Kilkenny, Cromwell proceeded to invest Clonmel, and here met with a still more obstinate resistance. Hugh O'Nial, a northern officer, with twelve hundred of his provincials, maintained the town with such valour, that in the first assault two thousand of the besiegers were lost; and Cromwell determined rather to starve, than force the city to submission. Harrassed and enfeebled by delay, he made the most pressing instances to lord Broghill to hasten to his assistance. On the other hand, Ormond laboured indefatigably to succour the garrison. Notwithstanding the infatuated obstinacy of the commissioners of trust, who defeated all his attempts, he

[r] Carte, Orm. Vol. II. p. 114.   [s] A. D. 1650.

he prevailed on lord Roche, a person of considerable power in the South, to collect a body of troops for the relief of Clonmel; but these were encountered and defeated by lord Broghill[t]. The Romish bishop of Ross, who had been particularly active in raising and animating these unfortunate troops, was taken prisoner in the engagement. A man so distinguished in his opposition to the parliamentarians could expect no mercy; Broghill, however, promised to spare his life, on condition that he should use his spiritual authority with the garrison of a fort adjacent to the field of battle, and prevail on them to surrender. For this purpose he was conducted to the fort; but the gallant captive, unshaken by the fear of death, exhorted the garrison to maintain their post resolutely against the enemies of their religion and their country, and instantly resigned himself to execution. His enemies could discover nothing in this conduct but insolence and obstinacy, for he was a papist and a prelate.

In the mean time, Cromwell was repeatedly called into England, where the alarm of a Scottish invasion rendered his presence absolutely necessary. But his reputation must be considerably impaired, should he abandon his present enterprize; he, therefore, continued to invest Clonmel. After a brave defence of two months, the garrison found their ammunition and provisions totally exhausted, without any prospect of relief. Hugh O'Nial withdrew secretly with his forces, and conducted them to Waterford; while the townsmen treated with the besiegers, and were permitted to surrender the city upon honourable terms. Cromwell now resigned his army to the care of Ireton, and embarked for England.

CHAP.

[t] Cox, Vol. II. part III. p. 16.

CHAP. II.

State of Ireland on the departure of Cromwell.—Attempt to recover Ulster from the parliamentarians. —Defeat and death of Heber Mac-Mahon.—Limerick refuses to receive a garrison from Ormond.— He applies to the clergy.—Their factious and insidious conduct.—Ormond threatens to retire from the kingdom.—The nobility alarmed.—The citizens of Limerick relent.—They invite Ormond to their town.—He is excluded by a tumult.—Traduced by the clergy.—Their assembly at James-town.—They require Ormond to depart from the kingdom.— Their declaration against his government.—Their excommunication of all his party.—Progress of the parliamentarians.—Irish prelates suspend, but refuse to revoke their excommunication.—They are enflamed by the king's declaration from Scotland.— Ormond's propositions to the commissioners of trust. —New general Assembly, influenced by the clergy. ---Ormond retires to France.—Marquis of Clanricarde, lord deputy.—Attempt on Limerick defeated. —Irish clergy disposed to a treaty with the parliamentarians.—The are intimidated.—yet still averse to the king's authority.—Their agent sent to the duke of Lorrain.—Occasion, progress, and event of the transactions with this prince.—Ireton prepares for the siege of Limerick,—crosses the Shannon,— and invests the city.---Valour of Henry O'Nial.--- Lord Muskerry marches to the relief of Limerick,--- is defeated by lord Broghill.---Limerick betrayed to
the

the besiegers.----Severe executions.------Ungenerous treatment of Henry O'Nial.---Death of Ireton.---Ludlow prepares for a new campaign.---General consternation.---The clergy still insolent.---Galway surrendered.---Extreme distress of Clanricarde.---He accepts terms,---and departs from the kingdom.---Acts for distribution of lands in Ireland.---Trials of Irish rebels.---Sir Phelim O'Nial seized.---His trial and execution.----Dispositions of the forfeited lands.---Oliver proclaimed lord protector in Ireland.---Henry Cromwell sent into Ireland.---Fleetwood lord deputy,---succeeded by Henry Cromwell.---His character and conduct.---He is created lord lieutenant on the accession of his brother Richard.---He resigns his office on the restoration of the rump-parliament.---Designs and proceedings of the royalists.---Their leaders.---Their success.---Convention of estates.---The king proclaimed in Ireland.

ALTHOUGH the faction and obstinacy of the Irish in opposing every reasonable provision for defence, had facilitated the progress of Cromwell; and although he had reduced several places of importance, yet a great part of the kingdom was still free from the power of the parliamentarians [u]. The province of Connaught was entirely possessed by the catholics; Waterford, Limerick, Galway, were in their hands, which might be made so strong, as to fear no force that Ireton could command, and were so situated for receiving succours by sea, that, if well supplied, they might maintain a war against the whole kingdom. They had the forts of Duncannon and Sligo, the castles of Athlone, Charlemont, Carlow, and Nenagh. They could readily collect forces in number more than double

of

[u] Borlase.

of their enemies. But they had neither union, order, nor resolution.

During the campaign of Cromwell, an attempt was made to recover Ulster from the parliamentarians, by a conjunction of the northern Irish with the British royalists of this province, under the command of the marquis of Clanricarde. The Irish refused to follow any leader but one of their own election; the British were persuaded by Antrim, that designs were formed to extirpate them, and refused to concur with the Irish, whom they easily suspected of the basest purposes; thus, was the design defeated. Ormond, however, judged it necessary to comply with the northern catholics, and permitted them to elect a general in the place of Owen O'Nial. Their election fell on Mac Mahon, the prelate of Clogher, a man, who by his ecclesiastical authority could collect, but was utterly unfit to command an army. The consequence were such as might be expected from a choice so injudcious. The bishop, contrary to the advice of his most experienced officers, ventured, with inferiour numbers, to encounter Sir Charles Coote near Letterkenny. In the action he displayed an intrepidity suited to his new character: but his army was defeated with considerable slaughter. In the pursuit, he had the misfortune of being taken prisoner, and was soon after executed by order of the English parliament. The victors proceeded to lay siege to Charlemont, which surrendered after a brave defence; Enniskillen had been already given up to Coote; and thus he had the honour of reducing the whole northern province.

Ormond, in the mean time, patiently contending

ing with his difficulties, formed a scheme for prosecuting the war with vigour and effect. He cast his eyes on Limerick, a place of the utmost consequence; and which, probably, would be soon attempted by the parliament forces. Could he prevail on this city to receive a garrison, he had no doubt of securing it; and, by the countenance of such a station, and the convenience of the river Shannon, to find quarters for his forces, to raise contributions for their support, to discipline and recruit his army, so as to be enabled by spring to meet the enemy in the field. He went to Limerick; he represented to the citizens the absolute necessity of their receiving fifteen hundred foot, and three hundred horse, not only for their own security, but the preservation of the kingdom: the citizens rejected his proposal.

ORMOND imputed this alarming obstinacy to the true cause w, the malignant practises of those clergy and their partizans, who, from their opposition to the peace, had uniformly persevered in distressing and traducing his government, exulting in his misfortunes, enflaming the general discontent, and artfully encreasing the dejection and terrour which drove men daily to consult their private security, by making compositions with the enemy. By advice of the commissioners of trust, he condescended to expostulate with the clergy. He summoned twenty-four of their bishops to attend him at Limerick, that he might confer with them and others of the nobility, and, by their advice and assistance, resolve on some effectual measures for the advancement of the king's service, and preservation of his people. However they really disregarded the king and his service, yet they obeyed the orders of the marquis, and assembled
with

---

w Borlase.

with apparent respect and submission. He conferred freely with them on the distracted state of affairs, represented the danger of that disobedience which the citizens of Limerick had discovered, the ruin that must attend the nation, and the dishonour to himself, should he be contented with a nominal authority, without the real power of a chief governour. If they had conceived any distaste to his administration, he desired they should express their sentiments with freedom, and proposed, that " ei-
" ther they would procure a due obedience to be
" yielded to him, or recommend some other way,
" by his quitting the kingdom, how it might be
" preserved."

WITH an affected deference they presented him some propositions for removing those discontents which prevailed among the people [x], most of them loosely expressed, general, and indeterminate. The most precise and important of their demands were, that the receiver-general should account for the sums levied since the peace, (a demand evidently calculated to encourage the suspicions they themselves had raised, of some misapplication of the public money), and that a privy council should be composed of the native nobility, spiritual and temporal, to assist the chief governour; by which they really meant to establish themselves in the administration of public affairs. Ormond readily consented that all those who had received any money for the king's service should be brought to a strict account; and, as to the second demand, he observed, the king alone could name a privy council; yet, if they would specify what particular acts were necessary to be done by such a council, he promised to qualify persons free

[x] Carte, Orm. Vol. II. p. 118.

from juſt exceptions, with ſufficient powers. They They could not object to theſe anſwers; they, therefore, publiſhed a declaration, that they would endeavour to root out of mens hearts all jealouſies and ſiniſter opinions of the marquis, and the preſent government deſiring his further directions, and promiſing the utmoſt care and induſtry on their part.

It was natural to expect that ſuch a declaration muſt have a favourable influence on the citizens of Limerick. Some of the biſhops undertook to perſuade them to receive a garriſon. Ormond himſelf deigned to practiſe with their magiſtrates and principal leaders. But his conciliating addreſs was ſecretly counteracted. They now refuſed to treat him with thoſe forms of reſpect due to his ſtation. The commanders of the city-guards neither came to him for orders, nor imparted to him thoſe they had received. No officer could gain admittance to him but by licence of the chief magiſtrate. A catholic lord, who ſerved in his army, was committed to priſon, for preſuming, by his order, to quarter a few ſoldiers within the liberties of the city. Exaſperated at ſuch inſults, Ormond retired, in diſdain, to Loghrea, whither he was followed by the biſhops.

Nor was it the leaſt part of his preſent mortification, that he was obliged to keep terms with theſe eccleſiaſtics, who, by their ignorance and preſumption, their illiberal artifice and duplicity, diſgraced their profeſſion, and became the moſt deſpicable of any order of men who ever acquired an influence in any country. In their private conferences with Ormond, they declared, that all the jealouſies of the people aroſe from their ſuſpicions of Inchiquin and
his

his puritanic forces; and even demanded, that all the English troops should be removed from the kingdom, as the most effectual measure for allaying the general discontent. To Inchiquin they, at the same time, professed the utmost attachment. He was of a noble Irish family; and, therefore, they observed, must be peculiarly dear to the Irish. Should he be invested with the government, he would be readily obeyed, and soon grow strong enough to oppose the enemy, and recover his country. These insinuations were communicated by these noblemen to each other, and only served to convince them that the clergy wished to get rid of both, and to make themselves absolute masters of the kingdom.

Every day afforded some occasion of discovering the hypocrisy of their public professions. The earl of Castlehaven [y], who had been appointed to command in Leinster, represented that the royal interests in this province were in danger of immediate ruin by the Irish inhabitants, who submitted in great numbers to the enemy, and, by their contributions, furnished the greatest part of their subsistence. It was proposed, that the bishops should issue their excommunication against those who were guilty of such compliances. But this engine of their authority was to be reserved for more factious purposes; they could not be prevailed on to employ it in the king's service. Ormond, wearied by their insolent and insidious conduct, declared his resolution of making use of the licence he had received from the king, and withdrawing himself and his authority from Ireland. However acceptable his departure might be to the clergy, yet the full power to which they aspired

[y] Carte, Orm. Vol. II. p. 121.

aspired was not yet completely secured. The nominal authority of chief governour they wished to be deposited with some one of their creatures, but were not agreed upon the person most likely to serve their purposes. The nobility and commissioners of trust were terrified at the thoughts of anarchy, and public confusion; and all united in endeavouring to detain the marquis. However indulgently they spake of the disobedience of Limerick, yet they promised to renew their instances with the citizens, and to reduce them to a just submission. The citizens were alarmed at the approach of some parties of the enemy; they seemed to relent; they no longer objected to accept a garrison; they required only that it should consist of such troops, and be commanded by such officers as they should chuse; that they should be quartered without the walls, and demand no subsistence from the city. Propositions were received from the parliamentarian general, offering them a free exercise of their religion, the enjoyment of their estates, churches, and church-livings, a free trade and commerce, without any garrison to be imposed on them, provided that they would allow his forces to march through their city into the county of Clare. The citizens rejected these propositions; and thus, seemed to return gradually to a better temper.

ORMOND, encouraged by these promising appearances%, suspended his purpose of embarking, and drew his few forces to Clare, within twelve miles of Limerick. Here he received a respectful invitation from the magistrates of this city, that he would honour Limerick with a visit, and regulate the garrison. He consented, on condition of being received

% Carte, Orm. Vol. II. p. 121. Borlase.

ed with the honours due to his station, and quarters being provided for his guards. But when he had advanced near the walls, he suddenly received intelligence, that a seditious friar, called Wolfe, had raised a tumult in the city to oppose his entrance, and gaining the keys, either by force or connivance, had set a guard on the gates, while other lawless incendiaries rifled the magazines, disposing of the corn at their pleasure. The bishops pretended to condemn these outrages, but refused to excommunicate the authors. They had even the presumption to intercede with Ormond for an officer of the name of O'Brian, who took a principal part in the tumult, and desired not only that he might be pardoned, but employed.

This incorrigible obstinacy and disobedience of Limerick, rendered it impossible for the marquis either to collect an army, or to keep it in a body, on either side of the Shannon. To complete his distress, the example of this city was soon followed by that of Galway, which refused to admit any garrison but such as should be appointed and commanded by the magistrates. Should the enemy pass the river, or pierce into Connaught by any other way, Ormond could have no retreat. The conduct of the disobedient cities demonstrated a purpose eitheir of yielding to the enemy at once, or of erecting an authority independent of the king. The refractory clergy were evidently possessed with this latter design. They had already petitioned several catholic powers for protection; they continued to inveigh with bitterness and malice against the administration of Ormond; and he suspected, not without reason, that the least prospect of advantage might induce some of their partizans to betray him to the enemy. In circumstances

so

so desperate, he naturally resumed his purpose of retiring from the kingdom.

No sooner had this purpose been intimated, when the clergy and their faction redoubled their clamours[a]. Among other proofs of Ormond's inviolable attachment to the royal cause, he had formerly rejected their own insidious overtures of placing him on the throne of Ireland, provided he would unite with the nuncio and embrace their religion. Yet now they imputed his resolution of retiring to a secret agreement with the parliamentarians. Not yet satisfied with the effect of such insinuations on the ignorant and bigotted, in the fullness of their hopes, and extravagance of their pride, they resolved on more direct measures for renouncing the king's authority, and the government of his lieutenant.

A LETTER signed by the popish archbishops of Dublin and Tuam, informed the marquis, that in the present melancholy state of public affairs[b], they and their brethren, the prelates of Ireland, had resolved to assemble at a place called James-town, to devise some measures for the defence of their religion, and the security of the nation. In a style sufficiently imperious, they declared their readiness to receive any proposals from the marquis, and did not want " willingness to prepare a good answer." The marquis replied, by a severe reprehension of their former conduct, to which he ascribed all the public calamities, and the destructive progress of the enemy, refusing to make any new proposals, yet allowing their convention, and expressing his wishes that it might be attended by some happy consequences. Instead of receiving overtures, they were thus obliged

[a] Carte, Orm. Vol. II. p. 126. [b] Borlase.

ed to make them; and they were quickly made in a strain of such insolence, as could not be expected even from these insolent ecclesiastics. They required that his excellency should speedily repair to the king, leaving his authority " in the hands of some " person faithful to his majesty, and trusty to the " nation, and such as the affections and confidence " of the people would follow."

It seems natural to expect, that an address of such a nature, framed by such men, and presented with such careless presumption, would have excited the indignation of the sensible and moderate, and exposed the authors to the severest punishment. But the ignorance of the vulgar had stamped such a degree of reverence and authority on the ecclesiastical character, that the dictates of the meanest of this order were superiour to all power civil and military. It was known, that when a regiment was detached on some particular service, a seditious friar, seizing the colours, had pronounced eternal perdition on those who should presume to march; and that the whole body, at his word, cast down their arms, and dispersed to their several habitations. Even those who were most zealous for the king, and most offended at the violence of their clergy, were yet so tender of their immunities, granted in the darkest periods of popery, and now revived in their full extent, that they could not harbour a thought so profane, as that of inflicting punishment on a churchman by any but an ecclesiastical authority. So that, if Ormond had attempted to correct the insolence of these prelates, or any other of the clerical faction, he must have not only determined by his single judgment, but executed his determination with his own hand. No

protestant

protestant officer was left about him, but the captain of his guard, he was, therefore, obliged to condescension and forbearance: at the desire of the commissioners of trust, he summoned the bishops to a conference; they refused to attend him; he expostulated with their agents, and endeavoured to convince them of the dangerous and ruinous nature of the proposition they had made. Unable entirely to suppress his disdain of a contemptible faction, he now declared that he would not remove from the kingdom until forced by inevitable necessity.

But the bishops were not to be dissuaded or deterred from their purpose. Without waiting any answer to their address, and even before it was presented, they had already drawn up, and now published, an insturment, entitled, " A declaration of the prelates " and dignitaries of the secular and regular clergy, " against the continuance of his majesty's authority " in the marquis of Ormond; for the misgovern- " ment of the subjects, the ill conduct of the army, " and the violation of the peace." In this declaration they magnified their own zeal and services, particularly in procuring vast sums of money for maintenance of the king's cause. They complained of abuses in the expenditure of these sums; of improvidence and ill conduct of Ormond, particularly in the fatal action of Rathmines; of his partiality to Protestants, his aversion to the Catholic religion, his cruel treatment of its professors and clergy, and his misrepresentations to the king: they threatened to present articles of accusation against him to his majesty, and enjoined the people to obey no orders but those of the congregation of clergy, until a general assembly should be convened. To give this edict greater weight, it was attended with a solemn sentence of excommunication, fulminated against all those who should adhere to the lord lieutenant, or give him subsidy, contribution, or obedience.

THE folly, the iniquity, and ingratitude of this proceeding, appear more strongly c, when we consider the progress of the parliamentarian forces, and the present situation of the marquis of Ormond. Immediately after the surrender of Clonmel, Trecrohan, a fort of great consequence, on account of the quantity of stores and artillery there deposited, was reduced, notwithstanding a brave attempt made by lord Castlehaven to relieve it. Huson, the noted republican, had taken Naas, Athy, Maryborough, Castledermot, and other places; Carlow was invested and reduced; Waterford was surrendered by Preston; the strong fort of Duncannon soon shared the same fate. Ireton, not yet prepared for the siege of Limerick, detached Ingoldsby and Sir Hardress Waller, to block it up at a distance, who gained some advantages over detached parties of the Irish, and some adjacent forts. While the parliamentarians ranged over the adjacent country, Ormond, with a few troops, and those hasty levies, which particular districts supplied by what were called their *risings-out*, contended at once with famine and a victorious enemy, and made the most desperate efforts to prevent them from passing the Shannon. In the mean time, Ireton and Sir Charles Coote advanced towards Athlone, and thus alarmed the Irish with the apprehensions of losing the whole western province. Clanricarde marched with his forces to oppose them, but the sentence of excommunication was published at the head of his troops, so as to discharge them from all obedience to government. The commissioners

c Carte Orm. Borlase

oners of truſt, the nobility, the more moderate of the clergy, ſome who repented of their violences, and would now retract them, all made the moſt preſſing inſtances to the congregation, remonſtrated, expoſtulated, conjured them in this dangerous juncture to ſupport the preſent government, and not to abandon their country to an enemy who ſought their utter extirpation. But neither danger, nor entreaty, nor the moſt obvious ſuggeſtions of duty or policy, could induce theſe prelates to revoke the ſentence of excommunication. In their infatuated pride, they conſented only with a ſtately reluctance to ſuſpend it, during the expedition made for the relief of Athlone. They proceeded to levy forces by their own authority, ſo that Ormond had now a new enemy to contend with; and, though their ſanguine hopes were in a great meaſure diſappointed, and ſome of their parties defeated, yet they ſtill continued their ſeditious clamours, invoking the full weight of divine wrath upon the people, for contempt of their own cenſures and thoſe of the nuncio, to which they impudently aſcribed all the calamities of the nation.

A NEW incident ſerved to enflame their violence, and to give ſome plauſible colour to their proceedings. Among other conceſſions of Charles, he now indulged the fanaticiſm of the Scots, by his famous declaration, in which he acknowledged the ſin of his farther in marrying into an idolatrous family, declared, that all the bloodſhed of the late war was to be charged to his father, expreſſed a deep ſenſe of his own former prejudices againſt the cauſe of God, his repentance for his paſt life, which had been a courſe of enmity to God's work; and, among other particulars, his utter abhorrence of the peace concluded by his father with the Iriſh papiſts, and ratified by

himſelf

himself, pronouncing it utterly void, on suppofition of the unlawfulnefs of any peace made with bloody and idolatrous rebels.

Nothing could be more convenient for the congregation of prelates [d], and their purpofe of enflaming the people, than this virulent declaration. They imputed it entirely to the reprefentations of the marquis of Ormond. "The king," faid they, "hath
" now withdrawn the authority of his lieutenant;
" he hath caft the whole Irifh nation from his fa-
" vour and protection. Why fhould we be bound
" by a peace which he fo folemnly difclaims? Why
" fhould we fubmit to an authority which he, in ef-
" fect, recalls? Let us remember our oath of affoci-
" ation; let us recur to our original confederacy;
" and, inftead of fighting in fupport of a treaty thus
" difowned, let us bravely hazard our lives and for-
" tunes to extort more favourable articles from the
" enemy."

Ormond well knew the ufe that muft be made of this declaration. He, at firft, regarded it, or affected to treat it, as a forgery; but foon received a private letter from the king, acknowledging that he had really fubfcribed it, apologizing for this fhameful tranfaction as the effect of fear and force, infinuating, that it could not be binding in Ireland, as it was done without the concurrence of a privy council, and earneftly preffing him to retire in time from this kingdom. He had hitherto contended without fufficient forces, without any of the provifions neceffary for war, againft an enemy powerful and well fupplied; he was betrayed, harraffed, maligned, and infulted. He could no longer fupport the conteft with

[d] Carte, Orm. Borlafe.

with the king's secret and open enemies. Yet to leave the factious and refractory without excuse, he addressed himself to the commissioners of trust. He told them, that since the declaration was by undue means obtained from his majesty, he was resolved at all hazards, and by all means, to assert the lawfulness and validity of the late peace, until the king should give some free and unconstrained assurances of his pleasure; provided, in the mean time, that the acts of the congregation of prelates should be revoked, or punished as an usurpation on the king's authority; that all due obedience should be paid to him, and some honourable maintenance secured, to enable him to support his present station, as he was now deprived of all his own fortune.

THE answer of the commissioners plainly discovered, that they were afflicted and scandalized at the exorbitances of the clergy. They expostulated with the prelates, but found them inexorable. They importuned the marquis to wait the result of a new general assembly which must be fired with indignation at the extravagant proceedings of the bishops, and meet, with the more determined resolution to controul them. The assembly was convened, but soon appeared too tender and submissive to the ecclesiastics. These men deigned to publish a protestation, that by their proceedings at James-town, they had no purpose to usurp on the king's authority, or the liberty of the people; graciously confessing, " that " it did not belong to their jurisdiction so to do." The assembly, contented with this protestation, passed no censure on their acts, demanded no security for their future peaceable demeanour. The marquis was justly incensed, and prepared for his departure. Every member of the assembly not totally infatuated

by

by religious bigotry, was alarmed at his purpose, and shuddered at the horrible consequences of anarchy. They besought him, at least, to delegate the royal authority to some person faithful to the king, and acceptable to the nation. The request was enforced by a respectful address from the assembly. Ormond answered, that he would comply with their desires, when he should first be satisfied, that the person entrusted with the king's authority would be secured from those insults he himself had experienced, and received with a just and honourable submission. As he had rejected a pass from Ireton, it now became necessary to hasten his departure, lest he might be intercepted by some parliament ships. He, therefore, appointed the marquis of Clanricarde his lord deputy, with directions to use, or decline the commission, as he should be encouraged, or deterred, by the proceedings of the assembly; and thus embarking at the port of Galway, after a tempestuous and dangerous voyage, he arrived in France.

Every consideration of personal interest deterred Clanricarde from engaging in a dangerous and invidious charge; and, in Ormond, he had a striking example of that treatment to which he might be exposed. But, in the ardour of loyalty, he was solicitous to preserve some appearance of the king's authority in Ireland, to protect the remains of his sincere adherents, and, by continuing the war, even under manifold disadvantages, and without any hopes of final success, to make a diversion in favour of the royal party in England. He was, therefore, satisfied to accept the government, provided he might be assured of due obedience. The general assembly had already engaged to obey the person to whom the
lord

lord lieutenant should delegate his authority. But the engagement was not expressed with sufficient precision, so as to found this obedience on the principle of loyalty and duty to the king. The bishops opposed an explanation, or any clause which might convey a reflection on their former conduct. They offered to bind themselves by a solemn oath, to pay as great obedience to Clanricarde, as any catholic clergy in catholic times had ever paid to a catholic governour. The assembly was satisfied with this declaration, but Clanricarde dreaded the insidiousness of these ecclesiastics; he required expressions more determined and explicit.

An instrument was at length prepared and presented[e], in which the assembly declared, that " the " lords spiritual and temporal, gentry, or people, " clergy or laity, shall not attempt to do any act to " discharge the people from yielding due obedience " to his majesty's authority vested in the marquis of " Clanricarde, or any other governour; and, in case " of any such act, that no person shall or OUGHT " to be led thereby; but, by their disobedience, " are subject to the penalties of the laws of the land " in force, *and practised in the reign of Henry VII.* " *and other catholic princes.* Yet, by any thing " herein contained, it is not intended that the nation " shall recede from the late peace, or obey any " new governour unduely nominated by the king, " now in the power of a party of the Scots, and " during his present unfree condition." The bishops, conscious of their former violences, obliged the assembly to subjoin an explanatory clause, " that by " the word OUGHT, it was not intended to have any " retrospect to any former proceedings of the clergy."

CLAN-

[e] Carte, Orm. Vol. II. p. 140.

CLANRICARDE, not yet satisfied, proposed clauses still more explicit; he dreaded some subterfuge couched under the expression relative to *Henry VII. and other catholic princes.* He was assured, that they meant nothing more than a provision for the catholic clergy, who, in cases of treason or felony, had not since these times enjoyed the privileges formerly annexed to their function, but had suffered without degradation or other ceremonies due to churchmen. He was entreated to accept of such declarations as the clergy were willing to subscribe, instead of affording them any pretence for condemning the proceedings of the assembly, and enflaming the people by their protests. He saw a general disposition to submit to the parliamentarians; that the clergy, in their blind zeal for demolishing the royal power, encouraged this disposition; that some immediate union, and the speedy exertion of some authority, were absolutely necessary to prevent the fatal consequences. The assembly was on the point of breaking up in confusion: he, therefore, hesitated no longer, acquiesced in the declaration, defective as it appeared, and declared, his acceptance of the government.

THE popish party of Ireland had now a chief governour of their own religion [e]. The protestant royalists were dispersed; some had engaged in the service of the parliamentarians, numbers accepted passes, and retired to foreign countries: lord Inchiquin and several other protestant officers, had embarked with Ormond; so that their forces were depurated from the defilements of heresy; and, though dispersed in different quarters, and under different com-

[e] Borlase.

commanders, yet, if collected, were by no means inconsiderable. Sir Charles Coote had been disappointed in his attempt upon Athlone. Ireton advanced to Limerick, and demanded that the citizens should receive his troops for their defence. They hesitated and debated; but lord Castlehaven arriving opportunely with his party[f], persuaded them to accept his assistance, and shut their gates against the enemy. Ireton could not venture on a formal siege in a season so advanced; he therefore, retired: so that Connaught remained still in the power of the Irish, together with a considerable part of Munster; and the possession of Limerick, Galway, and Sligo, might still enable them to carry on a war, not without some fair prospect of success.

But that fatal spirit which the nuncio had infused into the clergy and their creatures were still predominant, and defeated all the hopes of Clanricarde. Scarcely had he accepted the goverment, when some agents arrived from Ireton, and proposed to the assemby to abandon their desperate cause, and treat with the parliamentarians, who might grant more favourable conditions to the nation, than to particular persons. The proposition, though at first rejected, yet, by the influence of the clergy, was resumed and supported. Nicholas French, the popish bishop of Ferns, a distinguished partizan of the nuncio, and a virulent opposer of the royal authority, clamoured violently for a treaty. Clanricarde remonstrated, and enlarged on the treachery and the danger of such a measure. Several of the nobility, and other leading members of the assembly, expressed their warmest indignation at this forwardness of the clergy to abandon all the king's interests.

" It

[f] Castlehaven's Memoirs.

"It is now evident," said they, "that these church-men have not been transported to such excesses by a prejudice to the marquis of Ormond, or a zeal for their religion: their purpose is, to withdraw themselves entirely from the royal authority. It is the king and his government which are the real objects of their aversion: but these we will defend at every hazard; and when a submission to the enemy can be no longer deferred, we shall not think it necessary to make any stipulations in favour of the secret enemies of our cause. Let these men who oppose the royal authority be excluded from the benefits of our treaty."

The clergy were unaccustomed to such bold language; they began to fear, that men might be at length awakened to a just indignation at their absurd tyranny. They had an exquisite sensibility of their own danger; and, therefore, deemed it necessary to keep some measures with their opponents. Their opinion was suddenly altered; they concurred with the assembly in opposing any treaty with the enemy; and, when the lord deputy issued a proclamation, forbidding all persons to resort to the quarters of the common enemy, to enlist in their army, or to pay them contributions, the prelates deigned to enforce this act of state, by pronouncing sentence of excommunication on all those who should not pay it strict obedience. Yet, notwithstanding this compliance, they still retained their hatred of Clanricarde, the opposer of all their fantastical projects, and the zealous friend of Ormond; they still whispered the design of reverting to their original confederacy, without regard to the king's authority; or, as one of their order expressed it, " that idol of Dagon [h], a "foolish

[h] Carte, Orm, Vol. II. p. 159.

" foolish loyalty." They held their secret consultations; they indulged their airy hopes of establishing the papal power, and their own sovereign authority in Ireland, by the intervention of some foreign prince; and the bishop of Ferns, their most active partizan, was sent to Brussels, to solicit the duke of Lorrain to take their nation and religion under his princely protection.

Before the departure of the marquis of Ormond, the king [i], in his extreme necessity, had listened to a proposal of mortgaging the fort of Duncannon to this duke for twenty-four thousand pounds. Ormond was directed, if he approved of the contract, to deliver up the fort to persons appointed by the duke, upon receipt of the stipulated sum. But, as Duncannon was threatened with a siege, the security became precarious; difficulties arose about the manner of paying the money; and, after a course of evasion and insincerity, the agents of Lorrain retired, without bringing the treaty to any issue. It was afterwards renewed by lord Taafe, who arrived at Brussels with letters of credence from the duke of York, and earnestly pressed the duke of Lorrain to support the king's interests in Ireland, offering him the security of any place in this kingdom, for the repayment of such sums as he should advance.

The duke, to prevent any dispute about the title to his dominions, had married his cousin-german, Nicole, daughter of Henry duke of Lorrain and Bar, and heir-general of these duchies. But, being afterwards captivated by Beatrix de Cusance, widow to the count of Cantecroix, he married her, while the duchess

[i] Carte, Orm. Vol. II. p. 144—152.

duchess Nicole was still living, and wished to engage the court of Rome to pronounce his first marriage void, and to legitimate his children by his second consort. As his solicitations had hitherto proved ineffectual, he imagined, that by engaging with extraordinary zeal in defence of the catholic cause in Ireland, he might plead so much merit, that the pope must, at length, yield to his desires. Taafe, who was a forward undertaker, flattered his partiality to the children of the princess of Cantecroix, and proposed a match between her infant daughter and the duke of York. Lorrain was delighted with the prospect of such an alliance; and, probably, in the progress of the negociation, his views were gradually extended, and his ambition flattered by the hopes of acquiring the sovereignty of Ireland. Whatever were his designs or expectations, he received lord Taafe with particular favour, expressed the warmest zeal for the interest of his countrymen, and furnished him with five thousand pounds to purchase arms and ammunition, which arrived in the bay of Galway, when the assembly deliberated about treating with the parliamentarians, and had no small share in influencing their decision.

TAAFE was astonished at this munificence, which the duke declared was but an earnest of his future favour. He affected the utmost commiseration of the Irish catholics; declared that he was ready, if invited, to appear personally in their defence, with such supplies as would soon recover the kingdom; hinting, at the same time, that he should expect entire obedience, and that he could not consent to act by commission from any person whatever. Taafe could not venture to engage for such conditions. The king might be displeased; the marquis of Ormond,

mond, when he supposed to be still in Ireland, might not consent to resign the power and pre-eminence annexed to his station. On the other hand, the interposition of the duke seemed necessary to rescue his country from destruction. In these difficulties, he deemed it the safer course, to propose that the duke of Lorrain should send some person of distinction into Ireland to treat with those in authority. Stephen de Hennin Abbe de Saint Catherine was chosen for this purpose, and landed at Galway, while the bishop of Ferns was on his way to Brussels, with a commission from the disaffected clergy to treat with the duke, and to solicit his protection for their unhappy country.

No one could be more acceptable to the clergy and their creatures than this envoy of Lorrain. Though his letters of credence were addressed to the estates of the kingdom, yet, when he found that Clanricarde was vested with the authority of chief governour, he was too attentive to decorum not to apply immediately to him. To avoid all clamour or censure, the marquis appointed a committee, composed of bishops, nobility and gentry, to treat with the Abbe, to receive his proposals, and to report them, with their opinion and advice. His proposals were, that the duke of Lorrain, his heirs and successors, with the saving to his majesty's rights, and those of the subjects, should be accepted as protectors of Ireland, and while there resident, should have the supreme command of the militia, with power of convening general assemblies, and with other appendages of royal authority, until all disbursements were repaid. The committee, utterly regardless of their instructions, debated these proposals among themselves, excluded the more moderate

rate and loyal of their number, admitted others, without content of the lord deputy with whom they scorned to communicate. Clanricarde complained of this proceeding, as well as of the propositions offered by the envoy so derogatory to the king's honour and authority. The bishops insisted that they should be accepted, as the only means left to preserve the nation. They were desired to subscribe this their advice; they hesitated, and refused. The Abbe consented to some qualification of his demands; the marquis declared, that they were still inadmissible. He would not even admit the man who had dishonoured his master to an audience of leave; and, by this stately resentment, so intimidated the Abbe, that he consented to advance twenty thousand pounds on the security of Limerick and Galway, and to refer all articles relative to the protectorship to be adjusted by a treaty at Brussels. In consequence of this agreement, Sir Nicholas Plunket, and Geoffry Browne, were commissioned to treat with the duke of Lorrain, in conjuction with lord Taafe; and expressly instructed to carry on there negociation agreeably to the directions they should receive from the queen, the duke of York, and the lord lieutenant.

But all such limitations were immediately forgotten. On their arrival at Brussels, they found lord Taafe was gone to Paris, to communicate the lord deputy's transactions with the Abbe de Sainte Catherine, and to desire further instructions from the queen and lord lieutenant. French, the turbulent prelate of Ferns, attended the duke of Lorrain, and was graciously received. He was assisted by some other creatures of the disaffected clergy, and some agents sent from the cities not yet reduced. They con-

confidently affured the duke, that they could inveft him with the whole power of the kingdom. French inveighed againft the agents fent from the lord deputy, their oppofition to the nuncio, and the appeal againft his excommunication. In an hypocritical ftrain of fanctified virulence he declared, that this excommunication was confirmed in heaven; that all its oppofers, however great and exalted in the eye of man, were forfaken of God, and delivered up to Satan. In fincerity and evangelic charity he exhorted them, to make fuch an agreement with the duke of Lorrain, as would be profitable to their nation, and acceptable to heaven; to proftrate themfelves in the name of all the people before his holinefs, to fupplicate his apoftolic benediction, that the light of wifdom, the fpirit of fortitude, virtue, grace, fuccefs, and the bleffing of God might return to them. He affured them that God would never profper any treaty directed by the deputy, a man excommunicated for many juft caufes; and that the duke, when rightly informed, could never confent to negociate with agents deriving their authority from a whithered and accurfed hand.

PLUNKET and Browne received this infidious cant with too great attention. They difclaimed the lord deputy's commiffion; they pleaded another and more unlimited authority. In the name of the nation and people of Ireland, they figned a treaty with the duke, by which he was, in effect, invefted with the entire fovereignty of the kingdom, by the title of Protector Royal. Plunket, the greater bigot, was, at the fame time, perfuaded by the bifhop of Ferns, to fign a petition to the pope, by which, in the name of the nation, he profeffed an entire fubmiffion to the holy fee, and implored abfolution from the nuncio's cio's censures. Browne had the spirit resolutely to refuse his subscription. The name of lord Taafe was signed in his absence, without his consent or knowledge. The clergy now exulted in the happy progress of their schemes. They entertained their imaginations with the usual airy prospects of a glorious and triumphant church, and a stately hierarchy, protected by a catholic prince. But, whatever were the secret designs of the duke of Lorrain, he soon found that they could not be promoted by any further treaty with the Irish. He received from the lord deputy a formal protest against the unwarrantable proceedings of his agents, so contrary to his instructions, and so derogatory to the king's honour. He had thus, a fair pretence for declining any further treaty; and the king's interests in Ireland soon grew so desperate, that there was nothing left to purchase the assistance of Lorrain, even upon the most reasonable terms.

In he mean time, the expectation of an agreement with this prince transported the Irish clergy to the utmost axtravagance. Their synods were convened; they declared the duke of Lorrain protector of their nation; they excommunicated those who should presume to dispute this nomination; they took an oath of secrecy; they resolved, that the prelates of each province should chuse two persons to compose a new supreme council, with full powers to transact all civil and military affairs, by the direction, and with the consent of the clergy. They prepared a sentence of excommunication against the marquis of Clanricarde and his adherents, to be published at a convenient time; and this ridiculous usurpation of the whole power and authority of the kingdom, they called a rivival of the original confederacy. But they

they were soon roused from this dream of power and grandeur, to a dreadful sense of danger and calamity.

From the tedious and disgusting detail of the presumption and infatuation of these seditious cecclesiastics[k], we are now to return to the affairs of war, and the progress of the parlimentarians. Ireton, having made all provisions for an early campaign, and received some reinforcements from England, resolved to open the campaign by besieging Limerick[l]. As it was necessary to pierce into Connaught, in order to invest this city on all sides, Sir Charles Coote was directed to advance towards Sligo. The Irish prepared to relieve this place; when Coote, suddenly drawing off his men, passed, with some difficulty, over the Curlew-Mountains, and invested Athlone. Clanricarde, embarrassed as he was by faction and opposition, made some efforts to oppose him; but, before his forces could be collected, Athlone was taken; and Coote pursuing his advantage, marched against Galway. The deputy was solicitous to defend this important post; he summoned the earl of Castlehaven to his assistance; but scarcely had this lord marched a few miles, with a detachment of four thousand men, when a party, which he had left to defend a pass over the Shannon, suffered themselves to be overpowered by the enemy, and fled precipitately. His whole army caught the pannic, and dispersed with that ease and suddenness usual to the Irish, when indifferent to the cause in which they were engaged, and secure of a retreat among their kinsmen. At the same time, an officer called Fennel, who had been stationed at Killaloe, to defend this passage of the Shannon, abandoned his station either from treachery or cowardice; so that

[k] A. D. 1651. [l] Carte, Orm. Vol. II. p. 154.

that the English burst rapidly into the western province; and all provisions being made for the attempt on Limerick, Ireton commenced the siege in form.

Both the citizens and the clergy had promised all submission to the lord deputy; but when he proposed to shut himself up in Limerick, and to share their fortune, he was excluded with the same insolence which Ormond had experienced. At the approach of danger indeed, the magistrates deigned to accept some troops, of such number and quality as they chose; and appointed Henry O'Nial, who had so bravely defended Clonmel, to be their nominal governour, reserving all real power to themselves. A constant correspondence was maintained between the besiegers and citizens, by means of those Irish who had compounded and submitted to Ireton. It was industriously suggested, that the independents were by no means uncharitable to popery, or friends to compulsion in matter of religion; and, when the cruel executions of priests and prelates were mentioned, of which every day afforded new instances, these proceedings were imputed entirely to the virulent spirit of the presbyterian party. Such was the influence of these insinuations; and such the divisions and distraction within the walls, that in three days the citizens proposed to surrender. The bishops and clergy well knew, that Ireton would except several persons from the benefit of any articles, and dreaded that they would be made the first victims of his cruelty. They, therefore, opposed all motions for capitulating with particular zeal; while O'Nial exerted himself against the besiegers, with a spirit worthy of the reputation he had already acquired.

IN the mean time, lord Muſkerry, alarmed at the danger of Limerick [m], advanced from Kerry with a ſtrong party to its relief. Lord Broghill was detached to oppoſe him; and, after a ſharp engagement reſolutely maintained on each ſide, Muſkerry, was obliged to retire with conſiderable loſs. Notwithſtanding this diſappointment, Hugh O'Nial continued to make a brave defence, and in ſeveral ſucceſsful ſallies ſlew conſiderable numbers of the beſiegers. Winter now approached; and the ſeverity of the ſeaſon, and ſickneſs of his army, muſt ſoon have obliged Ireton to abandon his enterprize, when treachery and ſedition proved too powerful for the gallantry of O'Nial. His authority had ever been controuled by the magiſtrates, and of conſequence ſlighted by his officers. Of theſe a number aſſembled tumultuouſly, and reſolved to treat with the enemy, without objecting to any exceptions which might be made of particular perſons, with reſpect to quarter or confiſcation. The biſhops clamoured againſt the deſign of ſacrificing them to the fury of the enemy, and thundered an excommunication againſt the authors of ſuch impious council; but, in the hour of terrour, their ſpiritual authority was utterly neglected. Fennel, who had yielded the paſs of Killalloe, at the head of a ſeditious rabble of ſoldiers and citizens, ſeized two of the principal gates. The chief magiſtrate protected him from the authority of the governour. He turned the cannon on the town, inſiſted on capitulating, and ſent commiſſioners to Ireton. The garriſon were allowed to lay down their arms, and to march out unmoleſted, the citizens to remove with their effects; twenty-four perſons, clergy, ſoldiers and inhabitants

[m] Cox. Borlaſe.

habitants, were excluded from mercy; and Ireton, now master of the city, executed the severest vengeance on those who had been the most distinguished partizans of the nuncio, and most inveterate opposers of English government. Of all those who had been excepted from mercy, the bishop of Limerick alone escaped. O'Brian, the popish prelate, of Emly, was seized and instantly executed. Wolfe, the friar, who had seditiously excluded the marquis of Ormond from Limerick, now received the just reward of his presumption. With him were led to execution some magistrates, the most turbulent and seditious of the nuncio's faction. Fennel, notwithstanding his services, was tried for several murders and condemned to death. Geoffry Browne, on his return from Brussels, fell into the hands of an enemy, who little regarded his consequence with the Irish n, and suffered by the executioner*. The brave Henry O'Nial had so offended by his defence of the city, and so provoked Ireton by his former gallant behaviour at Clonmel, that the gloomy and intractable republican tried him by a court martial for a conduct which should have recommended him to

the

---

n Ludlow's Memoirs.

* 'He pleaded, saith Ludlow, "that it was not just to exclude him "from mercy, because he had been engaged in the same cause as we "pretended to fight for, the liberty and religion of his country." 'The deputy replied, that Ireland being a conquered country, the 'English nation might, with justice, assert their right and conquest; 'that they had been treated by the late government far beyond their 'merits, or the rules of reason; notwithstanding which, they had bar-'barously murdered all the English that fell into their hands, and rob-'bed them of their goods, which they had gained by their industry, 'and taken away the lands which they had purchased with their mo-'ney.—That touching the point of religion, there was a wide difference 'also between us; we *only* contending to preserve our natural right 'therein, *without imposing our opinions upon other men*; whereas they 'would not be contented, unless they might have power to compel all 'others to submit to their imposition on pain of death.' The men of *tolerant* principles, it seems, thought this a *full refutation* of the prisoner's plea.

the esteem of a soldier. O'Nial pleaded, that he had taken no part in the original conspiracy; that he had been invited into Ireland by his countrymen, and ever acted as a fair and honourable enemy. But Ireton was inexorable; and his pliant court shamefully condemned the Irish general to death. Some of the officers, more generous, expostulated with Ireton, and happily subdued his obstinacy: the cause was re-examined, and the court, with difficulty, consented to spare his life.

Galway, the great remaining resource of the Irish was now summoned to accept the conditions originally offered to Limerick [o]; and, in case of any refusal or delay, threatened with the same severities. The citizens, in the first impressions of terrour, were ready to treat, when Ireton caught the fatal infection which wasted several parts of Ireland, and died at Limerick. Encouraged by this event, the Irish of Galway grew resolute. They united under the command of general Preston, and addressed themselves to Clanricarde for assistance, promising all obedience to his authority. The marquis attended them in person, and summoned an assembly of nobility, gentry, and prelates, to meet at Galway, and concert measures for defence.

In the mean time, Ludlow was, for the present, entrusted with the command of the English forces [p], and exerted himself with due vigour to complete the reduction of the Irish. While the depth of winter suspended his operations, he issued orders against supplying the enemy with arms, or other necessaries; he required all persons to withdraw from their quarters, on pain of being treated as enemies; he directed

that

[o] Borlase.   [p] Ludlow's Memoirs, Vol. I.

that no quarter should be granted to those who had withdrawn themselves from protection, and joined the Irish since the arrival of general Cromwell. His officers executed these orders with diligence and severity. An universal dismay seized the whole Irish party. Numbers daily submitted, and secured the remains of their property by compositions. A submission was offered in the name of the nation, by an assembly held in Leinster: no sooner had Sir Charles Coote appeared before Galway, when the assembly there convened, prevailed on Clanricarde to send the like offer to Ludlow. But no general treaty of submission could be now admitted. The settlement of the nation (it was said) belonged to the parliament of England, who would distinguish those who accepted their protection, as well from such as had committed murders and massacres of the protestants, as those who obstinately opposed the authority of the commonwealth; so that individuals only, who should immediately lay down their arms, might expect favourable conditions. Nor did this extremity of distress allay the infatuated pride and turbulence of the Irish clergy and their creatures; they still talked idly of renewing the original confederacy; they still maligned and opposed Clanricarde; they still continued their seditious practices, and vented their contempt of that delusion of loyalty, to which they attributed all the misfortunes of the nation. In the midst of consternation, clamour, and confusion, Preston, the governour of Galway, fled by sea from the impending danger; and the city without the least regard to the authority of Clanricarde, was surrendered with an ease utterly astonishing to the besiegers.

THE reduction of a few inferiour towns was effected without difficulty; yet the marquis of Clanricarde

ricarde still continued some appearance of hostilities; from a vain hope of making a diversion in favour of the king's English enterprizes[q]. He pierced into the northern province, and being joined by some Ulster forces, took the castles of Ballyshannon and Donnegal: having maintained these posts for some time, he was obliged to fly from the superiour force of the enemy; his troops were dispersed, his resources utterly exhausted, and his person every hour in danger from the treachery of his followers. In this situation, he pursued the king's instructions, and accepted conditions from the republicans. He was allowed to reside unmolested in their quarters for some time, and then to transport himself and three thousand Irish into any prince's service in amity with England. He retired from a country lost to his royal master, by illiberal bigotry, frantic pride, the blindness of men intoxicated by an imaginary consequence, their senseless factions, and incorrigible perverseness, in contending against their own interests, and rejecting every measure necessary for their own security.

In the mean time [r], the parliament of England concerted measures for the final settlement and administration of Ireland. Lambert was appointed successor to Ireton, and prepared for his departure [f]; but as Cromwell's commission of lord lieutenant was speedily to expire, it became a question whether it should not be renewed, instead of sending Lambert as his deputy. Cromwell, conscious of his secret designs, artfully entreated that he might not be continued in this office, affecting to concur with those who deemed the title of lord lieutenant more suitable to a monarchy than a commonwealth; at
the

q Borlase.   r A. D. 1652.   f Ludlow.

the same time, he moved to employ Lambert in the character of lord deputy. The parliament refused to grant him any higher title than that of commander in chief of their forces in Ireland. Lambert, as Cromwell wished, was offended, and refused to accept this command. It was conferred on Fleetwood, who had lately married the relict of Ireton, and, of consequence, was particularly devoted to his father-in law, Cromwell.

Two acts relative to Ireland were now debated in parliament; one for confiscation of all the lands of rebels; another, for adjusting the claims of adventurers, and vesting them with their Irish estates. Before acts could be completely adjusted, Fleetwood was dispatched to Ireland, where he found scarcely the remains of war, and the Irish of all orders submitting to the terms imposed by their conquerors. They were to abide a trial [t], if accused of any murders committed in the beginning of the war; if convicted, they were to be incapable of pardon, and their estates entirely confiscated; those who had only assisted in the war, were to forfeit two thirds of their estates, and to be banished from Ireland; but among those excepted from pardon, for life, and estate, the marquis of Ormond, lord Inchiquin, Bramhal the protestant bishop of Derry, a man peculiarly obnoxious to the republicans, and the earl of Roscommon, were distinctly named.

The first employment of the new administration was to enforce these rigourous ordinances [u]. Commissions issued in the several provinces for the erection of an high court of justice, in order to try those who were accused of murdering the English. Lord Mayo,

[t] Cox.   [u] Borlase.

Mayo, in Connaught, colonel William Bagnal, in Munster[w], were condemned, not on the clearest and most exceptionable evidence. Lord Muskerry was charged with the assassination of several Englishmen, but honourably acquitted on his trial, and permitted to embark for Spain. So many authors of the first barbarous outrages of this war, had been cut off in the hostilities of ten years, had escaped into foreign countries, or died by famine and the plague, that two hundred only, on the severest inquisition, were condemned to death. In the northern province, which had been the great scene of barbarity, not one was brought to justice but Sir Phelim O'Nial.

From the arrival of Owen O'Nial, this barbarous conspirator had continued to act an inferiour part, without honour, esteem, or notice. During the administration of Clanricarde, when abler commanders had been gradually removed, he emerged from his obscurity, and gave the marquis some assistance; but was soon compelled, by repeated defeats, to shelter himself in a retired island. Hence lord Caulfield, heir of that lord, whose castle and person he had seized, and whom his followers had barbarously murdered, soon dragged him to justice. In the last period of his life, he discovered a spirit and resolution worthy of a better character. He was accused of exhibiting a commission from the late king for commencing the Irish insurrection: he acknowledged the charge; adding, that on seizing the fort of Charlemont he had found a patent with a broad seal annexed, which he directed to be taken off and fixed to a pretended commission. His judges, not satisfied with this allegation, pressed him

---

[w] Carte, Orm. Vol. II. p. 157.

FORFEIT lands were assigned to satisfy the arrears due to the English army; but this satisfaction was confined to those who had served from the arrival of Cromwell, in the year sixteen hundred and forty-nine. The distresses of those who had borne arms against the Irish before this period were much more lamentable; but they were infected by a mixture of the ungodly and malignant, and no provision could be now obtained for them except a small portion of lands in Wicklow, and the adjacent counties, not sufficient to discharge a fourth part of their arrears. The adventurers, persuaded that there were forfeited lands in one moiety of nine principal counties, sufficient to repay them, accepted this moiety as their full satisfaction; the other was assigned to soldiers. Connaught was reserved entirely for the Irish, under the qualifications determined by parliament. Here they were to confine themselves, and to enjoy their several proportions of land; that so, the new English planters might proceed without interruption, and and without that danger of degenerating, which former ages had experienced from an intercourse with the Irish; and the natives, divided by the Shannon from the other provinces, and surrounded by English garrisons, might be restrained from their old barbarous incursions. Notwithstanding all these assignments and provisions, the counties of Dublin, Kildare, Carlow, and Cork, remained still unappropriated. These, together with the lands of bishops, deans, and chapters, (of which a part was granted to the university of Dublin) were all reserved by parliament, to be hereafter disposed of at their pleasure. Courts were established at Dublin and Athlone to hear and adjudge all claims, which were to be exhibited and established within a limited time, that all proprietors might be freed from future litigation. Such arrangements

ments necessarily engaged more time than was at first imagined; were attended with complaints, disputes and jealousies; nor, in the distribution of lands, were the commissioners and their creatures inattentive to their own interests.

LITTLE progress had been made in this important affair, when intelligence was received in Ireland of an astonishing revolution. Oliver Cromwell had forcibly dissolved the parliament, delegated the government to another assembly called by the same name, which soon pronounced their own dissolution, and was now declared by his council of officers, protector of the commonwealth of England, Scotland, and Ireland. The news of this momentous change in English government was variously received in Ireland; by the army, who complained of partiality in the commissioners, with particular satisfaction; by some fanatics, who had for a long time insulted every party, with invective and resentment; by Ludlow, and other zealous republicans, with abhorrence and indignation. It was proposed to proclaim the protector; after the debates and opposition of a fortnight, Fleetwood, and the commissioners, with a few principal officers, at length, with difficulty, resolved, by the majority of one voice, that a proclamation should be issued. Ludlow retired from the offensive pageantry, declared his purpose of acting no longer as a commissioner, yet still kept his post of lieutenant general, possibly to preserve his influence in the army.

OLIVER, who was attentive to every part of his new dominions, sent his son Henry into Ireland, to sound the dispositions of the army, to reconcile men's minds to the usurpation, and, by cultivating those of greatest influence, to prepare the way for his future govern-

^a A. D. 1654.

ment of this kingdom. Henry was penetrating, juft, and generous. He foon difcovered, that the commiffioners had done little more than make orders for the diftribution of lands, referving large proportions to themfelves; fo that, in fome inftances, the ftate had been fcandaloufly defrauded. He was paticularly affected with the miferable condition of the courts of judicature, the delays and oppreffions occafioned by the want of able judges and lawyers; the univerfal defolation, arifing from the virulence of his countrymen againft the old inhabitants, which had fcarcely left a fingle houfe out of the walled towns undemolifhed. He endeavoured to reconcile the difaffected, and practifed with Ludlow to gain him to his father's intereft, but without effect. He departed, deeply impreffed with the neceffity of removing the obftinate republicans from every place of power they enjoyed in Ireland.

The instrument of government required that a parliament fhould be fummoned for the three nations, now united into one commonwealth. Thirty members were to be chofen for Ireland. The commiffioners were informed of this claufe, and directed to tranfmit their advice relative to the election of thefe members. They were of opinion, that in the prefent defolate and unfettled ftate of the nation, fuch an election was not to be attempted, as perfons might be chofen in fome places not well affected to the Englifh intereft. They, therefore, inclined to the opinion, that the protector fhould call the thirty members by writ to parliament. The fpirit of Ludlow was on fire at this ignoble purpofe; he ftepped out of his retreat; he exhorted the commiffioners not to refign the name and form of liberty, though the fubftance and reality had been tamely yielded; he defpifed the apprehenfions

they

they expressed of a popular election; and observed, that the very persons they desired could not fail to be chosen by the influence of government. Fleetwood complied; he apportioned the numbers to be chosen by the counties and cities; a private junto of the commissioners agreed on the persons to be returned; sheriffs were nominated and prepared for this purpose; and, for the most part, the elections were made agreeable to their desires.

But this service could not allay the suspicions which the wary proctor entertained of the commissioners. He put an end to their authority, and appointed Fleetwood lord deputy for three years, assigning him a new council to assist in the administration. They were instructed to improve the interest of the commonwealth in Ireland, to suppress idolatry, popery, superstition, and profaneness, to encourage godly and gifted ministers of the word, and to execute the laws against the scandalous and malignant, to provide for the advancement of learning, to attend to the revenue with diligence and œconomy, and to dispense with the orders of the late parliament and council of state for transporting the Irish into Connaught, if it should be for the public service.

This indulgence to the Irish did not escape the enemies of Cromwell. They had already observed his partiality to the cavaliers, and affected the greatest alarm at his assiduity in conciliating all parties to his interest, however odious and obnoxious. It was observed with no small jealousy, that the form of administration lately established in Ireland was more suited to a royal than a republican government, and indicated a settled purpose in Oliver of establishing a monarchical power in his family. The army was discontented

contented at the delays in affigning them their portions of land, and many of them utterly diffatisfied with the prefent government. When Cromwell had recalled a detachment to England, in order to ftrengthen him againft fome attempts of the royalifts, they mutinied, and exclaimed, that they had engaged to fight againft Irifh rebels, but in England they might poffibly be employed againft their beft friends. Ludlow [a] was regarded as the principal male-content; he took an active part in enflaming the difcontented, and was induftrious in difperfing feveral tracts * publifhed againft the protector. Oliver was offended and alarmed. He directed Fleetwood to require him to furrender his commiffion, and, in cafe of refufal, to fend him prifoner into England. Ludlow refufed to give up a commiffion he had received from the parliament; but, at length, was prevailed on to promife on his parole, that he would prefent himfelf before Cromwell; and, in the mean time, not to act againft the prefent government. In the prefent difcontents of England, fuch a man might prove dangerous. Cromwell, therefore, on recollection, ordered that he fhould be detained in Ireland; and care was fome time after taken that his regiment fhould be difbanded, fo as to diminifh his influence.

It cannot be expected that Ireland, at this period, fhould [b] afford any materials for the Hiftorian. The old

[a] Ludlow's Memoirs.   [b] A. D. 1655.

* An order was fome time after fent to Ireland, conceived in the full fpirit of arbitrary power. "That the printer" (for there was, but one) "in Dublin fhould not fuffer his prefs to be made ufe of "without firft bringing the copy to be printed to the clerk of the "council; who, upon viewing it, if he found any thing tending to "the prejudice of the comonwealth, or the public peace and wel- "fare, fhould acquaint the council with the fame, for their pleafures "to be known therein."

old inhabitants were completely broken and subdued; the English army waited with impatience to reap the fruits of their labours; and the great object of administration was, to suppress all murmurs and discontents, and to reconcile men's mind to the present government of England. For this purpose, Henry Cromwell was again employed, first as a military officer, and soon after as lord deputy, in the place of Fleetwood. He found the officers of the army discontented and refractory; they refused to join in an address to the protector, promising to support him against his enemies; at the same time, they had the hardiness to petition him to restore their former deputy. Their petition was, indeed, encountered by another from the opposite party, in favour of Henry Cromwell; and the liberal and equitable spirit of his administration, his justice, impartiality, and benevolence, soon reconciled them to their new governour. Though the nation depopulated and exhausted, and in this state of extreme poverty was oppressed with grievous assessments, though the military establishment could not be supported, and the partiality of Oliver to the officers who espoused his cause, prevented any scheme of a reduction; though his grants to particular creatures exhausted the revenue, and no supplies were sent from England; and though the affairs of Ireland were sometimes totally neglected amidst the more urgent concerns of the protector, yet his son Henry proved " a governour from whom he himself might learn;" (to use his own expression.) He established his authority firmly in the hearts of a people, who were ingenuous enough to acknowledge the merits of his administration, that the were entirely reconciled to his father's interests. When Oliver received a petition from the officers of his own regiment, publicly avowing their dissatisfaction at his government, addresses were transmitted

mitted from the army and the inhabitants of every county in Ireland, expressing their resolution of adhering to the protector against all those whose particular animosities endeavoured to re-embroil the public.

On the death of Oliver,[c] the same assurances of support were renewed to Richard, who confirmed his brother in the government of Ireland, by the new title of lord lieutenant. He summoned the members [d]chosen for Ireland to this parliament: the republicans, who were for adhering to the ancient law of the land, opposed the admission of thirty men known to be zealous advocates for the ruling power; but the court, with difficulty, at length prevailed, that they should sit and vote. The news of the dissolution of this parliament, and the intrigues of Wallingford-house, was brought to Ireland by Sir Charles Coote. The lieutenant exerted himself with peculiar vigour to support the tottering power of his brother. On the restoration of the rump-parliament, he laboured to prevent the disorders which might arise from this sudden revolution. He issued a proclamation to preserve the peace; and on consulting with his officers, sent agents to the council of state, with proposals relative to the civil and military government of Ireland. They were referred to the parliament, as it was called, who made some ordinances for the benefit of the adventurers and soldiers; and, at the same time, resolved, that the government of Ireland should be again administered by commissioners, that Henry Cromwell should be recalled, and Ludlow appointed to command the forces of the comonwealth in this kingdom.

HENRY

[c] Ludlow's Memoirs.   [d] A. D. 1658.

Henry had already declared to Fleetwood,[e] "that, although he could not promise so much affection to the late changes, as others very honestly might, because he could not promote any thing which inferred a diminution of his late father's honour and merit, yet he had such a tenderness for peace as to be content with the present government; and, therefore, thought it his duty to prevent those fears and jealousies which might give occasion to interrupt the public peace, by resigning his charge to any one whom they should send to receive it." The new commissioners were not acquainted with his sentiments, or suspected his sincerity. They dreaded his abilities, his popularity, and his power in Ireland: they imagined he would attempt to retain his authority by force. Sir Hardress Waller was employed to surprise the castle of Dublin; he was admitted without the least opposition, while Henry Cromwell retired to a house in the Phœnix-Park, having administered the government with such disregard to his private interest, that he could not immediately command so much money as might defray the expences of a voyage to England.

From the moment of the abdication of Richard Cromwell, the royalists of Ireland conceived the most sanguine hopes of the king's speedy restoration. Most of the old English race, and many of the original Irish, were sincerely devoted to his interests; and the Scots of Ulster were so dreaded by the usurpers, that the severest ordinances had been repeatedly made for excluding their countrymen from Ireland. The attachment of lord Broghill to the royal family, was justly suspected, notwithstanding his compliance with Oliver and his sons; so that on intelligence of the insurrection of

[e] Thurloe.

of Sir George Booth, Ludlow and the new commiſſioners threatned to confine him, unleſs he ſhould engage to keep the ſouthern province in peaceable ſubjection to the preſent government; a demand ſo unreaſonable, that they could not inſiſt upon it, as they would not venture to entruſt him with the ſole power of this province. It is ſaid, that even Henry Cromwell, *e* when deprived of his government, had once reſolved to declare for the king, though, on the arrival of the commiſſioners, he changed this reſolution.

These diſpoſitions in favour of the king were conſiderably promoted by the ſeverity and jealouſy of the commiſſioners. That the army might be modelled to the purpoſes of their faction, lord Broghill, Sir Charles Coote, and other ſuſpected perſons, were diſmiſſed: on the quarrel between the army and parliament, they proceeded yet further; more than two hundred officers were caſhiered without any trial, or any crime alledged to diminiſh the merit of their long trial, and painful ſervices. Broghill was, by birth and intereſt, determined to the ſide of monarchy. Diſguſted at the ſudden revolutions of power, the anarchy and confuſion of England, and evidently foreſeeing, that theſe events muſt end in the reſtoration of the king, he reſolved to ſecure his ſhare of merit; but cautious, dark, and deliberate, he concealed his intentions, and to the laſt diſclaimed all thoughts of what he called "a ruinous wickedneſs." *f* He laboured, at the ſame time, to engage all his officers, friends, and dependents, in his deſign. He communicated it to Sir Charles Coote, *g* who had already betrayed a diſaffection both to the rump-parliament and to the army. Coote, and his father, had engaged in the parliamentarian ſervice, not from principle, but intereſt. The ruin of this party was

e Carte, Orm. Vol. II. p. 201. f Thurloe. g Orrery's Mem.

was evidently approaching. Sir Charles had no way to atone for his oppofition to the royal family, but by a fpeedy and zealous declaration in favour of the king. He inftantly embraced the overtures of Broghill; and his ardour, like that of all new converts, was violent and unreftrained. He threatned, by his precipitation, to defeat the meafures of this lord; and was fcarcely reftrained from an untimely declaration.

In the mean time, Ludlow [h] was recalled to London, by the diffolution of the rump parliament. Colonel John Jones, one of the late king's judges was appointed to command the forces in Ireland, and feemed to exult in his addrefs, in reconciling the army to the new change of government. The commiffioners were fo refigned to the authority of Lambert and his officers, that they fuddenly changed their title from that of commiffioners of parliament, to commiffioners of the commonwealth. Peace and compofure feemed eftablifhed in Ireland, when the royal party burft from their concealment, and demolifhed the whole fabric of this republican government. Lord Montgomery, Sir Theophilus Jones, Sir Oliver Saint-George, Sir Audley Mervyn, and others [i] of confiderable weight and confequence, had by this time adopted the fentiments of lord Broghill and Sir Charles Coote. They formed a bold defign to feize the caftle of Dublin, and to fecure the perfons of the commiffioners. They affembled at Dublin, [k] on pretence of petitioning for a general council of officers, to deliver their fentiments on the prefent ftate of affairs. Their petition was rejected; when, by a fudden and defperate effort, they poffeffed themfelves of the caftle, made Jones their prifoner, feized Corbet and Tomlinfon, two of his colleagues,

on

[h] Ludlow. [i] Cox. [k] Carte, Orm. vol. II. p. 202.

on their return from a conventicle, and declared for a free parliament. In the mean time, Sir Charles Coote, impatient to be diftinguifhed by his zeal, fecured the town and fort of Galway, changed the governour, collected a confiderable body, confifting chiefly of the old Englifh, furprifed Athlone, marched to Dublin, and impeached Ludlow and the commiffioners of high treafon. The royalifts of other quarters poffeffed themfelves of Youghall, Clonmel, Carlow, Limerick, Drogheda; fo that in one week, moft of the confiderable garrifons of Ireland declared for a free parliament; a language, whofe real import was, by this time, generally underftood.

CHARLES was foon informed of thefe favourable appearances in Ireland. Lord Broghill invited him to repair immediately to this kingdom. Coote employed an emiffary to explain his intentions, and to give the warmeft affurances of his fervice. It was even debated in the king's council, whether he fhould not go directly to Ireland. Charles feemed refolved on this enterprize; but there was now great expectation from the proceedings of Monk; it was confidered, that this country muft of courfe follow the example of England; it was, therefore, thought proper to fufpend this refolution, until the iffue of Englifh affairs fhould be difcovered.

A COUNCIL of officers now affumed the government of Ireland. On a petition of the magiftracy of Dublin, they fummoned a convention of eftates. The council of ftate in England ordered this convention to be diffolved; but they proceeded in contempt of thefe orders. They declared their deteftation of the proceedings of the high court of juftice, and the late king's murder; and, having fecured the army, by providing

ing for the payment of the arrears, and their future maintenance, they published their declaration for a full and free parliament.

LUDLOW now arrived in the port of Dublin.[1] The council of officers attempted to seize this desperate republican, but in vain. Instead of venturing on shore, he went to Duncannon; and, by his letters to the commanders of several garrisons endeavoured to exasperate them against the dangerous proceedings of Dublin, and to confirm their attachment to the good old cause. But the parliament of England were so awed and influenced by Monk, that they soon recalled Ludlow, and their other Irish commissioners. Sir Hardress Waller was now the only dangerous opponent to the convention. He had sat as one of the late king's judges; and, although he had refused to sign an engagement to Lambert and his faction, and was zealous for the parliament, yet was he a determined enemy to monarchy, and, both by interest and principle, averse to every measure tending to a restoration. He mixed with the council of officers at Dublin; and, when a bold and virulent remonstrance was preparing to be transmitted to the English parliament, he artfully moved, that the council should be adjourned to the castle. The officers, justly suspecting a design to seize their persons, rejected this motion. Waller, with some partizans, contrived to possess themselves of the castle, and openly declared their intentions of bringing the leaders of the council to condign punishment. The incident was alarming. Sir Charles Coote, and Sir Theophilus Jones, mounted on horseback, rode through the streets exclaiming for a free parliament, and were soon followed by a vast concourse echoing their clamours.
The

---

1 Ludlow's Memoirs.

The castle was invested, and after a resistance of five days, Waller was reduced, and sent prisoner to England.

The convention and council of officers now proceeded without restraint or opposition, and avowed their design of restoring the king. [m] One point only remained to be debated, whether they should stipulate for a confirmation of estates to the adventurers and soldiers, or whether they should restore withou thim any previous condition. Possessed with high notions of their own consequence, they debated this point warmly. Coote contended for submitting all their interests implicitly to the king; and his opinion at length prevailed. He thus triumphed over the coldness and caution of lord Broghill, who, by affecting to proceed slowly and secretly, rendered himself suspected to several of the royalists. He seemed to apprehend, that the forwardness of the Irish subjects might give offence to the royalists of England: the ardour of Coote was not restrained by such considerations; hence arose an emulation between these leaders, which might have proved inconvenient, had there been a necessity for action. But a few inconsiderable fanatics, and some of the old Irish, with their popish primate, were the only persons who presumed to declare against the king. The Body of the nation caught the flame of loyalty, and waited with impatience for the declaration of Breda. This was readily accepted; Charles was proclaimed in all the great towns of Ireland with every manifestation of joy; and the convention voted a present of twenty thousand pounds to his majesty, four thousand to the duke of York, and two thousand to the duke of Gloucester.

CHAP.

[m] Carte, ut sup.

CHAP. III.

*Temper of different parties in Ireland at the restoration.—Irish catholics odious.—Ordinance against them.—Prelacy and the liturgy restored.—Petition in favour of dissenters suppressed.—*DECLARATION *for the settlement of Ireland.—Instructions for executing it.—Temper and proceedings of the Irish parliament.—Debates on the act of settlement in Ireland,—and in London.—Indiscretion of the Irish agents.—Colonel Richard Talbot.—The Irish agents dismissed with disgrace.—Thirty thousand pounds granted by parliament to the duke of Ormond.—*ACT OF SETTLEMENT *passed.—Court of wards abolished.—Objections to the act of settlement.—Courts of claims.—*NEW INTEREST *alarmed and provoked.—Plot for seizing the castle of Dublin.—Address of the house of commons, and Mervyn's speech.—Scheme of a general insurrection, detected and defeated.—Plan of an* ACT OF EXPLANATION.*—Ormond called to England.—Act of explanation debated.—Dissatisfaction of the Irish.—Objections of the commons at Dublin.—Proceedings of the Irish parliament.—Act of explanation passed.—Perplexities in the execution of it.—Bill for prohibiting the importation of Irish cattle into England.—Its effects on Ireland.—Motion for a perpetual prohibition.—Violence of the two English houses.—Their bill receives the royal assent.—Useful caution of the duke of Ormond. His endeavours to alleviate the distresses of Ireland arising from this bill,—to establish arts and manufactures, and to encourage learning in Ireland.—Practices against the duke of Ormond in England.—Dissimulation of the king.—Lord Roberts appointed lord lieutenant of Ireland.—His character and conduct.—He is succeeded by lord Berkley.*

THE restoration of Charles the Second[m] was an event of great expectation in every part of the English dominions; but in Ireland, after a desperate civil war of almost nine years, various contentions of violent and embittered factions, and various revolutions of power and property, it naturally roused the hopes and fears of men, and kept their attention to the most interesting objects of this life strained to a painful degree of anxiety. The old inhabitants, the new adventurers, catholics, fanatics, every denomination of protestants, and every party of Romanists, eyed each other with jealousy, with envy, with suspicion and aversion; impatient to be restored to their antient possessions, to be confirmed in their new acquisitions, to be pardoned for their delinquency, or to be rewarded for their services.

Of these, the Irish catholics were the most impatient. They, whom Cromwell had declared innocent of the rebellion, who yet were ejected from their estates, and obliged to accept some inferior portions of land in Connaught, now exulted in the extinction of a fanatical tyranny.[n] Even before the king had been proclaimed, many of them, disdaining the slow and formal procedure of law, re-entered on their patrimonial lands, and expelled the new intruders. Hence arose various riots and disorders, which obliged the convention to publish an ordinance, for preserving the peace and quieting possessions. Nothing could be more acceptable to the new English settlers than these instances of lawless outrage. They represented them in England as the first overtures to a new rebellion; and, in England, every rumour unfavourable to the Irish was received with peculiar avidity. Agents were sent from Ireland, who reported their conduct

[m] A. D. 1660. [n] Carte, Orm. vol. II. p. 205—216.

conduct and designs with every offensive aggravation, so that before the landing of the king, the act of indemnity was so prepared as to exclude all those who had any hand in plotting or contriving, aiding or abetting the rebellion of Ireland, by which the whole Romish party were in effect excluded: and when, by another clause, it was provided, that the act should not extend to restore to any persons the estates disposed of by authority of any parliament or convention, it was with some difficulty that an exception was inserted of " the marquis of Ormond, and other the protestants " of Ireland." Some other provisos were attempted, which must have utterly ruined all the old English families of this country; but they were suspended, and afterwards defeated by the marquis.

In the mean time, the severest ordinances lately made against the Irish Roman catholics were strictly executed. They were not allowed to pass from one province to another on their ordinary business; many of them were imprisoned, their letters were intercepted; their gentry were forbidden to meet, and thus deprived of the opportunity of chusing agents, or representing their grievances. No sooner had the king arrived in London, when the houses united in representing the danger to be apprehended from the recent violences of many natives of Ireland; and Charles was obliged to publish a proclamation for apprehending and prosecuting all Irish rebels, and commanding that adventurers, soldiers, and others, who were possessed of their manors, houses, or lands, should not be disturbed in their possessions, until legally evicted, or his majesty, by advice of parliament, should take further order therein.

The Irish convention, and their agents, who attended

tended on the king and the English parliament, were not yet satisfied. This proclamation might be recalled; another might be issued of a different tenour; several of the Irish daily solicited for letters to put them in possession of their former estates, and several were granted. An Irish parliament, duly composed, and speedily convened, was deemed absolutely necessary to secure the interests of the soldiers and adventurers. The king was urged to call such a parliament without delay: he answered, that it should be called in due time; for he had not yet leisure to satisfy the impatience of these bold petitioners. Several arrangements were previously to be made in the ecclesiastical and civil affairs of Ireland, both at this time remarkbly embarrassed and disordered. The convention had requested, that all impropriate and forfeited tythes and glebes, in the king's disposal, might be granted to the clergy; and that all escheated lands now exempted from the payment of ecclesiastical dues, might hereafter be made liable to the same. To this request Charles readily condescended; but who the ministers should be that were to receive these endowments was a point not universally agreed.

Besides the Scottish ministers in the northern province, some divines of the presbyterian judgment had lately gained possession of churches in Dublin, and the adjacent country, governed themselves in divine service by the directory, and preached the covenant with particular industry. They were indeed few, for the ecclesiastical benefices of Ireland were at this time too poor to tempt any numbers of these zealous missionaries from England. But they had courage, assiduity, and friends; and, on the king's landing, petitioned to have their model of church government established.

established. A petition of the same nature was promoted in the army of Ireland. The divines of the episcopal persuasion were alarmed, and remonstrated against these proceedings. They applied to Ormond for protection: Ormond proved their zealous and powerful advocate. He represented to the king, that episcopacy and the liturgy were as yet part of the legal establishment of Ireland; he proposed, that instead of trusting to the sense of a new parliament, composed of the adventurers and officers of Cromwell's army, the king should immediately proceed to fill up the ecclesiastical preferments of this country with men of worth, learning, and zeal for the established church. The advice was approved, and Charles immediately filled the four archbishopricks, and twelve episcopal sees, with the most eminent of the clergy of Ireland.

As a new great seal was not yet prepared, the patents, and, of consequence, the consecration of the nominated prelates were delayed for some months. The enemies of this order were elated; they imputed the delay to some secret reluctance or irresolution in the king. Their agents were busily imployed in every quarter of the kingdom; a petition prepared, to his majesty, that he would be graciously pleased to give order that their godly ministers of the gospel might be continued and protected; adventurers, officers, civil and military, men of every order and condition were solicited to subscribe this petition. On the return of the king, Monk had been appointed lord lieutenant, and lord Roberts deputy of Ireland; but as both continued in England, the administration was committed to Sir Charles Coote, and one major Bury, with the title of commissioners of government. Of these, Coote was well affected to the established church, Bury countenanced the petition. The officers of the army had

drawn

drawn it up, and were its chief promoters. In the ardour of their zeal they had incautiously betrayed their secret aversion to monarchy; and, in this their favourite petition, inserted several expressions reflecting on the present government. Of these Coote took full advantage, and, by pointing them out to his collegue, and alarming him with the consequences, prevailed on him to unite in suppressing the petition.

But however men's passions were at this time engaged by modes of church government and religious worship, the lands and possessions of Ireland were objects still more interesting to the several inhabitants. On the adjournment of the English houses the king had some leisure to attend to the distractions and competitions of this kingdom; and policy demanded, that he should make such establishments, as might, if possible, satisfy the different claimants, prevent all future litigation, and form a complete, peaceable, and lasting settlement. The variety of pretensions, as well as the unreasonable expectations both of parties and individuals, rendered this an arduous and perplexing task.

The interest of the adventurers, who, on the credit of those acts of parliament to which the late king assented, had advanced their money, and received their Irish lands from the usurpers, required particular regard, unless the king were to give the whole English nation an occasion to impeach his justice. The late merit of the protestant Irish army in returning to their duty, and, concurring chearfully in his restoration, claimed a competent provision for their pay. He had made a peace with the confederate Irish in the year sixteen hundred and forty-eight; and, however grievous the conditions, they were to be made good to those

those who adhered to the treaty, and honestly performed their engagements. Numbers of this party, when driven from their country, had expressed their loyalty and affection to the king during his exile, submitting to his commands with all chearfulness, and engaging in the service of France or Spain, as he deemed most consonant to his interests: such men could not now be excluded from his favour and protection. Some provision was due to those protestant officers, who, from the beginning of the Irish war, had faithfully served the king to the year sixteen hundred and forty-nine, and to whom Cromwell had denied any satisfaction for arrears on account of their attachment to the royal cause. Such various claimants, and such clashing interests, seemed difficult, if not impossible, to be satisfied. The king was willing to resign all his forfeitures; but all his forfeitures seemed insufficient for this purpose, to men best acquainted with the circumstances of Ireland. Various schemes were devised, considered, and rejected. Lord Broghill, now created earl of Orrery, Sir John Clotworthy, and Sir Arthur Mervyn, three bold and sanguine undertakers, at length formed an estimate of lands, which, when the adventurers and soldiers should be confirmed in their possessions, seemed, in theory, sufficient to compensate, or to *reprise*, as it was called, all the innocent or meritorious Irish. Charles eagerly adopted a scheme which promised to relieve his indolence from embarrassment and perplexity, and published his famous declaration for the settlement of Ireland.

By this declaration [o], in the first place, the adventurers were confirmed in the lands possessed by them on on the seventh day of May, sixteen hundred and fifty-nine,

---

[o] Carte, Orm. vol. II. p. 217.

nine, agreeably to the acts of parliament ᵖ of the seventeenth and eighteenth years of Charles the First; and all their deficiencies were to be satisfied before the ensuing month of May. These lands were to be held in free and common soccage.

IN the next place, the king confirmed to the soldiers the lands allotted for their pay (to be held by knights service, *in capite*) with an exception of church-lands, of estates procured by fraudulent means, and of lands possessed by those who were excepted in the act of oblivion and indemnity, or any others who, since the restoration, had endeavoured to disturb the public peace, or manifested an aversion to the regal government.

OFFICERS who had served before the month of June 1649, and had not yet received lands for their pay, were to be satisfied by estates, houses, and other securities allotted for this purpose. From these they were to receive immediate satisfaction of twelve shillings and six pence in the pound of their arrears, and an equal dividend of whatever should remain of their security.

PROTESTANTS, whose estates had been given to adventurers, or soldiers, were to be restored, unless they had been in rebellion before the cessation, or had taken out decrees for lands in Connaught or Clare. The persons thus removed were to be reprised, without being accountable for the *mesne* profits.

INNOCENT papists, although they had taken lands in Connaught, were to be restored to their estates; and

---

ᵖ Irish Stat. 14 and 15 Car. II. cap. 2.

and the persons, thus removed, to be reprised. If they had sold their Connaught lands, they were to satisfy the purchasers. But as the modelling of corporations seemed essential to the security of government, and as it was a point determined, that they should be formed entirely of English inhabitants, there was an exception inserted in this article. Those innocent papists, whose former estates lay within corporate towns, instead of being restored to their possessions, were to be reprised in the neighbourhood.

Papists who submitted and adhered to the peace of sixteen hundred and forty-eight, if they staid at home, sued out decrees, and received lands in Connaught, were to be bound thereby, and not relieved from their own act.

Those who had served abroad under the king's ensigns, and accepted no lands in Connaught, were to be restored to their old possessions, but not till the adventurers or soldiers, who now enjoyed them, should be reprised and satisfied for their disbursements.

The English parliament had already restored the marquis of Ormond and lord Inchiquin to their estates; and, in the present declaration, a provision was made for the interests of these lords, and some others, particularly of Monk, now duke of Albemarle, who received a considerable grant of Irish forfeitures. Thirty-six of the Irish nobility and gentry were also named as objects of the king's peculiar favour, to be restored to their estates on the same terms with those who had served abroad.

That no dispute might arise about precedency in restitution, it was directed, that innocent protestants and

and papists, who had no lands assigned in Connaught, should be first restored; then the innocent who had taken out decrees for such lands: the persons thus dispossessed were then to receive their reprisals; and, next in order, were those Irish to be restored to their lands who claimed the benefit of the peace concluded in sixteen hundred and forty-eight, or had served abroad under the king's ensigns. Should any lands remain after the necessary reprisals, they were assigned to the satisfaction of those who had furnished arms, ammunition, or provision, for the Irish war, previous to the year sixteen hundred and forty-nine; and from all the estates thus settled, restored, or reprised, a small rent was reserved to the crown.

To establish the particulars mentioned in this declaration, the king expressed his intention of convening a parliament in Ireland; and that, on the final settlement of this kingdom, an act of general pardon and oblivion should be passed, with an exception only of notorious murderers: that all frauds committed in decrees of forfeitures, should be reviewed and corrected; and that all judicial proceedings in the courts of law, or claims, should be ratified by parliament.

As a free gift from the adventurers and soldiers, the king graciously accepted one half year's rent from each of their two first years, to be applied to his own use, and that of the eminent sufferers in his service.

From all benefit of this declaration were excluded those concerned in contriving the surprisal of the castle of Dublin in the year sixteen hundred and forty-one, the late king's judges, they who signed his sentence, and the guard of halberdiers who assisted in the execution of it.

AND

AND as Charles abhorred the republican and fanatic spirit more than that of popery, he determined that the corporations should be formed entirely of men friendly to monarchy. His declaration was, therefore, closed by a provision, that nothing therein contained should extend to confirm the disposition of any lands, or tenements belonging to any city, or sea-town incorporated, either to adventurer, soldier, or any others; but that they should remain in his own hands, to be restored to such corporations as were found fit for his grace and favour; and that the persons, to whom they had been assigned, should be reprised as in other cases.

THE declaration thus framed, was transmitted to Ireland, with instructions for the execution of it, addressed to three new lord justices, Sir Maurice Eustace lord chancellor, the earl of Orrery, and Sir Charles Coote, now advanced to the dignity of earl of Montrath. The appointment [q] of these chief governours was immediately followed by the consecration of twelve bishops. This seemed a solemn revival of the ecclesiastical establishment, and was performed with such pomp, as indicated a kind of triumph over the puritanic party, who had hoped for the extinction of prelacy, and who had laboured to the last to effect some diminution at least of the ecclesiastical revenues, but were still disappointed, chiefly by the interposition of the marquis of Ormond.

THE declaration for the settlement of Ireland, however calculated to provide for all interests, yet did not satisfy the expectations of every party. To the adventurers and soldiers, indeed, the king vouchsafed
an

---

[q] Carte, Orm. vol. II. p. 212.

an enviable degree of favour. Nor was it without considerable repining, that the loyal officers who served before the year sixteen hundred and forty-nine, (or as they were stiled in these days, the FORTY-NINE-MEN) beheld what they deemed an unreasonable partiality to fanatics and republicans. They themselves had fought bravely against the Irish insurgents when their power was greatest, and the war most violent. Their known attachment to royalty had rendered them odious to the late usurpers. Their arrears remained unpaid; and now little more than half of these arrears were to be satisfied; nor were the securities assigned for this purpose deemed sufficient to discharge even this proportion of their demands. Those of the Irish, who pleaded their innocence or their merits, were still more provoked, that the restitution of their estates should be deferred until reprisals were found and assigned to the present unjust possessors. They objected to the choice of commissioners for executing the declaration, who were all, by interest and inclination, bound to the adventurers and soldiers; and the instructions sent to those commissioners, filled them with the most melancholy apprehensions.

IN these instructions they complained, that the qualifications necessary to ascertain their innocence were so severely stated that scarcely any of their nation could expect a sentence of acquittal. No ʳ man was to be restored as an innocent papist, who, at or before the cessation of the year sixteen hundred and forty-three, was of the royal party, or enjoyed his property in the quarters of the rebels, except the inhabitants of Cork and Youghall, who were driven into these quarters by force. No papist was to be deemed innocent,

who

ʳ Irish Stat. ut supra.

who had entered into the Irish confederacy before the peace of forty-eight: none who had at any time adheared to the nuncio, the clergy, or the papal power, in opposition to the royal authority, or who, having been excommunicated for his loyalty, had acknowledged himself an offender, and received absolution. Whoever derived the title to his estate from any who died guilty of these crimes; whoever claimed his estate on the articles of peace, and thus acknowledged his concurrence in the rebellion; whoever in the English quarters held correspondence with the rebels; whoever before the peace of forty-eight, sat in any assemblies or councils of the confederates, or acted by any commissions derived from them; whoever employed agents to treat with any foreign papal power for bringing forces into Ireland, or acted in such negociations, or harrassed the country as Wood-kerns, or "Tories," as they were called, before the departure of the marquis of Clanricarde, were all to be considered as guilty of rebellion, and incapable of restitution.

The popish party[s] exclaimed against the rigours of several of these qualifications, against the palpable injustice of the first. They pleaded, that abundance of catholics, averse to the rebellion of their countrymen and well affected to the crown, had lived peaceably in their own houses, lying accidentally within the quarters of the rebels, who, out of reverence to their characters, or favour to religion, left them unmolested, though they would not concur in their hostilities. They recalled to view the conduct of the lords justices in the begining of the rebellion, and their proclamation banishing all those on pain of death, who attempted to seek shelter in Dublin. They inveighed against
the

---

[s] Carte, Orm. vol. II. p. 220.

the cruelty of depriving men of their eftates, for refiding in the only places where government permitted them to refide; and, in a time of war and commotion accepting mercy from those whom they could not refift.

On the other hand, it was urged, that fuch men had not only given no affiftance to the crown, but favoured and fupported their rebellious countrymen: that their exclufion from the capital, was a proof that they were confider ed as enemies to the ftate; that, at the diftance of twenty years,[t] it was impoffible to prove particular acts of rebellion againft many who were moft guilty; that their place of refidence was now the only means of diftinguifhing between the innocent and criminal; and that fcrupulous adherence to this qualification was of abfolute neceffity to prevent multitudes of dangerous and difaffected papifts from recovering their power, embarraffing the kings government; and perhaps renewing the commotions of the realm, with all their tremendous confequences.

Such arguments received additional force from that violent and inveterate averfion which the new race of Englifh fettlers entertained to the catholics of Ireland. Full fraught with the puritanic fpirit, they abhorred their idolatrous and anti-chriftian worfhip. Enflamed with exaggerated accounts of their rapine, their murders, and maffacres, they fhuddered at their barbarity. They urged it as a point neceffary to the public peace, to crufh thefe enemies of God and man. They contended for the eftablifhment of what they called an Englifh intereft in Ireland, as the moft effectual fecurity of the crown: and both their principles,

[t] Ibid. p. 236.

ples, and their paſſion for power and riches, ſerved to extend their averſion indiſcriminately to all the old inhabitants, even of the proteſtant profeſſion. However unpolluted by the errours and exceſſes of popery, they yet were not ſufficiently heated againſt prelacy. However bravely they had fought againſt popiſh inſurgents, they had fought with equal bravery againſt republicans; and what was equally intolerable, their ſervices had now a fair claim to attention and reward.

In ſuch diſpoſitions, men waited impatiently for the meeting of that Iriſh parliament, which was to confirm the king's declaration by a law, and by which they hoped to be eſtabliſhed in their poſſeſſions, or to be redreſſed in their grievances. The parliament was convened [u]; and, as the adventurers and ſoldiers kept poſſeſſion of their lands and their intereſts in the ſeveral corporations, moſt of the members elected for the lower houſe were of their party. No catholics, and but few of the more virulent fanatics were returned [x]. Both houſes began with a declaration requiring all perſons to conform to the church-government and liturgy eſtabliſhed by law, in which they agreed the readier, and which they publiſhed with the greater expedition, before the non-conformiſts had encreaſed their power, by being fully ſecured in their eſtates. They concurred with equal eaſe in cenſuring the convenant, and oaths of aſſociation. The commons reſolved to addreſs the lords juſtices, that the term ſhould be adjourned, and the courts of law for ſome time ſhut up, in order to prevent the reverſal of outlawries, and the ejectment of adventurers or ſoldiers, before their preſent title ſhould be adjuſted by a ſtatute. The lords objected to ſuch a meaſure, not only as unconſtitutional, but of

[u] A. D. 1661.   [x] Carte, Orm. vol. II. p. 222.

of great prejudice to the old proteſtants. Yet, it was at length carried in their houſe to unite in this addreſs, and the juſtices condeſcended to their requeſt.

The commons hated and dreaded the popiſh party; and not ſatisfied with the preſent modelling of their houſe, laboured to exclude all of this party from ever ſitting in it. A bill had been tranſmitted for impoſing an oath of qualification on their members, calculated for this purpoſe. It was ſuppreſſed in England as unſeaſonable. They again attempted their purpoſe, by a reſolution, that no members ſhould ſit in their houſe, who had not taken the oaths of ſupremacy and allegiance; and, artfully involving other obnoxious perſons in the ſame incapacity, they added an excluſion of " all thoſe, and the ſons of thoſe, who had ſat in " the pretended high courts of juſtice wherein ſentence " of death had been pronounced on the late king, or " any of his majeſty's ſubjects, (except Thomas Scot, " who had been active in the reſtoration.)" This reſolution, when communicated to the juſtices, was condemned as an invaſion on the prerogative, in requiring qualifications different from what his majeſty had expreſſed in his writ. Provoked at what they deemed an unreaſonable partiality to papiſts, they revived the rumours of new plots and conſpiracies, received informations of many dark deſigns and ſuſpicious proceedings of the Iriſh, alarmed the government with the danger of public commotions; and, though all their induſtry could produce no material diſcoveries, yet it ſerved their purpoſe of loading an obnoxious party with additional odium, at a time when they were to contend with them for eſtates and ſettlements.

The great object of this parliament was the heads of a bill for ſettling the kingdom purſuant to the king's king's declaration. In the commons, where the NEW INTEREST of adventurers and soldiers was predominant, it was contended, that the declaration should be strictly observed, and confirmed exactly by a law. In the upper house sat several lords of the Irish race; several, who, by interest and inclination, were attached to the old English families of Ireland, and exasperated at the thought, that men of noble or reputable origin, settled in the kingdom for ages, loyal and zealous supporters of the crown, should be supplanted by a new colony of mean extraction and seditious spirit, who, though established by the usurpers, presumed to call themselves the only subjects in the realm on whom the king could depend. At the head of these stood the earl of Kildare, fortified by his powerful connections, and the proxy of Ormond, now created a duke[y]. They contended, that the king's declaration had been made on misinformation; that should it be adhered to literally, the hopes of the new interest indeed would be fully gratified, but no reprisals could be found either for the old protestants, for the Irish named as especial objects of royal favour, or NOMINEES (as they were called) for those who had served abroad, now stiled ENSIGN-MEN, or for those who should be adjudged innocent. To enlarge the fund of reprisals, they insisted, that a number of the most pestilent fanatics should, by name, be excluded from all advantages of the declaration: they examined the proceedings of the court of claims; here they found various subjects of complaint; the streets of Dublin were crowded with widows, who had entered claims for their jointures, and though most of their cases admitted no difficulty, not one had been restored. When restitution had been directed by the king to particular persons, they could obtain no order for their estates:

[y] Carte, Orm. vol. II. p. 228,

estates: the commissioners pleaded, that there were no reprisals for their present possessors; and, it was found on enquiry, that they had granted the lands allotted for the reprisals clandestinely to their own friends, under the notion of *cautionary* reprisals, or reprisals *de bene esse*. The lords deemed it necessary to put some stop to this scandalous abuse of power, and to petition the king, that these illicit grants should be revoked.

In another particular, they insisted on a remarkable defalcation from the claims of the adventurers. Soon after the English act of the seventeenth year of Charles the First, for vesting those who should advance money with the forfeited lands of Ireland, the parliament, in the distresses of the civil war, publish what was called the DOUBLING ORDINANCE[z]. It imported, that whoever should advance one-fourth part more than his original adventure, should have the whole doubled on account, and receive lands as for the whole doubled sum really paid; and that, if the adventurer refused to advance this fourth, any other person on paying it, should reap the same advantage, deducting only the original money paid by the first adventurer. The king, it was alledged, was by no means bound to ratify these stipulations. They were founded not on the act of adventurers, but an ordinance of parliament, which could be no longer binding than while that parliament subsisted; nor was the money thus raised at all applied to the service of Ireland; so that there was no foundation either in law, equity, or the king's declaration, for confirming such exorbitant advantages, by which the crown must unjustly lose more than sixty thousand pounds, which in land, by a moderate calculation, would amount to one hundred and forty-two thousand acres; and these, at

the

[z] Carte, Orm. vol. II. p. 225.

the rate of three shillings by the acre, to the sum of two hundred and twelve thousand pounds a year.

These objections were approved, notwithstanding all the efforts of Sir John Clotworthy, now lord Masfarene, who had been a considerable agent in the English parliament for the doubling ordinance; and was now particularly interested to support it. The affair was laid before the king; the king agreed to the propriety of satisfying the adventurers on this ordinance for the money they had really advanced, and no more. A clause for this purpose was inserted in the heads of the bill of settlement, which after various contests and delays, were at length prepared, amended, transcribed, and presented to the lords justices. Some weeks passed in adjusting clauses and provisos, which the justices took the liberty to insert. It was at length transmitted to England by three lords commissioned by the council, while each house of parliament nominated their agents to attend the king and council in England, and to solicit the immediate passing of the bill.

London now became the great scene of debate on Irish affairs[z]; and hither the Irish catholics also sent agents to plead their cause. The adventurers raised a considerable sum of money to be distributed among those who could support their interest. The Irish had neither money nor friends. The English nation regarded them with horrour. The council, before whom they were to appear, knew little of the conduct of individuals who deserved favour, and were ready to involve them all in the general guilt of massacre and rebellion. The duke of Ormond was the only person able and inclined to save them from ruin; and him they took care, in the first place, to disoblige[a]. He recommended a modest

[z] A. D. 1662.   [a] Carte, Orm. vol. II. p. 233-245.

modest extenuation of their crimes, an humble submission to the king's mercy, and a declaration of their desire to live peaceably and brotherly with their fellow-subjects for the future: they chose to plead the justice of their cause, their merits, and superiour pretensions to the king's favour. He was ready to approve himself their zealous advocate: they chose another advocate. Colonel Richard Talbot, son of Sir William, an eminent lawyer of Ireland, and brother of Sir Robert, a man highly revered by the Irish confederates, had, in the Low Countries, acquired the favour of the duke of York. His brother, Peter, an Irish Jesuit, was said to be entrusted with the secrets of the king's reconciliation to popery. Richard was well acquainted with the religion of the duke. By his interest he had been raised to station and consequence; which he enjoyed without moderation, ambitious, vain, and violent. Abundance of the Irish who were attached to the nuncio, and his party, when driven from Ireland, had entered into foreign service. When the king recalled his subjects from France, they repaired to Flanders, and helped to form his little army. Their sense of this merit effaced all remembrance of their former errours. Their expectations were extravagant. Ormond, who would not contribute to gratify them, and Clarendon, who opposed them, were perpetually the subjects of their abuse. They addressed themselves to Richard Talbot, as a rising favourite. He had served against the nuncio's party; yet the vanity of appearing popular led him to espouse the cause of these men. They followed the king to London; where they and their patron continued their invectives against Ormond and the chancellor.

THE Irish agents were easily induced to consider Talbot as the fittest person to support their cause.

Richard boldly promised them essential services, inveighing against the duke of Ormond, and his advice, as coming from a person by no means well inclined to their party. Fully possessed with the justice of their cause, and the influence of their patron Talbot, they yielded to his insinuations, rejected the measures proposed by the duke, and provoked him to withdraw from Irish affairs, and leave them to pursue the dictates of their own insolence and folly.

Their success was soon found not to correspond with their expectations. They made a bold demand to be relieved from the rigour of those qualifications of innocency which the king's instructions had prescribed; and that neither their claiming the articles of peace, nor paying contributions to the rebels, nor residing in their quarters, should be regarded as a proof of guilt. Thus, the greatest part of the rebels must be declared innocent, restored to their lands, resume their settlements in corporations and places of strength, so as to constitute all future parliaments of Ireland at their pleasure; to strike the English settlers in every part of Ireland with perpetual terrour; and, at any time, to revive the disorders of the kingdom with particular advantage. A demand which threatened such dangerous consequences, which, if granted, must defeat the purpose of the king's declaration, by leaving no reprisals for those whom he intended to gratify, was naturally received with disgust, and speedily rejected. It was by this time universally allowed, that there were not lands in Ireland sufficient for reprisals; and the stock was much diminished by a grant to the duke of York of all the estates possessed by the regicides; so that the restoration of the Irish appeared every day more desperate. To complete their mortification, the king declared his intentions of establishing and supporting an

English

English interest in Ireland. They imputed this resolution to the practices of Ormond; Talbot was employed to expostulate with him; and his expostulation was so indecent and intemperate, that he was committed to the Tower, and released only on an humble submission.

In a juncture so critical, common prudence must have dictated the most guarded and inoffensive conduct to the Irish. Yet they wantonly disobliged a nobleman, to whose abilities and equity the interests of all subjects of Ireland were intrusted; for the duke of Ormond was now declared lord lieutenant of this kingdom. At home, their enemies and competitors were indefatigable in endeavouring to load their whole party with the guilt of new conspiracies; and even manifest forgeries were received as solid proofs. In London, their agents boasted their loyalty, and that of their ancestors, in terms so pompous and confident, as if there never had been any rebellion in Ireland. They challenged, as their right, the exact performance of every article of the peace made in sixteen hundred and forty-eight. The king, who considered every concession as his free grace and favour, was shocked at this peremptory demand. Their adversaries laboured to convince him, that from the time, the circumstances, and the nature of this peace, it was in itself invalid, and could not possibly oblige him; and he listened to their reasonings with favour. While the Irish clamoured for justice, they submitted calmly to his mercy, and acknowledged, that both their properties and their lives were derived from this source. While the Irish inveighed with acrimony against English rebels and regicides, and involved all the adventurers and soldiers in this guilt, many of their judges, conscious of opposing the late king, were offended and exasperated. When their adversaries recriminated, by displaying all the horrours of the Irish massacres, the outrages of the war, their traiterous endeavours to subvert the English government, and to introduce a foreign power into Ireland, they were heard with favour and applause. And as the conduct of the Irish was intemperate, so their demands were inadmissible; nor would they propose any qualification, or listen to any expedient which might tend to accommodate any party but their own.

The very length and tediousness of various examinations and debates about the affairs of Ireland, were sufficient to weary the dissipated temper of the king. He was present in every council summoned on the settlement of this kingdom, in order to be acquainted with its several interests, or to persuade the world that if some hardships were to be imposed, they necessarily arose from the perplexities and embarrassments of various defections and usurpations, and from the duty incumbent on his office, of making the best provision for his people, which the state and circumstances of affairs could permit. When he issued his declaration, he was persuaded, that there were lands enough to satisfy all parties. He was now sensible of this mistake. One or other of the discordant interests must suffer; and Charles, who considered the settlement of Ireland as an affair rather of policy than justice, was readily persuaded, that the advantage of the crown, and the security of his government required, that the loss should be sustained by the Irish. Any other decision would be condemned by his council, and highly offensive to the English parliament.

The indiscretion and improvidence of the Irish soon afforded him a plausible reason for this determination, and put an end to all debates about the bill of settlement. They had provoked their adversaries to examine rigourously into the conduct of their party. The

charges

charges on each fide were violent and indifcriminate, and the great point now urged againft the Irifh was a defign of cafting off all obedience to the crown of England. To fhew that this had been their real purpofe, the induftry of their adverfaries had procured, and the proteftant agents now prefented to the committee for Irifh affairs, the original paper of inftructions given by the fupreme council of Ireland to the bifhop of Ferns, and Sir Nicholas Plunket, their agents to the court of Rome, a draft of inftructions to France and Spain, and a copy of the excommunication publifhed at Jamestown. By the inftructions it appeared, that the agents were commiffioned to make a tender of the kingdom to the pope, and, if he declined it, to any other catholic prince. Thofe to Rome were figned by Sir Nicholas Plunket, the others were in his hand-writing. With a ftrange and unpardonable inattention this very Plunket, a noted partizan of the nuncio, a man who received his knighthood from the pope, had been chofen by the Irifh party one of their prefent agents, and now ftood before the committee. The papers were read; he acknowledged his fignature and writing; they were prefented to the king and council, who received them with the utmoft indignation. An order was inftantly made, that no farther petition or addrefs fhould be received from the Roman catholics of Ireland, as they had been already fully heard; that the bill of fettlement fhould be engroffed without farther delay; and that Sir Nicholas Plunket have notice of the king's pleafure, that he forbear to come into his majefty's prefence, or to appear any more at court. Such was the conclufion of debates fo long protracted, and fo violently agitated. The bill was finifhed, tranfmitted, and foon after paffed by the Irifh houfes.

THE arrival of the duke of Ormond was now impatiently expected in Ireland, as the perfon who was to complete

complete the grand and momentous work of a national settlement[b]. The Irish parliament, in an extraordinary strain of generosity, presented him with the sum of thirty thousand pounds; his son, lord Ossory, was called by writ to the house of lords of Ireland. All men seemed solicitous to express their reverence for a nobleman, who had so long maintained the royal interests under every distress and difficulty, and was so highly and so deservedly the favourite of his royal master. The marriage of the king, the queen's reception, the forming of her court, and other particulars necessary to be adjusted on such an occasion, detained him for some time in London. At length he arrived in Ireland, attended by a magnificent train; and, some time after, gave the royal assent to the bill of settlement, with some others relative to the revenue, and one for abolishing the court of wards. The advantages, derived to the crown from this court, were compensated by the tax on hearths and chimneys, according to the precedent lately established in England.

The act of settlement was not so accurately devised as to guard against every reasonable exception[c]; nor was it possible that any act could be so framed as to satisfy every individual of every party. Many of the provisos inserted in it had been disapproved by the duke of Ormond; and the king would have at once struck out all the provisos, but the duke advised that they should stand, as it might not be difficult in the execution of the act to prevent the effect of those which were unreasonable or unjust; and, for this purpose, a clause was inserted empowering the lord lieutenant and council, to give such farther instructions to the commissioners appointed to execute this act as they should judge fitting. The Irish catholics now added to their former complaints,

that

[b] Carte, Orm. vol. II. p. 246.   [c] Ibid. p. 258.

that they had not been heard before the English council, nor their agents confulted on framing the bill. The forty-nine officers, whofe merits were inconteftible, found the fecurity of their arrears diminifhed by this act. Some doubtful expreffions in the king's declaration and inftructions were indeed explained in their favour; but, although the king had promifed to preferve their fecurity entire, yet the earl of Leicefter had obtained a provifo for charging it with fifty thoufand pounds, which he pleaded to be ftill due to him as lord lieutenant of Ireland, and colonel of a regiment. Other grants were made in prejudice to their fecurity; but nothing affected it more than one claufe, which provided, that the debts due for furnifhing the army in Ireland fhould be all paid out of this fecurity. Even the houfe of commons acknowledged the feverities impofed on thefe loyal officers; and, as foon as the act of fettlement had paffed their houfe, ordered a bill of explanation to be brought in, calculated chiefly for their relief.

Nor were the adventurers and foldiers, for whom the ampleft provifion feemed to have been made, lefs diffatisfied than others. Before the act had been tranfmitted, feveral more notorious fanatics, who dreaded to be excepted from all benefit of this act, precipitately fold their interefts for trifling fums. No fuch exception was admitted. But an additional number of Irifh nominees was inferted, which was confidered by the Englifh puritans as an unpardonable partiality to the popifh intereft. The provifion, made by this act for the eftablifhed church, was fcarcely lefs offenfive to thefe men. The regulation of demands made on the doubling ordinance, occafioned a large defalcation from their allotments; and fome of their moft powerful partizans

tizans were defeated in their interested purposes, by the clause enacting that no adventurer should be satisfied for more money than he had really advanced.

The execution of this act was entrusted to English commissioners, disengaged from all corners and interests in Ireland; and, therefore, likely to be most impartial: they sat in Dublin to receive claims, and hear proofs of innocency; and, notwithstanding those rigourous qualifications necessary for exculpating the Irish, more of their party were pronounced innocent than their adversaries wished or expected. In the first month of trials [d], thirty-eight persons were pronounced innocent, seven only nocent: in the second, seven were condemned, fifty-three acquitted: in the third, seventy-seven were found innocent, five pronounced guilty. These innocents were immediately to be reinvested with their estates, without any provision for reprising those who should be dispossessed; and, as the fund for future reprisals was known to be small, the adventurers and soldiers were confounded at these decisions. They had no leisure to reflect, that those of the Irish who were freest from guilt were naturally the most forward to present their claims: and that the proportion of innocents to nocents was so far from being extraordinary, that it was rather extraordinary that any should be found guilty on the first trials. In their fears for their property [e], they expected to be entirely dispossessed; in their suspicions of the king, they concluded that the commissioners were influenced by secret instructions, and that a scheme was formed to exalt the Irish upon the ruins of the English interest. The more violent declared for maintaining their possessions by the sword. Such a spirit was quickly caught, and readily propagated.

[d] Cox, vol. II.   [e] Carte, Orm. vol. II. p. 259—263.

propagated. Care had indeed been taken, as in England, to model the army, and to disband all those who were most inveterate enemies to monarchy. But the men, thus discharged, served to encrease the number and power of the discontented. The proceedings, which indicated so much favour to the Irish, were represented in England with every circumstance of odium and aggravation. Here, the old republicans were impatient of the present form, and provoked at the conduct of government. The act of uniformity had blasted all the hopes of the presbyterians, and the ejection of their pastors was insupportable. It was not only the wildness of some fifth-monarchy men[f] that attempted an insurrection: plots were deeply laid, and schemes deliberately formed, in order to restore the commonwealth. The malcontents naturally turned their eyes to Ireland, where the faction was numerous, enflamed by the apprehension of losing their estates, and encouraged by the divisions and unsettled condition of the kingdom. Agents were sent to try the dispositions of their friends in Ireland, and found them prepared for any desperate purpose. A number of officers, who had served in Cromwell's army[g], were easily encouraged to form a scheme of general insurrection. A private committee was appointed to conduct it; one of which discovered the design to the duke of Ormond. Some of the conspirators, impatient of delay, formed a separate scheme of seizing the castle of Dublin. This too was discovered and defeated.

THE great dependence of the conspirators was on the general dissatisfactions of the English party; and some proceedings of the commons at Dublin served to enflame

[f] Ludlow, vol. III. p. 166. [g] Carte, ut sup.

enflame thefe diffatisfactions, by countenancing complaints againſt the commiſſioners of claims. So many of the Iriſh had been pronounced reſtorable, notwithſtanding the rigourous qualifications of innocency preſcribed by the king's inſtructions, that they refolved to make thefe qualifications ſtill more rigourous. They took advantage of the claufe in the act of ſettlement, whereby the lieutenant and council were empowered to give farther directions to the commiſſioners, and propofed ſuch directions as tended to involve the whole Iriſh party in inevitable condemnation. To enforce their advice and requeſt, the whole houfe [h] attended the lord lieutenant; and their ſpeaker, Sir Audley Mervyn, in his uſual inflated ſtyle, pronounced a folemn comment on every article of the petition. It was received with cold civility: the commons refolved to appeal to the public: Mervyn's ſpeech was printed; and its quaintnefs and figurative obfcurity were not ill calculated for the time, and the temper of the people. Not contented with this ſtep, and not finding that their directions were adopted, the commons proceeded farther; and by an invidious refolution declared, "that " they would apply their utmoſt remedies to prevent " and ſtop the great and manifold prejudices and in- " conveniences which daily did, and were like to " happen to the proteſtants of Ireland, by the proceed " ings of the commiſſioners for executing the act of " ſettlement [i]."

THIS violence of the commons was refented by the king, and Mervyn's ſpeech did not pafs unnoticed. Some offenfive paſſages were difcovered in it, one particularly

---

h Journ. of the H. of Com. of Ireland, vol. II. p. 252.
i Carte, Orm. vol. II. p. 265.

ticularly, in which he afferted, that "this is the critical time in which religion, the eftablifhed religion, is in danger of being undermined, by tafting the predominancy of temper upon a popifh intereft." Profecutions were commenced againft the printers of this fpeech both in London and Dublin. The lord lieutenant[j], in a letter to the commons, reprefented the bad confequences of their vote, as well as the indifcretions of their fpeaker; by which, particularly, the confpirators had been encouraged in their late attempt upon the caftle of Dublin, as if the proteftant intereft and religion were in danger. They were fo far intimidated, that they retracted their vote, and declared their abhorrence of the fanatic plot; yet, their anfwer to the duke was fufficiently dignified, and foon followed, by an addrefs, reprefenting the danger arifing from recufants, and the confluence of popifh priefts, friars, and jefuits, and recommending bills for enforcing the oaths of fupremacy, and banifhing all popifh ecclefiaftics from the kingdom.

But Ormond[k] was now to guard againft other dangers and other enemies. His difcovery of the plot for furprifing the caftle of Dublin, did not put a ftop to the more general fcheme of infurrection. Meetings were ftill held in the capital[l]; correfpondences maintained with different parts of the kingdom, and efpecially the northern province; arms, and ammunition prepared, and numbers of difbanded foldiers engaged. Some lawyers, feveral prefbyterian minifters, Blood, who was afterwards fo diftinguifhed in London, fome members of the Irifh commons, and feveral republican officers

[j] Journ. of the H. of Com. of Ireland, vol. II. p. 297—317.
[k] A. D. 1663.
[l] Carte, Orm. vol. II. p. 266-270.

officers embarked in this design. Declarations were printed, and ready to be dispersed, encouraging all good protestants to unite for securing the English interest, averting the danger with which the three nations were threatened by the countenance given to popery, confirming the English subjects of Ireland in the estates they had purchased by their services, and establishing religion agreeably to the solemn league and covenant.

The zeal of these conspirators so far outran their discretion, that intimations of their purposes and proceedings were from time to time conveyed to the duke of Ormond. The utmost circumspection was necessary on his part; for however the common people submitted peaceably, or were well disposed to the present government, the army was still disaffected and discontented. Sir Arthur Forbes was sent into Ulster, where he soon discovered the design of an immediate insurrection, boldly ventured to seize one of the principal conspirators, though surrounded by his friends, and so intimidated the whole party by his spirited procedure, that the accomplices fled to Scotland. An attempt was made to engage Sir Theophilus Jones in this enterprize, and the whole scheme was rashly communicated to him. He instantly conveyed his information to the lieutenant; so that on the eve of the day appointed for seizing the castle of Dublin, and publishing their declaration, about five and twenty conspirators were seized, and a reward published for the apprehension of those who escaped. A weak government deemed it necessary to proceed with lenity against delinquents who had engaged in a popular cause. A few were condemned and executed, the rest received the king's pardon.

THE

THE discontents of the English parliament, and the profusion of the king, disabled him from sending remittances to Ireland, and making those provisions for a military establishment, which the security of his administration in this kingdom required. The state of property was still unsettled and disordered. Several insufficiencies were foreseen in the act of settlement, many others were discovered in the execution of it. The explanatory bill prepared by the commons was rejected. The king refused to accept of any scheme for a final accommodation of all interests, formed by an assembly which had given him unfavourable impressions of their temper, and which he had some thoughts of dissolving. He referred the whole affair to the lord lieutenant and council, and directed that they should prepare an entirely new bill. They proceeded with the caution necessary in a point so important, so delicate and difficult; where they were to consider not only what might be demanded on the principles of strict justice, but what in the present circumstances of the kingdom might be practicable and attainable, not what every individual of every party might expect; but a provision for the general welfare, as equitable and extensive as could be obtained from the English council and the Irish parliament. The purport of their bill, as transmitted from Ireland, was to explain some clauses in the declaration; to assign a better security to the forty-nine officers; to prevent the restitution of Irish lands and houses in corporations; to increase the stock of reprisals, by taking away a sixth part from adventurers and soldiers, and by other expedients, and to make provision for some deserving persons, whom the court of claims had not been able to relieve, by the determination of their power. In this particular there was a fairer demand for redress, as scarcely more than six hundred

hundred out of four thousand claims of innocency had been decided by this court.

The bill was attended by agents from the different parties. They were heard before the council [m]; memorials and replies presented; while individuals practised secretly with some men in power, particularly colonel Richard Talbot, who, for valuable considerations, engaged to obtain provisos in their favour. In the perplexity arising from various claimants and petitioners, the king wished to be assisted by the duke of Ormond. To enable him to provide for the security of his government, some money was remitted for payment of the army; levies were made in Ireland for the service of Portugal; one thousand of the most disaffected among the soldiery were thus drawn away, and replaced by troops from England. After these precautions, it was thought that the duke might be spared for some time without hazard. He was called into England, and his son, the earl of Ossory, appointed lord deputy during his absence.

Ormond had already laboured to form the new explanatory bill, in such a manner as to make the best provision for the several interests that could probably be obtained in the present state of affairs, and disposition of parties. To apply some remedy to the striking grievance of a number of Irish claimants abandoned to ruin, merely for want of the common justice of being heard, he had proposed, that the lord lieutenant and six of the privy council of Ireland should be empowered to nominate such other persons as innocents, of whose constant loyalty they had sufficient knowledge, and who should be thus entitled to the same advantages

[m] Carte, Orm. vol. II, p. 295.

advantages with those who were pronounced innocent by the court[n] of claims. But this proposal was rejected by the English council; and, on his arrival in London, he found all parties complaining, all weary of their unsettled condition, harrassed by expence and trouble, anxious for the event, and all disposed to relax something of their several pretensions, in order to obtain a final settlement. The London adventurers, a considerable and powerful body, wearied out by tedious disputes, proposed to resign their lands to the king, and to account for the *mesne* profits, on condition of being reimbursed their principal money, with interest upon interest, at the rate of three pounds *per cent*. the adventurers and soldiers in Ireland proposed to cut off all adventurers, who had issued their money after the rupture between the late king and parliament; the forty-nine officers consented to accept ten shillings in the pound for their composition. It was discovered by the diligence of Sir William Domville, attorney-general of Ireland, that one entire moiety of the adventurers money had been subscribed and paid, subsequent to the doubling ordinance; and, consequently, that one half of the lands set out to them ought to be retrenched. Great abuses were detected in the manner of setting out their satisfaction, in which the proceedings were clandestine and confused. In ameasurements, in returns of unprofitable lands, in various particulars, there appeared room for correction and amendment, so as probably to encrease the stock of reprisals, and to dispose the several parties to reasonable concessions.

The English council had ordered, that the lord lieutenant, calling to his assistance such of the privy counsellors of Ireland as were in London, the commissioners

[n] Carte, Orm. vol. II. p. 301. A.D. 1664.

sioners of claims, and the solicitor-general, (Sir Heneage Finch) should review what had been already deliberated relative to the affairs of Ireland, and offer such farther expedients as they should think fit, in order to the settlement of that kingdom. Almost ten months were spent in hearing and answering vast numbers of petitions, and in considering the provisos * to be inserted in the new bill. The agents of the several interests offered their proposals, pleaded, objected, contended, and complained. It was at length proposed

on

---

* One proviso in favour of the marquis of Antrim was a subject of particular clamour and complaint.—We have already seen the conduct of this nobleman, down to his opposition to the peace made by Ormond with the Irish. He was afterwards accused of being a spy on the royalists, of conveying intelligence to Jones and Ireton, of corresponding with Cromwell, of aspersing the memory of the late king, by charging him with encouraging the Irish rebellion, and of a treacherous opposition to his present majesty when in Scotland. Soon after the restoration he was committed to the Tower; but, as no charge was proved against him he was released, and sent to Ireland to abide his trial. He absolutely denied the charge of aspersing the late king; he called on the queen-mother to attest, that his intercourse with the rebels was by the late king's direction, and for his service; and, as he received no censure in Ireland, the king in consideration of his services to Montrose, and at the pressing instances of the queen-mother, allowed a clause to be inserted in the act of settlement, confirming the disposition he had made of his estate in trust for payment of his debts.

But the present possessors of his lands were to be reprised, and nothing but a positive establishment of his innocency could immediately eject them. The queen-mother was earnest and incessant in her applications; the king wrote to Ormond, that he should move the Irish council to transmit a bill for restoring Antrim to his estate. The council was unanimous that such a bill ought not to be transmitted. Antrim addressed himself by petition to the king; his cause was heard before the English council; they found him "innocent from any malice or rebellious purposes, and that his "correspondence with the Irish was in order to the service of the "late king, and warranted by his instructions." A certificate of this sentence was by the king transmitted to the lord lieutenant and council at Dublin, with an order for communicating it to the commissioners of claims. Ormond and his council remonstrated against this order. The adventurers petitioned against the favour
intended

on the part of the Irish catholics, that, for the satisfaction of their interests, the adventurers and soldiers should resign one-third of the lands respectively, enjoyed by them on the seventh day of May, 1659. The proposal was accepted; one-third of all the king's grants (with some exceptions) retrenched; and, on this principle, with consent of all the agents, the bill of explanation was at length framed, and presented to the privy council. Nothing remained but the addition of twenty persons to the list of nominees, whom the king was to restore to their estates, and, who were to be particularly mentioned in the new act. The choice of these was assigned to the duke of Ormond: and it was an office which could not but expose him to resentment and obloquy. Through the whole business of the settlement, he had acted a disinterested and honourable

---

intended for a man, whose guilt in opposing every accommodation with the Irish, and joining with the nuncio against the royal interest, was so notorious. But the intercessions in favour of Antrim were too powerful to be resisted. A new certificate was obtained from the king, addressed immediately to the commissioners; and Antrim, thus fortified, appeared before the court of claims. Some of the judges were of opinion, to adjudge him innocent at once, on the authority of the king's certificate; others contended for hearing the evidence against him: the evidence was heard, and clearly proved his guilt; yet the majority of the commissioners refused to decide in opposition to the king's testimony, and pronounced the marquis innocent.

This decision was to the last degree unpopular and odious. The adventurers and soldiers petitioned the king for relief against it, stating the evidence which appeared against the marquis, in its full force. The king superseded the decree of the commissioners; he declared, that he saw no reason why they should rest their judgment on his certificate, which only declared the authority and purpose of Antrim's intercourse with the Irish, without any justification of his subsequent conduct. He directed, that the marquis should abide a new trial. Antrim well knew the event of such trial; he now acknowledged his guilt, and petitioned to be supported by the king's mercy, since he could not be supported by his own innocence. Here the interposition of his powerful friends prevailed; and, by the act of explanation, he was restored to his estate. CARTE, ORM. vol. II. p. 277. COUNCIL BOOKS of IRELAND, MS.

able part. He had given up his own rights to facilitate a general accommodation: the debts and mortgages on his estate, which were contracted in the public service, he generously discharged, though forfeited to the king, and granted to him by the act of settlement. But the Irish,[o] in the bitterness of their disappointments, had no leisure to discover the merit of this conduct. It was declared in the new bill, that the protestants were, in the first place, and especially to be settled, and that any ambiguity was to be interpreted in the sense most favourable to their interests. It was also provided, that no papist, who, by the qualifications of the former act, had not been adjudged innocent, should at any future time be reputed innocent, or entitled to claim any lands or settlements. Thus, every remaining hope of those numerous claimants whose causes had not been heard, was entirely cut off. They complained of perjury and subornation in the causes that had been tried before the commissioners of claims; though such wicked practices were probably not confined to one party. But their great and striking grievance was that more than three thousand persons were condemned, without the justice granted to the vilest criminals, that of a fair and equal trial. Of this number, though many, and probably the greater part,[p] would have been declared nocent, yet several cases were undoubtedly pityable; and now, twenty only were to be restored by especial favour. The Irish pleaded their several merits, and, in judging for themselves, each claimed a preference. Those nominated by Ormond were allowed to be innocent; but others were equally worthy of favour, and could impute their disappointment only to the partiality of the lieutenant.

AND

o Irish Stat. 17 and 18 Car. II. cap. 2. A. D. 1665.
p Carte, Orm. vol. II. p. 304.

AND, however grievous the Irish deemed this explanatory bill, and however favorable it appeared to the new interest, yet, when brought to Ireland by the duke, it proved by no means acceptable to the commons. Some objected to it as not sufficiently secure [q]; some found themselves not so well provided for as they thought their merits had deserved; or, as others whom they deemed not more meritorious than themselves; and some, perhaps, were ready to reject every mode of settlement, in order to involve the nation in new disorders. Ormond could not venture to lay the bill immediately before a house of commons composed of such tempers, and who had discovered such turbulence in their former session. He first determined, that the vacant seats should be supplied, and laboured to procure members acceptable to government. In the mean time, nothing was so proper to employ them as the late plot, to which their own proceedings had given countenance. Several of their members, and even Mervyn, their speaker, were said to have taken some part in it; so that to remove all suspicions of his own conduct, every man was obliged to distinguish himself, by his zeal against the conspirators. On the first day [r] of their session, a letter from the king to the duke of Ormond was laid before them, condemning their former proceedings and votes relative to the commissioners of claims. Terrified with the fears of a dissolution, and a new parliament less friendly to their interests, they made the humblest submission to the king, acknowledged their errours, retracted their proceedings, and inveighed against the conspiracy. Seven of their members accused as accomplices, were instantly suspended from sitting in the

---

q Carte, Orm. vol. II. p. 314.
r Journ. of the H. of Com. of Ireland. vol. II. p. 230–256.

the house. They pleaded his majesty's pardon; yet, on examination of the evidence against them, they were expelled, and declared incapable of serving in the present, or any future parliament. A bill was prepared to disqualify them for holding any office, civil, military, or ecclesiastical; the lord lieutenant approved this zeal, and now entrusted them with the act of explanation.

In their debates on this interesting subject[s], their doubts and objections were freely proposed and considered, collected, and laid before the lord lieutenant in a petition. He exhorted them not to dwell minutely on niceties and scruples, at a time when their enemies, both abroad and at home, might be contriving the ruin of the three kingdoms. He alarmed them with some advertisements he had received from Lord Arlington, of an invasion intended by France in favour of the Hollanders, now at war with England. He assured them, that as the lieutenant and council were empowered to explain any difficulties, and to amend any defects in the act, every thing should be explained and amended agreeably to their wishes, and all obstructions to the happy settlement of the kingdom removed, if necessary, by new bills, to which he doubted not of his majesty's gracious consent. His answer was voted satisfactory; and, without one dissenting voice, they passed this famous act, which fixed the general rights of the several interests in Ireland, and established a final and invariable rule for the settlement of this kingdom.

Yet this was but the beginning of the great work of settlement. The rest depended on the execution of the act, and the application of the rule to particular cases. Five commissioners were appointed, who, in all matters of difficulty, were to resort to the lord lieu-

tenant

---

s Carte, Orm. vol. II. p. 220.

tenant and council. An infinite number of perplexed cafes produced perpetual applications to the ftate; and gave, for years, continual employment to the duke of Ormond, in providing for the impartial execution of this act, and defeating the attempts of thofe who laboured to evade it, by procuring grants and letters from the king.

SCARCELY had the act of explanation paffed, when the Englifh commons[t] feemed to envy that profperity of the fubjects of Ireland, which the fettlement of this kingdom promifed; and, notwithftanding all the folicitude expreffed for the interefts of a new colony of their fellow-fubjects, refolved on a meafure calculated at once to mortify and diftrefs them.

IT was found, that the rents of England had of late years decreafed to the amount of two hundred thoufand pounds annually[u]. The caufes of this alarming decreafe were, many of them, fufficiently obvious. Perfecutions had driven numbers of induftrious puritans to Holland and the American plantations; the trade with Spain had been diminifhed and interrupted; a ruinous commerce carried on with France[v], in which the balance againft England amounted to near a million yearly. The war with Holland had produced new obftructions to trade. The plague had leffened the confumption of provifions[x]; and even the gaiety and diffipation of the court had contributed to the public diftrefs, by feducing the nobility to London, and fuppreffing the old hofpitality of the country. But the interefted views of fome great men, who wifhed to embarrafs the adminiftration of Ormond, and to drive him from the government of Ireland, confpired with that

---

t A. D. 1666.
u Carte Orm. vol. II. p. 317.
v R. Coke's Detect. vol. III.
x Carte, ut fupra.

that difpofition which the Englifh nation hath at fome times difcovered, of exerting a feverity over the inferior members of their empire, and taught the commons to afcribe the decreafe of rents to another caufe, the importation of Irifh cattle. The annual value of the cattle fent to England, was far fhort of the deficiency difcovered in the value of lands; and, before the troubles of England, far greater numbers had been imported without any complaints, or any decreafe of rents: yet the Englifh commons, in a violent, and almoft unaccountable rage of oppreffion, had no leifure to attend to fuch confiderations. So early as the year 1663, they had paffed a temporary act for prohibiting the importation of fat cattle from Ireland after the firft day of July in every year. The inconveniences of this reftraint to both countries, were reprefented in the ftrongeft terms to the king. But in proportion as he feemed convinced of the impropriety of this meafure, the commons were the more enflamed. In the parliament held at Oxford, in the year 1665, a bill was brought in for a perpetual prohibition of importing all cattle from Ireland, dead or alive, great or fmall, fat or lean.

In vain did Sir Heneage Finch oppofe the bill by arguments drawn from natural juftice; from the rights of Englifhmen to which the fubjects of Ireland were entitled; from the mifery to which it muft reduce the whole kingdom of Ireland; from the mifchiefs which muft arife from forcing the Irifh to trade with other countries. In vain was it urged, that the bill would deftroy a trade highly advantageous to England, which, in return for provifions and rude materials, fent back every fpecies of manufacture; that the induftrious inhabitants of England, when deprived of Irifh provifions, muft augment the price of labour, and thus render their manufactures too dear to be exported; while thofe of Ireland, finding the value of provifions reduced, would be
the

the less inclined to labour, and in danger of falling into the ancient barbarism of the country; that they could not pay taxes, nor maintain the forces necessary for the security of government: all these, and other powerful arguments, were totally disregarded. Some gentlemen of Ireland appeared in behalf of their country, but were refused a copy of the bill. It passed the commons by a small majority. In the lords it was opposed, particularly by the earl of Castlehaven. Sir William Petty was heard before their committee, and pleaded the cause of a country, in which, by his abilities and diligence, he had acquired a considerable interest. The report was delayed, and the parliament prorogued.

In the mean time, Ireland experienced the greatest distress[y]; deprived of its usual trade with England, and disabled from any foreign commerce by the want of shipping, and the war with France and Holland; exposed to the attempts both of secret and open enemies, and every moment in danger of some violent insurrections, by the calamities and discontents of its inhabitants. The duke of Ormond was wary, vigilant, and diligent. He watched the proceedings of the popish party, and the futile attempts of the most turbulent of their clergy, to engage France in a descent on Ireland. With equal assiduity he laboured to discover the correspondence of the fanatics with those of England and Scotland. He every day received information of some secret practices or conspiracies, but received them at once with caution and magnanimity, without neglecting the proper measures for security, and without provoking the discontented.

The complaints of the soldiery for want of pay, was one great encouragement to the disaffected to form their

---

y Carte, Orm. vol. II, p. 323.

their schemes of insurrection, from a confidence, that the army would readily favour their designs. The garrison mutinied at Carricfergus, seized the town and castle, and acted with such desperate resolution as proved highly alarming to government in this time of danger. The earl of Arran, son to the duke of Ormond, was sent by sea to reduce them. The duke himself marched against them with the few forces on whose attachment he could rely. After some resistance, the mutineers surrendered: one hundred and ten were tried by a court martial, nine executed, and the companies to which they belonged were instantly disbanded. This petty commotion, with the rumours of vast preparations made in France for a descent on Ireland, procured the duke a supply from the English treasury of fifteen thousand pounds. He was thus enabled to give some content to the army, and to execute a scheme he had projected of establishing a body of militia in the provinces. As the French were expected to make their attempt on Munster, he visited this province, examined the state of its towns and forts on the coast, arrayed and armed the militia, a body of the greater consequence, as composed principally of veterans, whose valour and experience were well approved. From these cares he was recalled to Dublin, in order to prevent any commotion to which the disaffected might be encouraged by intelligence of the fire of London. A contribution for relief of the sufferers by this dreadful incident, was proposed by the lord lieutenant [z], and chearfully adopted by the privy council, nobility, and gentry of Ireland. Thirty thousand beeves, the only riches which the country now afforded, were subscribed for this purpose. But however pure and disinterested were the motives to this bounty, in England it received a malignant interpretation,

[z] Carte, Orm. vol. II. p. 329—337.

tion, and was induſtriouſly repreſented as a political contrivance to defeat the prohibition of Iriſh cattle.

THE experience of three years had now proved the effects of reſtraining the importation of cattle from Ireland. The rents of England had not increaſed; Ireland was ſo reduced as to be unable to pay the ſubſidies granted by parliament. But Buckingham, Aſhley, Lauderdale, and their party, had already vowed the deſtruction of the chancellor, and hated his friend Ormond, whoſe views and principles were ſo oppoſite to their own, and whoſe influence was a dangerous obſtacle to that ſcheme of power, which they meditated. Diſcontents were to be raiſed in Ireland; theſe might afford ſome pretence for removing their rival from his government; perhaps, ſome plauſible ground of an impeachment. The paſſions of undiſcerning men were eaſily enflamed. People were in general perſuaded, that all their diſtreſs aroſe from the importation of Iriſh cattle; the northern and weſtern members of the commons in particular, were tranſported to the utmoſt violence, and the bill of prohibition was eagerly reſumed.

THE king had expreſſed his utter abhorrence of this bill, and paſſionately declared, that it never ſhould receive his aſſent. The commons, on whom he depended for the maintenance of his war, were the more determined to mortify him with a full conviction of their ſuperiour power; by declaring in the preamble to the bill, that the importation of Iriſh cattle was a NUSANCE, they precluded him from attempting any diſpenſing power in favour of the Iriſh ſubjects. They paſſed the bill in a rage of obſtinacy, without the leaſt attention to argument or reaſon. In the lords it was amended, particularly by inſerting the words "detriment and miſ-"chief," in the place of "nuſance." When returned to the commons, their violence seemed to be suddenly allayed. Intelligence was received of an insurrection in Scotland; they began to discern some danger in exasperating Ireland; but the insurrection was quelled, and Ireland was again deemed insignificant. They insisted on their preamble; and, in a conference between the committees of both houses, neither seemed disposed to recede. Ashley, with an affected moderation, proposed, that instead of calling the importation a nusance, it might be declared to be felony, or a premunire. The chancellor suggested an amendment equally reasonable, and observed, that it might as properly be declared, "adultery."

Through the whole proceedings on this bill the lords carried on their debates with all the violence of men contending for their lives, with a shameful contempt of the order and dignity of their house. The duke of Buckingham, with all the plebeian meanness of national reflection, exclaimed, " none could oppose the " bill but such as had Irish estates, or Irish understand- " ings." This produced a challenge from lord Ossory, the admired and popular son of the duke of Ormond, which Buckingham declined to accept, chusing rather to complain to the house; and Ossory was sent to the Tower. The young earl was not dismayed. When Ashley inveighed against the Irish subscription, and all concerned in promoting it, Ossory observed, that "such " virulence became none but one of Cromwell's coun- " sellors." The partizans on each side caught the flame, and several lords seemed on the point of drawing the sword against each other. The commons apparently less enflamed, but inflexibly determined, refused to alter their preamble. Rather than resign their favourite expression, they resolved to give up the bill, and to introduce it without any amendments as a proviso to the bill of assessments.

assessments. They even offered to the lords interested in Irish estates, that if they would consent to their preamble, a year's liberty should be given for the importation of cattle. The king was alarmed at this obstinacy, and the danger of losing his supplies. He directed his servants in the house of lords to consent to the word " nusance;" and thus decided the fate of this bill. In giving it the royal assent, he could not forbear expressing his resentment at the jealousy conceived against him.

The English nation soon felt the inconveniences of an act[a], which wantonly put an end to an advantageous commerce. Discerning men saw the happy consequences which it must, in time produce to Ireland. For the present, however, the Irish subjects were cast into despair. All commerce was interrupted; war made it necessary to guard against invasion[b]; subsidies were due, but no money could be found. Ormond thought it both necessary and convenient to accept part of these subsidies in provisions, consulting at once the king's service and the ease of his distressed subjects. Nor was the king ill-disposed to alleviate the present difficulties of Ireland. With the consent of his council, obtained not without some reluctance, he, by an act of state, allowed a free trade from Ireland to all foreign countries, either at war or in peace with his majesty. He permitted the Irish, at the same time, to retaliate on the Scots, who, copying from England, had prohibited their cattle, corn, and beef. The importation of linen and woollen manufactures, stockings, gloves, and other commodities from Scotland was forbidden, as highly detrimental to the trade of Ireland.

The

a A. D. 1667.   b Carte, Orm. vol. II. p. 228.

The exportation of Irish wool was prohibited by law, except to England by particular licence of the chief governour. Yet, in the order of council for free exportation, wool was not excepted. The lords who had contended for the most unreasonable restraints on Ireland, and were declared enemies to Ormond, admitted in their debates, that wool should be included in the exportable articles. Such was their ignorance of the affairs of this kingdom, and such their inattention to the interests of England. Ormond suspected that some snare was laid, and some pretence sought for a future accusation, should he take too great liberties in an affair so delicate. Wool was not mentioned in the proclamation, nor would he consent to grant particular licences for exporting it. The Irish, forced by a necessity, which breaks through all laws and restraints, conveyed their wool by stealth to foreign countries, and have experienced the advantages of this clandestine commerce.

But the most effectual measure[c] which the Irish subjects could pursue to elude the violence of an oppressive law, was that of applying themselves to manufactures, and working up their own commodities; and in this they were countenanced and encouraged by the noble spirit of their chief governour.

Men of abilities and knowledge in commerce were encouraged to suggest their schemes for promoting industry, and preventing the necessity of foreign importations. Sir Peter Pett presented a memorial to the duke of Ormond, for erecting a manufacture of woollen cloth, which might at least furnish a sufficient quantity for home consumption. He chiefly recommended the making fine worsted stockings, and Norwich stuffs, which

---

c Carte, Orm. vol. II. p. 340.

which might not only keep money in the country, but be so improved, as to bring considerable sums from abroad. He offered to procure workmen from Norwich: the council of trade, lately established in Ireland, approved of his proposal; the duke of Ormond encouraged it, and erected the manufacture at Clonmel, the capital of his county-palatine of Tipperary. To supply the scarcity of workmen, Grant (a man well known by his observations on the bills of mortality) was employed to procure five hundred Walloon protestant families from Canterbury to remove to Ireland. At the same time, colonel Richard Lawrence, another ingenious projector, was encouraged to promote the business of combing wool, and making frizes. A manufacture of this kind was established at Carrick, a town belonging to the duke.

But of all such schemes of national improvement, that of a linen manufacture was most acceptable to Ormond. He possessed himself with the noble ambition of imitating the earl of Strafford in the most honourable part of his conduct, and opening a source of public wealth and prosperity, which the troubles and disorders of Ireland had stopped. An act of parliament was passed at Dublin to encourage the growth of flax and manufacture of linen. Ormond was at the charge of sending skilful persons to the Low-Countries, to make observations on the state of this trade, the manner of working, the way of whitening their thread, the regulations of their manufacture, and management of their grounds, and to contract with some of their most experienced artists. He engaged Sir William Temple to send to Ireland five hundred families from Brabant, skilled in manufacturing linen; others were procured from Rochelle and the Isle of Rè, from Jersey and the neighbouring parts of France. Convenient tenements were prepared

for

for the artificers at Chapel-Izod, near Dublin, where cordage, fail-cloth, ticken, linen, and diaper, were brought to a confiderable degree of perfection. Such cares reflect real honour on the governour, who thus laboured to promote the happinefs of a nation, and fhould be recorded with pleafure and gratitude, however we may be captivated by the more glaring objects of hiftory.

Nor was this excellent governour lefs affiduous to cultivate knowledge and learning in Ireland, fo as to root out that fuperflition by which the country had been enflaved, and to introduce that civility and refinement which give refpect and confequence to a nation. On the reftoration of the king, he found the univerfity of Dublin in the utmoft diforder, naturally refulting from the public confufions. Doctor Jeremiah Taylor, the pious and learned bifhop of Downe, was entrufted with the regulation of this feminary. The lord lieutenant wifely deemed it an important object of his adminiftration, to infpect the difcipline, to encourage the ftudies, and to promote the interefts both of the body and its particular members. When his enemies in England attempted to diminifh his confequence, by prevailing on the king to nominate an Englifhman to an Irifh bifhoprick, without his concurrence or recommendation, he thus expreffed his fentiments to the fecretary of ftate.

"It is fit that it be remembered, that near this city
"(of Dublin) there is an univerfity of the foundation
"of queen Elizabeth, principally intended for the e-
"ducation and advantage of the natives of this king-
"dom, which hath produced men very eminent for
"learning and piety, and thofe of this nation. And
"fuch there are now in this church; fo that while
"there are fo, the paffing them by is not only in fome
"meafure

"measure a violation of the original intention and in-
"stitution, but a great discouragement to the natives
"from making themselves capable and fit for prefer-
"ments in the church; whereunto (if they have equal
"parts) they are better able to do service than stran-
"gers, their knowledge of the country, and their
"relations in it giving them the advantage. The pro-
"motion too of fitting persons already dignified or be-
"neficed, will make room for, and consequently en-
"courage young men, students in this university;
"which room will be lost, and the inferiour clergy
"much disheartened, if, upon the vacancy of bishop-
"ricks, persons unknown to the kingdom and uni-
"versity shall be sent to fill them, and to be less useful
"there to the church and kingdom than those who are
"better acquainted with both."

* * * * * * *

WHILE the duke of Ormond employed his power in Ireland to the noblest purposes, his enemies in England laboured incessantly to disgrace him. His friend, the chancellor, had already fallen. Buckingham was impatient to complete his triumph, by supplanting Ormond in his posts of steward of the houshould and lieutenant of Ireland. The obstacle to this design arising from the general esteem and popularity which the duke enjoyed, was, if possible, to be removed, by finding out some ground of accusation in his conduct; and, for this purpose, the most malicious industry was used. They, whom Ormond had offended in his government, by denying their unreasonable requests, became the willing instruments, in the design of Buckingham. It was notorious, that he had given a commission for trying the mutineers at Carricfergus by martial law[d], in what his enemies called a time of peace, when

[d] Carte, Orm. vol. II. p. 356.

when an invasion was expected, when the mutinous troops had levied war, seized the king's forts, and maintained them by force of arms. An obsolete Irish law was discovered of the eighteenth year of Henry the Sixth, whereby it was enacted, that " no lord, nor " any other of what condition soever, shall bring or " lead hoblers, kearns, or hooded-men, neither English " rebels nor Irish enemies, nor any other people, nor " horses, to lie upon the king's subjects without their " consents, but upon their own costs, and without do- " ing hurt to commons of the county; and if any do " so, he shall be adjudged a traitor. Hence it was inferred, that the chief governour could not by law issue warrants for quartering soldiers on Dublin; and that Ormond (who was no barbarous lord, or leader of rebels, disguised ruffians, or enemies to the royal authority) had incurred the guilt of high treason, by maintaining the king's guards, and quartering the troops necessary for the safety of his government, agreeable to the usage of his predecessors. These two grand points of delinquency, with others still more frivolous, were formed into twelve articles of impeachment, which Buckingham and his creatures displayed in the utmost triumph.

The king expressed some indignation at these attempts against the duke of Ormond, and a resolution to support him yet seemed to discover the secret influence of Buckingham[e], by declining to send him any approbation of his conduct in quartering soldiers, or any directions for the future, leaving him entirely to the guidance of his own judgment, and to abide the hazard of any erroneous procedure. In Ireland, the discourses of the disaffected were bold and unrestrained,
and

[e] Carte, Orm. vol. II. p. 361. A. D. 1668.

and their expectations suited to their wishes. They, in times past allowed no benefit of laws to others, now clamoured for a strict and literal adherence to law. An opposition was made in many towns to quartering the army; while Ormond, with an undaunted attention to the security of the kingdom, continued to issue and enforce his warrants. In England every idle complaint of misconduct in the Irish government was eagerly received. Not only the enemies, but the friends of the lieutenant, were tempted to furnish materials for accusing him. The earl of Anglesey rejected the overtures of Buckingham with indignation, and gave Ormond notice of the designs formed against him. The earl of Orrery, who now enjoyed the presidental government of Munster, and seems to have aspired to the chief government of Ireland, was not actuated by the same generous resolution. He wavered between his dread of Ormond's power and sense of his integrity, and a desire of recommending himself to the English ministry. After some formal professions of friendship, he was gradually seduced into the purposes of those who sought the ruin of the duke. The earl prepared for a voyage to England; Ormond, dreading the insinuations of a disguised enemy, resolved to repair to the English court, and once more committed the government of Ireland to his amiable and gallant son, the earl of Ossory.

On the arrival of the duke in London,[f] he found the efforts to disgrace him still violent, notwithstanding the fair professions of Buckingham, his capital enemy. If the king felt no gratitude for his services, he was at least not totally divested of shame, and could not at once consent to abandon a servant so distinguished by his attachment. Attempts were made to

[f] Ibid. p. 367.

to poſſeſs him with an opinion, that great miſmanagements had prevailed in the revenue of Ireland, a point which, in the preſent neceſſities of the crown, it was ſuppoſed would irritate him moſt violently againſt his lieutenant. A long enquiry was held, and no ground of accuſation againſt Ormond could be diſcovered. Inſidious attempts were made to bring him to a voluntary reſignation of his government; when theſe proved ineffectual, the king was wearied with inceſſant applications to conſent to his removal; and the CABAL was by this time grown too powerful to be refuſed. On the repeated rumours of his diſgrace, Ormond repeatedly expoſtulated with the king. Charles reiterated the warmeſt aſſurances of attachment and protection. In one of their laſt interviews,[f] the duke was received with ſuch apparent cordiality of affection, as perſuaded him that his royal maſter was firmly determined to ſupport him againſt all his enemies, and unalterable in his reſolution of continuing him governour of Ireland. He was inſtantly informed, that the day before this audience, the king had poſitively promiſed the duke of Buckingham and his friends that he would remove him. He again expoſtulated, and Charles now ventured to confeſs, that he had entertained ſome thoughts of ſuch a meaſure. Lord Arlington was immediately afterwards employed to acquaint the duke of Ormond in form, that his majeſty intended to appoint a new lieutenant of Ireland, lord Robarts, lord privy-ſeal.

ORMOND could not entirely impute this change to perſonal enmity. He had diſcernment to diſcover,[*] that it muſt be attended with ſome extraordinary conſequences, though he could not fathom the deſigns of

[f] Carte, Orm. vol. II. p. 374.
[*] Immediately after his removal, the duke thus expreſſed himſelf in a letter to Sir Arthur Forbes.

SIR,

of the men now in power; defigns, which for the prefent lay deeply concealed, and whofe operation was neceffarily interrupted. Lord Robarts [g] was employed entirely for the purpofe of fcrutinizing the conduct of his predeceffor; but could not, by all his diligence, difcover any folid objections to the government of the duke, and had too much integrity to malign him. His temper was fullen, his addrefs and deportment folemn,

"SIR, White-Hall, 15 March, 68.

"I hope you have bin acquainted with as much as could be need-
"ful to your information, from what I have written to my fonne
"Offory, for you are in the firft ranke of thofe friends with whome
"I advifed him to confult in what might relate to the king's fer-
"vice, and the intereft of my family, which nether have, nor
"ever fhall bee feperated, though this alteration in government of
"that kingdome was contrived to that end by thofe who have fo
"long laboured with the king in it. All that is *paft*, is or will be
"knowen to you, when you have fo converfed with this gentleman.
"But if you are curious to know what *will bee*, you muft make a
"journey to Donaghadee, or further into Scotland, where pre-
"dictions are more plentiful. In earneft, no rules of ordinary
"forefight will now ferve the time. But thofe of honefty and loy-
"alty are in all events fafe, provided they are affifted by prudence
"and induftry. I am with all truth and reality, your moft affecti-
"onate humble fervant, ORMOND."
(*From the* ORIGINAL.)

To lord Offory he fpake his fufpicions yet clearer, although they were the fufpicions of a man, not acquainted with the true fecret of affairs. "If I am not much miftaken," faid he, "there is a
"purpofe to ftrike at the duke (of York's) command in the admi-
"ralty;——and that the aim is to drive him, by leffening his
"authority, to intemperate refentments, of which they will be
"ready to make fome ufe. When I fay *they*, I mean the duke of
"Bucks, your brother Arlington, and Sir Thomas Clifford, who,
"I think, have prevailed on the keeper to be inftrumental. All thefe
"do equally fear the duke fhould have credit with the king.—As
"for the duke of Bucks, I am confident he not only undervalues,
"but hates the king's perfon and his brother's, and has defigns
"apart, if not aimed at the ruin of them both," CARTE, ORM.
vol. II. p. 377.

g Carte, Orm. vol. II, p. 378--411. A. D. 1669.

solemn, ungraceful, and the more disgusting, as the Irish subjects had been habituated to the affable and conciliating manners of the duke of Ormond. By affecting to administer his government on principles different from those of his predecessor, he exposed himself to odium and contempt. Despised in Ireland, and useless to his faction in England, he was speedily recalled, and John, lord Berkley of Stratton, nominated his successor.

CHAP.

CHAP. IV.

Scheme for supporting the popish interest in Ireland.—History of the Irish REMONSTRANCE.—*Insolence of Peter Talbot. Partiality of lord Berkley to the anti-remonstrants.— Other instances of favour to the popish party.—Terrour of protestants.—Attempts to rescind the acts of settlement.— Spirited interposition of the English parliament.—Lord Berkley succeeded by the earl of Essex.—His Administration.—Essex recalled.—Interval of the duke of Ormond's disgrace.—Attempt on his life.—Attacks on his reputation.—His temperate conduct.—Ormond suddenly restored to favour,--and to the government of Ireland.—His administration.—The popish plot.—Peter Talbot seized.— Ormond's measures for the security of his government.— Complaints of his conduct.—He is censured by lord Shaftesbury in the house of Lords.—Reply of the earl of Ossory. —Attempts to remove the duke of Ormond.—Evidences of a popish plot encouraged.—Accused persons conveyed to London.—Trial of Oliver Plunket.—Attempts against Ormond renewed.—He is recalled to England.—Designs of the king and duke of York.—Ormond suddenly removed. —Earl of Rochester named lord lieutenant of Ireland.— Death of Charles the Second.*

THE administration of lord Berkley[k] opened a new and an alarming scene in Ireland[l]. He is said to have been made chief governour by the influence of the popish party, and from a thorough conviction of his attachment to their interests. However this may be, he was a creature of the duke of Buckingham[m]; and another creature, Sir Ellis Leighton, attended him as his

k A. D. 1670.
l Memoirs of Ireland, from Restor. p. 8.
m Carte, Orm. vol. II. p. 413.

his secretary, to be a spy upon his conduct, and to keep him firm to the purposes of the present English ministry.* The design of erecting arbitrary power upon the basis of popery was already formed; and, though deeply concealed, and cautiously and gradually developed in England, yet it was deemed neither indiscreet nor dangerous to make the first experiment in Ireland, with a contemptuous indifference to the principles and passions of its English inhabitants.

Some of the most powerful and factious partizans of the popish interest immediately followed lord Berkley into Ireland. And scarcely had he been seated in the chair of government, when their influence was discovered, by the conduct of the new lieutenant, to the more odious and dangerous of those parties into which the Irish Roman catholics were divided; and, by the countenance which, contrary to his public instructions, he shewed to those called ANTI-REMONSTRANTS, of whom it is here necessary to give some account.

From the days of Elizabeth, the measure of obedience due by papists to the civil power was a question frequently agitated in their schools and conventions. An enquiry into the nature and extent of the papal authority was necessarily involved in it; and, in these momentous points, the learned of their communion were by no means agreed. Several professed and taught a civil obedience to the queen; and hence, in all her wars, several of the Romish religion were distinguished by their services to the crown. To James, her successor, the most solemn declarations were occasionally tendered of an unreserved submission to his supreme temporal

---

* Vide Hume's Hist. vol. VI. p. 238. 4º.

temporal authority. In the diforders of the following reign the queftion was revived; and we have already feen the violences of Rinunccini, and his inveteracy to thofe who prefumed to decide againft the pope's authority even in temporals. We have alfo feen, that the clerical partizans of this nuncio, by imitating and even tranfcending his extravagance, brought down a dreadful chaftifement, not only on their whole order, but their whole communion in Ireland.

On the reftoration of Charles the Second[n], fome of the Irifh prelates and clergy, fmarting with the cruelty of the ufurpers, mortified at the expulfion of their party from their ancient inheritances, and dreading fome farther feverities from government, commiffioned Peter Walfh, a Francifcan friar, to prefent an addrefs to the king in London, to congratulate his acceffion to the throne of his anceftors, and to implore the benefits of the peace made with Ormond in the year fixteen hundred and forty-eight. Walfh knew how that peace had been violated by many of his brethren, and deemed it neceffary to obviate the objection againft tolerating the Romifh religion from its inconfiftency with the fecurity of a proteftant government. For this purpofe he drew up the REMONSTRANCE, as it was called, of the Roman catholic clergy of Ireland.

In this remonftrance[o] they acknowledged the king to be fupreme lord and rightful fovereign of the realm of Ireland; that they were bound to obey him in all civil and temporal affairs, and to pay him faithful loyalty and allegiance, notwithftanding any power or pretenfion, any fentence or declaration, of the pope

or

[n] Walfh's Hift. of the Irifh Remonftrance, Firft Treatife, Part i.
[o] Ibid.

or fee of Rome; that they openly difclaimed "all fo-
"reign power, papal or princely, fpiritual or temporal,
"in as much as it may feem able, or fhall pretend to
"free them from this obligation, or permit them to
"offer any violence to his majefty's perfon or govern-
"ment." They declared their refolution to detect
and oppofe all confpiracies and traiterous attempts
againft the king. They profeffed, that all abfolute
princes and fupreme governours, of what religion foever, are God's lieutenants upon earth; and that obedience is due to them in all civil and temporal affairs,
according to the laws in each commonwealth. They
protefted againft all doctrine and authority to the contrary; and declared it impious and againft the word
of God, to maintain that any private fubject may kill
his prince, though of a different religion.

The remonftrance thus framed[p] was prefented to the
duke of Ormond. He objected, that it was not figned
by the clergy, but offered folely on the authority of
Walfh, their procurator. One Irifh bifhop, and about
twenty-three of their clergy, immediately fubfcribed it.
Some few declined their fubfcription. Circular letters
were addreffed to the Irifh prelates in their feveral refi-
dences, inviting them to concur in an addrefs, which
was foon fubfcribed by an additional number of the
clergy, and by a refpectable collection of lay lords and
gentlemen. A declaration againft the temporal authority of the pope was by no means acceptable at Rome.
And, although the holy father would not openly inter-
pofe his immediate authority, yet the internuncio of
Bruffels, who had the care of ecclefiaftical affairs in
Ireland, and cardinal Barberini, were both employed to
cenfure the remonftrance in his name, as containing
propofitions already condemned by the apoftolic fee:
the

[p] Walfh's Hift. of the Irifh Remonftrance, Firft Treatife, Part i.

the former with greater violence declared, that it would do more mischief to the church than any persecution hitherto suffered from heretics. A powerful party was soon formed against the remonstrance, by those who would not openly acknowledge the authority or influence of these censures. Some, and particularly the Jesuits, proposed new forms of an address, which appeared equivocal, evasive, or ineffectual. Some objected to that of Peter Walsh, that it was inexpedient; others, that it was uncatholic; some, that it was condemned by the learned doctors of Lovain; some opposed it, as justifying the death of that holy martyr Saint Thomas of Canterbury; others reclaimed against the impiety of it, as being repugnant to the doctrines of Thomas Aquinas.

Such frivolous altercations were not entirely disagreeable to the state[q] as they would probably engross the attention of the Romish clergy, and prevent them from engaging in any practices against government. Some of their order had expressed their desire, that the remonstrance should be debated in a national synod. Reily, the Romish primate of Armagh, and French, of Ferns[r], wrote supplicating letters to the duke of Ormond, entreating permission to return to Ireland, and engaging to atone for past offences, by allowing the remonstrance. By this time the king was engaged in war with France and Holland; a descent on Ireland was expected, and some of the discontented Irish were practising secretly with France. In such a juncture it was supposed, that any secret conspiracies would be discouraged,[s] if the Irish clergy were to be convened expressly for the purpose of declaring their fidelity to the king

[q] Carte, Orm. vol. II. p. 511.
[r] Walsh. Hist. ut supra.
[s] Ib. first Treat. part ii.

king. Ormond allowed them to assemble; the agents of Rome laboured to prevent the design; but, after some vigourous opposition, the assembly was appointed to be held at Dublin, on the eleventh day of June, 1666, Reily, the popish primate, suddenly appeared in the synod, and, instead of performing his promise, practised zealously against the remonstrance. It was moved, that such of the clergy as had rendered themselves obnoxious to the laws, by their conduct in the Irish war, should implore the pardon of government. They answered[t], that they knew of no guilt or crime committed in this war. The whole proceedings of the clergy were intemperate and tumultuous. Their assembly broke up without any decision; the members, violently enflamed against each other, divided into two contending parties, those who supported, and those who opposed the remonstrance. It was not a sufficient triumph to this latter party that it had not been adopted by their assembly. They who had framed or subscribed, who approved or countenanced, or who had not opposed this profession of allegiance, were to be prosecuted and totally suppressed.

For this purpose, on the arrival of lord Berkley, provincial councils and diocesan synods were convened. The pope, who named the bishops, and commanded the preferments of regulars, easily formed his party. The remonstrants were every where dispossessed of their cures and stations; Peter Walsh, and his associates, were denounced excommunicate, and left without means of preserving their lives, but by submitting to their persecutors, or flying to foreign countries, where they were again in danger of being burnt as heretics for denying the power of the pope in temporal affairs

The

---

t Ibid Hist. Dedicat.

THE anti-remonstrants[u] had just now gained a distinguished and powerful partisan, Peter Talbot, created by the pope archbishop of Dublin, for the very purpose of chastising the opposers of his temporal authority. Peter, by conversing with his brother Richard, being favoured by Buckingham, and noticed by the king, had acquired a passion for political intrigue. The favour he enjoyed at the English court, rendered him an object of stupendous consequence to the popish clergy: and, to encrease their veneration, he had the confidence to declare publicly, that the king had appointed him to superintend their whole order in Ireland. He persuaded lord Berkley, that his influence in this country was irresistible. He had the hardiness to appear before the council at Dublin in the habit of his order and station, and Berkley was mean enough to permit this outrage on the laws, and to dismiss him unmolested, though he refused to join in any recognition of loyalty. Another incident made a deeper impression upon the protestant party[x] than things of more moment, which do not immediately strike the senses of the common people. Talbot proposed to celebrate a mass in Dublin, with extraordinary splendour. On this occasion he publicly applied to Sir Ellis Leighton to borrow some hangings and plate, which made part of the furniture of the castle. The secretary sent the utensils necessary for the pomp of his worship; and, in his compliment to Talbot, was said to have expressed a wish that high mass might soon be celebrated at Christ Church.

THE wretched remonstrants[y] felt all the insolence of this presuming prelate: they sought relief from lord Berkley, and the plainest dictates of justice and policy pleaded

[u] Carte, Orm. vol. II. p. 414. [y] Carte, ut sup.
[x] Memoirs of Ireland.

pleaded in their behalf; but Berkley, either through fear of Talbot, or in obedience to his private instructions, refused to interpose his authority for their protection. The body of Romish clergy were on the point of uniting in the doctrine of the pope's unlimited authority; a doctrine rejected in France, and other catholic countries, and to which the late miseries of Ireland were in a great measure to be imputed. The opposers of this doctrine requested to lay their case before the lieutenant. He refused them an audience. Margetson, the protestant primate, attempted to plead for them; he was reproved: they addressed themselves to the duke of Ormond: * the duke was their zealous friend; but Berkley complained of his officiousness, and openly declared, that he would consider any new orders from the council of England as the dictates of the duke, and pass them by unnoticed. Peter Talbot, and his colleagues, proceeded securely in the exercise of a foreign jurisdiction, and in his severities against those who presumed to maintain the odious doctrine of allegiance.

Nor was this indulgence to the Romish ecclesiastical jurisdiction the only favour shewn to Irish catholics [z]. It was soon followed by an order for granting commissions of the peace to professed papists, and admitting them to inhabit and trade in corporations. An attempt to establish [a] some popish aldermen, and a popish common council in Dublin, produced violent and lasting animosities

---

* Mr. Carte imputes it to the interposition of the duke of Ormond, that lord Berkley received a particular instruction, to protect those who supported the remonstrance, and were persecuted on this account. In a manuscript copy of his instructions (now before me) attested by Sir Ellis Leighton, the article relative to this matter stands last, and is evidently an addition occasionally made, and probably at the instances of Ormond.

[z] Carte, Orm. vol. II. p. 420. [a] Memoirs of Ireland.

fities in the city, and was at length effected, partly by fraud and outrage. Proteſtant ſubjects were aſtoniſhed; they poſſeſſed their imaginations with new plots and maſſacres. Croſſes * were diſcovered over all the doors of papiſts, a mark of diſtinction which was ſaid to ſecure the inhabitants from ſlaughter on the day of execution. It was whiſpered, and the popiſh party, in their vanity, encouraged the rumour, that Charles, in his exile, had promiſed the French king to reſtore the Iriſh to their eſtates, and the freedom of their religion: and ſuch rumours were countenanced by the attempts made by Richard Talbot to infringe the acts of ſettlement. †

THE

* Every trivial circumſtance was interpreted with the utmoſt malignity, by thoſe whoſe imaginations were poſſeſſed by rebellion, murder, and maſſacre. From theſe croſſes, the author of *Memoirs of Ireland from the Reſtoration*, hath, in his flaming zeal, adopted, or invented a dreadful tale of conſpiracy. But Story, in his hiſtory of the wars of Ireland, gives a fair account of this terrible phenomenon. On the popiſh feſtival, called Corpus Chriſti, the vulgar Iriſh, in their childiſh ſuperſtition, fixed a croſs of ſtraw in the front of their cottages: on the return of the feſtival, another was added. They were intended to ſecure the habitation, not from maſſacre, but witchcraft and evil ſpirits.

† At the time when the popiſh party could avow their deſigns, it plainly appeared, that nothing could content them but the utter abolition of theſe laws. For the preſent, however, they affected ſome moderation. In their private memorials to the king and duke, they repreſented the rebellion of forty-one as the act of a few, driven by fear and oppreſſion to take up arms: that the inſurgents had ſubmitted, adhered to the peace of forty-eight, and to the late king's ſervice. They acquieſced in his preſent majeſty's declaration, and the ſettlement of adventurers and ſoldiers, and deſired only a compenſation in money from the king's new revenues. At the ſame time, they magnified their own power and conſequence in Ireland, as well as their attachment to the crown, deſired to be reſtored to their habitations and freedom in corporate towns, to magiſtracies and military command; that the army ſhould be formed gradually of catholics, and the courts of law filled with catholic judges: they even hinted the propriety of admitting catholic prelates into parliament.

See the Appendix to King's State of the Proteſtants of Ireland. No. ii.

The favourable difpofitions which the court difcovered to the popifh party,[b] emboldened a number of their lords and gentlemen to grant a commiffion to Talbot for laying their grievances before the king and parliament of England. Purfuant to his procuration, he prefented their petition to the king and council. It fet forth, that the petitioners had been difpoffeffed of their lands by the ufurpers for their loyalty, had faithfully ferved his majefty; but that, for want of a juft reprefentation of their cafes, their eftates had been poffeffed by others. They prayed that fome impartial perfons fhould be appointed to hear and report their grievances; and that, in the interim, the king would fufpend his grants of any lands not yet difpofed of in Ireland. A committee was appointed to confider this petition. Ormond, one of the members, was alarmed at the bold and dangerous defign of overturning the whole fettlement of Ireland. Some errours had indeed been committed, but in attempting to correct them, many more, and thefe more dangerous might be introduced; fome grievances had been fuftained by individuals, but thefe were not to be redreffed by cafting the kingdom into general confufion. He preffed, that the petitioners might not be heard, nor their counfel admitted to object againft the acts. When this could not be obtained, he anfwered all their allegations fully; and Sir Heneage Finch, to whom, as attorney-general, all the papers were referred, made a report highly unfavourable to the petitioners. But the refources of the cabal were not yet exhaufted. Another committee[c] (from which Ormond was induftrioufly excluded) was empowered to revife " all papers and orders for the fettlement of Ireland, " to report what alterations had been made of matters
" once

[b] Carte, Orm. vol. II. p. 425. A. D. 1671.
[c] Ibid. Appendix. p. 91.

" once settled, and to represent the defects of papers
" or warrants for justifying any clauses contrary to
" the king's declaration, the first ground of settle-
" ment." Their report was erroneous: a third commission was issued, and many months wasted in search-
ing for materials to form another report.

In the mean time, Ireland[d] was a scene of general
alarm. The adventurers and soldiers, the forty-nine
officers, the Connaught purchasers, presented their several petitions, which were transmitted to England, and
all agreed in one great point, the maintenance of the
present settlement. In England, the people were not
indifferent to the conduct of Irish affairs. Terrified
by every indulgence to popery, suspicious of the king,
certain of the duke of York's dispositions, they complained and clamoured. The ministry was alarmed;
they dreaded the approaching parliament; they began to discern, that they had made too precipitate a
discovery of their purposes: they now affected to condemn the conduct of lord Berkley; they found it necessary to remove him from his government, and to
substitute the earl of Essex in his place.

The English parliament was not thus satisfied: a-
mong other spirited proceedings, they presented an
address to the king relative to the affairs of Ireland.
They petitioned, that he would maintain the acts of
settlement and explanation, and recal his late commission of enquiry, as highly prejudicial to many individuals, and dangerous to the peace and security of
that kingdom; that he would give order that no papists should be admitted justices of the peace, sheriffs,
coroners, or any magistrates in Ireland; and that all
licences to papists for inhabiting within corporations
should

[d] Carte, Orm. vol. II. p. 429.

should be recalled. They required that all popish prelates, and others, exercising ecclesiastical jurisdiction by the pope's authority, particularly Peter Talbot, pretended archbishop of Dublin, should be commanded to depart from Ireland, and all other his majesty's dominions; that all convents and seminaries should be dissolved, and all secular priests banished; that colonel Richard Talbot, assuming the title of agent of the Roman catholics of Ireland, should be dismissed from all command, civil or military, and forbidden access to his majesty's court: and lastly, that the chief governour of Ireland should have such orders and directions, as might tend to encourage the English planters and protestant interest, and suppress the disorders of the Irish papists.

The parliament was too formidable, for any slight or neglect of their representations. The commission of enquiry was superseded, and the king declared his resolution to maintain the acts of settlement. The obnoxious proceedings in the corporation of Dublin were reversed, and the ejected protestants restored to their places. The public countenance so inconsiderately shewn to the popish interest was for a time withdrawn; and the administration of lord Essex passed in the usual course of Irish government, without exhibiting any extraordinary or important incidents. His new rules[e] for regulating corporations, which he was by the act of explanation empowered to prescribe, were calculated to encrease the power of the crown, and to lessen the popular interest. The election of magistrates was confined by these rules to a few; and, in general, the approbation of the chief governour and council was required, before any magistrate could assume his office.
Strangers

[e] Irish Stat. vol. III.

Strangers and aliens were admitted to freedom in every town on easy terms. Such regulations could not but mortify the inferiour orders of citizens, who, in their ignorance and pride of association, are most susceptible of unfavourable impressions of government, and readiest to clamour against their superiours. The late violent proceedings and contests in Dublin had produced discontents and factions among the citizens, which[f], if we may believe lord Essex, were secretly fomented by Sir Ellis Leighton and Richard Talbot. The proceedings relative to the contest between the protestant and popish aldermen were ordered to be erased from the books of the corporation. The commons refused obedience to this order; they even questioned the authority of the lieutenant and council; and Essex, in his attempts to suppress their turbulence, discovered more of cold caution than the manly spirit of a good governour.

This chief governour, indeed, seems to have been particularly embarrassed through his whole administration, by his fears of the English factions, and the reports which might be spread in London to his disadvantage. He experienced numberless difficulties in executing the acts of settlement, in a country so " rent ' and torn," as he expressed it[g], that he could compare its distractions " to nothing better than flinging ' the reward upon the death of a deer among a pack ' of hounds, where every one pulls and tears what he ' can for himself." Private grants conferred by the king's letters produced deficiencies in the discharge of the Irish establishment, of which he complained, not with all the pliancy of a courtier: nor was he satisfied with the general management of the revenue, or with the

[f] Essex's Letters.   [g] Essex's Letters.

the farmers to whom it was entrusted. In the year 1675, he, with difficulty obtained licence to repair to England to lay the state of Irish affairs before the king: and although he was allowed to resume his government, neither Charles, nor his brother, seems to have been satisfied with a lord lieutenant whose integrity was more rigid than their own, who objected to several exceptionable and clandestine measures, however authorised, and even refused obedience to the royal orders, when not exactly conformable to law. Colonel Richard Talbot interested himself with particular forwardness in procuring a successor to the earl of Essex[h]. The office was said to be exposed to sale[i], and some noblemen sought for who would consent to purchase it, by an annual sum of money paid privately to the king, who was mean enough to engage in such traffic. But whatever designs were entertained of this nature, the kingdom was suddenly surprised by an unexpected, and apparently unaccountable disposition of the government of Ireland.

CHARLES had so implicitly yielded to the influence of his ministers[k], that for a long time he appeared totally estranged from the duke of Ormond. A horrid attempt was made on the life of this nobleman by Blood, who had formerly engaged in the design of seizing the castle of Dublin. As the duke returned from attending the prince of Orange to an entertainment in the city of London, Blood, with his accomplices, stopped and dragged him from his coach. Happily, in a refinement of cruelty, he resolved to hang him at Tyburn, which gave time to his domestics to fly to his rescue. When the assassin was seized in his attempt to

h Burnet's own Times.
i Memoirs of Ireland.
k Carte, Orm. vol. II. p. 420—447.

to rob the Tower of the regalia, and Charles defcended to confer with him, he freely acknowledged his attempt on the duke of Ormond. When this monfter was to be pardoned and rewarded, lord Arlington was employed to fignify the king's pleafure, that the duke would not profecute Blood, for reafons which he was commanded to deliver. " If the king," faid Ormond, " hath forgiven his defign of ftealing the crown, I " may eafily forgive the attempt upon my life. His " majefty's pleafure is a fufficient reafon, Your lord- " fhip may fpare the reft."

The earl of Offory, youthful, warm, and fpirited, could not preferve fuch temper on fuch an incident. He fufpected that the duke of Buckingham had been the firft mover of this attempt againft his father, nor did he conceal his fufpicions. While Buckingham ftood near the king, the earl advanced with his eyes glaring, and his afpect enflamed with indignation. " My lord," faid he, in a low and fullen voice, " I " well know that you were at the bottom of this late " attempt of Blood. Take notice; fhould my father " come to an untimely or violent death, I fhall confider " you as the affaffin: I fhall piftol you, though you " ftood behind the king: I tell it you in his majefty's " prefence, that you may be fure I fhall keep my " word."

Although his life was faved[1], yet the enemies of Ormond ftill laboured indefatigably to deftroy his reputation. He was accufed of mifconduct in his government, and mifmanagement of the Irifh revenue. On folemn examinations before the council, the charge proved falfe and frivolous. Yet the refuted falfehoods were

[1] Carte, Orm. vol. II. p. 451—461.

were frequently repeated, and the king, however he respected the virtues of Ormond; was yet obliged to treat him with a mortifying coldness. Such unworthy treatment could neither humble nor provoke the duke. He took his part in council, he attended daily on the king, without concealing his sentiments on public affairs, or betraying his resentment; without courting the king's mistresses for favour: without intriguing, or flying to any faction for revenge. He preferred that dignity and credit which both king and ministers had forfeited. Even in the drawing-room, his virtues and conciliating address attracted a little circle round him of those who were independent on the court. On such an occasion, the king, not daring to shew him any civility, was abashed and confounded. "Sir," said the profligate Buckingham, "I wish to know "whether it be the duke of Ormond that is out of "favour with your majesty, or your majesty with the "duke of Ormond; for, of the two, you seem most "out of countenance." In this state of disgrace, he still continued to speak his sentiments freely, nor was he mortified by opposition. He compared himself to an old clock cast into a corner; "and yet," said he, "even this rusty machine points sometimes right." When colonel Cary Dillon solicited his interest in some suit, declaring that he had no friends but God and his grace; "Alas, poor Cary!" replied the duke, "thou "couldst not have named two friends of less interest, "or less respected at court."

In Ireland he still enjoyed the utmost degree of popularity notwithstanding his disgrace. On visiting this country during the administration of lord Essex, he was received with every mark of affection and delight. Kilkenny, his place of residence, became instantly the seat feat of fplendour. Two hundred gentlemen were every day entertained at his table; and Dublin would have been exhaufted of all its inhabitants of rank, had not the duke determined to pay his refpects in perfon to the lieutenant. The cold civility with which he was received, in compliance with the Englifh miniftry, and poffibly from fome jealoufy of his fuperior popularity, only ferved to excite indignation, and to redouble the attention of all orders to this favourite duke.

It was now feveral years fince the king had fpoken to Ormond in any confidential manner, except when Shaftfbury was declared lord chancellor. On this occafion, Charles ventured to take him apart, and to afk his opinion of this meafure. " Your majefty," faid the duke, " hath acted very prudently in committing " the feals to lord Shaftfbury, provided you know how " to get them from him again." After this fhort conference the king relapfed into his former coldnefs. For almoft a year, he never deigned to fpeak to the duke, who, from his return to England, every day attended at the court. At length, in the month of April 1677, Ormond was furprifed by a meffage from the king, that he would fup with him. Their interview was eafy and chearful, without any explanation, or any difcuffion of paft tranfactions. On parting, Charles fignified his intentions of again employing him in Ireland. The next morning he faw the duke at a diftance, advancing to pay his ufual duty. " Yonder " comes Ormond:" faid Charles, " I have done all " in my power to difoblige him, and to make him as " difcontented as others, but he will be loyal in fpite " of me. I muft even employ him again, and he is the " fitteft perfon to govern Ireland." From this time he was defigned lord lieutenant, and nothing remained ed but to adjuſt with the earl of Eſſex the time and manner of his departure.

An appointment ſo unexpected[m] gave free ſcope to conjecture. Some imputed it to the king's deſire of quieting the ſuſpicions of a parliament juſt now convened, and diſcrediting the rumours of his intention to encourage popery in Ireland. Others, who had diſcovered that the duke of York was a great means of effecting it, raſhly pronounced that Ormond muſt have been reconciled to the intereſts of popery. The account adopted by Mr. Carte ſeems more probable, and more worthy of notice than ſuch vague conjectures. The duke of Monmouth was by this time grown a particular favourite both with the court and the populace. The earl of Shaftſbury and his party deemed him a proper inſtrument of their purpoſes, and wrought aſſiduouſly on his weakneſs and ambition. He was already maſter of the horſe; and both the ducheſs of Portſmouth and the treaſurer, earneſtly ſolicited the king to appoint him lord lieutenant of Ireland. The duke of York was alarmed. He could not bear that his rival ſhould get a taſte of ſovereignty, and become maſter of the whole power of a kingdom. He inſtantly reſolved to prevent it; and finding no competitor fit to be oppoſed to Monmouth but the duke of Ormond, laboured to reſtore him to the king's favour, and to the government of Ireland.

The firſt cares of Ormond's new adminiſtration were to render the Iriſh[n] army reſpectable, to have it duly exerciſed, and regularly paid; and, for theſe purpoſes, to inſpect the ſtate of the revenue, to correct abuſes in

---

[m] A. D. 1677. Carte, Orm. vol. II. p. 466.
[n] Ibid. p. 469—473.

in the grants of money, and to guard againſt thoſe miſrepreſentations to which he had been formerly expoſed. He found the kingdom defenceleſs; he wiſhed to provide for its ſecurity; ſupplies were abſolutely neceſſary, and no ſupplies could be obtained but from an Iriſh parliament. It was neceſſary, for many reaſons, that ſuch a parliament ſhould be convened. The decrees of the court of claims were to be confirmed; ſubjects were to be ſecured againſt any old title of the crown, by ſuch proviſions as the acts of ſettlement had not eſtabliſhed: commiſſions of enquiry into concealed forfeitures, with their train of lawyers, projectors, and ſolicitors, had grown to an enormous grievance, which required legal redreſs. The vexations and terrours of the people called for an act of general pardon and remiſſion of the crown debts. The abuſes committed in the revenue might be moſt effectually corrected, and prevented for the future by a parliament: but above all other conſiderations, money was to be raiſed by ſome additional duties; the king was deſirous of ſubſidies, and Ormond was impatient for an aſſembly that was to provide for the honour and ſecurity of his government.

But a new and alarming incident in England, interrupted all meaſures for the improvement of the ſtate of Ireland, and involved his adminiſtration in terrour and perplexity. As the duke returned to Kilkenny from viſiting the forts of Munſter, and particularly a fort he had juſt now erected at Kinſale, he received intelligence of what was called the popiſh plot, by a letter haſtily written, while Tonge and Oates were in their examination before the council. This was immediately followed by a more particular information from the ſecretary of ſtate, that the plot extended to Ireland, that Peter Talbot was engaged in it, and that persons were hired to assassinate the lieutenant. If the first report of a popish conspiracy could raise a general ferment in England, much more violent effects were to be expected in a country where the popish inhabitants were so numerous, and where protestants were possessed with an habitual horrour of their secret practices, where the first outrages of the late rebellion were remembered, related with every hideous circumstance of cruelty and carnage, and the imaginations of all the English race possessed with scenes of blood and desolation.

The least degree of inactivity on the part of government, the slightest hesitation or doubt of the reality of the plot in general, or of the particular circumstances relative to Ireland, would have been considered as dangerous and traiterous. Peter Talbot, however factiously inclined, was at this time utterly incable of taking any active part in a conspiracy. For two years violently afflicted with the stone and and stranguary, he had petitioned for a tacit permission to remove from Cheshire, and die in Ireland. Ormond, however, instantly signed a warrant to secure his person. The officer appointed to execute it found him at his brother's seat in the neighbourhood of Dublin. He probably had time to remove his papers; for, notwithstanding his extensive correspondence, nothing was found in his cabinet but a few letters of controversial divinity; and, as it seemed impossible to remove him in his present state of pain and languor, the security of his brother was accepted for his appearance. Such indulgence was liable to dangerous misrepresentation; and, therefore, on the return of the duke of Ormond to Dublin, Peter was removed to the castle, and attended with the care due to a person who seeemed on the point of death.

In the mean time, orders were iſſued that all officers and ſoldiers ſhould repair to their reſpective garriſons; that popiſh eccleſiaſtics ſhould depart from the kingdom, popiſh ſeminaries and convents be ſuppreſſed; and that all papiſts ſhould bring in their arms within twenty days to the perſons appointed to receive and depoſit them in the king's ſtores. Informations quickly multiplied; and directions were received from England to ſeize Richard Talbot, Lord Mountgarret and his ſon, and a colonel of the name of Peppard[a]. Lord Mountgarret, repreſented as a dangerous conſpirator, was of the age of fourſcore years, bed-ridden, and in a ſtate of dotage; and, to the further diſcredit of the evidences, no colonel Peppard was known, or could be found in Ireland. From the examination of Richard Talbot nothing alarming could be collected, nothing that might warrant his further detention; he was, therefore, by order of the Engliſh council, ſuffered to give ſecurity for his quiet demeanour, and to depart from Ireland.

In this time of terrour and alarm, amidſt the clamours of the vulgar, the violent and the deſigning, Ormond proceeded with temper, with ſteadineſs and vigour[b]. He diſarmed the papiſts, ſettled the militia, ſecured the garriſons, and kept the army untainted. A number of vagabond robbers, called tories, the remains or deſcendants of that race of barbarous plunderers which the Iriſh war had produced, concealed themſelves in the mountains and bogs of Ulſter, and other parts of Ireland, iſſued out occaſionally, and harraſſed the civil inhabitants by every kind of outrage. They were uſually concealed by their relations; ſometimes by the popiſh priest,

[a] Carte, Orm. vol. II, p. 479. [b] Ibid p. 481.

priest, who, notwithstanding all the formal proclamations of government, continued to exercise his function in the neighbourhood of these robbers. In a season of apparent danger, Ormond recurred to an extraordinary expedient, justified only by necessity, and the failure of all other means. A proclamation was published, directing, that the near relations of known tories should be committed to prison, until such tories were killed or brought to justice; and that any popish pretended parish priest of any place where murder or robbery were perpetrated by these tories, should be committed to prison, and thence transported, unless within fourteen days the guilty persons were killed or taken, or such discovery made, that they might be apprehended and brought to justice.

But this instance of rigour did not satisfy many protestants, who, in their zeal, their terrour, and perhaps some secret inclination to a new rebellion and new forfeitures, called for more severe and irritating measures[c]. They proposed, that those of the Irish who still enjoyed the old rank of chieftainry, who had lost their estates, and were, therefore, likely to engage in any desperate purpose, should be secured, so as to restrain their septs from rebellion. But Ormond thought it unjust to imprison men merely because they might do mischief, and before they had discovered any dangerous dispositions. If all suspected persons were to be seized, it seemed difficult to say how or where they were to be kept; how many might be thus driven to desperate courses, and whether their followers might not rather be provoked than intimidated. It was well known how much the imprisonments, and other severities

of

[c] Carte, Orm. vol. II. p. 484.

of Sir William Parsons, had contributed to hurry numbers into the last rebellion; and neither the duke nor the privy council deemed it prudent to make another experiment, whether the same measures might be attended with the same effects.

It was also proposed to expel those papists from corporate towns, who, though formerly excluded, had yet been licensed to return[d]. But, whatever had been the occasional indulgence of government to this obnoxious party, it was well known the English inhabitants had contributed to the abuse they now inveighed against. They themselves had received the papist Irish into towns, because they could not live without them. They wanted servants, tenants, and tradesmen; the Irish furnished all these, and were encouraged. Whatever danger arose from their re-admission into towns, the evil could not be immediately remedied, without desolating these towns, and driving numbers to a vagrant life. In an affair so delicate, where the violation of the law was evident, and its strict enforcement dangerous, Ormond and the council took a middle course. They issued a proclamation, that none of the popish religion should come into the castle of Dublin, or any other fort or citadel, without special order from the lord lieutenant; that fairs and markets should be held without the walls of some principal cities, to which papists were to resort unarmed. Such of them as had lately been admitted into these cities were removed; and from others, where popish inhabitants chiefly abounded, all the idle and useless were expelled; and none suffered to remain but merchants, artificers, and other necessary persons.

[d] Carte, Orm. vol. II. p. 480---485.

An administration conducted with temper, by which the protestants were secured from false alarms of danger, without relaxation of that care and vigilance which the time required, and without irritating the popish party by oppression or wanton severity, was not entirely agreeable to the passions and prejudices of many English subjects in Ireland. The more violent attempted to drive the duke of Ormond from his course of moderate measures, by alarming him with fears of assassination[e]. Letters were dropt in Dublin, intimating a design of this nature, and several pretended to give an account of what they heard or suspected of this design. But the Duke was not to be moved by dark and inexplicable informations; and the next step of those who were dissatisfied with his conduct, was to transmit their complaints to England. The lieutenant, by all his influence, by all his expence in procuring intelligence, could find no reason to apprehend an insurrection in Ireland; yet letters were sent into England, insinuating that the protestants of this country were in the utmost danger, and little care taken for their defence[f]. Ormond was accused for not seizing the Irish chieftains, of not expelling papists from corporate towns, of commanding them by proclamation to deliver up their arms, instead of sending his soldiers to disarm them; by which every garrison must have been abandoned, and the army scattered in loose files, exposed to destruction, and utterly incapable of executing their orders in any reasonable time, even if no commotion should arise; as, by the computation of Sir William Petty, there were about fifteen papists now in Ireland to one protestants. But these complaints, however unreasonable and absurd, were received

with

[e] Carte, Orm. vol. II. p. 481. [f] Ibid p. 484. [g] A. D. 1679.

with avidity by the prevailing party in England. The licentiousness of the press, the virulence of private slander, the prejudices and credulity of the vulgar, the artifice of popular leaders, all conspired to load the duke of Ormond with the odium of being popishly inclined. Lord Shaftsbury conveyed the insinuation into the house of lords, with sanguine hopes of removing Ormond from his government. To sound the temper of the peers, he recommended to their consideration the state of Ireland, a country too much neglected, managed with too great inattention to the English interest, and too dangerous partiality to the popish party. The earl of Ossory was witness of these reflections on his father. He started up, and in the unadorned language of a soldier, and with the warmth of filial affection, expressed his astonishment at these insinuations against the duke of Ormond, briefly recounted those actions of his life which had raised his zeal for the royal service and the interest of protestants above suspicion; then, with a firm and elevated voice, with an eye darting indignation and contempt on Shaftsbury, he proceeded thus: "And now
" my lords, having spoken of what he has done,
" I presume, with the same truth, to tell your
" lordships what he has not done. He never advised the breaking of the triple league; he never
" advised the shutting up of the exchequer; he
" never advised the declaration for a toleration;
" he never advised the falling out with the Dutch,
" and joining with France; he was not the au-
" thor of that most excellent position, Delenda
" est Carthago, that Holland, a protestant country, should, contrary to the true interest of England, be totally destroyed. I beg your lordships

" will be so just as to judge of my father, and of
" all men, according to their actions and coun-
" sels [h]."

Nothing could have happened more convenient to the purposes of Shaftsbury than an insurrection in Ireland [i]; he was disappointed, and provoked at the tranquillity of this country, and at that moderate administration which maintained it: he was impatient to remove Ormond from his government, but the king firmly declared, that he never should be removed: he attempted to change the Irish council which had concurred in the measures of the lieutenant: the king rejected the proposition; he would not change any of his ministers in Ireland; for he would not, as he expressed it, resign this kingdom to the parliament. Shaftsbury and his party were thus obliged to proceed indirectly, and to procure orders for the council of Ireland to transmit severe bills against popish recusants. Should they refuse, they must be removed; should they obey, the Irish might be driven to rebellion. Orders were transmitted to the lord lieutenant and council, to prepare laws for excluding papists from either house of parliament, or any office in Ireland, agreeably to those already enacted in England; and that a proclamation should be issued for encouraging all persons to make farther discoveries of the horrid popish plot. The bills were not transmitted till after the dissolution of the English parliament: the proclamation was immediately published.

It reflected particular discredit on the popish plot in England, that a year had passed before one evidence

[h] Carte Orm. vol. II. Append. p. 90. [i] Ibid. p. 491—497.

evidence could be found of any like conspiracy in Ireland, where the papists were so numerous, and whither their brethren of England might naturally have resorted for assistance. The fears and suspicions of those who were most heated against popery and the Irish, formed imaginary dangers. An invasion was suddenly expected from France. Informations of such a design were transmitted to England by lord Orrery, and eagerly received. One ship was particularly named to have conveyed a vast number of arms and military stores to the port of Waterford. The vessel was instantly seized, searched, and instead of containing all the formidable preparations for rebellion and massacre, was found to be freighted only with salt. Such futile alarms served as hints to those whom the hope of gain, or revenge, prompted to embrace the encouragement given to informers, and assisted them in framing their malicious tales. One Bourke, of the county of Waterford, a man of flagitious character, had been committed to prison by De la Poer, earl of Tyrone. He instantly accused the earl as engaged in promoting an invasion; but, however implicitly the accusation was believed in London, it proved, on the clearest evidence, false and malicious. David Fitzgerald, a protestant of the county of Limerick, at first seemed a more reputable evidence, though he commenced informer in prison, and on the point of being tried for high treason. He was acquitted, and his information received by the duke of Ormond. He named some men of figure as accomplices in the design of an insurrection; but his narrative was confused, improbable, and inconsistent. The persons accused freely offered themselves to be tried in that place where
their

their converfation was known, and where the confpiracy was faid to be carried on. But Shaftfbury now boafted that he could produce important difcoveries of an Irifh plot. It was refolved to try the culprits in London. Fitzgerald was fent for; and though he attempted to efcape, was forcibly dragged to give his evidence in London.

But one witnefs, however credible, was not fufficient. More were fought for; nor was it extraordinary, nor is it any fair ground for national reflection, that uncommon induftry and encouragement procured fome more witneffes in Ireland. Some of the inferiour popifh clergy, of extreme poverty and profligate lives, confented to become informers. The haunts of tories were fuccefsfully ranfacked for others; and all thefe men fuddenly appeared in London, not in their original ftate of meannefs and barbarifm, but in a decent garb, and with the appearance even of affluence [k]. Happily the perfons accufed by Fitzgerald efcaped by the remorfe of their accufer; who, at length, freely acknowledged the bafenefs and falfehood of his information. Oliver Plunket, the popifh archbifhop of Armagh, was not fo fortunate. He fucceeded Reily in this ftation: and during the government of lord Effex, lived quietly in Ireland, recommending a peaceable fubmiffion to government, and expreffing his abhorrence of all political intrigues. He even exerted his fpiritual authority to reftrain the turbulent temper of Peter Talbot, and to confine him within the duties of his profeffion. But fome of the inferiours of his clergy, men of lewd lives and brutal manners, were provoked by his cenfures and correction, and
formed

[k] Carte, Orm. vol. II. Append. p. 109.

formed the design of accusing him. He was conveyed to London; but, as these evidences had neither honesty to swear the truth, nor sense to devise a consistent tale, their first attempt was defeated.--- The jury, even in these days of passionate credulity, could not find a bill against Plunket[l]. But the informers gained some accomplices, they framed their accusation a-new, and made another attack[m]. Plunket was accused of obtaining his title and station for the purpose, and on an express compact, of raising seventy thousand men in Ireland by the contributions of the popish clergy, whose whole revenues could not equip a single regiment. This formidable body of insurgents was destined to join twenty thousand men to be furnished by France, and who were to make their descent at the port of Carlingford, a place the most inconvenient, and even impossible for the purpose. The witnesses of Plunket were detained by contrary winds, and other untoward accidents; so that he had little to urge against his accusers but the improbability of their evidence, and solemn asseverations of his own innocence. The wretched man was condemned, and executed for a plot which he explicitly denied at his death, with the most solemn disavowal of all equivocation; and which, if he had confessed, no man at all acquainted with the circumstances of Ireland (as he pertinently observed) could have given the least credit to his dying confession.

THROUGH the whole melancholy progress of perjury and subornation, the duke of Ormond acted with the utmost caution[n]. He discouraged no informations; he discovered no violence in the prosecution of them. He gave his enemies in England no

l Burnet, Vol. I. p. 282. m State Trials, Vol. III. n A.D. 1680.

no pretence for accusing him of remissness, or inattention to the security of his government; but he gave them no hopes of concurring in their favourite measures. On the afflicting death of his son, the gallant earl of Ossory, they renewed their efforts to remove him from the goverment of Ireland[o]. Even the more virtuous of the popular party could not be satisfied at the power and favour enjoyed by a nobleman, bred in the most exalted notions of loyalty and hereditary right, known to enjoy a good degree of confidence with the duke of York, and supposed to be an enemy to the scheme of exclusion. For the very same reason, the king resolved to continue him in his present station. Lord Essex laboured to be restored to the government of Ireland; his friends espoused his pretensions; old clamours were revived against the duke; new calumnies suggested and propagated; but such dishonourable means defeated their own purposes[p]. Ormond stood the attack unmoved: and when the apprehensions excited by an infamous train of informers were allayed; when notwithstanding the vote of an English parliament that there was a plot in Ireland, no traces could be discovered; when, after the first fit of popular fury, the credit of the plot and its evidence declined in England; and, on several trials in Ireland the accused were clearly acquitted, the minds of all subjects in this kingdom were relieved from a state of terrour and anxiety[q]. Trade and industry increased, and the composed state of public affairs enabled Ormond to commit the sword of state to a deputy, the earl of Arran, and to repair to England, whither he was called by the king, at the instances of the duke of York.

It

[o] Carte, Orm, Vol. II. p. 508. [p] A.D. 1681. [q] Ibid. p. 519.

It is not to be doubted, but that the king in the present course of arbitrary measures which he adopted, wished for the countenance of a servant so generally respected as the duke of Ormond; and that the duke of York, knowing the instability of his brother, sought to keep him steady and determined by the authority of such a counsellor[r]. Were it to the present purpose to enter into a detail of Ormond's conduct in England, it might not appear to form the most brilliant part of his life. The very facts which his biographer hath recited with so much satisfaction, prove him to have displayed the most unbounded attachment to the crown, by being an active agent in the most odious and obnoxious measures. But, to his honour, it must be observed, that he was by no means admitted into all the most secret councils and purposes of the king and duke. After two years residence in London, he prepared to return to his government[s]. He solicited zealously for an Irish parliament; but the prospect of a considerable supply could not reconcile the king to this measure. Ormond ascribed this reluctance to the probable cause, the severity of some bills transmitted against papists during the violence of the popish plot, and he approved the apparent moderation of the king in defeating these bills. Nor do his suspicions seem to have been roused by another measure which produced considerable clamour. As it was resolved that an Irish parliament should not be convened; and as it was necessary for the quiet of Ireland, that estates should be confirmed to their proprietors, against all fraudulent or captious attempts, a commission of grace was issued for remedy of defective titles. The scheme of this commission was formed by the duke of York; and the protestant

[r] A. D. 1682. [s] Carte, Orm. Vol. I. p. 535.

testant party had too good reason to conclude, that the real design of this novelty was to make a narrow inspection into titles, and to discover what advantages might be made for depriving protestants of their possessions, and restoring them to the Irish[t].

However this may be, the duke of Ormond had scarcely returned to Ireland, when he received surprising proof that designs were formed with respect to this country, in which his concurrence could not be expected[u]. Charles now lived in an indolent enjoyment of that superiority which he had acquired over all the opposers of his power. The party which had made such desperate efforts to circumscribe the king within the strict limits of the constitution, and to exclude the duke of York from the succession, was totally subdued. By the discovery of the Rye-house plot, their leaders were exposed to the rigour of the law; and the people, who confounded the design of assassination with that of an insurrection, looked on the whole party with horrour, and seemed to contend with each other, in a passionate zeal, for laying themselves and their liberties at the feet of their sovereign. The reins of government were committed to the duke of York. The duke affected activity and penetration. He represented to his brother the necessity of securing and perpetuating that superiority he had now acquired; he reminded him of those distresses to which the crown had oftentimes been reduced, from the want of a sufficient army implicitly devoted to its service. He turned his attention to Ireland, a country which, if duly managed, would with an implicit devotion conform to his wishes. In this country the revenue was considerably improved, though

---

t Memoirs of Ireland.   u Carte, Orm. Vol. II. p. 539. A. D. 1684.

though in the hands of farmers, whose contracts, however advantageous to themselves, had not always been performed[w]. Sixty-one thousand pounds had been yearly drawn from the Irish treasury for the garrison of Tangier. By the demolition of this fort, the country had been eased of this grievous burden; and tranquillity and improvement promised new accessions of wealth to Ireland. Here then the king was taught to look for such a military establishment as might give respect and stability to his government. But it was not the present army of Ireland for whose attachment the duke of York could so peremptorily engage: he regarded it as an assemblage of factious fanatical republicans, comprehended under the general name of protestants, not reconciled to the present favourite doctrines of absolute submission and obedience; the descendants of those who resisted his royal father, and pursued him even to the scaffold, nurtured in the same principles, and ready for the same purposes. He advised the king to fix his reliance on another party, that of the catholics, who, notwithstanding all their grievances, were unalterably devoted to the crown, and the presumptive heir; whose principles and interest must attach them firmly to his service, and whose zeal must be enlivened by being at length restored to favour and consequence, and relieved from the oppression of sectaries and rebels.

CHARLES hastily adopted this scheme, rather in careless compliance with his brother, than from that deliberate reflection which an affair of such importance merited. It was speedily resolved to remove the duke of Ormond from the government of Ireland, as his powers could not be diminished, and his

[w] Carte, Orm. Vol. II. p. 472—525.

his principles were known to be repugnant to this new design. Scarcely had this design been suspected at court, when, as usual, insinuations were whispered against the conduct both of Ormond and his son Arran. Colonel Richard Talbot, who had been allowed to return from exile, and probably was admitted to the secret councils of the duke of York, inveighed with his usual violence against the administration of Irish affairs, and represented it as a matter of absolute necessity to make a general reformation in the council, the magistracy, and the army of Ireland. The duke of Ormond had but just resumed his government, when, (as he expressed it) "before his head was settled from the agitation of the sea," he received private assurances of his intended removal. These were soon followed by a letter from the king conceived in the following terms.

"*Newmarket, October* 19, 1684.

"I find it absolutely necessary for my service, that
"very many, and almost general alterations should
"be made in Ireland, both in the civil and military
"parts of the government; that several persons
"who were recommended and placed by you (and
"who were fit to be so at that time) must now be
"removed[x]. For which reason, and others of the
"like nature, I have resolved to put that govern-
"ment into another hand, and have made choice
"of my lord Rochester, who is every way fit for it;
"and, in one respect, fitter than any other man can
"be, which is, that the near *relation he has to
"you

[x] Carte, Orm. Vol. II. Append. p. 111.
* The daughter of lord Hyde, now earl of Rochester, had lately been married to the young earl of Ossory, grandson to the duke of Ormond.

" you makes your concerns and those of your fami-
" ly to be his, and he will have that care of them
" which I desire may be always continued. And,
" because I would have this alteration appear with
" all the regard and consideration that I have for
" you, I offer to yourself to propose in what man-
" ner you would wish it to be done; and after-
" wards, if you choose to stay in that country, all
" whom I employ shall pay you all the respect
" your merit and long constant services can expect;
" and, whenever you come hither, you shall re-
" ceive the same marks of my kindness, esteem,
" and confidence you have hitherto had; and this
" you may depend upon. Nothing I have now
" resolved on this subject shall be public till I hear
" from you, and so be sure of my kindnesses.

CHARLES REX."

Thus was the favourite design revealed. The total alteration in all departments could be intended only to introduce the catholic party. The person destined to the government was to be abridged in his most essential powers. He was not to interfere in any military matters, or to name the lowest commissioned officer in the army. This whole province was to be assigned to a lieutenant-general; and Talbot, the well known patron of the popish party, was to be invested with this station and authority. Ormond was comforted in his disgrace, by finding that the charge of forming a popish party was not committed to him. " I was
" much to seek," said he in a letter to Sir Robert Southwell, " what it could be that was fit for the
" king to command, and yet would be hard to
" impose upon me to execute. For such things
" the king was pleased to say were to be done by
" my

"my successor; but now I think that riddle is
"expounded in the restraints put upon my lord of
"Rochester; one whereof is, that he shall not
"dispose of the lowest commissioned office in the
"armyy. I confess it would have been very uneasy
"to me to have continued in the government upon
"those conditions; and I should have thought it
"not very dutiful to have refused to serve the king
"upon any terms, or in any station. From this
"difficulty, I thank God and the king I am deli-
"vered, and I am so well pleased that I am, that
"if it had been told me this was one of the
"charges intended, I should have owned my re-
"move from the government for a greater favour
"than my placing in it in the most prosperous
"time."

Nor doth the earl of Rochester seem to have been insensible to the mortification of assuming the government with such limitations; at least he discovered some reluctance to assuming it. The king seemed again disposed to change his measures and his counsellors; and in this sudden fluctuation, it was natural for a nobleman of figure and consequence, allied to the royal family, not to be very forward to hazard his interest at court by retiring to another kingdom. All projects, with respect to the management of the Irish affairs, appeared suspended. The hopes of the Protestant subjects revived, those of the Romanists in Ireland were proportionally depressed, when the death of Charles the Second, attended with the immediate recal of the duke of Ormond, produced a total revolution in the passions and prospects of the several inhabitants, and opened a new scene in this country, worthy of being distinctly considered.

y Carte, Orm. Append. Vol. II. p. 118.

CHAP. V.

The accession of James the Second.---Its influence on the catholics and protestants of Ireland.---New lords justices.---Their conduct.---Effects of Monmouth's rebellion.----Militia disarmed.----Talbot ennobled.---Earl of Clarendon appointed lord lieutenant of Ireland.---The nation in ferment.----Protestant party plundered by robbers; and harrassed by informers.---Attempt to invalidate the acts of settlement.----New lord chancellor.----Popish judges and privy counsellors.---Favours to the popish clergy.---Tyrconnel arrives in Ireland,---models the army.---His insolence and meanness.---His schemes.---Assisted by Nagle.---Tyrconnel appointed successor to Clarendon.---View of Tyrconnel's character.---More changes in the courts of law.---Quo-warranto against the charter of Dublin.---Other charters resigned or seized.---New corporations.---Attempts on the university of Dublin.---General distress.---Attempts to remove Tyrconnel.---He meets the king at Chester.---His design against the acts of settlement.---His agents insulted in London.---Birth of a prince.---Ridiculous triumph of papists in Dublin.---Enterprize of the prince of Orange.---Its effects in Ireland.---Rumours of a popish massacre.---Confusion in Dublin,---and in other parts of Ireland.---Lord Antrim's regiment excluded from London-Derry.---Conduct and proceedings of the garrison.---Association of northern protestants.---Terrour and artifice of Tyrconnel.---Reserve of William.---Hamilton sent to practise with Tyrconnel.---His advice.---He is sent against the Northerns.---Their retreat.---They assemble

assemble at Colerain.---They fly to Derry.---Lundy suspected.---Bravery of the garrison.---James lands at Kinsale.---His arrival at Dublin.---He marches against Derry.---George Walker.---Lundy abandons the passes.---Garrison of Derry provoked.---Declare for a brave defence,---appoint their governours,---regulate their operations.---Their resolution.---Kirk arrives in Lake-Foyle.---He retires.---The garrison still obstinate.---Barbarity of Mareschal Rosen.---Piteous distresses of the garrison.---They are relieved in their extremity.---The siege raised.---Conduct and successes of the Enniskilleners.---Battle of Newtown-Butler.

FOURTEEN years had elapsed since the royal brothers first betrayed their purpose of establishing a popish interest in Ireland[a].--- Here they deemed the experiment less hazardous, and here the experiment was made in consequence of their private agreement with France. Terrified by the spirited remonstrances of an English parliament, they suspended their attempts. They renewed them when the royal authority seemed above controul; Charles with a careless acceptance of any measures which promised to confirm the ascendency he had acquired; James, with a bigoted and passionate affection for popery. When his schemes and his power were apparently on the point of ruin, he suddenly found himself invested with sovereignty. He ascended the throne amidst the acclamations of a triumphant faction, which he mistook for the univerfal joy of all his subjects. His religion had not been concealed; it was now openly and formally avowed.

SUCH

[a] A.D. 1684.

SUCH a prince, unexpectedly seated in such triumph on the throne of England, naturally inspired the popish subjects of Ireland with the most extravagant expectations. They already saw the victory of their religion over all its adversaries; they fancied themselves already restored to the possessions of their fathers; and, roused from that depression they had so long endured, they enjoyed the flattering prospect of redress, of power and consequence, of royal favour, of every advantage to be derived from a king of their own religion. Ormond, whom the violent and bigoted of their party considered as a mortal enemy, was removed from his government, with evident impatience of his continuing in power, even for the shortest time [b]. He was directed to resign the sword immediately to two lords justices. The age and infirmities of the duke were assigned as the cause of his removal; and, in public, Ormond affected to believe this to be the real cause. During his administration a stately hospital had been erected near Dublin for the reception of old soldiers; hither he invited the military officers to an entertainment, and, at the conclusion, holding his glass filled to the brim, he thus addressed himself to the company. "See, gentlemen!---They "say at court I am old and doating.---But my "hand is steady, nor doth my heart fail; and I "hope to convince some of them of their mistake. "---This to the king's health."

BUT however Ormond concealed his sentiments of the king's real purpose, the protestant subjects of Ireland felt the most melancholy apprehensions. They saw the popish gentry crowding in triumph to the

[b] Secret consults of the popish party. State tracts, Vol. III. Memoirs of Ireland.

the capital, busy in consultation, intemperate in their expressions of joy, vaunting their own loyalty, traducing and reviling others. Every rumour of their meetings was received with terrour, and every violent expression reported with dismay. Imaginary dangers were discovered in the choice of a new council, though composed of protestants, and in the appointment of two lords justices, who had repeatedly approved their fidelity in this station; Boyle, primate and chancellor, and Forbes Earl of Granard. In this time of fear, Boyle was considered by the puritans as a churchman little removed from popery; Granard was regarded by the churchmen as a sectary invidiously advanced to divide the protestant interest. The prelate was indeed impressed with high notions of loyalty, and the earl had married a lady of presbyterian principles; he was the protector of the northern puritans, had humanely screened their teachers from those severities which in England proved both odious and impolitic, and gained them a pension of five hundred pounds annually from government.

But whatever difference was apprehended in the political or religious sentiments of these governours, they now concurred amicably in support of the general interest of protestants, and of the public tranquillity. Futile informations were every day received from papists of plots formed against the king, by those whom they called fanatics [c]. Reports were made by protestants of expressions, violent and dangerous, used by popish gentry in their private meetings. But all such officious accusations were equally discouraged. Yet so intolerable was the insolence of papists, and so violent were the clamours of both parties

[c] A. D. 1685.

parties, that Granard intimated a desire of being dismissed from his station. James thought his service so necessary for the present, that in a letter, written with his own hand, he assured him, that nothing should be done in Ireland prejudicial to the protestant interest. These assurances were communicated; and the justices laboured to allay the fears of protestants, by representing the improbability of any scheme being meditated in favour of popery, when the English and Scottish subjects were so numerous and powerful, possessed of all the force and authority of the kingdom.

The effects of these prudent endeavours to preserve the public peace, were soon discovered on the attempts made in Scotland and England to disturb the government of James. The forces of Ireland marched with alacrity to the northern province, to be transported, if necessary, and to serve against the adherents of Argyle. During the rebellion of Monmouth, the popish subjects every moment flattered themselves that some puritans at least would endeavour to raise an insurrection in favour of this popular duke: it was even whispered, and believed, that the earl of Granard intended to share his fortunes. But, to the utter disappointment of all such expectations, no commotion was attempted, no signs of disloyalty appeared; every subject of Ireland expressed an abhorrence of Monmouth's attempt, and a resolution to support the reigning prince. Still the virulent and designing of the popish party spread their futile rumours of plots and insurrections, and affected a deadly terrour of fanatics. The vulgar of their communion were assured, that the protestants had formed a conspiracy to cut them off by a general massacre; that they

assembled

assembled frequently by night, and were on the point of executing their bloody purpose. Some were really alarmed; many pretended fear. They abandoned their dwellings, and concealed themselves from the imaginary danger. Tales were framed, informations taken by magistrates, and transmitted to the state. The lords justices, to allay the ferment, found it necessary to issue a proclamation against " night-meeting," a new species of crime, the invention of malignant and designing men, who wished to give their party the merit of being persecuted; and, by loading their adversaries with odium, to justify any severities that might hereafter be inflicted on them.

JAMES now felt himself possessed of that vigour which a prince derives from a discomfited rebellion. He declared his purpose of employing popish officers in England, and even cautioned his parliament against the presumption of objecting to this exercise of prerogative. In Ireland he proceeded with still less reserve. A letter to the lords justices and council informed them, that the contagion of Monmouth's rebellion had been extensively diffused; that, for the safety of Ireland, it was judged necessary to recall the arms of the militia, and to deposite them in the king's stores. This militia was entirely formed of protestants, embodied, armed, and disciplined by the duke of Ormond. The order for resigning their arms was received with consternation by men trained to an habitual horrour of the popish Irish, and who now expected to be exposed defenceless to their fury. This consternation was encreased by the intemperance of papists, who exulted over their rivals, and threatened them with the vengeance of government, should they betray their
rebellious

rebellious purposes, by retaining any arms, even those of their own property. The justices were not without their fears that the proclamation for disarming them might be attended with some commotion. Primate Boyle was employed to practise with the citizens of Dublin, and laboured to dissipate their terrour. He exhorted them to display their loyalty, by chearfully depositing their arms in the king's stores, where they would be well preserved, and lie at hand ready to be resumed on any danger. The citizens resigned their arms with a better grace, by pretending to yield to the force of his arguments. Their example influenced other quarters of the kingdom, and in all places the orders of government were obeyed without apparent reluctance.

The disarming so considerable a body of protestants was but the beginning of that great work which James now meditated, and which, to the utter dissatisfaction of the impatient Irish, was to be disclosed gradually, and with some degree of caution. A new chief governour was now destined for Ireland, who might act with greater authority, and a more cordial compliance with the king's wishes than could be expected from the present lords justices. All thoughts of employing the earl of Rochester in this kingdom had ended with the life of Charles the Second. He was advanced by his brother-in-law to the dignity of lord high treasurer of England. Talbot, the great patron of the Irish, was created earl of Tyrconnel; and scarcely had the rebellion of Monmouth been subdued, when the Irish catholic clergy, in the fulness of their zeal, and pride of imaginary consequence, framed a petition to the king, that he would be pleased to establish this earl in such authority

thority in Ireland, as might secure them in the exercise of their functions ᵈ. But James could not yet resign himself to such counsellors. Talbot had but just now been ennobled, and might be well contented to serve the king's purposes in a station inferiour to that of chief governour. He was unpopular, and even odious to many of the English nation; and the king himself knew that he was precipitate and incautious. For the present therefore, he complied with his more moderate counsellors; and the earl of Clarendon, his other brother-in-law, was appointed lord lieutenant of Ireland.

The king's near affinity to Clarendon, and the exalted principles of loyalty and submission which this lord professed, and which was indeed the fashionable language of courtiers, persuaded James that he might not be averse to promoting his designs; nor were they entirely concealed from him. In his public instructions, the king intimated a desire of introducing catholics into corporations, and investing them with magistracies and judicial offices ᵉ. At the same time, some condescension was to be shewn to the terrours and suspicions of the protestant party. The new lord lieutenant was commanded to declare, that his majesty had no intention of altering the acts of settlement ᶠ. Thus, by ascertaining the bounds which he was not to pass, James reserved the liberty, and almost intimated his purpose of indulging the Irish catholics in every other particular.

Lord

---

d King's State of the Protest of Ireland, Appendix No. ii.
e Clarend. Let. Vol. I. p. 113. 4to. f Ibid Vol. II. p. 283.

LORD CLARENDON, in his speech to the privy council on receiving the sword of state, expressed his satisfaction at assuming the administration in such perfect peace and quietness. But in this he was insincere, or greatly deceived; for, at this juncture, Ireland was in considerable ferment. No sooner had the protestant militia been disarmed, than those savage banditti, called tories, issued in vast numbers from their private haunts, to the extreme terrour and annoyance of the civilized and industrious. The English were defenceless against their ravages; the Irish would not suppress their friends and kinsmen. The grievance was so manifest and urgent, that Clarendon was empowered to restore some arms to those who were fit to be entrusted, and most exposed to depredation; but he was too cautious to exercise this power with the necessary speed and alacrity g. In the mean time, the protestant subjects not only became a prey to robbers, but were exposed to the malice of another set of miscreants still more detestable. A number of informers suddenly started up in various quarters, and laboured to involve their neighbours in the guilt of treason. They tortured their inventions for plausible fiction, or ransacked their memories for the casual conversations of several years past, in order to accuse the English inhabitants of words spoken against the king when duke of York. The protestant who exacted rent from his tenant, he who repelled the violence of a tory, he who had at any time given any offence to his neighbour, was suddenly accused, sometimes imprisoned, exposed to a litigious prosecution, or harrassed with continual apprehensions from revenge and perjury. Informations multiplied in every part of Ireland, and

g Clarend. Let. Vol. I.

and were daily heaped on the lord lieutenant. He saw clearly through their falsehood and malice, yet could not venture openly to discourage them, as the king retained an unprincely resentment of offences committed against him before his accession, and as he affected a particular jealousy of the protestant subjects in Ireland.

THE Irish catholics were no strangers to this prepossession of the king, nor were their leaders inattentive to take advantage of it. Though they could not yet attempt to subvert the acts of settlement, yet they prepared a petition for the relief of those who had suffered by these acts; an application not in itself entirely unreasonable, but justly offensive in the manner of it; for it was agreed to chuse agents from the several counties, who, without any intervention of the lieutenant, were to repair to England, and address themselves directly to the throne. The more moderate of their party refused to concur in a proceeding disrespectful to the governour, who had acted with lenity, and even some degree of indulgence to the Irish catholics[h]. Their next petition, therefore, was conveyed to him: and in this they had the hardiness to desire a general reversal of the outlawries occasioned by the rebellion of the year sixteen hundred and forty one. This, as Lord Clarendon expresses it, " would " greatly alarm the English, and perhaps startle " some of the Irish too, who had gotten new " estates." And, however the case of some particulars might have merited attention and favour, yet the petition, if granted in its full extent, must have been considered as the previous step to an utter subversion of all establishments of property. But

[h] Ibid Vol. I. p. 27. & alib.

But the Irish knew no moderation in their demands. Their gentry crowded round Whitehall, and were graciously received. Hither Tyrconnel had repaired on the arrival of lord Clarendon in Ireland. He made such representations of Irish affairs as suited the interests of his party, or gratified the violence of his passions, and was heard with perfect confidence by his deluded master.

It soon appeared that the power of this lord was irresistible, and that the most violent and offensive measures were most agreeable to the cabinet. The seals of Ireland were suddenly taken from primate Boyle, and a new chancellor was sent from England, Sir Charles Porter, a man whose distressed circumstances promised to render him implicitly submissive to the court [i]. Three protestant judges, without any reason assigned, any objection alleged against their conduct, were at once removed; in their places, two popish lawyers of Irish birth, Nugent and Daly, and one Ingolsby, an Englishman, were raised to the bench; and when Ingolsby declined this preferment, Rice, another Irish lawyer, not of an unexceptionable character, was chosen to supply his place. In vain did lord Clarendon represent, that the admission of Roman catholics into offices of trust and honour, without taking the oath of supremacy, was contrary to law. To James such language was impertinent and uncourtly. All these new popish judges, and some popish lawyers, were admitted into the privy council of Ireland, an honour not hitherto conferred on men of their rank [k]. Rice was ashamed of such advancement, and hesitated; Nagle, an active and skilful lawyer of the popish

[i] Clarend. Let. Vol. I. p. 88.   [k] Vol. I. passim.

popish party, and greatly favoured by Tyrconnel, declined to accept an honour which would interfere with the business and solid advantages of his profession.

Even the rumours of such changes and appointments were sufficient to alarm the English protestants [1]. Traders sold their effects, and abandoned a country in which they expected a speedy establishment of popery, and a total confusion of property. To console him for the loss of his regiment, the earl of Granard was appointed president of the council, an office hitherto unknown in Ireland: but, declining to accept this honour, and declaring his purpose to retire from public business, he encreased the apprehensions of his party by thus discovering his own. The Irish, instead of waiting quietly for the effects of the king's favour, seemed rather solicitous to augment the terrour of their rivals. They boasted their correspondence with Whitehall, and their intelligence of every purpose of their favourite monarch. They talked with confidence of alterations to be made in the army; they whispered their expectations of some extraordinary changes in ecclesiastical affairs. The archbishoprick of Cashel was vacant, nor could the king be persuaded to fill it up. The popish clergy did not scruple to report that he had written to the pope to nominate a new archbishop. And although this seems to have been the mere suggestion of their vanity, yet it soon appeared that the revenue of this, and other vacant fees, were reserved for the maintenance of popish bishops. Orders were issued by the king's command that the catholic clergy should not be molested in the exercise

[1] Clarend. Let. Vol. I. p. 107. & passim, A. D. 1686.

cife of their functions; and thefe were foon followed by a notification of the royal pleafure, that their prelates fhould appear publicly in the habit of their order. The proteftant clergy were prohibited from treating of controverfial points in the pulpit. In this particular their conduct was ftrictly watched; and whoever prefumed to glance the flighteft reflection on popery, was inftantly delated to the king, and marked as difaffected and feditious.

To encreafe that gloom now evidently impreffed on every proteftant, the earl of Tyrconnel arrived in Ireland with power to command and regulate the army, independent of the lord lieutenant, with particular orders for the admiffion of Roman catholics to the freedom of corporations, and the offices of fheriffs and juftices of the peace, and with a number of new military commiffions, whereby the old proteftant officers were fufpended, and the worft and meaneft of the catholic party fubftituted in their place m. His natural violence was enflamed by the extravagant adulations with which the popifh party received their patron and protector, and prompted him to the moft infolent and contemptuous treatment of the lord lieutenant. He raved of the iniquity of the acts of fettlement, of mifconduct in the whole adminiftration of Ireland, of the bafenefs and difloyalty of particular perfons. He proceeded to execute the king's commands with furious impatience: officers and private men were difmiffed from the army, without any plaufible caufe affigned, frequently with abufe and contumely, fometimes with injuftice and cruelty. Their places were fupplied by Irifh catholics; and, in all preferments, thofe Irifh only were
taken

m Vol. I. Let. May 8. July 29.

taken in, who entertained the higheſt notions of the authority of the pope. The vulgar, in their aſtoniſhing ignorance, when they had taken the oath of fidelity, imagined that they had ſworn fidelity to the pope and their religion, and declared that their prieſts had forbidden them to take any other oath.

The king's inſtructions to Tyrconnel implied no more than that all ſubjects indiſcriminately ſhould be admitted to ſerve his majeſty, without regard to their religious principles; but this lord iſſued ſtrict orders that none but catholics ſhould be admitted into the army. Lord Clarendon was offended, and remonſtrated againſt a conduct which muſt enflame the jealouſies already raiſed amongſt the king's ſubjects. Tyrconnel was for a moment confounded, and had the meanneſs to deny his own orders. But lord Roſcommon, with the ſpirit of a ſoldier, aſſerted to his face, that he and other officers had received theſe orders from him in terms the moſt peremptory and explicit [n].

The bolder and more violent of the popiſh party declared, that in a few months not one proteſtant would be left in the army; and now that they had gotten arms, they would ſpeedily regain their lands. Some of the old proprietors cautioned the tenants againſt paying any rent to their Engliſh landlords; and, with the ſame inſolence, ſome popiſh clergy forbad the people to pay tythes to proteſtant incumbents.

The earl of Clarendon was every day alarmed with intelligence of theſe extravagancies, and every day

[n] Clarend. Let. July 22.

day insulted by the violence of Tyrconnel. He was even accused of reluctance in obeying the king's orders, because he did not at once pour in numbers of catholic freemen into every corporation, and establish catholic magistrates in every county, before he could inform himself of their claims, characters, and qualifications. The principles in which he had been trained taught him an implicit submission to his sovereign; and that it was his part only to represent the impropriety and danger of such orders as he disapproved, without presuming to disobey them, or to retire from his station. Agreeably to these principles, he remonstrated both to the king and Sunderland against the heat and presumption of Tyrconnel; yet with a pliancy which at this day reflects no honour on his character, declared the utmost readiness to execute the king's purposes, whatever they might be, though in a manner less offensive and alarming o.

To quiet the suspicions and fears of protestants, he recommended a commission of grace for confirming titles, and a general pardon for offensive words spoken against the king while duke of York, to put an end to litigious prosecutions. But Sunderland returned no answer to his representations, and was even suspected of secreting his letters from the king: nor did James vouchsafe any explanation of his sentiments. He now positively refused to repeat his former assurances of maintaining the acts of settlement by proclamation. Tyrconnel was left at liberty to proceed in his usual course of violence p. Having already filled one complete moiety of the army with Irish catholics, he hastened to England, denouncing the terrour of his

o Vol. I. passim.   p Clarend. Let. Vol. II. p. 18.

his influence against all those who had not served the king with sufficient ardour. He was attended by Nagle, the ablest, most acute, and artful of the Irish lawyers, a violent impugner of the acts of settlement, and who was now to employ all his artifice to persuade the king, if not utterly to rescind, at least to invalidate these acts. The case of many sufferers who could not be restored to their estates from the want of lands to reprize the present possessors, afforded arguments sufficiently plausible, and which a man of his abilities could enforce with great advantage q. But several of the king's counsellors retained a warm affection for what was called the English interest in Ireland; they dreaded the violence of Tyrconnel and his projector, and the danger of breaking in on those establishments of property which had subsisted for twenty years, and by which the country had been remarkably improved. Their representations had some effect upon the king. Nagle could not immediately be admitted to kiss his hand, and was at length received with evident coldness. But his patron, and the more violent of the popish party, resolved to make some use of his abilities. They employed him to write a treatise on the injustice of the acts of settlement. It was published in the form of a letter from Coventry, and hence known, and much spoken of in those days, by the name of " The Coventry " Letter."

IN the mean time, Clarendon was accused to the king of male-administration in several instances, alleged without regard to candour or veracity.--- His defence was clear and satisfactory; but his brother, Rochester, refused to renounce his religion, and

---

q Secret Consults, &c.

and was removed from his office of treasurer. He himself was not found an instrument suited to all the designs, wildly conceived and hastily pursued by the bigoted or insidious counsellors of a bigoted and deluded king. The appointment of a successor to lord Clarendon became an object of deliberation in the cabinet. Several lords were proposed and rejected by the king. Sunderland, the present minister, flattered the partialities of his master, by recommending the unworthiest and most dangerous of all the competitors[r]. Tyrconnel stipulated to pay him an annual pension from the profits of the Irish government, and by his interest was appointed chief governour of Ireland, with the inferior title of lord deputy.

AND here, it may not be improper to view the character of this lord more nearly than it hath been hitherto exhibited. A native of Ireland, descended from the race of old English of the Pale, he came into the world about the time when this race were particularly united with the original Irish; and from concurring in their political intrigues, were led to concur in their insurrection. From his infancy he imbibed his sentiments in religion and politics from the most bigoted to popery, and the most hostile to English government. In his youth he had been witness of the carnage at Drogheda; and, on his escape from this infernal scene, naturally retained a violent abhorrence of fanatics, in which denomination he included all of the protestant party. Obsequiousness and vivacity recommended him to the royal brothers on the continent, at a time when an obsequious and lively associate was particularly suited to the vacant hours of their exile. Here he discovered

[r] Memoirs of Ireland.

covered his resentment and his spirit in no very honourable manner, by proposing to assassinate Oliver Cromwell. When provoked by the supposed injuries of his party, he afterwards threatened to turn his poignard on the duke of Ormond: but in such menaces he discovered more of passion and malignity than of resolution. He was incautious and precipitate; virulent in his censures, with a disregard to truth which even became proverbial; furious in his animosities to a degree of apparent frenzy, yet not with that placability which sometimes attends the sudden start of passion; his revenge was steadily and unalterably pursued; his attachment to the popish party was merely factious, without attention or regard to the different modes of religion, for his life was profligate, and his conversation profane. In the vanity of that power he gradually acquired, he insulted his superiours, and tyrannized over those below him: to the one his deportment was vulgar, to the other brutal. If, at any time, he condescended to artifice and insinuation, this violence to his natural temper was soon discovered, for the least disappointment cast him into a paroxism of rage. Every step of his exaltation was gained by bribery and flattery, and enjoyed without temper, justice, or decency.

To this popish delegate of a popish prince, lord Clarendon resigned the sword of state, in a general and violent agitation of the kingdom [s]. He embarked at the port of Dublin, attended by fifteen hundred protestant families of Dublin, who abandoned a country where the peace, the property, and the lives of protestants were exposed to the malice of the meanest and most malignant of a party now exulting

[s] Clarend. Diary.

exulting in the fulnefs of their triumph, with their friend and patron in fupreme authority, attended by popifh minifters and officers of ftate. Sir Charles Porter had not proved fo pliant as the king expected. He demeaned himfelf to all parties with that equity and impartiality which fuited his ftation, and declared againft being inftrumental in any illegal or clandeftine defigns. He was removed from his office, and Sir Alexander Fitton placed at the head of the Chancery in Ireland, a man convicted of forgery, and publicly ftigmatized, but who redeemed the infamy of his character by conforming to the king's religion. An appointment fo odious and alarming was foon followed by fubftituting Nagle, the popifh lawyer, as attorney-general, in the place of Sir William Domville, a proteftant long diftinguifhed by his loyalty and abilities. Nugent and Rice were advanced to the ftation of chief judges; Irifh papifts were chofen to fucceed them, and three proteftants only were fuffered on the benches, Keating and Worth, who were fuppofed implicitly obedient, and Lyndon, a man of meannefs and infignificance t. In courts thus fupplied were the validity of outlawries and forfeitures, the titles of proteftants, and the claims of papifts to be determined.

ALMOST the whole army of Ireland was by this time formed of Irifh catholics, and a number of proteftant officers deprived of commiffions which they had purchafed, and gradually driven from the kingdom, fought fhelter in Holland, poured out their grievances to the prince of Orange, and were by him protected and employed u. The admiffion of catholics into the feveral corporations had proceeded

---

t Secret Confults, &c.   u A. D. 1687.

ed slowly during the administration of lord Clarendon; and some more compendious method was to be devised, to invest this party with the whole power of the kingdom, and especially the power of modelling all future parliaments. Tyrconnel addressed himself to the city of Dublin, and without the decency of assigning any plausible pretence, recommended to them to resign their charter to the king. They hesitated; he grew more peremptory; they still delayed their answer; in a rage of passion he loaded them with reproaches, and thundered out the severity of the royal vengeance on their perverseness. It was vain to urge reason to the deputy, or to expect justice from him. Their recorder was dispatched to Whitehall; introduced to the king by the duke of Ormond, presented their petition, setting forth their loyalty and services, and imploring the continuance of their charter. The application was rejected with disgrace. A quo warranto was immediately issued, and judgment hastily pronounced against their charter. Many other corporations were dissolved by the same procedure within the short course of two terms. Some corporations were either flattered or intimidated into a surrender of their charters. In several instances, a new charter was granted to such men as the attorney-general approved, who were put in possession of the corporation by a popish sheriff; and the former possessors left to bring their action before popish judges against the intruders; or, where these had greatest power, the ancient members were imprisoned for their disobedience.

In forming the new corporations it was the general rule, that in great cities where the English interest
had

had been predominant, two thirds of the members should be catholics, and one third protestants; but those called protestant were chosen from quakers, or other enthusiasts, from the poor, the profligate and contemptible [x]. And although lords and gentlemen of the adjacent country were taken into every corporation, yet it was found necessary, in order to complete these bodies, to receive an additional number of the most scandalous and barbarous Irish; so that in one northern city, a man was made chief magistrate who had been condemned to the gallows.

From the invasions made by James on the learned bodies of England, it cannot be expected that the university of Dublin, the only protestant seminary in Ireland, should have been entirely unattempted [y]. It was indeed an object of particular envy to those who wished to make the whole island papal; and lord Clarendon had not yet been removed, when the king's mandate was presented to the governours of the university, directing them to admit one Green, a Roman catholic, to a professorship, with all its emoluments and arrears of salary. It was styled in the king's letter a professorship of the Irish language; and so ignorant were his advisers, that no such establishment had ever been made. The founder and his grant, the office and its emoluments, existed only in their imaginations. Green was thus disappointed; but the university expected some farther attacks with the most melancholy apprehensions. They shared in the general consternation of protestants on the appointment of Tyrconnel to the government of Ireland; and with the timidity of retired men,

seem

[x] Secret Consults, &c.   [y] Archives of Trin. Col. Dub. MS.

seem to have expected every violence from a popish administration.

In these terrours they resolved to convert most of their plate into money, for the purpose of erecting new buildings or purchasing new lands[z]. The consent of their visitors was obtained, and the consent of Clarendon for transporting the plate (duty free) into England, as to a better market. In the mean time, Tyrconnel arrives, is informed of this transaction, seizes the plate in the port of Dublin, and deposits it in the king's stores. The more moderate of his advisers, ashamed of this tyranny, interposed, and prevailed on him to restore it to the university. The plate was sold; when, in an instant, all the absurd fury of Tyrconnel was rekindled. The purchaser appeared before him. Nugent, the lord chief justice, with astonishing impudence, accused him of purchasing stolen goods, the property of the king, and obliged him to give security to prosecute the governours of the university. Happily Nagle was possessed of more reason and temper, and by the authority of his opinion, defended them from any further outrage. But the terrour of this senseless violence of Tyrconnel had not yet subsided, when another letter from the king directed that one Doyle should be admitted to a fellowship, without taking any oaths but the oath of a fellow. The man was wretchedly insufficient, and scandalously profligate; but he was lately reconciled to popery, and the merit of his conversion was to be rewarded. Yet here again the ignorance of his patrons happily defeated the purposes of their party. The oath of a fellow included in it the oath of supremacy, and this Doyle refused to take. The terms

[z] Archives of Trin. Col. Dub. MS.

terms of the king's mandate were so explicit, that the popish judges directed him to procure a second letter; and his character was proved to be so infamous, that his friends were ashamed to make any farther effort in his favour. The vexation of Tyrconnel at this disappointment was expressed in a manner worthy of him: he stopped the pension annually paid to the university from the exchequer; and which at this time made the most considerable part of their subsistence.

And now the kingdom every where resounded with complaints of the meanness, the ignorance, and brutality of popish sheriffs, scandalous partialities in the courts of justice, the insolence and barbarities of military officers, robberies unrestrained and unpunished, broils wildly raised, and murders wantonly committed, a fearful decay of trade, and a defiance and contempt of law [a]. Outlawries were daily reversed; the sons of rebels and murderers stood foremost in the favour of government; hinds and menial servants gained offices of trust and authority, and insulted their former masters. Indigent men, suddenly advanced, had no other means of supporting their new stations, but by involving themselves in debts which they were neither able nor inclined to discharge, and even forcing goods from tradesmen, who trembled at their brutal arrogance. The credit of merchants was destroyed; numbers of artificers were reduced to beggary, or driven to other countries for subsistence; and so ignorant were the popish ministers, that they beheld such instances of public calamity without concern, as if it were only the calamity of protestants.

But

[a] Secret Consults, &c. King's State of the Protestants of Ireland.

But the alarming increase of the Irish revenue had its full impression on those English ministers, whose views were not solely confined to the establishment of popery [b]. They imputed it to the misconduct of Tyrconnel; they inveighed against his violence. Lord Belasis declared with particular warmth, that his folly and madness were sufficient to ruin ten kingdoms, and urged the king to appoint a wiser and more temperate governour for Ireland. To avert the impending storm, Tyrconnel obtained permission to attend his royal master, now in his progress at Chester. He committed his government to the hands of chancellor Fitton and lord Clanricarde, reminding these and his popish counsellors of the fulness of that power they had now acquired in the kingdom; and, with hideous indecency, praying God to damn them should they ever part with it. Rice, chief baron of the exchequer, attended him to Chester; and his abilities were of use. James listened to his representations of the state of Ireland; and these were so plausibly calculated to recommend his patron, that the king accounted himself justified in remitting Tyrconnel to his government. Several addresses were sent from Ireland to Chester. That of the university declared, that while they retained their religion they could not depart from their loyalty. James, in his short answer, assured them that he had no doubt of the loyalty of any of the church of England. Yet Tyrconnel was instructed on his departure to dismiss almost all the protestant officers now remaining in the army [c].

[b] Memoirs of Ireland, Secret Consults, &c. Col. Dub. MS.
[c] Archives of Trin.

THE popish ministers of Ireland were by this time so secure and confident, that, as they had no common enemy to contend with, they found leisure to contend with each other [d]. One Sheridan, secretary of state and commissioner of the customs, had been restrained by Tyrconnel in his practice of selling employments; fired with resentment, and relying on the countenance of his kinsman, father Petre, he resolved to ruin the lord deputy. With the assistance of the popish primate, he drew up an accusation against him, which was transmitted to London, and which Tyrconnel encountered by a particular detail of his briberies, and other sinister practices. The progress of their contest was too mean and insignificant to merit a recital. It is sufficient to observe, that the influence of Sunderland proved superior to that of Petre. Sheridan was dismissed from his employments; but the triumph of Tyrconnel was not without some mortification and disgrace. To revenge himself on the popish primate, the king was made to solicit the pope that he would appoint a coadjutor to this prelate. Odescalchi, in his contempt of James, absolutely rejected this slight request. Petre, and his associates of the clergy, represented to the king and queen how injurious these altercations of Tyrconnel and Sheridan must prove to the catholic cause, and what advantage its enemies must derive from their quarrels. They expressed the utmost contempt of the lord deputy and his conduct, a man whose services amounted to nothing more than dispossessing protestants of their places, and this effected by raising public discontents and general calamity. The earl of Castlemain, who, since his embassy to Rome, had received no mark of royal favour, was recommended as a person

[d] Secret Consults, &c.

person worthy to be entrusted with the government of Ireland, and qualified to answer all the king's purposes.

The pope was said to have united in recommending Castlemain[e]. The ministers of France laboured to counteract him. They sent intelligence to Tyrconnel of these secret murmurs and designs. Tyrconnel, on consulting with his friends, Rice and Nagle, deemed it necessary by some brilliant measure to convince the king both of his zeal and abilities. He proposed to convene an Irish parliament, which, as the sheriffs were popish, and the corporations modelled agreeably to his wishes must prove entirely at the devotion of government. Heads of a bill were framed, with a plausible semblance of relieving the distressed and injured Irish, which unhinged the whole settlement of Ireland, and gave the king power over the greater part of its lands. Rice was commissioned to lay this favourite scheme before the English council, and Nugent obtruded himself as his colleague. They were received coldly by the ministers; but James, without any previous conference with the cabinet, where he apprehended some opposition, introduced their scheme to the privy-council, declaring warmly against the iniquity of the acts of settlement. To those who yet retained a regard to the interests of their kinsmen and countrymen, it appeared at first view so violent and dangerous, that the agents were with difficulty admitted to be heard. And however plausibly Rice supported his project, the weakness and futility of Nugent rendered it contemptible. They were insulted even in the royal presence, and dismissed with disgrace. The populace were soon informed of their ill success; they attended them

[e] Secret Consults, &c.

them with potatoes elevated on poles, and roared out in scorn, " Room for the Irish ambassadors!" Such are the general accounts of this transaction. Sunderland, in his apology, claims the merit of their disappointment; and declares, that he rejected a bribe of forty thousand pounds offered for his support of this project.

The Irish catholics were mortified at this severe disappointment; but their mortification was soon allayed by the birth of a prince [f]. Before they were indulged with any hopes of the queen's pregnancy, they had disposed of the succession agreeably to their own wishes and ignorant conceptions [g]. They declared that Fitz-James, natural son of the king, should be legitimated by the pope, and thus become inheritour of the crown. There was now no occasion for such devises; their joy was unbounded, and they generally expressed it by the most senseless insolence and outrage. The popish lord mayor of Dublin indeed displayed his triumph over the protestant party by a ludicrous instance of severity. He committed the officers of Christ Church to durance, because " their bells did not ring merrily enough" on this happy occasion [h].

Ireland now exhibited a gloomy scene of oppression and dejection, of insolence and despair, of power exercised without decency, and injuries sustained without redress. That English interest, which princes and statesmen had wisely laboured to establish in this country, was discouraged, depressed, and threatened with final extirpation. But new changes and new commotions were at hand. The pride,

[f] A. D. 1688.   [g] Claren. Lett. Vol. II. p. 139.   [h] King's State of the Protestants.

pride, the obstinacy, and the bigotry of the king, his headstrong and insidious counsellors, his foreign enemies, the spirit of the old republicans not yet extinguished, the just and general indignation of subjects whose rights had been trampled down with scorn, their well-grounded fears for the constitution, their solicitude for religion, all conspired to produce a revolution, the most glorious and important of those events which dignify the annals of the British empire.

THE enterprize of the prince of Orange was yet a secret to James, when Tyrconnel, we are assured, received intelligence of his design from Amsterdam, and conveyed it to the king[i]. It was received with derision both by Sunderland and his master. But this infatuated prince was soon awakened to a dreadful sense of his danger: and, on the first certain assurance of an invasion, Tyrconnel was directed to transport four thousand forces to England. Every day ushered in new advices and reports. In Ireland they were received with agitation and astonishment: English and Irish alike rushed in crowds to Dublin, impatient for intelligence, and eager to confirm their hopes or allay their fears, by conferring with their associates. The Irish catholics still affected to despise the prince of Orange and his attempt. They exclaimed that the States of Holland were weary of him; and, therefore, were sending him on a desperate enterprize, to end his days on a scaffold like the duke of Monmouth. Nugent, the lord chief justice, delivered these sentiments from the bench, and spoke with delight of English rebels hung up every where in clusters. But advices were soon received that the prince had landed, that
James

[i] Secret Consults, &c. Memoirs of Ireland.

James was deserted by his subjects, that the prince advanced, that he every day gained new adherents. The Irish and their chief governour forgot their pride, and sunk at once into consternation. Tyrconnel descended to flatter the protestants, to boast of his equal and impartial government, and to court them to make the most favourable representations of his conduct. The English protestants, on the other hand, were roused from their dejection; and no sooner had they received intelligence of commissioners being sent by the king, and a treaty opened with the prince of Orange, than the most spirited among them proposed to seize the castle of Dublin. But the uncertainty of events in England, the well known severity of James, should he once be extricated from his present distress, and some hopes that Tyrconnel would of himself abandon the government, operated on the more cautious, and defeated this design. In the mean time, new commissions were issued by Tyrconnel for levying forces. They were granted to all who would accept them, without paying even the fees of office. The popish clergy enjoined their people to take arms in this time of danger. In every quarter of the kingdom an armed rabble suddenly started up, who called themselves the king's soldiers, and, unpaid and unrestrained by government, supported themselves by open depredations. The English inhabitants endeavoured to defend themselves against these maurauders, and the whole country seemed gradually to decline from the order and security of social and civil life.

A LETTER addressed by an unknown person to lord Mount Alexander, in the county of Down, warned him of a general massacre intended by the
Irish.

Irish. The style was mean and vulgar; nor was the information on that account less plausible: it was confident and circumstantial, and pointed out Sunday the ninth day of December, as the precise time when this bloody design was to be executed, without distinction of sex, age, or condition[k]. The like intelligence was conveyed to some other gentlemen of the northern province[l]. And whether these letters were the contrivance of artifice, or the effect of credulity, their influence was wonderful. Men habitually possessed with horrour of Irish barbarity, who in the very scene of all the sufferings of their fathers, had listened from their infancy to hideous narratives of the insurrection in the year sixteen hundred and forty one, who were now exposed to the insolence and violence of the Irish, and ready to catch the alarm at the least appearance of commotion, could not hesitate a moment to give credit to these informations. They were confirmed by some suspicious circumstances. Popish priests had announced to their congregations what they called " a secret intention," and enjoined them to stand ready armed to obey their orders[m]. It was remembered that a friar of Derry had preached with unusual energy on the subject of Saul's destroying the Amalekites, and the iniquity of sparing those whom divine vengeance had devoted to destruction. Lord Mount Alexander's letter was instantly sent to Dublin; copies multiplied; the intelligence was conveyed through all orders of men. In a moment the capital became a scene of uproar and confusion; the guards of the lord deputy stood astonished; the castle bridge was drawn up, while a tumultuous crowd of

[k] Mackenz. Narrative. Impartial Account of Passages in Ireland, from the Notes of an eye-witness, 4to. Lond. 1689. [l] Harris's Life of King Wil. Append. No. xxi. [m] Mackenzie.

of men, women, and children ran precipitately to the fhore, imploring to be conveyed away from the daggers of the Irifh. In vain did Tyrconnel defpatch two lords to affure them of fecurity and protection; their remonftrances were drowned in clamour, fhrieking, and wailing. An unufual number of veffels lay in the harbour; the people crowded them in an extafy of terrour and impatience, leaving their lefs fuccefsful friends ftupified with expectation of the fatal blow.

The dreadful intelligence was foon conveyed to every part of Ireland[n]. In fome places it was received on the very day affigned for the maffacre. The people ftarted fuddenly from their devotions, fled aftonifhed, propagated the panick, and thus fwelled the crowds of fugitives; fome gained the coaft, and were tranfported to England, others fought fhelter in walled towns and proteftant fettlements, leaving their effects and habitations to the mercy of Irifh plunderers. In the northern counties, where the proteftants were moft numerous, they collected the arms ftill left among them, refolving to defend themfelves, and already meditating the defign of rifing againft the prefent government.

Of all the northern cities, Derry, or LondonDerry (as it was called) afforded principal fhelter to the fugitive proteftants. Seated on the weft fide of the Lake Foyle, it maintained a communication, by a ferry, with a county called by the fame name with the capital; it was furrounded by a firm wall ftrengthened by baftions, but was by no means fufficient to fuftain the fiege of a regular army.

[n] Impartial Account, &c.

army [o]. On the firſt alarm of an invaſion of England by the prince of Orange, Tyrconnel had recalled the garriſon of this city to Dublin. It conſiſted of a regiment well diſciplined and appointed; it was under the command of lord Mountjoy, ſon of primate Boyle; and being for the moſt part compoſed of proteſtants, was acceptable to the inhabitants. Tyrconnel ſoon perceived the errour of leaving this city to the government of the townſmen, and detached the earl of Antrim's regiment, conſiſting entirely of papiſts, Iriſh and Highlanders, to take their quarters in Derry. A body of twelve hundred men, tall and terrible in their aſpect, followed by a crowd of women and children, arrived at a village called Limavaddy, within twelve miles of Derry, at the very moment when the inhabitants received the informations of an intended maſſacre, and were deliberating on this important intelligence. The proprietor of this village was terrified at the diſorder and turbulence of a body, which in this time of ſuſpicion, ſeemed rather the inſtruments of ſlaughter and barbarity, than the regular forces of government. He inſtantly deſpatched the moſt alarming accounts to Derry of the number, appearance, and deſtination of his gueſts, conjuring the citizens to ſhut their gates againſt the barbarous crew. His letter found them already alarmed by the general reports of danger. They were collected in their ſtreets, conferring earneſtly, ſome reſolute, ſome wavering, ſome wiſhing to exclude the popiſh forces without appearing to take part in the attempt. Tomkins and Norman, two aldermen, conſulted the biſhop: the biſhop, cautious from years and by his principles, an enemy to reſiſtance, preached peace and ſubmiſſion

---

[o] Walker's Diary of the Siege of Derry. Mackenzie.

sion. Some graver citizens concurred with him; others affected to concur. The troops approached; two of their officers were already in the town to provide quarters; an advanced party appeared within three hundred yards of the Ferry-gate. In this critical moment, nine young men of the populace, with an enthusiastic ardour, drew their swords, snatched up the keys of the city, raised the drawbridge, locked the Ferry-gate, were instantly joined by numbers of their own rank, secured the other gates, assembled in the great square, deaf to all timid counsels and remonstrances, seized the magazine, and were soon countenanced and applauded by men of better condition. The body of inhabitants caught the same spirit, and declared for a brave defence. Their numbers were quickly encreased by a conflux from the neighbouring districts; the magazine afforded them some few arms, and a small quantity of ammunition. Phillips of Limavaddy, the man who first encouraged them to this enterprize, was chosen their governour. They threatened to fire on the king's soldiers, and conjured their neighbours to concur with them in defence of their lives, their properties and religion.

To the society of London they immediately transmitted an account of their dangers and proceedings; and Cairnes, the most considerable of their party, was commissioned to solicit succours from the prince of Orange [p]. At the same time, their magistrates and graver citizens, anxious for the event of an enterprize commenced under every disadvantage, addressed themselves to lord Mountjoy, and, by his mediation, to Tyrconnel [q]. They set

[p] Mackenzie. [q] Apology for the Protest. of Ireland. State Tracts, Vol. III. Mackenzie.

set forth their utter inability to restrain the populace, terrified by the rumours of a massacre, and the outrages of the new raised regiment; ascribing their insurrection to providence, who had stirred them up for their own safety and the public peace, against the wild attempts of the northern Irish. They declared their resolution to confine themselves entirely to self-defence, without violating their allegiance; at the same time, they represented the vast number of northern protestants who had been driven to take arms from the same fears, and for the same purposes.

TYRCONNEL, too late, perceived his errour in withdrawing his garrison from Derry, and endeavoured to correct it [r]. Lord Mountjoy, and Lundy his lieutenant-colonel, were instantly remanded to Ulster with six companies, and ordered to reduce this city. Mountjoy, a protestant lord, was highly acceptable to the inhabitants; his popish forces they detested. They disclaimed all mutinous and seditious purposes, but still expressed their firm purpose to defend themselves. After various conferences, Mountjoy was admitted upon conditions. It was particularly stipulated, that a free pardon should be granted within fifteen days; that, in the mean time, two companies only should be quartered in the city; that the forces afterwards admitted should be formed one half of protestants at least; that until the pardon was received the citizens should keep the guards; and that all should be left at liberty who desired to remove. Tyrconnel had now the mortification of finding the people of Derry assuming the power of purging and modelling his forces, and dismissing and disarming his popish soldiers,

[r] Walker's Diary.

soldiers. Mountjoy assumed the command of their city, and was obeyed as a friend and associate. By his advice the arms were repaired, money chearfully subscribed, ammunition purchased in Scotland, and Cairnes the agent earnestly solicited to procure supplies.

THE northern protestants beheld the spirit of the men of Derry with a generous emulation[s]. Enniskillen, the only borough town in the county of Fermanagh, situated on an island in the narrow part of Lake Erne, and inhabited by a few resolute protestants, refused admittance to two companies of Tyrconnel's popish army [t]. In Downe, Donnegal, Tyrone, Armagh, Monaghan, parties arose under the direction of Mount Alexander, Blaney, Rawdon, Skeffington, and other leaders. Their associations were published in the several counties, declaring, that they had united for self-defence and the protestant religion; that they resolved to act in subordination to the government of England, and to promote a free parliament. County councils were nominated, and a general council, to meet at Hillsborough, which appointed officers, and directed the operations of the associated body.

THE Northerns had the fairer opportunity of forming and strengthening this association, as Tyrconnel trembled in the capital, and seemed on the point of abandoning the kingdom [u]. His counsellors represented the vanity of contending with the prince of Orange, and the desperate circumstances of James. He seemed convinced, and ready to resign his government; professed to wait only until it

[s] Hamilton's Actions of Enniskilleners. [t] Mackenzie. [u] Secret Consults, &c. Memoirs of Ireland.

it should be demanded from him, and peevishly asked whether he should cast the sword of state over the castle wall. He prevailed on some protestants to notify these his sentiments to their friends in London. Keating, the judge, in a letter to Sir John Temple, enlarged on the distracted state of Ireland, and the jealousies both of protestants and catholics, declaring, that the army was ready to disband, and that the deputy only waited for directions from England. In the present unsettled state of affairs in London, such informations were flattering. That momentous interval between the flight of James and the investiture of William with the sovereignty, engaged this prince too busily, and agitated him too violently, to allow any attention to the affairs of Ireland. The English subjects of this kingdom had been lately deprived of a powerful advocate, by the death of the duke of Ormond. Their applications were now made to lord Clarendon; and soon after the arrival of the prince in London, some gentlemen of Ireland requested this lord to present them to his highness, in order to lay before him the state of their country [x]. Clarendon was by no means acceptable to the prince: he had, with great severity, condemned the forward desertion of his son lord Cornbury; and although he himself soon followed his example, yet he was thought cold to the interests of the prince of Orange, and affected to treat the design of seating him on the throne with indignation and disgust. It is also said, that William had some secret intimations, that on the settlement of the nation Clarendon entertained hopes of returning to his Irish government; that Tyrconnel hated him, and that nothing was so likely to confirm him in a desperate opposition

[x] Clarend. Diary.

sition, as any countenance shewn to this lord and his pretensions y. However this may be, he could not be admitted to the prince without various delays, and was at length received with coldness. When the prince was obliged to receive a formal address of the protestant subjects of Ireland, sensible that it was not at present in his power to assist them, he returned a concise and phlegmatic reply: " I thank you; I will take care of you z."

WHAT he had neither leisure nor power to attempt openly, William laboured to effect by practising secretly with Tyrconnel. Richard Hamilton, a popish general, sent into England on the first alarm of an invasion, was, in some sort, his prisoner a. He was esteemed a man of honour, had served with reputation in France, but was banished on account of his imprudent addresses to the king's daughter, princess of Conti b. He was recommended to the prince as one who had considerable influence on Tyrconnel. He proposed to repair to Ireland, and confer with his friend the deputy, expressing the utmost confidence of persuading him to resign his government, and promising to return should he prove unsuccessful. William readily embraced this overture. Hamilton arrived at Dublin; but, instead of executing his commission, advised Tyrconnel to maintain his station, assuring him that the affairs of England began to wear an aspect favourable to James, and that nothing but the firmness of his friends was necessary to reinstate him. Tyrconnel was thus determined in his measures, and Hamilton continued, and was employed in Ireland.

STILL

y Secret Consults, &c. z Clarend. Diary. a Memoirs of Ireland. b Mem. de la Fayette.

STILL the deputy found it neceſſary to diſſemble. He aſſured the proteſtant lords of his readineſs to ſubmit to the prince of Orange. By the warmth of his expreſſions, which was miſtaken for the effect of conviction and ſincerity, he perſuaded lord Mountjoy to repair to James, in conjunction with the chief baron, Rice, to repreſent the weak condition of Ireland, and the neceſſity of yielding to the times, inſtead of exaſperating his Engliſh ſubjects by a futile attempt to conquer England by his Iriſh powers. He even intimated, that if the king ſhould refuſe to ſurrender Ireland, he ſhould regard the refuſal as the effect of force, and deem himſelf fully warranted to reſign his authority. In accepting this unpopular commiſſion, Mountjoy was careful to ſtipulate with Tyrconnel that no more levies ſhould be made, no more arms or commiſſions given out, no more troops commanded into Ulſter, no perſons impriſoned, no private houſe diſturbed by ſoldiers [c]. He departed, and on his arrival at Paris was committed to the Baſtile, while Rice employed himſelf in ſoliciting ſuccours for the ſervice of his maſter. At Dublin Tyrconnel grew outrageous; he utterly denied the ſtipulations made with Mountjoy; the arms yet remaining in the hands of the proteſtants were wreſted from them by his ſoldiers in every place ſubject to his power, their horſes ſeized, their perſons inſulted, and their houſes plundered. Temple, ſon of Sir William, at whoſe inſtances Temple had been employed, was pierced too deeply by theſe melancholy effects of his advice, and in the bitterneſs of vexation put an end to his own life.

THE deputy was farther encouraged by a meſſenger from king James, aſſuring him that he would
soon

---

[c] Harris's Life of King William, Append. No. xxiii.

soon appear in Ireland with a powerful armament [d]. He had too long suffered the northern associators to proceed unmolested, awed by lord Inchiquin in Munster, who appeared in arms with more zeal than strength; in Connaught, by lord Kingston, who stood at the head of the protestants in this province, and preserved a communication with their brethren of Ulster. The northerns had attempted to reduce Carricfergus, but without success; and, though their powers were greatly magnified, yet the men were inexperienced, their officers unskilful, their ammunition utterly insufficient, their arms such as they had secreted on the general order for disarming protestants. These defects were supplied by zeal and ardour. On assurance of supplies from England, they boldly proclaimed William and Mary in the north eastern towns. But their exultation was speedily allayed. A proclamation by the deputy commanded them to lay down their arms, and to dissolve their assemblies; and they had the mortification to find it subscribed by lord Granard, and some other protestant counsellors [e]. General Hamilton marched against them with a formidable body of troops [f]. They abandoned Newry; they retired gradually to Dromore; here they were overtaken by the enemy; they fled before their superiour numbers, and were pursued with slaughter; they gained Hillsborough, but quickly abandoned this town, resigned the castle, and continued their flight. They seemed entirely broken; several fled to Britain, others accepted protections from the Irish army. But, by the spirit and authority of Mount-Alexander, Rawdon, and other leaders, about four thousand,

[d] Secret Consults, &c. Memoirs of Ireland. [e] Apology for Protest. of Ireland. State Tracts, Vol III. [f] Mackenzie.

thousand, were still kept embodied, and took their station at Colerain, in order to prevent the enemy from passing the river Bann: at the same time, those of the north-west poured into Enniskillen as their place of refuge.

The Irish army were so totally engaged in riot and plundering, that the confederates had time to collect, and to fortify Colerain g. Hither lord Blaney found it necessary to lead his party from Armagh. The garrisons of Charlemont, and Mountjoy were informed of his motions, and attempted to intercept him, by seizing the bridge at a place named Artrea. He was more alert, and secured the pass just at the moment of their approach. They advanced; he drew up his men and marched to attack them; they fled, were pursued and slaughtered; and this inconsiderable advantage served to animate the Northerns. Colerain was attacked, and the enemy bravely repulsed; but the place was not long found tenable. The Irish, after a successful skirmish, passed the Bann in boats, and the Northerns hasted by various routs to Derry, before the enemy should cut them off from this their last refuge.

From the time of lord Mountjoy's departure, the government of this city, and the principal direction of the north-eastern counties had been resigned to Lundy, a man who flattered the protestants by declarations of attachment to their cause, and resolution of fighting bravely, at least against the tyrannical and illegal government of Tyrconnel. Notwithstanding these public professions, he was suspected of retaining a regard to James and his

---

g Impartial Account of Passages in Ireland, &c.

his service. He had frequently disappointed the expectations of the associate-protestants, obliged them to abandon posts thought sufficiently tenable, and by an inactive and irresolute conduct, which was not attributed to any defect of courage, became generally suspected. William in his embarrassments was obliged to trust and to employ him; and, when an officer of the name of Hamilton was sent to Derry with arms, ammunition, and money, a commission from the new king was delivered to Lundy to command in the town, and to administer the oaths to all officers civil and military [h] Some refused the oaths; Lundy would not consent to take them publicly, alleging that he had already sworn on board Hamilton's vessel. Murmurings and discontents were thus excited among the people; some prepared to abandon a city ready to be betrayed, when Cairnes, their agent, happily arrived from London, with assurances from king William, that troops and supplies were prepared for their relief and the general service of Ireland. He conjured them by no means to desert a cause so glorious, and which must speedily prove so triumphant. They forgot their suspicions; they declared for a brave defence; the garrison was regulated; provisions distributed; Lundy seemed to have caught the spirit of the people, and announced his resolution of marching to engage the enemy.

In such circumstances, the garrison received a new alarm, and the enemy became still more formidable. James had cast himself into the arms of the French king. Louis commiserated his fallen state, and hated William, who had just declared war against him. Preparations were made for the service

---

[h] Walker's Diary. Mackenzie.

service of the royal exile; and James, after a mortifying attendance on the ministers, and after various difficulties and obstacles raised by their intrigues, at length effected his embarkation. Fourteen ships of war, six frigates, and three fire ships, attended him at Brest *. About twelve hundred forces of his own native subjects in the pay of France, and one hundred French officers, formed his army [i]. The count de Lausun was destined to command it. He conferred the Garter on this favourite; but, as he had not influence sufficient to make him a duke of France, Lausun was disgusted, and declined to take part in the expedition. Mareschal Rosen, a German officer, was substituted in his place as lieutenant-general [k]. Louis, we are told, in the ardour of generosity, offered to supply him with a French army. But James seemed to have caught the fire of heroism from his protector, and earnestly replied, that "he would recover his dominions by the assistance of his own subjects, or perish in the attempt." They parted with mutual expressions of tenderness and affection; and Louis, to dispel the gloom of his friend, gaily expressed his wish never to see him more, as the best he could form for his interest.

He sailed from Brest, and on the twelfth day of March landed at Kinsale, resolving, contrary to the sentiments of some of his adherents, to make Ireland the scene of his operations, where his party was numerous, and where he might support a brilliant

[i] Mem. de la Fayette. [k] Reresby.

* In fixing on this number, I follow Ralph, and the tract quoted as his authority. Reresby's magnificent account of this embarkation seems only the echo of those rumours which James's party industriously spread in England, with the artifice or vanity usual on such occasions.

brilliant appearance of loyalty¹. At Cork Tyrconnel appeared to congratulate his master, and expressed his zeal by ordering a magistrate to execution who had declared for the prince of Orange. James instantly created him a duke. In a stately progress he arrived at the capital; and on the twenty-fourth day of the same month made his triumphant entry, followed by a splendid train of French, British, and Irish, attended by the Count d'Avaux, in the character of Ambassadour of France, met by the magistrates, and the whole body of popish ecclesiastics, secular and regular, in their proper habits, with the host born in solemn procession, and adored devoutly by the king, amidst the acclamations of those who favoured his cause, and those who could not resist his power.

Addresses were instantly poured upon him from all orders of people. That of the protestant established clergy touched gently on the distraction of the times, and the grievances they had experienced. He assured them of protection and redress *. To the university he was still more gracious: he promised to defend, and even to enlarge their privileges. But his fairest declarations were received with coldness and suspicion, when all the remaining protestants of the privy-council were removed, and their places supplied by d'Avaux, Powis, Berwick, the bishop of Chester, and others of his zealous adherents. He now issued five several proclamations: by the first, he ordered all protestants who had lately abandoned the

l Kennet. Ralph.   m A. D. 1689.

* This account is taken from the appendix of Lesley's answer to King. As the address and answer are there stated at large, it seems to deserve more credit than the representations of some English writers.

the kingdom to return and accept his protection, under the severest penalties, and that his subjects of every persuasion should unite against the prince of Orange: the second was calculated to suppress robberies, commanding all catholics, not of his army, to lay up their arms in their several abodes: a third invited the country to carry provisions to his troops: by the fourth he raised the value of money: and the last summoned a parliament to meet at Dublin on the seventh day of May.

AFTER these first formal acts of sovereignty, James naturally deemed the reduction of the Northerns a peculiar object of his attention. With respect to Derry, the great seat of what in his court was called rebellion, we are told that different counsels were proposed [n]. Some declared for sending an irresistible force which should at once take the city by storm; others were for blocking it up, and reducing it by famine; others again for pressing it by a slow siege, so as to inure the Irish forces to fatigue and discipline, and to teach them the arts of war. Fatally for the interests of James, this last measure was adopted; but to encourage the besiegers, and to confound the stubborn insurgents, he resolved to appear in person, and lead his forces to the walls.

AMONG these resolute and active Northerns who took arms against Tyrconnel and his master, was George Walker, a clergyman of a Yorkshire family, and rector of a parish in the county of Tyrone [o]. The danger and turbulence of the time, when the assistance of every man became necessary, called him forth in the defence of law, liberty, and

[n] Burnet.   [o] Vindication of Walker's Diary.

and religion; and in a cause the most glorious that a citizen can espouse, he was zealous and indefatigable. He raised a regiment, and commanded it. He flew from post to post, conferred with the leaders, and animated the people, who were the more convinced of their danger when a man of his peaceable profession appeared in arms. As the enemy grew more formidable by the arrival of James, he felt an increasing ardour. He hastened to Derry; he informed Lundy of the approach of this king, reminded him of his former declarations, entreated him to give the enemy battle before their whole strength was collected, and his garrison diminished p. Lundy still affected vigour; as the Irish had passed the Bann, he was now to prevent them from crossing the Finn-Water: he stationed his forces for this purpose; but, in the hour of danger, he refused to support them, shamefully abandoned his own post, and hid himself within the walls of Derry, shutting the gates against many of those who sought the same refuge.

In the mean time, two English colonels, Cunningham and Richards, arrived in Lake Foyle with two English regiments. They notified their arrival to Lundy, whose orders they were to obey, advising him to secure the passes he had already abandoned, that if a battle should be necessary, he might engage to more advantage with their reinforcement to support him. On his return to Derry he received their letter; his written answer directed them to land; his messenger delivered his orders, that they should leave their men on board, and come to the city with some of their
officers

p Walker's Diary. Mackenzie.

officers to consult on the measures necessary in the present juncture, when there were not provisions for ten days, though all unnecessary persons should be removed. Eleven officers from the ships and five of the town formed a council of war, in which it was readily agreed, in consequence of Lundy's representations, that the place was by no means tenable; that the English regiments should not land; that the principal officers should privately withdraw from the town, and leave the inhabitants to make the best conditions in their power with the enemy q. These resolutions were communicated to the town-council, where it was resolved to offer terms of capitulation to James, who now advanced slowly towards the city.

These proceedings were not long a secret to the people; they saw their leaders flying, the English regiments preparing to return to England with all the provisions intended for their relief, although Lundy assured them they should land. They exclaimed against the governour, the council, and every suspected officer; they roared out for vengeance against their betrayer. In the phrensy of rage and terrour, they slew one officer as he was hastening to escape from the city, another they wounded. In this moment of distraction, Murray, a brave and popular captain, arrived at the head of a reinforcement, and, although Lundy commanded him to retire, insisted on entering the town, and was received with acclamations. To the soldiers who eagerly crowded around him, he inveighed against the base purpose of surrendering to a cruel and perfidious enemy, and was heard with rapture. While he expostulated with Lundy, they

rushed

q Walker's Diary.

rushed to the walls, pointed their cannon, and fired on James and his advanced party, who approached to take possession of the city. While the more cautious and timid sent a deputation to apologize for this violence of an head-strong populace, they with one voice declared for defence. Governour, councils, magistrates, at once lost all authority. Lundy resigned all care of the city, and concealed himself in his own house. The garrison chose for themselves two new governours, Walker, the gallant ecclesiastic, and one major Baker, that if either should fall they might not be left without command. By direction of these men they were formed into eight regiments, amounting to seven thousand and twenty men, three hundred and forty-one officers.

When the first sudden agitation had subsided, their resolution grew composed and deliberate [r]. They suffered the timid to depart unmolested. Lundy, by connivance of the new governours, escaped to the ships in a disguise suited to his meanness, bending under a load of match. The stores were viewed, orders issued, and obeyed with regularity; each regiment had its own ground, each company knew its own bastion; they repaired each to their post without any military parade, but without confusion or disorder. Eighteen clergymen of the established church, and seven non-conformist teachers, chearfully shared the labours and dangers of the siege; and, in their turns, every day collected the people in the cathedral church, and by the fervour of their devotions, and those strains of eloquence which their circumstances inspired, animated and enflamed their hearers. Some jealousies, however,

[r] Walker's Diary.

however, broke out from thefe different religious parties, even in the hour of their common danger; and one diffenting teacher pronounced thofe unworthy to fight for the proteftant caufe, who fhould refufe to take the covenant. But the difcreet and pious of both parties prevailed, preached obedience and mutual union, and laboured to elevate the people to the utmoft pitch of that devotional fpirit which renders courage irrefiftible.

AND here one might dwell with aftonifhment on this defperate attempt of a garrifon, in a town meanly fortified and miferably fupplied; as yet encumbered with thirty thoufand fugitives who could give them no affiftance, and affailed by twenty thoufand befiegers. But the plain, unftudied, unadorned effufions of their brave governour, Walker, rife above all elaborate defcriptions. "It did be-
"get" faith he, "fome diforder among us and
"confufion, when we looked about us and faw
"what we were doing, our enemies all about
"us, and our friends running away from us [s].
"A garrifon we had, compofed of a number of
"poor people frightened from their own homes,
"and feemed more fit to hide themfelves than to
"face an enemy. When we confidered that we had
"no perfons of any experience in war among us,
"and thofe very perfons, that were fent to affift us,
"had fo little confidence in the place, that they no
"fooner faw it but they thought fit to leave it;
"that we had but few horfe to fally out with, and
"no forage; no engineers to inftruct us in our
"works; no fire-works, not fo much as a hand-
"granado to annoy the enemy; not a gun well
"mounted in the whole town; that we had fo
"many

[s] Walker's Diary, 4to. Lon. p. 22.

"many mouths to feed, and not above ten days
"provision for them in the opinion of our former
"governours; that every day several left us, and
"gave constant intelligence to the enemy; that
"they had so many opportunities to divide us, and
"so often endeavoured it, and to betray the gover-
"nours; that they were so numerous, so powerful,
"and well appointed an army, that in all human
"probability we could not think ourselves in less
"danger than the Israelites at the Red Sea; when
"we considered all this, it was obvious enough
"what a dangerous undertaking we had ventured
"upon. But the resolution and courage of our
"people, and the necessity we were under, and the
"great confidence and dependence among us on
"God Almighty, that he would take care of us and
"preserve us, made us overlook all those difficul-
"ties."

WITH minds thus possessed, they resisted both the persuasions and the assaults of their besiegers. They made their sallies in a manner unauthorised by military rules. Any officer that could be spared engaged in the adventure, and any soldiers who pleased followed his standard†. Such were the repeated successes of this irregular war, that when the besiegers battered the walls, the garrison had the hardiness to advise them to spare their labour and expence, as their gates were ever open, and wider than any breach they could make. Eleven days James continued his assaults with repeated mortifications, and without any prospect of success. Impatient of his disappointments, he left the camp and returned to Dublin, peevishly exclaiming, that if his army had been English they would have brought

† Walker's Diary.

brought him the town piece-meal. The only exploit performed in his northern expedition was that of reducing the fort of Culmore, and this he was suspected to have achieved by the help of money.

The garrison of Derry still continued to defeat all the attempts of their besiegers, and to harrass them by successful sallies. But they were soon threatened with more terrible enemies, disease and famine. The heats of summer proved even pestilential to men fatigued and confined, and their scanty and unwholesome diet enflamed their disorders. In the heaviness of their affliction, and their melancholy forebodings, they discovered in lake Foyle thirty ships, which they doubted not had been sent to their relief from England. These indeed contained troops, arms, ammunition, and provisions, under the command of Kirk; but Kirk was too much hardened against the distresses of his fellow creatures to make any hazardous attempt in favour of the garrison. He was alarmed at magnificent accounts of the force and dispositions of an enemy who were cast into consternation at his appearance. He hesitated, and returned no chearful answer to the signals of the besieged. The enemy, encouraged by this irresolution, prepared to oppose his passage. Their batteries were planted, and their forces ranged on each side the lake where it grew narrow towards the city, and from two opposite forts they stretched a boom across the water, formed of strong timber joined by iron chains, and strengthened by thick cables.

The fleet, to which the garrison looked for relief, set sail and disappeared. With great difficulty, and after repeated disappointments, they at length

length received the afflicting intelligence from Kirk, that, as he found it impossible to force a passage by the river for his stores and victuals, he had sailed round to lake Swilly, if by any means he might give some diversion to the enemy, and send supplies to the protestant forces collected at Enniskillen. He comforted them, at the same time, with an assurance that he would still relieve them; that more forces were hourly expected from England; that both there and in Scotland affairs were entirely favourable to the new government; that, by the intelligence he had gained, the besiegers could not long continue to invest them, advising them, at the same time, "to be good husbands of their provisions." From this advice they drew a melancholy presage of all their future sufferings.

EVERY day the garrison was lessened by disease, and the wretched survivors more and more enfeebled by fatigue and hunger[u]. Baker, one of their governours, died; they chose an officer of the name of Mitchelbourne to succeed him. When numbers of them were scarcely able to support their arms, they threatened death to any who should mention a surrender. General Hamilton endeavoured to move them by persuasion; they reproached him with his own treachery. Rosen, who was sent to command the siege, and conducted it with vigour and address, thundered out dreadful menaces against them; and thus, by convincing them that no mercy was to be expected, confirmed their resolution. Outrageous at this obstinacy, he declared, that if the town were not surrendered by the first day of July, all of their faction through the whole country to Balyshannon, Charlemont, Belfast, Innisowen, protected

[u] Walker's Diary.

protected and unprotected alike, should be given up to plunder, and driven under their walls, there to perish, unless relieved by a surrender of the town. The appointed day arrived, but the garrison continued their defence. On the next morning a confused multitude was seen hurrying towards the walls. At a distance they were mistaken for enemies; the garrison fired on them, but happily without any damage to the thousands of miserable protestants, of all ages and conditions, infirm, old, young, women, infants, goaded on by soldiers whose ears were tortured with their shrieks, and who executed their hideous orders with tears. The afflicting spectacle transported the garrison to fury. Numbers of the wretched sufferers, thus driven to perish beneath their walls, conjured them with bended knees and lifted hands, by no means to consider their distress, but to defend their lives bravely against an enemy who fought to involve them all in one common slaughter. A gallows was now erected in view of the besiegers; they were assured, that all the prisoners taken by the garrison should be instantly executed, unless their friends were allowed to depart. Confessors were even admitted to prepare them for death; but Rosen was still unmoved. Happily the intelligence of his barbarous intentions flew to Dublin [x]. The protestant bishop of Meath remonstrated to James; he answered that he had already ordered these captives to be released, observing, that such severities were usual in foreign service, however shocking to his subjects. Those, who survived a confinement of almost three days without sustenance or shelter, were thus permitted to return to their habitations, where the ravages of the soldiery had left them no means

[x] King's State.

means of comfort. Some of their ablest men were stolen into the town, and five hundred useless people crowded among them, and passed undiscovered, notwithstanding the vigilance of the enemy y.

The garrison, with a confirmed horrour of the besiegers, continued their obstinate defence, and even made desperate and successful sallies when they were too much weakened by hunger to pursue their advantage z. The flesh of horses, dogs, and vermin, hides, tallow, and other nauseous substances, were purchased at extravagant prices, and eagerly devoured. Even such miserable resources began to fail, and no means of sustenance could be found for more than two days. Still the languid and ghastly crowds listened to the exhortations of Walker; still he assured them from the pulpit that the Almighty would grant them a deliverance. While their minds were yet warm with his harangue, delivered with all the eagerness of a man inspired, they discovered three ships in the lake making way to the town. Kirk, who had abandoned them from the thirteenth day of June to the thirtieth of July, at length thought fit, in their extreme distress, to make an hazardous attempt to relieve them; an attempt which he might have made with less danger at the moment of his arrival, and which possibly might still have been deferred, had he not received some intimations of a treaty for surrendering. Two ships laden with provisions, and convoyed by the Dartmouth frigate, advanced in view both of the garrison and the besiegers. On this interesting object they fixed their eyes in all the earnestness of suspence and expectation. The enemy, from their batteries, from their musketry, thundered furiously
on

y Walker. z Ibid.

on the ships, which returned their fire with spirit. The foremost of the victuallers struck rapidly against the boom, and broke it, but, rebounding with violence, ran aground. The enemy burst instantly into shouts of joy and prepared to board her; on the crowded walls the garrison stood stupified by despair. The vessel fired her guns, was extricated by the shock, and floated. She passed the boom, and was followed by her companions. The town was relieved and the enemy retired.

Of seven thousand five hundred men regimented in Derry, four thousand three hundred only remained to be witnesses of this deliverance; and of these more than one thousand were incapable of service. The wretched spectres had scarcely tasted food when they had the hardiness to march in quest of the enemy; and some few men were lost by adventuring too boldly on their rear guard. They retired in vexation to Strabane, having lost eight thousand men by the sword and by various disorders, in a siege of one hundred and five days.

During the whole course of this siege, James's army had been considerably embarrassed in their operations by the Enniskillen men, so were these protestants named who had collected about Enniskillen, chosen Gustavus Hamilton governour of their little town, and proclaimed William and Mary[a]. Lord Galmoy marched to reduce them, and invested Crom castle, their frontier garrison, seated on lake Erne. As he found it impracticable to bring up his cannon, he recurred to a ridiculous artifice: eight horses were employed to draw two pieces formed of tin, bound with cords, and so coloured as

[a] Hamilton's Actions of the Enniskilleners.

as to resemble cannon. With this new species of artillery he threatened to batter the castle. The garrison returned a defiance; and being reinforced from Enniskillen, sallied, and drove the enemy from their trenches, returning in triumph with considerable booty, and the tin cannon which had been drawn up with so much apparent difficulty. Galmoy thus became contemptible; he soon rendered himself detestable. On his march he had taken two youths prisoners, with whom he found commissions from the prince of Orange. He now proposed to exchange them for one of his own officers. The officer was returned, but the youths were executed; and the Northerns thus confirmed in their dread and abhorrence of an enemy that kept no faith. Their numbers daily encreased, their excursions were so successful, and both their numbers and successes were so magnified, that the ruling party at Dublin expected them speedily at their gates. But their real numbers were insufficient for any considerable enterprize, nor were they furnished with arms or ammunition, until their victory over a party of the enemy at Belturbet, and the arrival of Kirk supplied their necessities. They thus became so formidable, that a plan was formed to attack them at once by three different armies. For this purpose, Macarthy, a gallant and experienced officer, lately created a peer, encamped at Belturbet with seven thousand men; Sarsefield, another general equally distinguished, led an army from Connaught; Fitz James, duke of Berwick, prepared to attack them from the North. But the ignorance of their danger proved the means of their deliverance. They knew only of the motions of the Connaught army. They marched out with a rapidity unexpected and astonishing; they surprised

the

the enemy's camp, and routed them with considerable slaughter. Against the Duke of Berwick they were less successful. As he approached to Enniskillen, some companies, sent to seize a post which they might defend against his numbers, ventured beyond the bounds prescribed, were surprised, and cut to pieces; but at the approach of Hamilton, the governour, Berwick retired.

MACARTHY, the remaining general, was still more formidable: with an army which had already suppressed lord Inchiquin in Munster, he marched towards Enniskillen, and invested Cromp. An officer, called Berry, was detached to the relief of the castle; but, as the enemy advanced against him with a superiour body, found it necessary to retreat. He was pursued; a skirmish followed, in which the Enniskilleners were victorious; and the arrival of the main bodies on each side, the one commanded by Macarthy, the other by Wolsley, one of Kirk's officers, produced a general engagement near Newtown-Butler and Lisnaskea; and from both these places the battle hath taken its name. The inferiour numbers of the Northerns were supplied by an undaunted resolution, and an abhorrence of the enemy. They defeated and pursued them with great slaughter, granting quarter to none but officers. About two thousand fell by the weapons of an enemy transported by zeal and resentment, about five hundred plunged into lake Erne, and but one of all the multitude escaped. The same number were made prisoners, and with these their general, Macarthy. Stung with the disgraceful issue of his expedition, he rushed upon the enemy from a wood, whither he had been driven with a few horsemen, was

---

b Hamilton's Actions of the Enniskilleners.

was desperately wounded, and conducted to Ennis-killen, expressing fear that his wounds might not prove mortal. The news of this victory was soon conveyed to the army which retired from Derry; and served to precipitate their flight.

CHAP. VI.

James returns to Dublin.---His parliament---Bill for repealing the acts of settlement.---Cruel act of attainder,---passed,---concealed,---and discovered. ---Other acts of his parliament.---James levies money by his prerogative.---His brass coinage.--- Meanness and cruelty of his government.---His contest with the university of Dublin.---Sufferings of the university,---and of the protestant clergy.--- Insolence of popish clergy,---and bigotry of James. ---Levies raised for the service of Ireland.--- Landing of Duke Schomberg.---Carricfergus surrendered.--Schomberg advances.---Newry and Carlingford burnt by the Duke of Berwick.---Irish retreat to Drogheda.---Schomberg encamps at Dundalk.---His distresses.---James offers battle.--- Schomberg declines it.---Conspiracy in his camp.--- Excursions and success of the Enniskilleners.--- Misery of the English camp.---Schomberg reinforced, ---decamps,---removes his sick,---retires to winter quarters.---Disappointment and discontents of the English parliament.---Enquiry into the conduct of the war in Ireland.---William resolves to undertake the Irish war.---Action at Cavan.---James and Schomberg reinforced.---Action in the Bay of Dublin.-----Charlemont surrendered.-----William lands at Carricfergus,---advances southward.--- His vigour.---His force.---Council held by James. ---He resolves to defend the passage of the Boyne.--- Situation of his army.---William's army encamped near the river.---William wounded.---False rumours of his death.---Deserters, and their reports. ---William resolves to pass the river.---Schomberg disgusted.

disgusted.---Disposition of the forces.---Battle of the Boyne.---James's army defeated.---They retreat in good order.---James assembles the magistracy of Dublin.---His ungracious speech.---He flies to France.---William advances towards the capital.

WHILE the armies of James proceeded so unsuccessfully in the northern province, this prince returned to Dublin; and here, in all the state of sovereignty, assembled his parliament[c]. In the upper house, a number of new popish lords, and several whose outlawries had been reversed, gave a weight to their party which could not be balanced by four or five protestant lords still remaining in the kingdom, and three prelates summoned by writ to this assembly[d]. The commons were almost entirely composed of men named by Tyrconnel, returned from such counties as were subject to his power, or such corporations as he had previously modelled. The university returned two protestant members, and about four more were admitted from other places. The session was, as usual, opened by a speech from the throne, in which James commended the exemplary loyalty and zeal of his Irish subjects; declared his abhorrence of invading either the rights of conscience, or those of property; that it was his firm purpose to establish liberty of conscience wheresoever he had power, without any other test or distinction but that of loyalty; that he would readily consent to any wholesome laws for the good of the nation, the improvement of trade, and the relieving such as had been injured by the late acts of settlement, " as far forth " as

c A. D. 1689. d King's State.

" as might be confiftent with reafon, juftice, and
" the public good^e." He enlarged on the genero-
fity he had experienced from the moft Chriftian
king; and concluded with repeating his fenfe of
their fignal loyalty. Fitton, in the upper houfe,
and Nagle, fpeaker of the commons, enlarged on
this fpeech; it was echoed by a joint addrefs; and
a bill was immediately brought in, containing a recognition of the king's title, and an abhorrence of
the prince of Orange and his ufurpation^f.

A DECLARATION was now publifhed by James,
addreffed to all his fubjects of Ireland. In this he
expreffed a fatisfaction, that fince his arrival in this
kingdom he had demonftrated the falfehood and
malice of his enemies, by his favour to proteftant
fubjects, and his protection of their properties, privileges, and religion; hoping that his fubjects of
England would hence form a judgment of what
they might expect from him; and affuring all his
fubjects of a full pardon, if they fhould return to
their obedience within twenty four days after his
appearance in England. The moft obvious rules
of policy muft have dictated a conduct conformable
to this declaration. But in his prefent petty feat
of royalty, James found himfelf totally enflaved by
different factions, and it is faid to have expreffed a
fenfe of his condition. The ambaffador d'Avaux,
affected to take the lead in his council, and James was
fervilely attentive not to afford him any pretence of
complaint. All preferments in his army were given
to Frenchmen, to the utter difcontent and indignation of the Irifh. The Irifh were confoled by their
afcendency in the new parliament, and with their
ufual violence refolved to feize the opportunity of
providing

e Leflie's anfwer to King. Append.   f King's State.

providing for their own interests, without even a decent attention to the difficulties and embarrassments of their King. Instead of providing relief for the sufferers by the acts of settlement and explanation, the commons with a tumultuous shout of joy, received a bill for the repeal of these acts g. Daly, the popish judge, inveighed so violently against it, as to incur the censure of the commons, who insisted on calling him to the bar, and obliging him to beg pardon. But in a transport of joy, on some false intelligence of the surrender of Derry, they remitted this severity. In the lords, to whom the bill was hastily sent up, the protestant bishop of Meath argued against it both on the principles of justice and of policy; and this, as we are told, by the direction and desire of James h. Whatever unfavourable opinion he had formed of the acts of settlement, and however his Irish ministers had possessed him with the hardships their countrymen had sustained from these acts, yet nothing could more provoke the English, even of his own party, than his countenancing this bill i. It therefore seems natural to expect, that he must have expressed some disapprobation of it. But it was not only a favourite object of the Irish, but warmly recommended by the French ambassadour; and their united powers were not to be resisted. When an address against the bill was presented by the purchasers under the acts of settlement, James coldly replied, "that he could not do evil, that good might result from it." When some peers proposed to enter their protest, he observed, that protests were usual only in rebellious times.

THE

g True account of the State of Ireland, by a person who, with great difficulty, left Dublin. Lond, 1689. h King's State. i Leslie.

THE bill for repealing the acts of settlement was thus passed, with a preamble which exculpated the Irish from rebelling in sixteen hundred and forty-one; and a clause whereby the real estates of all those who dwelt in any of the three kingdoms, and did not acknowledge king James's power, or who aided or corresponded with those who rebelled against him, since the first day of August sixteen hundred and eighty eight, were declared to be forfeited and vested in the king [k]. Thus, by a strain of severity at once ridiculous and detestable, almost every protestant of Ireland, who could write, was to be deprived of his estate.

BUT this Irish parliament was not contented with recovering the estates of their ancestors, and expelling the protestant proprietors, by virtue of their present act [l]. In the fulness of triumphant insolence, they resolved on a proscription as virulent as that of Rome. An act was passed by which a number of persons in the service of the prince of Orange, those who had retired from the kingdom, and did not return in obedience to the king's proclamation, numbers who were resident in Britain, and therefore presumed to be adherents to the new government, were all attainted of high treason, and adjudged to suffer the pains of death and forfeiture, unless they surrendered within certain periods assigned. It was provided, that the estates even of those who were detained abroad by sickness, or nonage, should be seized by the king; and, in defiance of justice and humanity, they were to prove their own innocence before they could be restored. Two thousand four hundred and sixty one persons, of all orders and conditions, peers, peeresses, prelates, baronets,

[k] King's State. [l] King's State, Appendix.

baronets, knights, clergy, gentry, and yeomanry, were included in this dreadful sentence. Their names were haftily collected by their respective neighbours, and received with so much ease and precipitation, that Nagle, on presenting the bill to James, declared, that " many were attainted on " such evidence as satisfied the house, and the rest " on common fame." It was so framed as to preclude the king from all power of pardoning, after the first day of November, 1689. In the mean time, a statute which affected the lives and properties of so many thousands, was carefully concealed from them, and lay unknown in the custody of the chancellor [m]. At length, when four months had elapsed from the day limited for pardoning, Sir Thomas Southwell obtained a view of this fatal act for the instruction of his lawyer, who was to draw a warrant for his pardon, which James had promised. Nagle was surprised and enraged at this discovery: after some evasions, he insisted that the king was merely a trustee for the forfeitures, and had now no power of pardoning Southwell. Nothing remained for James but to reproach his attorney-general for having framed an act intrenching on his prerogative.

Of the other acts made in this assembly, the more remarkable were a supplement to the bill of attainder, by which the personal estates of absentees were vested in the king; one declaring that the parliament of England cannot bind Ireland, and against writs of errour and appeals to England; one for liberty of conscience; another which took away the provision formerly made for ministers in towns corporate; and one for entitling the Romish clergy

to

[m] King.

to all tythes and ecclefiaftical dues payable by thofe of their own communion. In fome few inftances James is faid to have ftill difcovered an attention to the fentiments of the Englifh: he oppofed and defeated a bill for the repeal of Poyning's law; nor would he confent to eftablifh inns of court in Ireland for the education of law ftudents, a point fo long and fo ardently purfued by the Irifh catholics.

But the execution of his government correfponded with the enormous exceffes of his legiflature [n]. The parliament had granted him a monthly fubfidy of twenty thoufand pounds to be levied from lands. A tax fo grievous was yet infufficient for his purpofes. While the parliament yet fubfifted, he iffued a proclamation by virtue of his prerogative royal, impofing another tax of the fame rate on all chattles. Some of his own council ventured to remonftrate againft this arbitrary proceeding, and reminded him of the advantage it muft give his enemies. But James had forgotten all fcruples, for he could not obtain money from France. He refented the interpofition of his counfellors; he infulted them with their own declaration, that it was a branch of his prerogative to levy money. "If I cannot do this," faid he, "I can "do nothing."

An exhaufted country could fcarcely fupply thefe demands; and oppreffive as they were, yet an extenfive military eftablifhment required new refources. In defiance of law, reafon, and humanity, the king chofe one refource, which has rendered his name horrible to Irifh proteftants. By feizing the tools and engines of one Moore, who, by virtue of

[n] King.

a patent of the late king, enjoyed the right of a copper coinage in Ireland, he established a mint in Dublin and Limerick [o]. Brass and copper of the basest kind, old cannon, broken bells, household utensils, were assiduously collected; and from every pound weight of such vile materials, valued at four pence, pieces were coined and circulated to the amount of five pounds in nominal value. By the first proclamation they were made current in all payments to and from the king and the subjects of the realm, except in the duties on importation of foreign goods, money left in trust, or due by mortgages, bills, or bonds; and James promised, that when this money should be decried, he would receive it in all payments, or make full satisfaction in gold and silver. His soldiers were now paid in this coin; it was poured on the protestant traders. The nominal value was raised by subsequent proclamations; the original restrictions were removed, and this base money was ordered to be received in all kinds of payments. As brass and copper grew scarce, it was made of still viler materials, of tin and pewter. It was obtruded on protestants with many circumstances of insolence and cruelty. Old debts of one thousand pounds were discharged by pieces of vile metal, amounting to thirty shillings in intrinsic value. Attempts were made to purchase gold and silver at immoderate rates with the brass money; but this was quickly forbidden on pain of death; and when protestants attempted to exonerate themselves of these heaps of coin, by purchasing the staple commodities of the kingdom, James, by proclamation, set a rate on these commodities, demanded them at this rate, returned his brass on the proprietors; and, with all the meanness of a trader,

---

[o] King. Simon on Irish Coins.

trader, exported them to France [p]. It appeared indeed, in the end, that James was the only gainer by this iniquitous project; and that in the final course of circulation, his own party became possessed of the greatest part of this adulterate coin, just at the time when William had power to suppress it by proclamation [q]. Yet certain it is, that during that melancholy interval in which the popish party was predominant, protestants felt all the distresses arising from a state of war and disorder, aggravated by the wanton insolence of their adversaries. If they attempted to purchase corn, or other provisions with the brass coin, these were instantly seized for the king's use, and the proprietors imprisoned, as men who intended to supply the enemy. "We "were at a loss," saith archbishop King, "what "the meaning of taking away corn from protestant "farmers, house keepers, and bakers should be, "when there was no scarcity in the kingdom.— "But Sir Robert Parker, and some others, blabbed "it out in the coffee-house, that they designed to "starve one half of the protestants, and hang the "other; and that it would never be well till this "were done. We were sensible that they were in "earnest by the event, for no protestant could get "a bit of bread, and hardly a drop of drink in "the whole city of Dublin. Twenty or thirty "soldiers stood constantly about every bake-house, "and would not suffer a protestant to come nigh "them [r]." Such representations are sometimes derided as the fictions of an enflamed party. But however improbable these instances of senseless tyranny may appear, they are confirmed by undoubted traditions

[p] King. [q] Simon on Irish Coins. Append. [r] King's State, p. 139, 4to.

traditions received from the sufferers, and transmitted with every circumstance of credibility.

In the midst of public disorder, of all that opposition already made to James, and all the dangers which threatened him, he was still resigned to the popish clergy, and with an unmanly bigotry still adopted all their measures for the extension of popery. A school erected at Kilkenny by the duke of Ormond, was converted into a popish seminary by a new charter [s]. Repeated disappointments had not discouraged his priests from their attempts on the university of Dublin; nor was James deterred by the consequence of his invasions on the English universities. In a few months after his arrival in Ireland, a mandamus was presented to the governours of the university of Dublin, in favour of Green, who had been already disappointed of his imaginary professorship [t]. He was now destined to another office, that of senior fellow of Trinity College. At a time when this society shared deeply in the general calamity, when no rents could be received, when their pension from the Exchequer was withheld, when their daily food was purchased by selling some part of their remaining plate; when the terrours of royal vengeance were thundered in their ears, and James and his forces at hand to execute their threats, the governours undauntedly refused obedience to the mandamus. They pleaded their own cause before Sir Richard Nagle; they urged the incapacity of Green, and the false allegations of his petition, "But there "are much more important reasons," said they, "drawn as well from the statutes relating to reli-"gion, as from the obligation of oaths we have "taken

[s] Harris's Life of King William. Append. [t] Archives of Trin. Col. Dub. MS.

" taken, and the interest of our religion (which
" we will never desert) that render it wholly im-
" possible for us, without violating our consciences,
" to have any concurrence, or to be any way con-
" cerned in the admission of him." The issue of
this unequal contest was speedy and decisive. In
a few days fellows and scholars were forcibly ejected by the soldiers of a prince, who had promised not
only to defend, but to augment their privileges;
the property of particular members, the communion plate, library, and furniture of the community
were all seized; their chapel was converted to a
magazine, their chambers into prisons [u]. The
members of the society obtained their personal liberty only by the intercession of the bishop of
Meath; and this, on the express condition, that three
of them should not meet together on pain of death.
Petre is said to have possessed James with the design
of conferring this college on the Jesuits. In the
mean time, one Moore, a popish ecclesiastic, was
nominated provost, a man of liberal sentiments,
and a lover of letters; who, with the assistance of
Macarthy, another of his own order, preserved the
library, books, and manuscripts, from the ravages
of a barbarous army.

The protestant clergy were by this time deprived, for the most part, of their subsistence [x]. They
could recover no dues from non conformists; for
these were, by the late act for liberty of conscience,
exempted from the jurisdiction of the ecclesiastical
courts. They could demand no tythes from the
numerous body of Roman catholics; while popish
incumbents, who every day multiplied by the death,
cession, or absence of protestants, exacted them

from

[u] Archives of Trin. Col. Dub. MS.   [x] King's State.

from all parties. Yet in the day of persecution, both clergy and laity felt an unusual fervour of devotion, and crowded to their places of worship. The popish government was offended, and possibly alarmed at these meetings. A proclamation was issued, confining protestants to their respective parishes, which, in effect, excluded great numbers from public worship, as, in several parts of Ireland, two parishes or more had but one church. But the popish clergy were for measures more direct and violent. By the assistance of magistrates, they seized churches for their own use, not in the country only, but the capital. The protestants remonstrated to James; he acknowledged his promise of protecting them, and published a proclamation against these outrages. But the clergy and their votaries disdained obedience to any orders repugnant to the interests of the faith. A contest now arose between the priests and their king: and in this contest James had the exquisite mortification of finding himself foiled and defeated. His order of restitution was sometimes evaded, by representing the church demanded for the protestants as a place of strength; and, therefore, improper to be entrusted to their custody. Christ Church in Dublin was seized, and could not be restored, because some arms were said to be concealed in it. When no such frivolous pretences could be urged, the priests and popish magistrates retained the churches with a contemptuous disregard of the repeated orders of a king, whose authority in ecclesiastical affairs they totally renounced. And whatever impotent resentment he expressed at this insolence, yet he still resigned himself servilely to the clergy; and seemed only solicitous to employ his momentary power for making Ireland what he called a catholic kingdom. An order was issued in the name of his governour of Dublin, that no more than five protestants should meet together, even in churches, on pain of death. The alarm of an invasion indeed was pleaded for this severity; but vulgar bigotry was ever the predominant principle of James. At the very moment when the formidable powers of his enemies were gathering round him, he thought himself worthily employed in filling the diocese of Meath with popish incumbents, and erecting a Benedictine nunnery in Dublin y.

An administration at once so tyrannical and contemptible, owed its duration to the English factions, and those distresses and embarrassments which William bitterly experienced in his elevation. The tempest in the political system was allayed, but the agitation still continued. The new king was surrounded with secret and avowed enemies. The war with France was declared; and Louis was his mortal foe. Insurrection was already meditated in Scotland; England was a scene of various discontents. It was scarcely possible for William in his complicated dangers, his fears, his suspicions, his management of parties, to proceed in the service of Ireland with necessary vigour. The English forces could not be spared; and, perhaps it was deemed hazardous to send them against the late king. New levies were ordered, and speedily completed; but the arms of the tower had been embezzled; others were to be sought in Holland; nor was it found easy to raise money on parliamentary grants[z]. In the mean time, the neglect of Ireland became a subject of popular complaint. The vulgar might

suggest

---

[y] Harris's Life of King Will. Append.   [z] Impartial History of Occurrences in Ireland, 4to. p. 6.

suggest reasons for it suited to their own sentiments; but they, who affected discernment, ascribed it to the counsels of lord Halifax, who was said to have persuaded his new master, that the commotions of Ireland would force all parties to a full and final settlement of England. The sea fight of Bantry Bay, and the adventure of lord Dundee, retarded the succours destined for Ireland; and, at the same time, encreased the popular discontents.

The levies for the service of this kingdom consisted of eighteen regiments of foot, and five horse; the men, strangers to war; the officers, sons of English gentry, employed in order to ensure their attachment, and equally unexperienced with their soldiers. The chief command was assigned to duke Schomberg, (for William had conferred this title on his general, together with the Garter) and to him count Solmes, another foreign officer, was second in command. Schomberg, who knew little of political expediency, or the intrigues of the cabinet, expressed his impatience of delay[a]. He proposed to march the troops immediately to Port Patrick in Scotland, whence they might be conveyed in a few hours to Ireland, without a tedious preparation of transports necessary for a longer voyage. His overture was coldly received. At length, on the sixteenth day of July, when the most affecting intelligence had arrived of the distresses so bravely supported by the garrison of Derry, he was introduced to the house of commons, returned thanks for their generous donation of one hundred thousand pounds, took a solemn leave, and declared his resolution of exposing his life in Ireland for the service of the king and of their house. On the twentieth he arrived

[a] Kennet.

rived at Chester; a great part of his forces were still at a distance; transports, clothing, tents, provisions of every kind, were found insufficient; twenty two days were wasted in endeavouring to supply all defects; the season of action was already too far spent; Schomberg could delay no longer. On the twelfth day of August he set sail, with about ten thousand of his forces, and part of the artillery. On the next day he appeared in the bay of Carricfergus, and landed near Bangor, in the county of Downe.

The forces stationed by James in the neighbouring garrisons might have opposed his landing with great advantage; but no such attempt was made. Those of Belfast and Antrim retired at his first appearance, some to Lisburne, most to Carricfergus, as the place of greatest strength. The laws of war forbad him to proceed until he had reduced this town; having sent detachments to take possession of the places abandoned by the enemy, he marched with a considerable force and laid siege to Carricfergus. This town was encompassed by a wall and fosse, and defended by bastions, but without any covered way [b]. Its citadel, surrounded with high walls, and fortified by two round towers at the land entrance, served to defend the gate. The whole of it was irregular, conforming to the curve of the rock, which is a precipice over the sea near forty feet high, but to the land not exceeding twenty. The town and castle, if well defended, might have checked the progress of Schomberg. But on the first approach of the besiegers, the garrison parleyed. They demanded liberty to send to king James for succours, or for licence to surrender [c].—The demand was scornfully rejected, and the siege carried

[b] Harris's *Life* of King Will. [c] Impartial History, &c.

carried on in form, while six ships battered the town from the sea. The garrison, in the next place, required to march out with the honours of war; Schomberg insisted on making them prisoners. But after the hostilities of some days, in order to prevent delay in a season so advanced, he allowed them to march with their arms and some baggage, and to be conducted to the next Irish garrison. His soldiers murmured at this indulgence; and such was the resentment of the Ulster Scots for the outrages they sustained from these men, and such their virulent enmity to popish troops, that, without regard to faith, they fell furiously upon the garrison, wrested their arms from them, plundered the more helpless, and were restrained from murder only by the vigorous interposition of the general.

The remainder of Schomberg's army had by this time arrived; but as the artillery horses were still detained at Chester he ordered the train and other necessaries to be conveyed by the fleet to Carlingford, while his army advanced to Lisburne, to Hillsborough, to Dromore, to Loughbrickland, through a desolated country [d]. The protestants had abandoned it on the first commotions of the North; and now the popish inhabitants fled precipitately with all their cattle and effects, or were forced forward by the progress of the English army. In this march, the Enniskilleners, (who, together with Kirk's forces, had joined the Duke at Carricfergus) formed the advance guard, in all the pride of victory, when their successes had been completed, by gaining Sligo, from which the Irish garrison, commanded by Sarsefield, fled precipitately on a false alarm of danger [e]. The English beheld these men, whose exploits

[d] Impartial History, &c. [e] Hamilton's Actions of the Enniskilleners.

exploits had been so celebrated, with surprise and disappointment [f]. Instead of a regular and well disciplined battalion, they found them a militia without any of the pomp, and scarcely furnished with the conveniencies of war; their equipage mean and unseemly, and their horses of the low breed of their country. Yet with this disadvantageous appearance, they retained an undaunted spirit, and a contempt of the enemy. They beheld their reconnoitering parties with impatience, and lamented the scrupulous discipline of Schomberg, which prevented them from flying to the attack. While the general too cautiously restrained these men from their irregular war, and proceeded with a scrupulous conformity to military rules, the enemy gained time to burn down Newry in their retreat; and while the duke of Berwick was thus employed, one of his parties set flames to Carlingford. Schomberg, by a trumpet, threatened to give no quarter, should the enemy continue these barbarities; they abandoned Dundalk, without injuring the town; and hither the English army advanced, encamping at about the distance of a mile northward from the town, in low and moist ground, with the mountains of Newry to the east, the town and river to the south, and on the north hills and bogs intermixed.

Such were the exalted ideas which James's officers had formed of Schomberg and his army, that they entertained little hope of opposing him, and were said to deliberate whether it might be expedient not only to abandon their present station at Drogheda, but to retire from Dublin [g]. Tyrconnel had the honour of diverting them from a resolution so inglorious. He hastened to the main army at

[f] Impartial History, &c. [g] Ibid.

at Drogheda, confifting of about eight or ten thoufand; he affured them of an immediate reinforcement, to the amount of twenty thoufand more. Thefe troops were inftantly poured in from the fouthern province: it was therefore finally refolved to maintain their prefent ftation.

HITHERTO duke Schomberg had marched through a country full of bogs and mountains, where the enemy's cavalry could not annoy him [h]. The country before him was plain and open, where the fuperior numbers of the enemy could eafily furround his army, and cut off all communication with their fhips and their northern friends. The fleet on which he depended for artillery and provifions had not yet arrived at Carlingford. His men, undifciplined and ignorant, had already experienced the hardfhips of their prefent fervice, wafted by a fatiguing march in rain and tempeft, in cold and hunger, through a country difpiriting by its afpect, and by the inclemency of the feafon rendered ftill more dreary and diftreffing. Several had funk under thefe feverities; the fick lay languifhing on the roads, and gave full employment to parties detached from every regiment in the army to collect and convey them to the camp. In fuch circumftances, Schomberg deemed it imprudent to advance. The enemy were elated with intelligence that "he halted." Marefchal Rofen at once pronounced, that "he muft be in want of fomething;" and immediately drew his forces towards Dundalk, while the duke fortified his camp, fo as to make it impoffible for the enemy to force him to an action.

[h] Impartial Hiftory, &c.

His soldiers in a confined and unwholsome station, in the midst of damps and winter showers, without sufficient food, fewel or covering, attended by surgeons who had provided for the cure of wounds, but neglected the provisions necessary for diseases, soon grew languid and distempered [i]. The sick were at first removed to Carlingford. But an unfriendly climate and inclement season soon weakened the whole army by fluxes; and a burning fever was caught from the garrison of Derry. While the attention of a vigilant and humane commander was fixed on the distresses of his soldiers, the enemy approached. One party was detached to seize the pass at Newry, so as to fall on the rear of the English; but, on the first appearance of opposition, retreated to Sligo. Another presented themselves before the camp, but at the sight of some cavalry retired to their main body. The whole army was then drawn out with James at their head, and displayed their royal standard. The duke observed them calmly, and when his officers were impatient to engage, "Let them alone," said he, "we "shall see what they will do." They still advanced; Schomberg was still composed, insisting that their appearance indicated no intention of fighting. They drew up in regular array, as if to storm the camp. The duke then dispatched orders to his cavalry to return, on an appointed signal, from foraging, and the foot were commanded to stand to their arms. These orders were received with joy; even the sick and languid seized their muskets in full confidence of victory, and only solicitous to be relieved from their present distress. But at the moment when an engagement seemed inevitable, James drew off his forces to Ardee. His army affected

[i] Impartial History, &c.

fected aſtoniſhment and vexation at this retreat; as if the ſtorming duke Schomberg's camp were an enterprize of no danger, they imputed his apparent irreſolution to a miſtaken tenderneſs for his Engliſh ſubjects; and Roſen exclaimed, " Had your ma-" jeſty ten kingdoms, you would looſe them *k*." The Engliſh on the other hand ſuſpected, that the enemy's motions had been intended only to countenance a conſpiracy formed by ſome French papiſts to betray the camp. On the ſucceeding day the deſign was diſcovered; the principal accomplices were executed, and a number of popiſh ſoldiers diſarmed, and tranſported to Holland *l*.

WHILE Schomberg confined his other forces, and was aſſiduous in exerciſing and training his inexperienced troops, the Enniſkilleners were allowed to make their uſual excurſions. About a thouſand of theſe brave Northerns ſuddenly attacked a ſuperior body of the enemy on their march to Sligo, ſlew their commander, routed the party, and gained a conſiderable booty. But the joy of this victory was ſoon allayed by the loſs of James-town and Sligo, from which Sarſefield drove the garriſons. A French officer indeed, having poſſeſſed himſelf of a fort, and being ſupplied with proviſions, bravely maintained his poſt, and at laſt capitulated upon honourable terms. Sarſefield attempted to ſeduce his men to the ſervice of king James: one only accepted his gold, his horſe, and furniture, and the next day rode off to the camp of Dundalk.

HERE the diſtreſſes of the army every day encreaſed. The fleet indeed gradually arrived at their place of deſtination, and furniſhed ſome proviſions;

k Hiſtoire d' Ireland par Magehagan. *l* Impartial Hiſtory, &c.

visions; but the contagion had spread too widely, and raged too violently to be subdued. The English, unaccustomed to severities, confined to a low and moist station, drenched with perpetual showers, without the means of health, or the relief necessary in sickness, died daily in great numbers. Several of their most distinguished officers caught the infection, languished, and expired. The men accused their general of an intention to protract the war, and of indifference to their calamity. They imputed it to the coldness of his years, and even to dotage, that they were confined to a pestilential spot, instead of being led against an enemy they were confident of defeating. He ordered that they should build huts for shelter; in listless despondency they slighted his orders, and thus encreased their own distress; indifferent to all expedients for relief, as they superstitiously conceived that they were fated to destruction. They recounted the calamities of former times, by which Dundalk was distinguished; they listened to narratives of tremendous meteors hovering over the very place on which they lay, of shrieks and groans heard in the air, the sure prognostics of calamity. Every day rendered them more and more habituated to spectacles of misery, till at length they were deprived of all remains of sensibility. Their companions died unnoticed; the survivors used their bodies for seats or shelter, and when these were carried to interment, murmured at being deprived of their conveniencies.

The enemy, who encamped on firmer and more elevated ground, insulted their miseries [m]. They imputed it to the judgment of Heaven, that the heretical army (seated in a valley, and surrounded with

[m] Impartial History, &c.

with mountains) was overwhelmed with rains, while they themselves enjoyed an unclouded sky: yet, in the end, their calamities became equally grievous, and their numbers were equally diminished.

While they prepared to retire to winter-quarters, Schomberg was reinforced by some regiments from England and Scotland. To prevent these troops from catching the infection, and to preserve the remains of his army, he resolved to abandon his fatal station, and, for the present, pitched a new camp beyond the town. The men now clamoured at being drawn from their huts, which they had at length consented to build, and exposed in shattered tents to the severity of the season [a]. The sick were ordered on board the ships; the ships could not contain their numbers. Waggons were provided to convey them to Belfast; some died on their first attempt to remove; the officers were employed in attendance on the sick; the general, at the age of fourscore years, afflicted with this scene of wretchedness, exposed to the violence of a dreary and tempestuous season, stood for hours at the bridge of Dundalk, commanding, encouraging, directing every means for alleviating the miseries of his men [o]. Scarcely had they been disposed in the waggons, when at the first violent motion several expired, and the roads were strewed with their carcasses. An army thus wasted was suddenly alarmed with advice that the enemy was at hand. Even the faint and diseased catched at their arms, and still confident of victory, cried out, " the papists " shall now pay for our being detained so long in " such dismal quarters." Happily the alarm proved false. It was now time for Schomberg to dispose

[a] Impartial Hist. p. 31. [o] Ibid. p. 35.

pose of that part of his army which remained in the northern towns. Hither he retired without any interruption from the enemy, (except one futile and ill conducted attempt to seize the pass at Newry) and hither his soldiers conveyed the infection of their camp.

The people of England had possessed their minds with the most brilliant expectations from duke Schomberg's army. His distresses had been concealed from them; they were assured that his camp was in a flourishing condition, supplied abundantly with every necessary p. But instead of reducing Ireland, they found him entrenching himself against an enemy they were long habituated to despise, and confining his operations to the protection of the northern province. Their pride was exasperated at the disappointment; the factious were delighted at this new occasion of loading the king's ministers with odium. From the first rise of the war in Ireland, the English commons affected to discover an attention to this kingdom, possibly with the greater zeal, as it was apparently neglected by the king. They studied means for relieving those protestants who fled from Ireland. Their artificers were allowed to trade in English corporations; their clergy to hold benefices in England consistently with their Irish preferments, until these should be recovered; their gentry they recommended to be supplied from the estates of those who were in arms against the present government q. Enraged at repeated intelligence of the distress sustained by the brave garrison of Derry, they enquired into the delays and misconduct in the service of Ireland; and when the king hesitated to communicate the minute books of that

p London Gazette. q Commons Journals, April 9, 1689. June 25--29.

that committee of the privy-council who managed the affairs of this kingdom, they resolved that his advisers were enemies to the king and kingdom. When these were obtained, and found insufficient for their satisfaction, they examined witnesses [r], they enquired with particular accuracy into the conduct of Lundy, now a prisoner in the Tower, and they addressed the king that he might be transmitted to London-Derry, there to be tried by a court-martial.

In the midst of this ferment, George Walker arrived in London with an address to the king from the inhabitants of Derry. He was received with the utmost grace, and immediately presented with five thousand pounds[s]. The city of London invited him to an entertainment; the populace crowded round him with acclamations; and the eyes of all were turned with wonder and delight on this military clergymen; for he reassumed the habit of his original profession, and by this slight circumstance seems to have rendered himself an object of greater favour and attention [t]. With the house of commons he was equally a favourite. He petitioned them for some relief for the widows and orphans of those who perished in the defence of Derry, and for the clergy of the city. They addressed the king to distribute ten thousand pounds for this purpose. Walker received their thanks from the speaker, and was desired to present the thanks of the house to those who had served under him. They consulted him upon the affairs of Ireland; and now, more exasperated by the event of Schomberg's expedition, they greedily received his information, that the misfortunes

[r] Aug. 12.
[s] London Gazette.
[t] Commons Journals. Novem.

misfortunes of the duke arose entirely from the misconduct of one Shales, purveyor to the army, by whose default his grace wanted artillery, horses, and carriages, the soldiers bread, their horses shoes and forage, and the surgeons medicines. In their rage they multiplied addresses. They first desired that persons should be sent into Ireland to take account of the numbers and condition of the army; then, that the king should order Shales to custody: but this had been already ordered. As the man had been employed by James, he was the more obnoxious to those who affected attachment to the present government. The house again desired that the king would inform them by whose advice Shales had been employed [u]. To this question he declared that he could return no answer; but, at the same time, to allay the resentments of the house which pointed directly at his ministers, he proposed that the commons should nominate commissioners, to take care of all preparations necessary for the service of Ireland. This gracious condescension served to check their animosity for a moment, but not to extinguish it. They indeed desired to be excused from such a recommendation, leaving it " to his majesty's great wisdom to nominate fit per-" sons." But they soon remonstrated with new violence against miscarriages in the army, the fleet, and in Ireland; and resolved, that the king should be addressed to take these into consideration, to find out the authors, and to entrust the management of affairs to persons unsuspected, and more to the safety of his majesty and satisfaction of his subjects. But it is no part of the present work to trace the progress of faction and competition in this assembly.

It

[u] Commons Journal. December.

It is only pertinent to obferve, that William, irritated, mortified, and diftracted by contention, inftead of retiring, as he once propofed, to Holland, and relinquifhing a fovereignty attended with the moft exquifite vexations, chofe new friends, refolved to call a new parliament, to commit the reins of government to his popular queen, and to undertake the war of Ireland in perfon.

THE firft report of this defign[x] was a confiderable encouragement to the Englifh army in Ulfter. Duke Schomberg had retired to winter quarters with about half thofe numbers he had brought to Ireland; and, although the diftempers of his army were not immediately fubdued, yet care and conveniences, wholefome food, and warm quarters, foon reftored them to an unufual degree of vigour. Several regiments were broken one into another, and officers fent to England for recruits. The Ennifkilleners made fome excurfions with their ufual alertnefs; nor were the Irifh regiments ftationed at Ardee entirely inactive. Early in the month of February, Schomberg received intelligence that the enemy were collecting about Dundalk, in order to difturb his frontier garrifons. Some troops were detached to watch their motions; but it foon appeared that their defign lay another way. The Ennifkilleners had furprifed their garrifon at Belturbet, and fortified the place: their prefent purpofe was to recover it. The gallant Northerns, under their victorious leader Wolfey, marched from the town, hoping to furprife them in Cavan. But hither the duke of Berwick had already arrived with a confiderable reinforcement; and the Northerns,

[x] Impartial Hiftory, &c.

to the number of one thousand, were encountered by four thousand Irish. The sudden violent impression of a spirited enemy had a greater effect in this petty action, than perhaps is usually experienced in more extensive engagements. The Irish at the first onset fled from those who had been accustomed to victory. The northern forces burst into the town, and were plundering it, when those of the enemy who had fled to the fort sallied out to renew the engagement. Wolsey could recall his men from their present disorder, only by setting fire to a town stored with all manner of provisions. Thus forced from their prey, they completed their victory, with considerable slaughter.

The spirits of the English army were elevated by such petty successes. Cloaths, arms, ammunition, and provisions arrived from England; and to animate them still farther, seven thousand well-appointed troops of Denmark landed at Belfast, under the command of the prince of Wirtemberg. Schomberg was now employed in furnishing his frontier garrisons with stores; nor was James less assiduous in forming his magazines and preparing for the campaign. If he really expressed a resolution of trusting to his own subjects for success, he had by this time forgotten such heroic sentiments. He now accepted five thousand French troops, under the conduct of count Lauzun; and in their place an equal number of Irish was transported to France. However such an exchange might have been warranted by theory or authority, James had the mortification to find his new auxiliaries refractory and disobedient. They knew and acknowledged no superior but Lauzun; and this general attended,

not

not to the interest of the king, but that of his troops: he considered himself as in an enemy's country, and lived at free quarter.

A trivial incident served to encrease the mortification of this unhappy prince[z]. The only frigate, he yet retained of that royal fleet which once obeyed him, lay in the bay of Dublin ready to convoy some small vessels to France laden with various goods, for which he had obtruded his brass coin on the proprietors. Some firing was heard from sea; James flattered himself that it was occasioned by some of his subjects of England returning to their allegiance. The strand was quickly crowded; James himself rode towards the shore at the head of his guards, and thus became spectator of the gallantry of Sir Cloudesly Shovel, who had sailed with a few ships from Belfast, and now, after some resistance, took the frigate with the whole convoy.

But what afflicted James still more sensibly was the loss of Charlemont. This fort was esteemed so strong and so well provided, that Schomberg in his progress did not venture to attack it. In spring, when his forces were capable of action, Caillemote, a brave French officer, was posted on the Blackwater, and harrassed and streightened the garrison: as the season advanced, the castle was more closely invested, and the governour summoned to surrender. This governour, O'Regan, a brave Irish officer, but of rude and vulgar manners, deigned no other reply, but that "The old knave Schomberg shall "not have this castle." A detachment of five hundred men sent to its relief, with a small quantity
of

[z] A. D. 1690. Impartial History, &c.

of ammunition and provisions, was suffered to march in after a slight resistance. They soon found that their additional numbers only served to hasten on that famine with which the garrison was threatened, and, therefore, attempted to return, but were repeatedly driven back with slaughter. O'Regan, incensed at their ill-success, swore that if they would not force their way, they were to expect no entertainment within, and obliged them to lodge on the counterscarp and dry ditch within the palisadoes. The distresses of the garrison, and the detachment thus excluded, soon became intolerable, and the governour, of consequence, less arrogant. He proposed terms of capitulation, and was allowed to march out with all the honours of war.

In the mean time [a], several new regiments, English, Dutch, and Brandenburghers, arrived in the northern province; and the army was every day encouraged with assurance that William was speedily to land. The hopes of pay, the expectations of preferment, the desire of having their sovereign a witness of their meritorious conduct possessed both officers and soldiers. They impatiently expected the king; and, on the fourteenth day of June, received him at Carricfergus in a transport of joy. He came, attended by prince George of Denmark, the young duke of Ormond, the earls of Oxford, Scarborough, and Manchester, and other persons of distinction; was met by duke Schomberg, the prince of Wirtemberg, Kirk, and other officers; received an address from the northern clergy, presented by Walker, and published his proclamations for the suppression of rapine, violence, and injustice.

His

---

a Impartial History, &c.

His military genius prompted him, and the present distracted state of England, together with the formidable preparations of France, obliged him to a vigourous prosecution of the war. From Belfast he advanced to Lisburne and Hillsborough. Here he commenced the exercise of his civil authority [b], by an act highly acceptable to the inhabitants of the northern province. The teachers of dissenting congregations, which abounded in this province, had acted with zeal against the cause of popery and the late king. One of this order had the merit of first encouraging the populace to shut the gates of Derry; several had patiently endured the hardships of the siege; and in every part of Ulster these ministers had shared deeply in the distresses of war. William now issued his warrant, granting them an annual pension of twelve hundred pounds, to be paid by the collector of customs in the port of Belfast [c]; a pension afterwards inserted in the civil list, and made payable from the exchequer. His forces were ordered to take the field; and when some cautious counsels were suggested by his officers, he rejected them with indignation. " I came not to Ireland," said he " to let grass grow under my feet." At Loughbrickland, his whole army assembled from their different quarters, and were joined by the king and his train. William ordered them to change their encampment, that he might review the regiments on their march to the new ground. The officers imagined, that on a tempestuous and dusty day, he would content himself with a general view from some convenient station; but they saw him dart quickly into the throng, riding eagerly from place

[b] Harris's Life of K. Wil. Walker's Diary.
[c] Impartial History, &c.

place to place, examining every regiment and every troop diftinctly and critically. His foldiers were thus pleafed and animated, every man confidering himfelf as under the immediate infpection of his royal leader, who took his quarters in the camp, was the whole day on horfeback, at the head of an advanced party, viewing the adjacent country, reconnoitering, or directing the accommodations neceffary for his foldiers. When an order was prefented to him to be figned for wine for his own table, he paffionately exclaimed, that his men fhould be firft provided; "Let them not want," faid he, "I fhall drink water." An army of thirty-fix thoufand men, thus animated, and excellently appointed, advanced fouthward to decide the fate of Ireland, while the fleet coafted flowly in view, to fupply them with every neceffary, and thus to encreafe their confidence.

Six days had elapfed from the time of William's landing, when James received the firft intelligence that a prince, who, he confidently believed, muft be detained in England by faction and difcontent, was already on his march to meet him. He committed the guard of Dublin to a militia, under the command of Lutterel, the governour, and marched with fix thoufand French infantry[d], to join the main body of his army, which, at the approach of the enemy had retired from Dundalk and Ardee, and now lay near Drogheda, on the banks of the river Boyne. His numbers were about thirty-three thoufand. His council of officers reminded him, that the naval armament of France was completed, and the fleet perhaps already on the Englifh coaft; that

[d] Impartial Hiftory.

that Louis had promised, as soon as the squadron attending on William should return, he would send a fleet of frigates into the Irish seas to destroy his transports; that he would be thus fatally detained in Ireland, while Britain was threatened by foreign invasion, and the domestic enemies of the reigning prince concerting an insurrection. In such circumstances they advised him to wait the event of those designs formed in his favour, not to hazard an engagement against superiour numbers, to strengthen his garrisons, to march to the Shannon, with his cavalry and a small body of foot, and thus to maintain a defensive war against an enemy, which, in a strange and unfriendly climate, without provisions or succours, must gradually perish by disease and famine. James on the contrary contended, that to abandon the capital, were to confess himself subdued; that his reputation must be irreparably ruined; that the Irish, who judged by appearances, would desert; and what was of still more moment, his friends in England and Scotland must be dispirited, and deterred from their attempts to restore him. He expressed satisfaction, that he had at last the opportunity of one fair battle for the crown. He insisted on maintaining his present post; and from such animated language, his officers concluded that he meant to take a desperate part in the engagement: yet, with an ominous precaution, he dispatched Sir Patrick Trant, one of his commissioners of revenue, to Waterford, to prepare a ship for conveying him to France in case of any misfortune.

WILLIAM was no stranger [e] to the motions of the French, and the machinations of his enemies. Whatever

[e] Impartial History, &c.

ever was the proper conduct for James, it was evidently his interest to bring their contest to an immediate decision. On the last day of June, at the first dawn of morning, his army moved towards the river in three columns. He marched at the head of his advanced guard, which by nine o'clock appeared within two miles of Drogheda. William, observing a hill west of the town, rode to the summit with his principal officers, to take a view of the enemy. On their right was Drogheda, filled with Irish soldiers. Westward of the town on the farther banks of the river, their camp extended in two lines, with a morass on the left, difficult to be passed. In their front were the fords of the Boyne, deep and dangerous, with rugged banks, defended by some breast-works, with huts and hedges, convenient to be lined with infantry. On their rear, at some distance, lay the church and village of Donore; three miles farther was the pass of Duleek, on which they depended for a retreat. The view of their encampment was intercepted by some hills to the south-west; so that Sgravenmore, one of William's generals, who counted but forty-six regiments, spoke with contempt of the enemy's numbers. The king observed, that more might lye concealed behind these hills, and many be stationed in the town; "But it is my purpose," said he, "to be speedily acquainted with their whole "strength."

His army was now marching into camp[f]; when William, anxious to gain a nearer and more distinct view of the enemy, advanced with some officers, within musket-shot of a ford opposite to a village called Old-bridge; here he conferred for some time
on

[f] Impartial History, &c.

on the methods of paſſing, and planting his batteries; when, riding on ſtill weſtward, he alighted and ſat down to refreſh himſelf on a riſing-ground. Neither the motions of William nor of his army were unnoticed. Berwick, Tyrconnel, Sarſefield, and ſome other generals, rode ſlowly on the oppoſite banks, viewing the army in their march, and ſoon diſcovered the preſent ſituation of the king. A party of about forty horſe immediately appeared in a plowed field oppoſite to the place on which he ſat. In their centre they carefully concealed two field pieces, which they planted unnoticed under cover of a hedge, and retired. William mounted his horſe; at that moment the firſt diſcharge killed a man and two horſes on a line, (at ſome diſtance) with the king: another ball inſtantly ſucceeded, grazed on the banks of the river, roſe, and ſlanted on his right ſhoulder, tearing his coat and fleſh. His attendants crowded round him, and appeared in confuſion. An univerſal ſhout of joy rung through the Iriſh camp, at the news that Orange was no more. It was conveyed rapidly to Dublin; it was wafted to Paris: Louis received it with exſtacy; and the guns of the Baſtile proclaimed the meanneſs of his triumph.

While ſome ſquadrons of the enemy's horſe drew down to the river [f], as if to purſue a flying enemy, William rode through his camp, to prevent all alarms or falſe reports of his danger. On the arrival of his artillery, the batteries were mounted, and the cannonading continued on each ſide, not without ſome execution, till the cloſe of evening. Some deſerters were received, and gave various accounts of the ſtrength and diſpoſition of the enemy. One who

---

[f] Impartial Hiſtory, &c.

who appeared of some note, spoke so plausibly [g], and, at the same time, so magnificently of their numbers, that William seemed disconcerted. To Sir Robert Southwell, his secretary of state, who had given him different intelligence, he expressed his suspicion that the enemy was really stronger than he imagined. Southwell communicated the king's doubts to Cox, his under-secretary, through whose channel the intelligence had been conveyed. Cox, with an acuteness which seems to have laid the foundation of his future fortune, led the deserter through the English camp; and when he had surveyed it, asked to what he computed the amount of William's forces. The man confidently rated them at more than double their number. The king was thus satisfied that his reports arose from ignorance and presumption. Other deserters made reports more unfavourable to the enemy; and the king was assured, that James, in expectation of a defeat, had already conveyed part of his baggage and artillery to Dublin.

About nine at night, William called a council of war [h], not to deliberate, but to receive his orders; and here he declared his resolution of passing the river in front of the enemy. Duke Schomberg, with the caution natural to his years, endeavoured to dissuade him from this hazardous enterprize; and when he could not prevail, insisted, that part of the army should be immediately detached to secure the bridge of Slane, about three miles westward of their camp, so as to flank the enemy, and to cut them off from Duleek, the pass through which they might retreat. It is generally imputed to the indifference with which his counsel was received, that this general retired in disgust, and received the order of battle in

[g] Harrison's life of king Will.   [h] Impartial History, &c.

in his tent, declaring that, "it was the firft ever fent to him." Nor did James difcover more attention to this important pafs of Slane. In his council of war, Hamilton recommended that eight regiments might be fent immediately to fecure the bridge. James propofed to employ fifty dragoons in this fervice; the general, in aftonifhment, bowed, and was filent.

WILLIAM directed[i] that the river fhould be paffed in three different places; by his right wing commanded by count Schomberg, fon of the duke, and general Douglas on the weft, at fome fords difcovered near the bridge of Slane; by the centre commanded by duke Schomberg, in front of the Irifh camp; and by the left wing led by the king himfelf, at a ford between the army and the town of Drogheda. At midnight William once more rode through his camp with torches, infpected every poft, and iffued his final orders.

EARLY on the fucceeding morning[k], count Schomberg with the cavalry, and Douglas with the infantry, which compofed the right wing, marched towards Slane with greater alacrity than the troops fent from the other fide to oppofe them. They croffed the river without any oppofition except from a regiment of dragoons ftationed over night at the ford, of which they killed feventy, before their retreat could be fecured. They advanced and found their antagonifts drawn up in two lines. They formed, mixing their horfe and foot, fquadron with battalion, till on the arrival of more infantry they changed their pofition, drawing the horfe to the right, by which they confiderably out-flanked
the

[i] Impartial Hiftory, &c. [k] Ibid.

the enemy. But they were to force their way through fields enclosed by deep ditches difficult to be surmounted, especially by the horse; who, in the face of an enemy, were obliged to advance in order: beyond these lay the morass still more embarrassing. The infantry were ordered to plunge in, and, while the horse found a firm passage to the right, forced their way with fatigue and difficulty. The enemy, astonished at their intrepidity, fled instantly towards Duleek, and were pursued with slaughter.

By the time when it was supposed that the right wing had made good their passage [1], the infantry in the centre was set in motion. The Dutch guards first entered the river, on the right opposite to Oldbridge. The French protestants and Enniskilleners, Brandenburghers, and English, at their several passes to the left, plunged in with alacrity, checking the current, and swelling the water, so that it rose in some places to their middle, in others to their breasts, and obliged the infantry to support their arms above their heads. The Dutch had marched unmolested to the middle of the river, when a violent discharge was made from the houses, breastworks, and hedges, but without execution; they moved on, gained the opposite banks, formed gradually, and drove the Irish from their posts. As they still advanced, the squadrons and battalions of the enemy suddenly appeared in view behind the eminences which had concealed them. Five of these battalions bore down upon those Dutch who had already passed, but were received firmly, and repulsed. The efforts of the Irish horse were equally unsuccessful. Two attacks were bravely repelled, when the

[1] Impartial History, &c.

the French and Enniskilleners arrived to the support of the Dutch, and drove back a third body of horse with confiderable execution.

In the mean time, general Hamilton[m] led the Irish infantry to the very margin of the river to oppose the paſſage of the French and English. But his men, although ſtationed in the poſt of honour at the requiſition of their officers, ſhrunk from the danger. Their cavalry proved more ſpirited. A ſquadron of Danes was attacked with ſuch fury and ſucceſs, that they fled back through the river. The Iriſh horſe purſued, and, on their return, fell furiouſly on the French huguenots, who had no pikes to ſuſtain their ſhock, and were inſtantly broken. Caillemote, their brave commander, received his mortal wound, and when borne to the Engliſh camp, with his laſt breath animated his countrymen who were paſſing the river. As he lay bleeding in the arms of four ſoldiers, he collected ſtrength to exclaim repeatedly in his own language, " A la " gloire, mes enfans! a la gloire!" " To glory, " my boys! to glory!" The rapidity of the Iriſh horſe, the flight of the Danes, and the diſorder of the French, ſpread a general alarm, and the want of cavalry ſtruck the minds even of the peaſants, who were but ſpectators of the battle, ſo forcibly, that a general cry of " Horſe! horſe!" was ſuddenly raiſed, was miſtaken for an order to " Halt," ſurpriſed and confounded the centre, was conveyed to the right wing, and for a while retarded their purſuit. In this moment of diſorder, duke Schomberg, who had waited to ſupport his friends on any dangerous emergency, ruſhed through the river, and placing himſelf at the head of the huguenot forces,

[m] Impartial Hiſtory, &c.

forces, who were now deprived of their leader, pointed to some French regiments in their front, and cried, " Allons, messieurs; voila vos persecu-" teurs." Come on, gentlemen, there are your " persecutors." These were his last words. The Irish horse, who had broken the French protestants, weeled through Old-bridge, in order to join their main body; but were here cut down by the Dutch and Enniskilleners. About sixteen of their squadron escaped, and, returning furiously from the slaughter of their companions, were mistaken by the huguenots for some of their own friends, and suffered to pass. The wounded Schomberg in the head, and were hurrying him forward, when his own men fired and slew him. About the same time, Walker of London-Derry, whose passion for military glory had hurried him unnecessarily into this engagement, received a wound in his belly, and instantly expired.

AFTER an uninterrupted firing of an hour, the disorder on both sides occasioned some respite. The centre of the English army began to recover from their confusion. The Irish retreated towards Donore, where James stood during the engagement, surrounded by his guards; and here, drawing up in good order, once more advanced. William had now crossed the river at the head of Dutch, Danish, and English cavalry, through a dangerous and difficult pass, where his horse, floundering in the mud, obliged him to dismount, and accept the assistance of his attendants. And now, when the enemy had advanced almost within musket shot of his infantry, he was seen with his sword drawn, animating his squadrons, and preparing to fall on their flank. They halted, and again retreated to Donore. But here, facing about vigourously, they charged with such

success

success, that the English cavalry, though led on by their king, was forced from their ground. William, with a collection of thought which accompanies true courage, rode up to the Enniskilleners, and asked, ' What they would do for him?" Their officer informed them who he was; they advanced with him, and received the enemy's fire. But, as he wheeled to the left, they followed by mistake; yet, while William led up some Dutch troops, they perceived their error, and returned bravely to the charge. The battle was now maintained on each side with equal ardour, and with variety of fortune. The king, who mingled in the hottest part of the engagement, was constantly exposed to danger. One of his own troopers, mistaking him for an enemy, presented a pistol to his head : William calmly put it by. " What," said he, " do not you know your friends?" The presence of such a prince gave double vigour to his soldiers. The Irish infantry were finally repulsed. Hamilton made one desperate effort to turn the fortune of the day, at the head of his horse. Their shock was furious, but neither orderly nor steady. They were routed, and their general conveyed a prisoner to William. The king asked him whether the Irish would fight more. " Upon my honour," said Hamilton, " I believe they will; for they have yet a good body of horse." William surveyed the man who had betrayed him in his transactions with Tyrconnel, and in a sullen and contemptuous tone exclaimed, Honour! YOUR honour!

NOR was this asseveration of Hamilton well-founded. The right wing of William's army had by this time forced their way through difficult grounds, and pursued the enemy close to Duleek. Lauzun,

Lauzun rode up to James, who still continued a
Donore, advising him to retreat immediately, as h
was in danger of being surrounded. He marche
to Duleek at the head of Sarsefield's regiment; hi
army followed, and poured through the pass, no
without some annoyance from a party of Englis
dragoons, which they might easily have cut t
pieces, had they not been solely intent on flying
When they reached the open ground, they drev
up, and cannonaded their pursuers. Their officer
ordered all things for a retreat, which they mad
in such order, as was commended by their enemies
Their loss in this engagement was computed a
fifteen hundred; that of William's army scarcel
amounted to one-third of this number *.

HER

* Burnet assures us, that all Tyrconnel's papers were taken in t
camp, and those of James afterwards found in Dublin; from whi
the king learned the design of the French to burn his transpor
" Among the earl of Tyrconnel's papers," saith the right revere
historian, " there was one letter writ to queen Mary at St. Ge
" mains, the night before the battle, but it was not sent. In it,
" said, he looked on all as lost; and ended it thus, *I have now no bu
" in any thing but in Jones's business.*" This he explains, by telling
from the information of lord Carmarthen, that this Jones was e
ployed to assassinate king William. He says, that Sir Robert Sout
well inspected all the papers and letters of Tyrconnel, and gave h
copies of two. In one he writes, that Jones is come; that his p
position was likelier to succeed than any yet made; but that
demands were high, *if any thing can be high for such a service.*
another he writes, that Jones had been with the king, *who did
like the thing* at first; but, he adds, we have now so satisfied him
conscience and honour, that every thing is done that Jones desir
Sir Robert Southwell, it seems, informed Burnet also, that Na
furnished this Jones with money, and a poignard *of a particular co
position*, together with a Bible bound without a Common Prayer, th
if seized, he might pass for a dissenter.

The authority of Sir Robert Southwell, who attended William
secretary of state, is indeed very considerable: else we might possi
be tempted to rank the *poignard of a particular composition*, with th
silver bullets of which we read in the reign of Charles the Secon
And still the whole narrative would appear less dubitable, if
bishop had explained how papers of such consequence were suffered
remain in James's camp, when he had already sent the baggage
Dubl

HERE was a final period of James's Irish royalty. He arrived at Dublin in great diforder, and damped the joy of his friends, who, at the intelligence of William's death, every moment expected to receive him in triumph. He affembled the popifh magiftrates and council of the city[n]: he told them, that in England his army had deferted him, in Ireland, they had fled in the hour of danger, nor could be perfuaded to rally, though their lofs was inconfiderable; both he and they muft therefore fhift for themfelves. It had been deliberated, whether, in cafe of fuch a misfortune, Dublin fhould not be fet on fire; but on their allegiance he charged them to commit no fuch barbarous outrage, which muft reflect difhonour on him, and irritate the conqueror. He was obliged, he faid, to yield to force, but would never ceafe to labour for their deliverance; too much blood had been already fhed; and Providence feemed to declare, againft him; he, therefore, advifed them to fet their prifoners at liberty, and fubmit to the prince of Orange, who was merciful. The reflection[o] on the courage of his Irifh troops was ungracious, and provoked their officers to retort it on the king. They contended, that in the whole of the engagement, their men, though not animated by a princely leader, had taken no inglorious part. They obferved, that while William fhared the danger of his army, encouraging them by his prefence, by his voice, by his example, James ftood at fecure diftance a quiet fpectator of the conteft for his crown and dignity. "Exchange kings," said

Dublin, in expectation of a defeat; and how letters of any confequence fhould, after an interval of feveral days, be feized in Dublin, when James, or his minifters at leaft, were left at full leifure to deftroy or to remove them.

n London Gazette.   o Impartial Hiftory, &c.

said they, " and we will once more fight the battle." Their indignation was encreased, when they saw the prince, who inveighed against Irish cowardice, fly precipitately to Waterford, breaking down the bridges to prevent a pursuit, and instantly embark for France. They, who did not impute this conduct to a defect of spirit, at least complained, that his Irish adherents were shamefully sacrificed to his interests and designs in England. Nor did the officers of William express entire satisfaction at his conduct. They complained, that the enemy were not pursued with sufficient vigour, without weighing the disadvantage sustained by the loss of duke Schomberg, or the danger of pursuit through a difficult pass and an unknown country. They contended, that at the very moment of victory, ten thousand men should have been detached to Athlone and Limerick, to seize these important places, and prevent the Irish from re-assembling. But they were strangers to those anxieties which oppressed the king's mind. He every moment looked for an invasion in England, and, expecting to be recalled, deemed it imprudent to divide his army, or to remove to any distance from the coast. Drogheda was summoned; the Irish governor hesitated, but being assured, that if the cannon were brought up, no quarter was to be expected, he surrendered on condition that the garrison should be conveyed, unarmed, to Athlone; and William now advanced slowly towards the capital.

CHAP.

CHAP. VII.

Dublin in confusion.—Conduct of Fitzgerald.—King William encamps at Finglass.—Address of the protestant clergy.—The king's declaration, and commission of forfeitures.—Irish prepare to renew the war.—Waterford and Duncannon reduced by William.—His anxieties.—He returns to Chappel-Izod, and resolves to embark.—He is diverted from his Purpose, and joins the army.—General Douglas marches against Athlone.—His progress,—his ill success,—his retreat.—William besieges Limerick.—Vigorous defence of the garrison.—English artillery surprised by Sarsefield.—Siege still continued.—A breach,—a storm.—English repulsed.—William raises the siege, and embarks for England.—Enterprize of the earl of Marlborough.—Cork reduced.--Fort of Kinsale surrendered.—English forces retire to Winter quarters.—General disorder and distress.—Rapparees.—Civil administration at Dublin.—Attempt on the English frontier.—Action at the Moat of Grenoge.—Arrival of Saint Ruth.—Ballymore reduced.—March to Athlone.--The English town forced.--Efforts to gain the Irish town.--Resolution of the besieged.--Preparations for passing the river,--suspended,--resumed.--The passage.--Athlone taken.--Proclamation of pardon.--Saint Ruth retires to Aghrim.--The situation of his army.--English march to the attack.--The battle obstinately maintained.--Death of Saint Ruth.--Final defeat of the Irish.--Galway besieged, and surrendered on honourable conditions.--Situation of the

Irish in Limerick.—Preparations for the siege.—Cautious procedure of Ginckle.—Successful attempt to pass the Shannon.—New declaration published by the general.—Second passage of the river.—Attack at Thomond-bridge.—The garrison discontented.—A parley.—English prisoners released.—Their distresses.—Terms of capitulation proposed by the garrison,—rejected by Ginckle.—Treaty renewed.—Articles of capitulation settled and signed.—War of Ireland finally concluded.

IT doth not appear that James, on retiring, gave any orders to his officers, or any instructions for continuing the war[a]. But although he had renounced the assistance of the Irish[b], yet the interests of their religion were involved in his cause; nor had they any hopes of recovering the lands of their ancestors, or securing those they still retained, but by contending against the new government. Most of his army marched through Dublin, bending their course to Limerick and Athlone, with indignation at their king, affecting to rejoice at his flight, which relieved them from the embarrassment of a leader who had no spirit for enterprize, no sincere concern for their interests. The metropolis was now threatened with all the evils of anarchy[c]. The civil officers of James had already fled, or were preparing for flight; no detachment had been sent by William to secure the city. The protestant prisoners were set free, with violent animosity against their persecutors, breathing revenge, and ready for every outrage. They assembled in small parties, they held their consultations, and were on the point of forcing and rifling the houses of papists, when Fitzgerald,

[a] A. D. 1690.   [b] Impartial History, &c.
[c] Harris's Life of K. Will. p. 271.

gerald, a military officer of the family of Kildare, who had been delivered from his confinement, suddenly appeared among the populace, and dissuaded them from their purpose. His character and family commanded their obedience; and, with the assistance of some gentry and clergy, he assumed the government of the city, gained the keys of the castle, persuaded the main-guard, composed of about thirty popish militia, to lay down their arms, put them in the hands of protestants, and sent expresses to king William's camp to request immediate assistance.

In this interval of danger and terrour, Fitzgerald, was every moment alarmed. It was whispered that one thousand of the enemy were returned. The suburbs were already set on fire, he flew to extinguish the flames, and the incendiaries vanished. In the mean time, the populace, still impatient for plunder, broke into the house of Sarsefield; he rushed among them, and by persuasion, by menaces, by violence, restrained their outrages. Still they clamoured that the enemy were returning; he sent new expresses to the king, and at length received nine troops of horse, under the command of Auverquerque and Sgravenmore, attended by the duke of Ormond, (a person more acceptable to the citizens) and these again were reinforced by the Dutch guards. William d, in the mean time continued to advance slowly, and encamped at Finglass, a village within two miles of the capital. Hence he entered the city and repaired to the cathedral church of Saint Patrick, to return thanks for his victory; but, still attentive to the discipline and duties of a general, returned immediately to his camp. Here the protestant

d Impartial History, &c.

testant clergy attended him with an address, congratulating his arrival, praying for his success, expressing their loyalty, and entreating him not to think unfavourably of them for continuing in Ireland, and submitting to a power which they could not resist, and by which they had been enabled to serve both the church and his majesty. He answered in the usual manner, that he came to free them from popish tyranny, and doubted not, by the divine assistance, to complete his design; permitting them to appoint a day of solemn thanksgiving, and to compose an occasional form of prayer.

WILLIAM now published a declaration calculated, to detach the lower orders of subjects from their leaders [e]. He promised pardon and protection to labourers, common soldiers, farmers, plowmen, and cottiers, to townsmen and artificers, who remained at home, or should return to their dwellings and surrender their arms. He commanded all tenants of protestant subjects to pay their rents to their respective landlords, and that the tenants of those who were concerned in rebellion should detain their rents, until the commissioners of his revenue should signify to whom they were to be paid. As to the desperate leaders of the rebellion, he declared his resolution of leaving them to the event of war. A pardon so confined, and which indeed expressly warned the gentry who adhered to James, that they had no part to take but that of obstinately continuing the war, is imputed to the influence of those English who were impatient for forfeitures [f]. They were gratified by a commission issued for seizing and securing all forfeitures accruing to the crown by the rebellion of the Irish, although no courts of judicature

[e] Impartial History, &c. [f] London Gazzette. Harris's life of K. Will.

ture were now opened for proceeding regularly and legally The commissioners seized without mercy; they harrassed the country, yet made but inconsiderable returns into the exchequer. They pleaded the defects of their commission, and that, as they were not sufficiently empowered to dispose of their seizures, these were frequently retaken by force. Thus the impatience of William's English adherents only served to confirm the Irish in their aversion to the new government; and by a shameful disregard, and almost perpetual violation of his protections granted to the peasantrys, they forced this order also to crowd their old leaders, and to take arms for their security.

Thus the Irish prepared to renew the war, possessed with every passion and every principle which renders an enemy dangerous and desperate. They were exasperated at the aspersions cast by James upon their national character, and impatient to redeem it. They saw their religion on the point of being utterly extinguished, and their remains of property ready to be seized by strangers; no security in submission, no reliance on any promises of pardon. Their leaders found leisure to collect and enflame their party by the undecided conduct of king William. The joy of his late success was instantly allayed by intelligence of the bloody victory gained by Luxemburg, in Flanders, over prince Waldeck and his confederate army; his mind was still impressed with alarm and anxiety from the motions of the French navy; eight days had passed since his victory at the Boyne, when he at length resolved to divide his army; and, while he marched southward, Douglas, one of his generals, was detached with ten regiments

regiments of foot, and five of cavalry, to reduce Athlone[h]. Scarcely had William advanced thirty miles from the capital, when he received the afflicting intelligence of Tourville's success over the united fleets of England and Holland. He was now doubly solicitous to gain a secure station for his transports; and, for this purpose, to reduce Waterford and Duncannon. He hastened his march; Wexford had already declared for him, and now received his garrison; Clonmel was abandoned by the Irish; Waterford was summoned; the garrison, after some hesitation, demanded the enjoyment of their estates, the freedom of their religion, and liberty to march out with arms and baggage. This last article only was admitted; they accepted it, and surrendered. The fort of Duncannon threatened a more obstinate resistance: the governour demanded time to consult Tyrconnel; and, when refused, boldly declared, that he would take it; but on the approach of the army, and the appearance of Sir Cloudsley Shovel, with sixteen frigates, he accepted the same conditions with Waterford.

HAVING thus obtained the immediate object of his enterprise, William, again alarmed by the second appearance of the French navy on the coast of England[i], deemed his presence necessary in this kingdom, where dejection and discontent operated violently on the minds of all his subjects. The charge of completing the reduction of Ireland was committed to his generals; the necessary orders issued for his departure; and from the camp he returned to Chappel-Izod, in the neighbourhood of Dublin. Here, while employed in receiving petitions, and redressing the grievances arising from perpetual violations

[h] Impartial History, &c.   [i] Ibid.

lations of his protection, he received new difpatches, informing him, that the French fleet had retired; that all their boafted enterprifes amounted to nothing more than the deftruction of fome fifhing boats, and the inconfiderable village of Tinmouth, in the Weft; that the terrours of his friends were diffipated, and the fecret machinations of his enemies, difcovered and defeated. Such pleafing intelligence diverted him from his purpofe; he now refolved to profecute the Irifh war, and returned to his camp.

In the mean time, Douglas proceeded in his expedition to Athlone[k]. He marched as through an enemy's country; his men plundering, and even murdering with impunity, in defiance of the royal proclamation, or the formal orders of their general. As he advanced, the Irifh peafantry appeared fucceffively in confiderable bodies to claim the benefit of king William's declaration; and were fucceffively enfnared by affurance of protection, and expofed to all the violences of the foldiers. An army, abhorred and execrated, at length appeared before Athlone. To the fummons fent by Douglas, the governour, Grace, a brave old officer, returned a paffionate defiance; " Thefe are my terms," faid he, " firing " a piftol at the meffenger." His garrifon confifted of three regiments of foot, nine troops of dragoons, and two of horfe, with a larger body encamped at a fmall diftance to fupport them, all violently exafperated againft the befiegers, and encouraged by falfe rumours of the death of William, of infurrections and of invafions in England. That part of Athlone, which lay on the eaftern fide of the Shannon, and was called the Englifh town, Grace deemed indefenfible; he had, therefore, fet fire to it, and broken

the

[k] Impartial Hiftory, &c.

the fair stone bridge built by Sir Henry Sidney, in the reign of Elizabeth, resolving to maintain the Irish district on the West. About two hundred yards above it, he raised some breast-works, cast up redoubts, and other works near the end of the bridge, and mounted two batteries, besides those of the castle, which stood on an eminence, and commanded the river.

Douglas thus found the enemy stronger and better disposed than he expected 1. His works were carried on with sufficient vigour; and he commenced his operations by playing on the castle from a battery of six guns, but without any considerable effect. He found his train utterly insufficient for the enterprize he had undertaken; he lost his best gunner by a shot from the town; in a few days his men grew faint and sickly from scanty provisions, his horses weak from want of forage, it was rumoured that Sarsefield had actually marched with fifteen thousand men to raise the siege, and to cut off the retreat of the English forces. The spirits of the garrison were on fire, and their efforts redoubled, while Douglas formed the inglorious resolution of retiring. He decamped at midnight, unmolested; and, in his terrour of the enemy, marched by devious and painful routes to join the royal army. The protestant inhabitants of the country near Athlone, who had enjoyed the benefit of Irish protections, were thus exposed to the utmost severities. On the approach of the besiegers they declared in favour of the English; and were, therefore, forced to attend them in their retreat; they abandoned their habitations and their harvests, and the miserable pittance of provisions

which

1 Impartial History, &c,

which they carried with them became the prey of a necessitous and merciless army.

Douglas found the king advancing to Limerick [m], the great seat of the Irish force, anxious for intelligence of the numbers and situation of the enemy. He was assured that count Lauzun, with other Frenchmen of distinction, had already abandoned the town, and prepared to return home; that all the forces of their nation yet in Limerick, amounting to three thousand, had declared their resolution of capitulating separately, and retiring from the kingdom, but were diverted from this purpose by the clamour and importunities of the Irish; that Boileau, one of their generals, had undertaken the command of Limerick, and occupied it with his troops, while the Irish forces lay encamped on the Connaught side, ready to supply him with men and provisions, and had already secured the adjacent passes of the Shannon. Limerick, like Ahtlone, consisted of two distinct towns, the English and Irish; the former almost surrounded by the river, and united to the other by a bridge. It was fortified by strong walls, bastions, and ramparts, and defended by a castle and citadel. It was deemed hazardous to attempt it only on one side [n]. But William, possibly from an expectation that the French would still retreat, and the Irish of consequence surrender, resolved on the attempt, though the season was advanced, and his army reduced to twenty thousand. At present he had but a field train; however, his artillery, consisting of six twenty-four pounders, and two eighteen pounders, was on the road from Dublin, escorted by two troops of horse.

[m] Correspondence of Clarke, secretary at War, MS. Trin. Col. Dub.
[n] Impartial History, &c.

ON the ninth day of August, William decamped [o], and began his approaches to the town, through grounds intersected with ditches and hedges lined with Irish infantry, who retreated gradually as the pioneers levelled the inclosures, until they came to a narrow and incumbered pass between two bogs, terminated by an old fort built by Ireton, and communicating with the town by three different lanes. Of these, the broadest was occupied by the Irish horse, while their musketeers were drawn up under cover of the hedges on the right and left. As the English army advanced in order, two field pieces were so planted as to bear upon the enemy's horse; and after some discharges forced them from their ground, while their infantry were attacked, and after some resistance, driven under the walls. Ireton's fort, and another advantageous post, were gained without resistance, and immediately mounted with field pieces to annoy the town and outworks. Encouraged by this success, William encamped within cannon shot of the walls, without the usual precautions for security, and before his artillery arrived, summoned the governour to surrender. Boileau addressed his answer, not to the king, to whom he would not give his royal titles, but to Sir Robert Southwell, the secretary. He expressed his surprize at the summons, and declared his resolution of meriting the good opinion of the prince of Orange, by a vigourous defence of the place entrusted to him by his majesty [p]. But this spirited answer, William was assured, by no means corresponded with the sentiments of his garrison, who were prevented from an immediate submission only by the remonstrances of the governour, the duke of Berwick, and Sarsefield.

[o] Impartial History, &c. [p] Clarke's Correspondence, MS.

Sarsefield. And, to animate his hopes still farther, Ginckle, his Dutch general, gained a ford about three miles from the town, which the enemy abandoned at his approach, and where a strong detachment was now posted on each side of the river.

The garrison, on their part, prepared for a vigourous defence. They learned from a French deserter the situation of the king's tent, and on this quarter directed all the fury of their artillery; so that Willam found it necessary to remove q. Among other articles of intelligence, the deserter informed them of the train expected from Dublin, its route, its motions, the nature, and number of its convoy. The enterprising spirit of Sarsefield was enflamed. He saw the desperate situation of his party, numbers of French troops already retired to Galway, and preparing to embark, those still in the town wavering and desponding, the Irish of themselves unequal to the enemy. Should they receive their cannon and other necessaries attending it, they must soon become masters of Limerick. He, therefore, resolved to make one bold effort to intercept them, the last he could attempt for his countrymen with any prospect of success; should he fail, he resolved to abandon their hopeless cause, and retire to France. With a party of chosen cavalry, he crossed the Shannon at Killalloe, about twelve milles above the English camp, marched by private ways well known to his men, lurked in the mountains, and waited the approach of the artillery and its escort. His motions were not unknown to the besiegers. They were informed that Sarsefield had crossed the Shannon on some secret expedition, of consequence enough, to be entrusted to an officer so distinguished

q Impartial History, &c.

ed; the information was at first received with indifference; but being conveyed to William, he ordered Sir John Lanier to march with five hundred horse, and meet the train. Lanier executed his orders, but not with due alacrity. In the mean time, the artillery advanced within seven miles to the rear of the English camp. The officer who commanded the convoy, apprehending no danger at so small a distance from the army, encamped, loosely on a plain, without precaution or discipline. The main body of the convoy was retired to rest, their horses at grass, their baggage and cannon carelessly disposed, when Sarsefield rushed suddenly upon them, in a moment cut their centinels and waggoners to pieces, fell on the convoy, as they started from their sleep and attempted to regain their horses, and slaughtered or dispersed the whole party. He now collected the connon, carriages, waggons, and ammunition; the cannon he filled with powder, fixing their mouths in the ground, and laying a train to the heap, fired it on his retreat. The hideous explosion announced the success of this enterprize to Lanier and his party; who, when the havock was already over, arrived in view of the enemy's rear, and made a futile attempt to intercept them. Sarsefield was better acquainted with the country, and returned triumphantly to Limerick.

The news of this disaster was received in the English camp with consternation immediately succeeded by clamour and murmuring[r]. It was imputed to the neglect of lord Portland and count Solmes, to the general indifference of the great officers to the king's service, or any other object but their own emolument, and to the secret disaffection of Lanier, who

[r] Impartial History, &c.

who had formerly been a favourite of king James. While the army thus gave vent to their indignation, each agreeably to his paffions and fentiments, William alone maintained that compofure which was unaccountable to his foldiers. They fufpected him of having no real defign to conclude the war, but only to keep the enemy cantoned about Limerick, and to preferve the conquefts he had already made. But it was obvioufly his intereft to complete the reduction of Ireland without delay. Two of his cannon had efcaped uninjured in the general havock, fome others were brought from Waterford. With thefe he furnifhed his batteries, and, after the interruption of a week, renewed his operations with vigour. The befieged, on their part, encouraged by the late fuccefs, animated by their officers, fired with emulation at the brave defence of Derry, and equally inveterate againft their affailants, defended themfelves like men whofe interefts were to be decided by one final effort. Without entering into a minute detail of all the incidents of this fiege, let it be fufficient to obferve, that from the opening of the the trenches on the eighteenth day of Auguft, both the affault and the defence were maintained with vigour; and William, who took an active part in every operation, was frequently expofed to danger; when, on the twenty-feventh, a breach was made twelve yards in length, and the king ordered the counterfcarp, and two towers on each fide of the breach, to be affaulted. Five hundred grenadiers in the fartheft angle of the trenches leaped over, ran towards the counterfcarp, were furioufly oppofed, but, in the midft of a tremendous fire, diflodged the enemy, and purfuing even to the breach, many were actually in the town, while the Irifh ran from the walls in confufion. The regiments appointed to fecond them ftopped

ped at the counterscarp, agreeably to their orders. They, whose ardour had hurried them within the walls, thus found themselves unsupported, their ammunition spent, and the enemy, who discovered their distress, rallying and powering down upon them. They prepared to retreat, but many of them were killed, and almost all wounded. The Irish again marched to the breach, and defended it in a rage of valour. Even their women mingled with the men, encouraged them, advanced before them, defied the besiegers, and assailed them with stones. For three hours a perpetual fire both of great and small arms was maintained on each side. One regiment of Brandenburghers, seized a battery, but the powder catching fire, they were almost all blown into the air. The breach was still obstinately defended; where the walls were entire, the besiegers, who had no scaling-ladders, wasted their fire to no purpose, and were exposed defenceless to all the fury of the enemy. Five hundred of their numbers were slain, and more than one thousand desperately wounded, when William at length ordered a retreat. On the succeeding morning, a drummer was sent into the town to demand a truce for the purpose of burying the dead; but the governour haughtily refused it. The English army, still undismayed, was impatient for another assault. But a disappointment so severe in an advanced season, when heavy rains were expected, which might render the roads impassable to the artillery, determined the king to raise the siege: He ordered the batteries to be disarmed; and his forces, drawn gradually off, retired by slow marches without any molestation from the garrison. Here too, as at Athlone, the army was attended by a melancholy troop of protestants, who dreaded the fury of an exulting enemy, and followed the camp with

so

so much of their effects as they could carry with them, without abode or settlement to shelter themselves and their children, and without any security from the indiscriminate ravages of the soldiery.

The friends of William describe him as supporting this defeat with astonishing composure and serenity; his enemies insist, that he was transported by his vexation even to the excesses of savage barbarity [f]. We are told, that to free himself from the incumbrance of his sick and wounded, the houses in which they lay were set on fire; but unfortunately for this insolent defiance of truth, his sick and wounded had no houses to shelter them, and were indeed carefully conveyed to Cathel and Clonmel [t]. Again, we are assured, that William on his retreat was asked what should be done with his prisoners? that he answered peevishly, " Burn them !" and that his orders were literally obeyed, and one thousand destroyed by fire. Such enormous and ridiculous falsehoods appear scarcely calculated to impose even on the vulgar and ignorant; yet the zealous impugners of heresy have found their account, it seems, in propagating and transmitting them.

Here was the period of William's personal enterprises in Ireland. While his army lay at Clonmel, he proceeded to Waterford, and with prince George, the duke of Ormond, and other attendants, embarked at Duncannon fort [u], leaving the command of his forces to count Solmes and Ginckle, and committing his civil government to two lords justices, lord Sydney and Thomas Coningsby, with a blank in their commission to be filled by a third name.

But

---

[f] Macgeoghan. Dominicana.
[t] Porter, quoted by the author of Hibernia
[u] Harris's Life of K. Wil. Appendix.

But notwithstanding the advanced season, the campaign was not yet ended. The earl of Marlborough had continued unemployed in England; and seems to have become obnoxious to the king, by the part which he and his consort had taken in the quarrel with the princess of Denmark. Impatient of his present inactivity, he formed a project for raising his own character, without being overshadowed by the king's personal interposition, or rivalled by his foreign generals. He represented the importance of Cork and Kinsale, places the most convenient for pouring succours into Ireland from France; and which, if once gained, would enlarge the quarters of the army, secure all the sea-ports from Dublin to the South, and favour the English traffic to the West Indies [w]. All apprehensions from the French navy were dissipated; those of England and Holland were refitted; all internal disorders were allayed; five thousand forces lay in England ready for any service; with these, and such reinforcements as might be spared in Ireland, he engaged to reduce these two towns [x]. The proposal was accepted, and the embarkation prepared at Portsmouth, while William yet lay before Limerick. While men indulged their conjectures, the real object of this expedition remained a profound secret, until it was too late for the enemy to guard against it.

On the twenty-first day of September the earl arrived in Cork-road, drove the enemy from a battery, sent some armed boats to seize their guns, and landed without further opposition. Ginckle, on whom the chief command devolved by the departure of count Solmes, detached Sgravenmore to his assistance
with

[w] Impartial History, &c. [x] Clarke's Correspondence, MS.

with nine hundred cavalry; and these were soon followed by four thousand foot under the prince of Wirtemberg, who expressed an ambition to share in this expedition. The operations of the siege had been already carried on with success when Wirtemberg arrived, and threatened to defeat the whole enterprize. He claimed the chief command by virtue of his superior rank; Marlborough insisted on the priority of his commission; he reminded the prince that his troops were merely auxiliaries, or rather Danish mercenaries, and that he himself led the forces of his own nation. The dispute grew warm and alarming; but, by the interposition of La Mellionere, a prudent French officer, was happily accommodated. The earl was persuaded to share the command with his rival, rather than retard the king's service. He commanded on the first day, and gave for the word, "Wirtemberg." The prince felt the full force of this politeness, and on the next day, when he received the command, the word was, "Marlborough."

The siege was now carried on, but not without some further contest between these generals[y]. The garrison gradually abandoned their outworks; a breach was made in the wall, and the besiegers prepared for an assault. When, for this purpose, they were on the point of crossing a marsh at low water, the governour parleyed, and proposed terms of capitulation. Marlborough, who had now the command, insisted that the garrison should became prisoners of war. Wirtemberg condemned this severity, and contended, that more favourable terms should be granted. The dispute continued until the tide returned, and the water was at the highest. But

[y] Original Letter of Sgravenmore in Clarke's Correspondence, MS.

But now, the governour imagining all danger over, broke off this conference. The generals were provoked at his collusion; the breach was enlarged, and the Dutch and English, encouraged by the duke of Grafton and other volunteers, bravely passed the river, wading to their shoulders, and exposed to the enemy's fire, and posted themselves under the bank of a marsh, which served as a counterscarp to the city wall[z]. Here the duke of Grafton was borne away mortally wounded, the most respected of all the sons of Charles the Second. The soldiers lamented the fate of this gallant lord, but without dismay prepared for a general assault. But now the garrison, whose ammunition was exhausted, renewed their parley, and consented to become prisoners of war, with all their officers, of whom several were of considerable note. The protestant prisoners were set at liberty; the protestant magistrates resumed their offices, and proclaimed the king and queen. All papists were ordered on pain of death to surrender their arms; a precaution absolutely necessary, as there were more than five thousand prisoners in the town.

THE severity of winter was approaching, and not a moment to be lost. On the very day of Marlborough's entry into Cork, a detachment was sent to summon Kinsale[a]. The governour returned a scornful answer, threatening to put the messenger to death. The town itself was scarcely tenable; he, therefore, set it on fire, and placed his reliance on the two forts, the old, or Castle-ny-fort, and the new, which the late duke of Ormond had completed, and called Charles-fort. The first of these was taken after a brave resistance, in which the governour, several officers, and half the garrison were slain. The

[z] Impartial History, &c.   [a] Ibid.

The reduction of Charles-fort appeared of still greater difficulty; and Marlborough could not conceal his disappointment, at finding it so much stronger than he expected. To his summons the governour carelessly replied, that " it would be time enough " to talk on this subject a month hence;" but being vigourously pressed for ten days, when the besiegers were preparing for a general assault, he parleyed and capitulated. In this critical time, when delay might prove fatal to the English forces, he was allowed conditions more favourable than those granted to Cork. The garrison marched out with arms and baggage, and was conducted to Limerick. Thus, in twenty-three days, the earl of Marlborough effected his brave purpose, to the utter mortification of those who had represented the undertaking as injudicious and impracticable. The king did justice to his merit; the people were delighted at the success of their native general.

WHILE the fate of Cork and Kinsale remained yet uncertain [b], Ginckle could by no means venture to dispose his forces in winter quarters, for the enemy was alert and elevated. No sooner had the siege of Limerick been raised, than Boileau retired with his French troops, and joined his countrymen who were recalled, in consequence of the shameful representations of Irish cowardice made by James, and still waited at Galway for transports. The Irish were by no means mortified at their departure. The superiority which these foreigners affected to assume, the partiality which James had discovered to his French auxiliaries, and the preference given to their officers in all promotions, disgusted and exasperated the natives [c]. The French spoke with contempt of the meanness of the Irish; the Irish affected

---

[b] Impartial History, &c.   [c] Walker's Diary.

to ridicule the pomp and pageantry of the French. They cursed those proud fellows who strutted in their " leathern trunks," so they called their great boots, and lamented that they were ever preferred to their own brave countrymen. Hence arose frequent broils and quarrels; and now the separation was equally agreeable to both parties. The Irish were left to the command of Sarsefield, their countryman, so distinguished by his valour, and so popular by his late success. They resolved to exert their native strength with double vigour [d]; and, transported by their victorious defence of Limerick, talked wildly of crossing the Shannon, piercing through Leinster, and setting fire to the capital. Their necessities might drive them to some desperate excursions; Ginckle, therefore, still kept his forces posted in different parts about the Shannon, ready to embody, and to oppose any sudden attempts. But, on the reduction of Cork and Kinsale, the general, conceiving that the ardour of the enemy must be abated, ventured to withdraw his troops into winter-quarters.

He soon found reason to regret that he had not so formed his frontier line as to secure the passes and castles along the Shannon. The Irish, inured to the severity of winter [e], acquainted with every road, urged by necessity, heated with animosity, made their excursions with success, surprised his smaller parties, ravaged, plundered, set houses and villages in flames, and spread a general terrour and consternation. The miserable inhabitants, of whatever party or denomination, fled from the outrages of the soldiery to their respective friends, but found no security or protection. The contending armies were equally

[d] Impartial History, &c.   [e] Ibid.

equally distressed; and soldiers, unpaid and unprovided, spurned at all discipline with impunity, and supplied their wants by violence, without distinction of parties, and without regard to formal protections, or the faith of promises. To aggravate the distresses arising from a rapacious soldiery, the country swarmed every where with robbers and murderers, who lived in a state of savage nature, unrestrained by the laws of peace or war. The northern province had from the earliest times harboured a particular species of Irish called Creaghts, who issued from their retreats with their wives, children, and cattle, roved in search of subsistence, without any certain abode or destination, and plundering every district which they visited, were dreaded and detested by their countrymen. In the civil war commenced in sixteen hundred and forty-one, we have seen them particularly active, and forming the army of Owen O'Nial: nor had they been entirely suppressed on the conclusion of this war; but, during the reign of Charles the Second, continued their depredations: and, under the name of Tories, became a peculiar object of the attention of government. They seized the occasion of present disorders; and when, at every mass, the priests exhorted all men to take arms, and stand prepared for war, they multiplied, and were soon distinguished by the title of * RAPPAREES,

from

---

* A LATE ingenious writer ascribes the outrages of these men to the ease with which they procured subsistence, and resolves their manners into their diet, which, he ventures to assert, consisted of potatoes alone. I am obliged to observe, in justification of my own account, that they were really driven to their excursions by necessity; that the Creaghts, whom all the narrators and the Gazettes of these times speak of as synonimous with Rapparees, fed on the milk of their kine, and wandered to find pasture; that this species of rovers, who now proved so offensive, existed, lived by rapine, and were abhorred by their own countrymen, long before the potatoe was known in Ireland; and that neither at this time, nor for some years after the Revolution, were potatoes the general diet of Irish peasantry.

from the Irish name of their half-pike, a weapon easily procured by the most barbarous. Many were influenced by example, and many driven by necessity to unite with them. They, who received protections from William's generals, and were yet plundered by his soldiers, ran with particular animosity to swell the numbers of these ravagers. In summer they hung about the English camp; every straggling soldier they killed, even for the sake of his arms or cloathing; and, in the rage of national hatred, frequently mangled his dead body. In winter, they appeared in the different quarters with all the marks of humility and abasement. Their weapons were carefully concealed, but lay ready for execution. They assembled in the dead of night in solitary places, projected their excursions, rushed suddenly on their prey, vanished at the first appearance of opposition, and were again readily collected. Through the whole dreary season of the year, the English forces were every where harrassed in pursuit of these miscreants. The Irish soldiers were frequently permitted to join their troops, and to share and encourage their disorders; the English frequently found it necessary to repel them by another body of maurauders of their own party, who were called Protestant Rapparees.

To give some check to such hideous aggravations of the calamities of war[f], the new lords justices at Dublin laboured to give form to the civil government. All indictments of high-treason were removed to the superiour courts, now furnished with judges. Lords lieutenant, and deputy lieutenants, were appointed in the several counties, subject to the English power; commissions granted to the officers of

[f] Impartial History, &c.

of the militia, who were armed, in order to defend their properties, and a privy council conftituted of fuch men as were efteemed moft attached to the new government. The commiffion of forfeitures, found of prejudice to the fubjects, and of little advantage to the crown, was fuperfeded; a variety of proclamations publifhed, to regulate trade and commerce, to reftrain the difaffected, and to promote the public peace. With a particular, and perhaps a neceffary feverity, it was ordained, that papifts of every county fhould be refponfible for the ravages committed by thofe of their communion; and that where any number of rapparees were collected, no popifh prieft fhould be fuffered to recide. Some weak attempts were made to correct the diforders of the army; but the officers treated the civil power with difregard; the foldiers acknowledged no fuperiours but their officers; the foreigners knew no diftinction between the different inhabitants of Ireland; the people exclaimed in the bitternefs of grief, that the army were worfe than rapparees; yet they had the candour to acknowledge, that the Dutch were honourably diftinguifhed by an inoffenfive modefty.

NOTHING but a general reduction and fettlement of the kingdom could end thofe calamities which Ireland had experienced for ages *j*, with little interruption, and which now oppreffed the nation. But feveral officers of William's army were fufpected of fecret reluctance to a final decifion of the prefent war, which might call them from Ireland to a feverer fervice, and againft an enemy more dangerous than the Irifh had as yet appeared. Several of his privy counfellors alfo, were faid to be equally averfe to fuch extenfive offers of pardon as might
break

j Impartial Hiftory, &c.

break the power of the enemy, by inducing numbers to lay down their arms. It was ever the private interest of officers of state, and the great English settlers in this kingdom, that rebels should be exterminated rather than reconciled. Ginckle, indeed, was possessed with more liberal sentiments, both as to a vigourous prosecution of the war, and the indulgence due to those who might be inclined to submission. Winter did not pass, without several skirmishes between the troops of each army, and almost perpetual action between the militia and the rapparees [h]. The general projected an incursion into Kerry, a country over-run with Irish, and which supplied their army with many necessaries. The possession of this part of Ireland was deemed of such consequence, that great preparations were made for the expedition; and Shovel, now on the coast, was directed by the lords justices to attend the orders of Ginckle with his fleet. The general, on this occasion, made pressing instances to be furnished with a declaration of pardon to repenting rebels. But this was not agreeable to the sentiments of the privy council. The justices hesitated; they required that overtures of submission should first be made by considerable bodies of the enemy: they pleaded their limited instructions, and that the letter of lord Nottingham, which directed them to treat with rebels, did not authorise them to publish a declaration so extensive as was required; they expressed their desire, that Ginckle should publish offers of pardon in his own name, and promised to ratify them at any hazard, should they be found absolutely necessary for the service. This reluctance and hesitation, which proceeded from a fear of disobliging some powerful members of the privy council, was,

[h] Clarke's Correspondence, MS.

was of the less consequence at present, as the general found it impracticable to penetrate into Kerry through broken roads, and in a dreary season.

The enemy, on their part[i], made several efforts to break in upon the English frontier. A magazine of forage was provided at Athlone for five thousand horse and dragoons for ten days, which indicated some design of more than ordinary moment. It soon appeared[k], that the enemy intended to attack the English garrison at Molingar; and for this purpose they were now employed in fortifying Bellymore, a little town between this garrison and Athlone. The garrison was reinforced; and Ginckle himself arrived at Molingar, and led about two thousand foot and one thousand horse against a considerable body of the enemy, encamped near Ballymore[l]. They drew up with an appearance of resolution. The pass which they occupied was secured by palisadoes; but the Irish, in their ignorance and precipitation, pointed the palisadoes inward towards themselves, so as to secure, instead of restraining the enemy. They were quickly put to flight, and pursued to a place called the Moat of Grenoge, from which the skirmish took its name; here they again drew up, but were driven into the town, where they attempted to entrench themselves, but soon abandoned the design, and fled finally to Athlone, in the utmost consternation. In this action the Irish lost about three hundred men, and several officers; with their baggage, a quantity of arms, and five hundred horses; and so great was the terrour and confusion at Athlone, that the gates were shut against the fugitives,

---

i Clarke's Correspondence, MS. k Impartial History, &c.
l Pultney's Letter in Tindal's Continuation.

gitives, of whom many fled for shelter to the bogs, and many perished in the river.

This action was of the greater consequence[m], as it defeated a design on the English garrisons, which might have proved fatal to the operations of the ensuing campaign, and as it damped the spirits of the Irish, a people violently affected either with good or bad fortune, and encreased the confusion now subsisting in their councils. Tyrconnel had been sent to France to solicit succours, and returned with a miserable pittance of eight thousand pounds, and some cloathing, wretchedly insufficient. The money was distributed as a donation among the soldiers, but could not allay their discontents and their suspicions of the insincerity of France. Tyrconnel himself appeared gloomy and desponding; he had served his master without conscience, and was now disgraced without reason. James committed the administration of his civil affairs to Sir Richard Nagle and Sir Stephen Rice; and, as Tyrconnel declared for moderate measures, and for securing the remains of the nation by a submission, he was accused of treachery. To this it was imputed, that in France he had recommended to send officers, stores, and provisions to Ireland, without any troops. Sarsefield, whose military genius determined him to seek security in arms, and rather to die bravely in the field than to abandon the cause in which he was engaged, opposed the temporizing councils of Tyrconnel. The officers who declared for war reviled and insulted him. They still flattered their followers with hopes of assistance from France; that Louis would speedily send his triumphant navy against Cork and Kinsale; that

arms,

[m] Impartial History, &c. Clarke's Correspondence, MS.

arms, cloaths, and other neceffaries, for twenty-five thoufand men, were every day expected; that England was ftill difcontented, fecret defigns ftill formed in favour of James, and that the weaknefs of government was evidently manifefted in the diftreffes to which the Englifh forces in Ireland were abandoned. Some French officers gradually arrived, and repeated the affurances of fpeedy fuccours [n]. At length monfieur Saint-Ruth, a man who boafted his fervice againft the heretics of France, and had lately the honour of reducing Savoy, landed at Limerick with a commiffion of chief commander. Sarfefield was juftly difcontented; nor could the title of earl of Lucan, which he received from James, reconcile him to this unneceffary and unreafonable partiality to a foreigner. Saint-Ruth, who was not fupplied with thofe vaft ftores which the Irifh had expected, refolved on a defenfive war, ordered the towns on the Irifh fide of the Shannon to be ftrengthened, and with the main army took his ftation behind Athlone.

Ginckle, on his part [o], had been confiderably retarded by the want of money, provifions, and other neceffaries. Thefe were, however, gradually fupplied, new reinforcements arrived from England: and while the lords juftices iffued fuch orders to the militia, as might fecure the exteriour quarters of the kingdom, the army affembled at Molingar, as it was refolved to open the campaign by the fiege of Athlone. Ginckle was attended by a number of gallant officers, fired with emulation, and tenacious of the honour of their refpective countries, the princes of Wirtemberg and Heffe-Darmftadt, Talmafh, the Englifh general, Mackay the brave Scot, who had reduced

[n] A. D. 1691.   [o] Clarke's Correfpondence, MS.

reduced the Highlanders, Sgravenmore, La Melloniere and Rouvigny, Tetteau the Dane, the Dutch count Naſſau, all already diſtinguiſhed in the Iriſh war. A conſiderable train of artillery arrived from Dublin; but the army, when collected, was inferiour to that of the enemy; a defect abundantly ſupplied by the confidence of the men, and the gallantry and experience of their officers.

THE campaign opened auſpiciouſly by the reduction of the fort of Ballymore[p], which the enemy encouraged by the convenience and natural ſtrength of the place, had fortified in the winter, and occupied with a thouſand of their choiceſt forces. No attempt was made either to relieve or to abandon this place. The governour was threatened with military execution, if he did not ſurrender within two hours. He demanded to march out with the honours of war; and, when this was denied, ſuſtained the attack for one day; but, at the ſight of ſome armed boats, launched on the lake which encompaſſed the defenceleſs ſide of the Iſland on which his fort was built, he and his garriſon cried for mercy, and were admitted priſoners of war. As the place lay convenient for maintaining a communication between Athlone, Molingar, and Dublin, Ginckle ordered the breaches to be repaired, and additional fortifications to be made; nor did he march forward until theſe works were finiſhed, and an Engliſh garriſon ſtationed in the fort.

ON the eighteenth day of June[q], the general advanced with a party of horſe, within a few miles of Athlone, and from an eminence ſurveyed the town, and the ſituation of the Iriſh army, which lay encamped

[p] Story's Wars of Ireland.   [q] Ibid.

camped on a neck of land between two bogs, at a distance of two miles from the Shannon. The next day his army was in motion through lanes lined with Irish infantry, who gradually retired at the approach of their enemy; and, as if they had been stationed as guides to lead them forward by the nearest ways, poured into the English district of Athlone. Here, though the houses had been laid in ruins, yet Douglas, in his expedition of last year, had not found time to demolish the walls. These were repaired and strengthened, and the enemy seemed resolved to defend both sides of the river. A battery of ten guns soon made a considerable breach, and orders were given for the assault. The enemy defended the breach; but, after some loss on each side, were driven to the bridge, (by this time repaired) and ran with such confusion into the Irish town, that many were crushed to death, and many plunged into the river from the battlements, and perished. But now the assailants, in the ardour of their success, found new difficulties to encounter. The arch of the bridge nearest to the Irish town was again broken. The enemy lay entrenched on the other side, and from their works fired furiously on the English district. The ford between the two towns was deep, narrow, and stony. At another place towards Lanesborough, he formed a scheme for passing by a bridge of pontons; but the enemy discovered the design, and guarded the pass. Ginckle now saw no means of forcing his way but by the bridge: here, while his batteries and mortars played incessantly, he carried on a wooden-work for the purpose of throwing planks over the broken arch. Though his workmen were by no means sheltered from the batteries of the enemy, they had almost completed their design, when a serjeant and ten men

in

in armour rushed from the opposite side, attempted to destroy their works, and were all slain. Another party repeated the desperate attack, and with more success; they resolutely cast down the beams and planks into the river, and two survivours returned in triumph.

The general, not yet disconcerted, made another effort to force a passage to the town^r, and carried on his works by a close gallery on the broken arch, which was soon completed; and now, after an obstinante contest of nine days, when several breaches had been made both in the walls and the castle, it was resolved in a council of war, to pass the Shannon by three different ways. One party was appointed to force the bridge, another to cross the ford below it, and a third to pass by floats and pontons about nine hundred feet farther. In the morning, when this bold effort was to be made, and the army stood ready to be commanded, the pontons were not prepared without some delay, the Irish were informed by deserters of the intended enterprize, and their troops were seen marching in great numbers from their camp into the town. The besiegers still persevered; money was distributed among the soldiers to animate them in an attempt of so much danger; the choicest of the Irish forces were drawn to the works, and on each side all was anxiety and agitation; when, in this moment of suspence, the enemy's granadoes set fire to some fascines on the broken arch; the flames quickly caught the gallery; the fire and smoak were blown into the faces of the besiegers with insupportable violence; nor could they prevent the utter destruction of that part of their gallery which extended towards the enemy. The attack

---

r Story's Wars of Ireland.

attack was countermanded; the Irish exulted; and Saint Ruth expressed his confidence in the security of Athlone, by inviting a number of gentlemen and ladies to his camp, and entertaining them with all the ease and elegance suited to a time of perfect peace.

IT was now expected that the siege must be immediately raised; and the English, by drawing off some of of their cannon, seemed to countenance such expectations. Ginckle, without delay, convened another council, in which it was warmly debated whether the besiegers were to retire, or still to attempt the passage of the Shannon. To remain for any time in their present situation was impossible, as the forage was destroyed for several miles; to retire before an exulting enemy was inconvenient and dispiriting, might open them a way to the very walls of Dublin, might force the army back to the northern province, and confine them to a defensive war. On the other hand, the consequences of an unsuccessful attack were evidently fatal, and Ginckle seemed inclined to retire [f]. The duke of Wirtemberg, and other general officers, contended, that no brave action could be performed without hazard; that on all great attempts they had hitherto experienced the undaunted bravery of their own troops, and the inferiority of the enemy. They reminded Ginckle that the passage by the ford was not so dangerous as they had at first imagined, that three Danish criminals had tried it on promise of their lives, passed and returned [t], and thus pointed out the way to victory [u]. Mackay, the Scottish general alone, in the caution and positiveness of age, opposed the design, and from the

[f] Story's Wars of Ireland.   [t] Dalrymple, from MS.
[u] Memoirs of Mackay,

the beginning declared against attempting to pass the river in the face of a town and an army*. The others thought only of the glory attending such a daring enterprize, and each contended for the honour of leading on the troops. Ginckle gave such a degree of opposition as might increase their ardour, and engage their pride, in the success of a design in which they had borne down the opinion of their general; and it was finally resolved to attempt the passage on the next morning. To encourage the English forces, they were assured by deserters, that Saint-Ruth, in full confidence that the siege must be immediately raised, had detached three of his worst regiments to man the works; and, to enflame their pride, the Irish all night insulted them from the opposite banks of the river, and exclaimed in derision, " that they had but ill earned the money " yesterday distributed by their officers.

IN the rotation of duty, the command of the passage devolved on Mackay [w]: but Ginckle, unwilling to entrust it to the officer who alone had declared against the attempt, consigned it to Talmash; Mackay

---

* In some circumstances of this siege I deemed it necessary to follow Sir John Dalrymple, who professes to write from MS. memoirs of general Mackay. Such memoirs, if written by the general, or under his direction, are of undoubted authority with respect to the operations, in which he took so considerable a part: in other particulars their authority may be fairly contested. For instance, we are told, from these memoirs, that on the first repulse of the English, and the burning of their works, when Saint-Ruth expected that the siege must be raised, a sudden pannic seized the protestants of Ireland, and the citizens of Dublin barricaded all the avenues of the city. Now, it evidently appears from the original correspondence between the lords justices at Dublin and the English camp, that this event was not known in the capital until intelligence was received of the taking of Athlone on the succeeding morning: nor was it possible indeed, that in so short an interval it could have been conveyed through the different parts of Ireland, so as to have any extensive influence on the protestant party.

w Dalrymple, from MS. Memoirs of Mackay.

Mackay complained of this indignity; the English general modestly relinquished his pretensions, entreating permission to attend as a volunteer. That the enemy might not be alarmed by any extraordinary commotion in the camp, or the English town, it was resolved to make the attack at the ordinary hour of relieving the guards [x], when a double garrison might appear without notice or suspicion. Two thousand men were appointed for this service; and, at the signal given, by tolling the church bell, their advanced guard boldly entered the river [y], amidst the acclamations of their companions. Mackay, their commander, waded by the side of his men; he was followed by La Melloniere, Tetteau, the prince of Hesse, and other officers; Talmash attended as a volunteer, encouraging the men. Wirtemberg, having his horse shot under him, was conveyed through the river on the shoulders of his grenadiers. The English from their works and batteries, fired furiously upon the enemy; the enemy with equal fury thundered on those who were passing the ford; but the detachment advanced intrepidly through fire and smoak, gained the opposite banks, and mounted the breaches next the river. Some flew to the assistance of their friends, who were laying planks over the broken bridge, others to support the pontons, while the Irish fled with astonishment to their camp, and not without considerable slaughter. Thus, by a surprising effort of valour, the English gained the town, and possessed the works which remained entire towards the enemy's camp, within half an hour from their first entrance of the river.

On this occasion Saint-Ruth betrayed a carlessness

[x] Story. [y] Dalrymple; from Mackay's Memoirs. Story.

ness and confidence utterly unworthy of a commander[z]. On receiving the first intelligence that the enemy were passing the ford, he exclaimed that it was impossible; that they could not presume to attempt the town while he and his army lay so near. Sarsefield replied calmly, that he knew the enterprize was not too difficult for English courage, and pressed him to send speedy succours. The Frenchman was offended; Sarsefield retorted his disdain; when a messenger in breathless consternation just found words to inform them that the enemy were in the town. Saint-Ruth dissembling his vexation, proudly commanded that they should be driven out again; and some fruitless efforts were made for this purpose. But now the English possessed the works opposite to his camp, and pointed their own cannon against the enemy. Saint-Ruth retired in vexation; the French officers exclaiming against the Irish, the Irish execrating their French general and his countrymen. The castle of Athlone followed the fate of the town; the governour and five hundred men were here made prisoners of war; and twelve hundred more of the enemy's numbers were either slain or taken during the course of the siege.

SAINT-RUTH had hitherto[a], it is said, flattered himself with hopes of reducing Ireland to the dominion of the French monarch. He solicited the Irish to swear allegiance to his master; all orders were issued in the name, not of James, but of Louis[q]. Such, at least, was the intelligence given by deserters; and, to confirm it, the English, saw with surprize, the standards of France waving in the town of Athlone. The reduction of this place, in view of this general

---

[z] Story.   [a] Story. London Gazette.
[q] Narrative of the progress of General Ginckle. 4to. Lond. 1691.

general and his army, was a dreadful mortification to his hopes, and such a diminution of his character, as required some immediate effort to redeem it. Those of the Irish who inclined to the French interest, were still amused with expectations of powerful succours, and still implicitly obedient to Saint-Ruth. They, who had bravely sustained the fury of battle, imputed their late misfortune to the weakness and inexperience of their associates, and still entertained hopes of better success, when their men should be more inured to danger, and their general less confident and more cautious. They, who had fled in the hour of trial, were stung with reproach, and impatient for an occasion to retrieve their honour. They, who were most affected with the neglect and insincerity of the French king, who espoused the cause of James from principle, who had fought for the freedom of their religion, or the recovery of what they called their property, reflected seriously on the alarming situation of their party. They knew the real power of English government; they had no hopes of pardon, no prospect of subsisting but by some desperate exertion of valour[c]. "It is your fault," said their prisoners to the English officers, "that you have so many enemies. We "are sensible of our unhappiness in depending on "the French; but you have made it necessary for "us; we must, and will, and are preparing to fight "it out." Thus, the whole Irish party, with different views, and from various motives, concurred in the resolution of bringing their long-protracted contest to a final decision in the field.

The English general, on his part, had experienced the inconveniences of war in an exhausted country

[c] Clarke's Correspondence, MS.

country irregularly and scantily supplied from England, and was equally impatient for an immediate decision. He was now employed in repairing the fortifications of Athlone; and, before he advanced in search of the enemy, it was deemed highly necessary to publish such a proclamation, and encouragement to those who should submit, as might break the force of the enemy, and possibly prevent the necessity of an engagement. But here the great English subjects of Ireland interposed, and laboured to defeat any accommodation with the Irish [d]. " I " did very much hope," said the secretary of the lords justices in a letter to Ginckle, " that, upon this " progress over the Shannon, some favourable de- " claration might have been emitted to break the " Irish army, and save the expence of a field battle. " But I see our civil officers regard more adding fif- " ty pounds a year to the English interest in this " kingdom, than saving England the expence of " fifty thousand. I promise myself it is for the " king's, the allies, and England's interest, to re- " mit most or all of the forfeitures, so that we could " immediately bring the kingdom under their ma- " jesties obedience." Ginckle was so possessed with the necessity of a proclamation of pardon, that he published one on the fifth day of July, which the justices, in deference to the privy counsellors, seemed inclined to disavow; but the propriety of this measure was so evident, and the occasion so pressing, that in two days after a proclamation was formally signed and published by government, offering a free pardon to all soldiers and officers who should surrender within three weeks, with a reasonable payment for their horses, arms, and furniture; to all governours of garrisons who should surrender their posts; to all officers

[d] Clarke's Correspondence, MS.

officers who should bring with them their regiments, troops, or companies, a free pardon and full possessions of their estates; liberal rewards to those who had no landed property; and to all a free exercise of religion, with such security in this particular as a parliament of Ireland might devise, and which the king would endeavour to procure, so as to convince the Irish of the difference between the blessings of English government and the tyranny of France.

This proclamation, however liberal and extensive, was yet published too late for the desired effect. Some of the Irish sued for protections; and, even of the rapparees, numbers laid down their arms. But Saint-Ruth collected his forces from the several garrisons, posted them advantageously, and resolved to wait the approach of the English; and the great body of his forces was equally determined to set their fortune on one desperate effort. Ginckle was no stranger to their purpose, and to strengthen his army drew off every detachment that could be spared from every English post[e]. The protestants were terrified at the defenceless state to which their districts were thus reduced. Even in the capital, the lords justices were alarmed, and formed a camp of militia to guard against any incursions of the enemy.

The fate of Ireland was now ready to be decided. Whether the English power was to be at length unalterably established in this harrassed country, or whether it was to be once more exposed to the calamities of a tedious intestine war, seemed to depend on the event of a few days, and the minds of all men were of consequence strained to a painful pitch of anxiety

[e] Clarke's Correspondence, MS,

anxiety and expectation [f]. On the tenth day of June Ginckle marched from Athlone, and encamped along the river Suc, in the county of Roscommon, a pass which the Irish might have maintained with advantage; but it soon appeared that they had taken their station to greater advantage, about three miles farther to the south-west. Their camp extended more than two miles along the heights of Kilcommeden, with a rivulet on their left running between hills and morasses, and these again skirted by a large bog, in breadth almost a mile; on the side of which stood the ruins of an old castle, called by the name of the neighbouring village, Aghrim, entrenched and occupied by infantry, and commanding the only pass on that side to the Irish camp. All along the front, at a distance of about half a mile from their encampment, the bog extended to their right, where was another pass through a range of small hills opening into wider ground. The slope of Kilcommeden, even to the edge of the bog, was intersected by hedges and ditches communicating with each other, and lined with Irish musketeers. Ginckle with eighteen thousand men, was now to attack an enemy amounting to twenty-five thousand, thus posted, and who wanted only an additional number of cannon to take full advantage of their situation. Saint-Ruth, from his eminence, had a full view of the motions of the English; he saw them cross the river and prepare to give him battle; he drew out his main army in front of his camp. He rode to every squadron and battalion; he reminded the Irish officers, that their future fortune depended on the issue of one encounter; that they were now to fight for their honours, their liberty and their estates; that they were now to establish their religion, for which he himself

[f] Story.

himself had displayed an extraordinary zeal, on such a firm basis, as the powers of hell and heresy should never shake; that the dearest interests and most honourable engagements of this life, and the ravishing prospects of eternal happiness called for a vigorous exertion of that valour which their enemies affected to deny them. The priests ran through the ranks, labouring to inspire the soldiers with the same sentiments; and, we are told, obliged them to swear on the sacrament, that they would not desert their colours.

On the twelfth day of July at noon[g], (for the fogs of the morning had hitherto prevented them) the English advanced in as good order as their broken and uneven ground would admit. It was, in the first place, deemed necessary to gain the pass to the right of the enemy. A small party of Danes, sent to force it, fled instantly at the appearance of a still smaller party of the enemy. Some English dragoons were next employed, were boldly opposed, were sustained by other bodies; the enemy retreated; as the assailants pressed forward, they found themselves encountered by new parties; but, after an obstinate contest of an hour, they forced their way beyond the bog; nor possibly was Saint-Ruth displeas'd to have an opportunity of fighting one wing of the English separately, in a place where, if defeated, their retreat must prove fatal. The skirmish served to convince Ginckle both of the spirit and of the advantages of the enemy. It was now debated whether the battle should not be deferred to the next morning; and, with difficulty, resolved, to prevent the enemy from decamping in the night, and prolonging the war, by an immediate renewal of the engagement. By the advice of general Mackay,

it

[g] Story.

it was resolved to begin the attack on the enemy's right wing, which would oblige Saint-Ruth to draw off some forces from his left, so that the passage by Aghrim castle would be rendered less dangerous for the English horse, and the whole army be enabled to engage. About the hour of five in the evening, the left wing of the English, both horse and foot, advanced boldly against the enemy, who obstinately maintained their posts. The musqueteers, supported by their cavalry, received and returned the English fire, defending their ditches until the musquets of each side closed with the other; then retiring by their lines of communication, flanked their assailants, and charged them with double fury. The engagement was thus continued for one hour and a half, when Saint-Ruth, as was foreseen, found it necessary to draw a considerable part of the cavalry from his left to support his right wing. Mackay seized the favourable moment, and, while the cavalry were in motion to gain the pass by Aghrim castle, several regiments of infantry in the centre were ordered to march through the bog extending along their front, and to post themselves on the lowest ditches, until the horse should gain the passage, and wheel from the right to support their charge. The infantry plunged into the bog, and were instantly sunk to their middle in mire and water; they floundered on unmolested, but no sooner had they gained the opposite side than they received a furious fire from the hedges and trenches occupied by the enemy. They advanced still undismayed; the Irish retired on purpose to draw them forward; transported with ardour, they forgot their orders, and pursued almost to the main battle of the Irish. Both horse and foot now poured down upon them, assailed them in front, in flank, forced them

from

from their ground, drove some of them back into the bog, pursued them with slaughter, took several prisoners of note; while Saint-Ruth exclaimed in an extacy of joy, "Now will I drive the English to the very walls of Dublin."

His attention was soon diverted to the English cavalry on his left, commanded by Talmash[h], who seeing the alarming disorder of the centre, pushed with incredible ardour close by the walls of the castle, through all the fire of the enemy, forcing their way through a narrow and dangerous pass, to the amazement of Saint-Ruth, who asked what the English meant? "To force their way to our left," replied his officers, "They are brave fellows!" said the general, "it is pity they should be so exposed."

Mackay, Talmash, Rouvigny, now gradually pressed forward from the right[i], bearing down all opposition; the infantry of the centre rallied, advanced, and regained their former ground; the left wing fought bravely; and was bravely opposed. Saint-Ruth saw that the fortune of the day depended on making an impression on the enemy's cavalry in their rapid progress from the right. He rode down from his station on the hill of Kilcommeden, and, having directed one of his batteries where to point their fire, led a body of horse against them. In this critical moment, a cannon-ball deprived him of life. His body was conveyed away, and the intelligence of his death ran through the lines. His cavalry halted, and, as they had no orders, returned towards their former station. The Irish beheld this retreat with dismay; they were counfounded and disordered; their disorder increased; Sarsefield, on whom

[h] Story. [i] Ibid.

whom the command devolved, had been neglected by the proud Frenchman ever since their altercation at Athlone. As the order of battle had not been imparted to him, he could not support the dispositions of the late general. The English, in the mean time, pressed forward, drove the enemy to their camp, pursued their advantage until the Irish, after an engagement supported with the fairest prospect of success, while they had a general to direct their valour, fled precipitately, the foot to a bog, the horse towards Loughrea.

During the heat of this action[k], some Danish forces stationed at the extremity of the left wing, kept several bodies of the enemy in awe. When they perceived the advantage at length gained by the battalions in the centre, they charged their opponents, to prevent their falling back to the relief of their associates. The Irish received them intrepidly, and continued the contest for some time; but, on the general rout of the army, fled with their countrymen. In the battle, and in a bloody pursuit of three miles, seven thousand of the Irish army were slain. The unrelenting fury of the victors appeared in the number of their prisoners, which amounted only to four hundred and fifty. On their side, seven hundred fell, one thousand were wounded. All the cannon, ammunition, tents, and baggage of the enemy were taken, with a great quantity of small arms, eleven standards, and thirty-two colours destined as a present to the queen. Such was the crowning victory of the English army.

Night put an end to the pursuit, and till morning the victors lay on their arms amidst the heaps of
their

[k] Story.

their slaughtered enemies [l]. After a few days of necessary refreshment to the troops, Ginckle led them through a desolated country to Galway, which he deemed necessary to be reduced, before he should attempt Limerick, the great and final refuge of the Irish. The garrison of Galway consisted of seven weak regiments; but they expected considerable reinforcements [m]. D'Ussone, a French officer of distinction in the town, assured them of succours from his royal master. An Irish partizan, who was known and celebrated by the name of Balderog O'Donnel, promised to march to their relief at the head of six or seven thousand northern rovers; and some assistance was expected from the garrison of Limerick. With such hopes, lord Dillon, the governour, returned a defiance to the summons of Ginckle, and declared, that he, D'Ussone, and all his officers were unanimous in their resolution of defending the town. But, after a resistance of a few days, it was found that the attempt, made to throw some troops into the town from Limerick, was frustrated by the vigilance and bravery of the besiegers; that O'Donnel's followers, alarmed at the defeat of Aghrim, had deserted him with the usual instability of the Old Irish; and that he, with the remains of his wild troop, amounting to six hundred, was preparing to make terms with English Government [n]. The townsmen and magistracy declared warmly for surrendering, and, although they were at first imprisoned for their presumption, yet the garrison quickly adopted the same sentiments. The Irish had been busily employed in finishing a fort to the south-east of the town, which commanded a great part of the wall on that side. A detachment crossed the river, and, conducted

[l] Story.   [m] Clarke's Correspondence, MS.   [n] Story.

conducted by a deserter, surprised and seized the fort. The governour parleyed, a cessation was granted, and a treaty of capitulation commenced. Talmash, and other officers, elevated by success, were utterly averse to granting any terms. But Ginckle wisely considered that the season of action was gradually wasting; that the Irish war was a grievous embarrassment to the continental interests of the king, and a dangerous encouragement to the disaffected in England. William he knew, was impatient to be freed from an oppressive and vexatious burden. To prevent another year of bloodshed in a country already wasted by distress, to extricate the king at once from difficulties grievous and dangerous, he resolved to grant such conditions to Galway, as might convince the whole Irish party of the infatuation of their perseverance in a desperate cause, and dispose them to an immediate submission. The garrison was allowed to march out with all the honours of war, and to be conveyed to Limerick, with liberty to those who desired it to continue in the town, or to repair to their respective habitations. A free pardon was granted to the governour, magistracy, freemen, and inhabitants, with full possession of their estates and liberties under the acts of settlement and explanation. The Romish clergy and laity were allowed the private exercise of their religion, their lawyers to practise, and their estated gentlemen to wear arms. Nor were these favourable terms without their effect; several considerable parties daily revolted from the Irish, and were either entertained in the army on taking the oaths of fidelity to the king and queen, or dismissed peaceably to their habitations, at their own option.

THE capitulation of Galway was considered in England

England as an event immediately to be attended by the final reduction of Ireland[o]. In full assurance that Limerick must surrender, the queen gave orders that a fleet of transports should be prepared, for conveying ten thousand foot, and six hundred horse from Cork and Kinsale to the assistance of her royal consort in Flanders. An interval of one month was happily allowed for this embarkation, and the design was farther postponed until the reduction of Limerick should be effected, an enterprize in which the generals employed in the service of Ireland saw more danger and difficulty than were discovered in the English cabinet. Sarsefield now adventured over the Shannon with all the forces he could collect, amounting to seven thousand, resolving to desolate the country, and threatened the city of Cashel with fire and slaughter: and, although he was soon obliged to retire, as the garrison of Cashel was reinforced, and the English advanced towards Limerick, yet the Irish spoke with confidence of meeting the enemy, and once more trying their fortune in the field [p]. Ginckle proceeded gradually and cautiously; and as the time limited for the submission of the Irish, by a former proclamation of government, was expired, he enlarged the term by a new declaration, promising pardon and protection, favour and encouragement, to all those, who by a timely submission should contribute to safe the effusion of blood.

THE town to which he approached [q], notwithstanding the apparent resolution of the garrison, was a scene of contention, discord, and suspicion. The French and Irish parties, the moderate and the violent,

[o] Clarke's Correspondence, MS.   [p] Story
[q] Clarke's Correspondence, MS.

lent, those who were for fighting to the last, those who wished to save the remains of their country by submitting, all contended with an acrimony encreased by their misfortunes. Tyrconnel expired in the bitterness of vexation: the vulgar Irish imputed his death to poison, administered by those who detested his moderate counsels; others were confident that he had been tried, condemned, and executed, for a private correspondence with the English. Three new lords justices now assumed the civil government in the name of the abdicated king, Fitton, Nagle, and Plowden; and, like Tyrconnel, declared for submission. Sarsefield was brave, violent, and enterprising, and of consequence averse to all compositions. The French generals expected succours from their own country, and declared for war. Some of the Irish officers had already engaged in a private correspondence with the English, and were solicitous to secure their own particular interests; others, with more generous sentiments, declined any composition which should not include the whole party of Irish catholics. Among these different factions, they, who favoured the French interest, and contended for a vigourous prosecution of war, were encouraged by new intellligence of twenty ships of war speedily to arrive, under the command of monsieur Chateau-Renault, and for the present became predominant. Nor were the English less divided in sentiments, some condemned all overtures made to the enemy; others with more condescension to the king's views, were for terminating the war on any terms, some advanced to Limerick in full confidence of success; others, recollecting the misfortune of the former attempt on this town, desponded, and proposed to fortify Loughrea, and other places, so

as

as to secure good winter quarters in case of any disappointment or delay.

The memory of the former siege seems to have made a deep impression on Ginckle[r]. He strengthened his army by withdrawing every garrison that could be spared; he secured the passes of the Shannon; some English ships lay in this river, under the command of captain Cole, to favour his operations; sir Ralph Delaval cruised off Cape Clear, to intercept the French succours. Some Irish garrisons were reduced which threatened to interrupt the communication between the camp and Kerry; a district reserved for his winter quarters, and in which extraordinary efforts were made to suppress the Irish party. His artillery was brought up under a strong escort, with every possible precaution. The government at Dublin were alarmed at his delays; they dreaded the approach of winter, and the arrival of the French fleet; they urged the general to make some resolute attempt without delay. But the general knew his own strength, the advantages of the enemy, the danger and the fatal consequences of a repulse. He contented himself with ordering Cole to burn the country and destroy the forage on the Clare side of the Shannon, the district on which the besieged depended for support.

By this time Ginckle was seated before the town, to which he advanced on the twenty-fifth day of August[s]. His approaches were made in the same manner as in the former siege. The Irish seemed determined against trying their fortune without the walls; and, after a feeble resistance, abandoned Ireton's, Cromwell's, and some other forts to the besiegers.

[r] Clarke's Correspondence, MS.   [s] Story.

besiegers. Every precaution was now taken for the security of their camp; and for several days their cannon and mortars played furiously upon the Irish town, which lay on the same side of the river with the besiegers. The houses were in flames, the inhabitants terrified, and, removing from the danger, formed a sort of camp to the north-east, where they hoped to lie secure from the enemy on the other side of the river. New batteries were raised against the English town. But it seemed of little advantage to the besiegers to set fire to houses abandoned by the inhabitants, and plundered by the soldiers, or to make breaches in the walls which they could not venture to storm, as the garrison was healthy; well supplied, and in numbers equal to their assailants. The only effectual means of reducing the town was to invest it on all parts, by gaining the opposite side of the river, and to cut off the garrison from all intercourse with the county of Clare, by commanding the bridge which opened to this quarter, and was called Thommond-bridge. It was resolved to make a bold effort to gain the other side of the river. To conceal the design, Ginckle gave such orders as indicated a purpose of raising the siege. The Irish saw his batteries dismounted with shouts of joy, and, lulled as they were in perfect security, never once suspected any danger, until a bridge of tin boats was almost completed in the darkness of night. A considerable body of forces was thus conveyed into an island, from which the river was fordable to the main land. Four regiments of Irish dragoons, commanded by an officer of the name of Clifford,* were

---

* The vulgar malice of the Irish propagated a report, that colonel Henry Lutterel commanded at this post, and treacherously betrayed it to the enemy. This report has been adopted by some precipitate writers of memoirs, and Lutterrel was unjustly and fatally pursued by popular odium.

were posted near the passage. Clifford was of the number of those who contended for a timely submission, and not displeased that the garrison should be so pressed as to force them into such a measure. To this it is imputed, that he suffered the English troops to pass gradually over, scarcely with the shew of resistance. The Irish horse, in their encampment, now heard of the enemy's passage with astonishment; the inhabitants, who lay near them, were in confusion; some prepared to seek security in the mountains, others ran for shelter to the town, but were refused admittance. In this uproar and confusion several were killed, and the slaughter must have been greater, had not the English forces been restrained from pursuing by their general, who apprehended an ambuscade.

Notwithstanding this success, it was debated whether the siege should be carried on, or converted into a blockade; such were the difficulties foreseen in reducing the town. Though the besiegers had made a lodgment on the other side of the Shannon, though their pontons were secured by a fort, yet the King's-Island, as it was called, which lay northward of the English town, was still in possession of the enemy; its soil low and marshy, the season far spent, and little hope of success, unless this important post could be secured. Ginckle, who probably

odium. He was indeed of the number of those who saw the folly of an obstinate resistance to the present government, and had contrived to notify his own desire of being reconciled to king William. He had by some means offended Tyrconnel, who procured him to be tried by a court-martial for holding a traiterous correspondence with the enemy. But though the court was formed entirely of Tyrconnel's creatures, yet Lutterel was honourably acquitted. He was, however, still confined in the castle of Limerick, where he lay at the very time when the English passed the river. See lord West-Meath's letter to W. Harris, Life of K. William. Appendix, No. lxii.

† Story.

probably held a secret intelligence with some officers of the garrison, and hoped to prevent the effusion of blood by offers of grace, issued a declaration, promising the garrison and inhabitants of Limerick, who should submit within eight days, pardon for all offences, restitution of their estates, and all other benefits of the proclamation published by the lords justices, from which no act of parliament debarred them, as they were falsely made to believe by those who sacrificed their country to the tyranny and ambition of France. This declaration was not attended by any immediate effects. The counsels of the English general were various and fluctuating; the intelligence of deserters uncertain and contradictory. It was dangerous for the besiegers to continue in their present station on the approach of winter; it was hazardous to divide an army sufficient only for assailing the town on one side. At length, however, it was finally resolved, to lead another body of troops across the river. On the twenty-second day of September, Ginckle, Wirtemberg, Sgravenmore, with a powerful party of both cavalry and infantry, marched over the bridge of boats, animated with intelligence of the reduction of Sligo by the earl of Granard. Their advanced guards were at first repulsed, were sustained, repelled the enemy in their turn; the party still advanced, and about the hour of four in the evening, the grenadiers, supported by four regiments, were ordered to assault the works which covered Thomond-bridge. Here the contest was for some time desperately maintained. The grenadiers were transported by their ardour, and pressed forward, even contrary to orders. The Irish, when pushed from their ground, were reinforced, and renewed the engagement; but through the fire of their musquettry, through the tremendous discharge of their

their cannon, the English forced their way undauntedly, and, at length, by the most obstinate efforts of valour, broke, routed and pursued the enemy. A French major, who commanded at Thomond-bridge, fearing that the grenadiers would enter with his own party, ordered the draw-bridge to be raised, and thus left the fugitives to the mercy of their pursuers. Before the carnage could be stopped, six hundred filled the bridge, even to the battlements, with their carcasses; about an hundred and fifty were forced into the river and perished; one hundred and twenty-six, officers and soldiers, were made prisoners, with an inconsiderable loss on the part of the assailants.

The besiegers now made a lodgment within ten yards of the bridge [u], astonished at their own success, and at a loss to account for the conduct of the enemy, in not hazarding a general engagement when the English forces were divided, rather than suffer the town to be surrounded. But the garrison was by this time weary of the war; the dissensions of their leaders every day encreased; the late behaviour of the French officer at Thomond-bridge, exasperated the whole Irish party; they exclaimed with the utmost virulence against such treacherous allies; they resolved to seek their security in a timely accommodation, before they were reduced to such a state of distress as might cut them off from all hopes of advantageous terms. On the twenty-third day of September, when the garrison had for many hours fired from their batteries with unusual fury, they closed the evening with beating a parley. A cessation was granted, and continued for three days, in order to give time for the horse, (which since the late re-encounter

[u] Story.

counter had encamped at some distance) to take advantage of the capitulation now projected. An amicable intercourse was thus opened between the two armies; but it exhibited a spectable neither honourable to the Irish, nor conciliating to the besiegers. About two hundred and forty English prisoners were led out to be surrendered to their friends. While the inhabitants continued in the town, they had received all charitable relief, particularly from the protestants: but, from the moment of their departure, were abandoned unheeded to disease and famine, and the fire of the besiegers. Thirty of their number had been killed; the survivors tottered feebly on; some fainting on their first exposure to the air; some expiring by the way; some writhing with the torture of wounds never dressed; and all hideous and ghastly. But, however the passions of the soldiers might be enflamed by such an object, Ginckle had urgent directions to terminate the war on any conditions [w]: and, as he sent to the secretary at war on the first parley, for " the king's letter " touching lord Lucan," (so Sarsfield was called by both parties) he was probably instructed to practise with this lord, and, if possible, to entice him to the service of king William.

On the last day of the cessation the Irish leaders offered their terms of a capitulation [x], which was to include the whole body of their party not yet reduced. They required an act of indemnity for all past offences, with a full enjoyment of the estates they possessed before the present revolution; freedom for the Roman catholic worship, with an establishment of one Romish ecclesiastic in each parish. They demanded that Roman catholics should be declared fully

[w] Clarke's Correspondence, MS.

fully qualified for every office, civil and military; that they should be admitted into all corporations; and that the Irish army should be kept up and paid in the same manner with the king's other troops, provided they be willing to serve. Ginckle replied, that stranger as he was to the laws of England, yet he understood that such demands were equally inconsistent with these laws, and with his own honour. In return for the English prisoners, he ordered those of the Irish to be restored, but not in the same wretched condition, for they had been treated with humanity, and their sick and wounded carefully attended. He now gave orders for new batteries, as if resolved to continue the siege.

By a second deputation y, he was desired to propose such terms, on his part, as he could grant. The season was far advanced, the continuance of the siege dangerous, and the event still precarious; he, therefore, made little difficulty to renew the treaty. If the Irish offered terms, not as a conquered people, the general made his propositions as to men who claimed attention and indulgence. He consented that all Irish Roman catholics should enjoy the exercise of their religion, as in the reign of Charles the Second; and promised, that their majesties would endeavour to procure them farther security in this particular, when a parliament could be convened. He engaged that all included in the capitulation should enjoy their estates, and pursue their callings and professions freely, as in the reign of Charles the Second; that their gentry should be allowed the use of arms, and that no oath should be required of any, except the oath of allegiance. Should it still be disagreeable to any of their party to reside in Ireland on these conditions, or should their army chuse

to

h Story.

to engage in any foreign service, he consented that all those of every quality who wished to retire with their families and effects, should have free liberty, and be conveyed to the continent at the expence of government.

Such liberal concessions were mortifying to those Irish who had already submitted on less favourable terms. They were detested by those protestants who lived in an habitual hatred and horrour of the Irish, enflamed by late transactions; they were provoking to those who studied the extension and security of the English interest, or were impatient to enjoy the estates of their enemies. But they were necessary to the king's immediate views and interests; nor is it just to this prince not to allow something to his equity and humanity. He knew the Irish had engaged in the present quarrel not without some plausible and pardonable motives: that they fought for a king of their own religion, by whom they hoped to be restored to those advantages their ancestors had forfeited, or of which they themselves had been deprived in the conflict of parties. The most indifferent and unprincipled among them were necessarily obliged to take some part. Should they oppose the revolution, they were attainted by English government; should they support it, they were at the mercy of the Irish parliament convened by James. In this necessity they were naturally determined to the popish prince, who was for a considerable time acknowledged even by the protestants of Ireland, where the just and generous sentiments of liberty had not been generally imbibed, and where James was present to enforce his authority.

The garrison, on their part, with a secret pride and

and satisfaction, accepted the concessions of Ginckle as the ground of a treaty [z]. Sir Theobald Butler, an acute and artful lawyer of the Irish party, was directed to reduce the several points settled in different conferences to a set of formal articles [a]. Some superiours of the popish clergy were in the town, and attended the progress of the treaty. Probably they conferred privately with Butler; and, without any great violation of charity, we may impute it to their zeal for the catholic cause, as well as to the subtility of their lawyer, that he ventured to insert in his draft many particulars exceeding his instructions. They did not escape the observation of Ginckle [b]; he remonstrated warmly to lord Lucan; and the honour and temper of this lord happily prevented all farther contests. The artcles of capitulation were reduced to the original intention and agreements of the parties. On the first day of October the lords justices arrived in the camp*. On the third the capitulation was finally adjusted and signed, the civil articles by the chief governours, Porter and Coningsby, the military by the general, not many days before a formidable French fleet arrived in the Shannon, with forces [c], arms, and provisions for the relief of Limerick.

It is not the intention of this history to enter into any detail of events subsequent to this important transaction. The war was now concluded, the contest for power finally decided in Ireland, and the authority of the crown of England unalterably established.

APPENDIX.

---

* We are told that they had already prepared a proclamation, offering terms still more advantageous to the Irish than those granted by the general; but, on the first intelligence of a treaty, they suppressed it. Hence it was called the SECRET PROCLAMATION, because, though printed, it was never published. See Harris. Writers of Ireland, in the article Cox.   z Clarke's Correspondence, MS.   a Story
b Clarkes Correspondence, MS.   c Story.

APPENDIX.

The CIVIL and MILITARY ARTICLES of LIMERICK, exactly printed from the Letters Patents; wherein they are ratified and exemplified by their Majesties, under the Great Seal of England.

GULIELMUS & Maria Dei gratia, Angliæ, Scotiæ, Franciæ & Hiberniæ, rex & regina, fidei defensores, &c. Omnibus ad quos præsentes literæ nostræ pervenerint salutem: inspeximus irrotulament. quarund. literarum patentium de confirmatione geren. dat. apud Westmonasterium vicesimo quarto die Februarii, ultimi præteriti in cancellar nostr. irrotulat. ac ibidem de recordo remanen. in hæc verba. William and Mary, by the grace of God, &c. To all to whom these presents shall come, greeting. Whereas certain articles, bearing date the third day of October last past, made and agreed on between our justices of our kingdom of Ireland, and our general of our forces there on the one part: and several officers there, commanding within the city of Limerick, in our said kingdom, on the other part. Whereby our said justices and general did undertake that we should ratify those articles within the space of eight months, or sooner; and to use their utmost endeavours that the same should be ratified and confirmed in parliament. The tenour of which said articles is as follows, viz.

ARTI-

APPENDIX.

ARTICLES agreed upon the third Day of October, One Thousand Six Hundred and Ninety-one.

BETWEEN the Right Honourable Sir Charles Porter, Knight, and Thomas Conningsby, Esq; Lords Justices of Ireland; and his Excellency the Baron de Ginckle, Lieutenant General, and Commander in Chief of the English Army; on the one Part.

AND the Right Honourable Patrick Earl of Lucan, Piercy Viscount Gallmoy, Colonel Nicholas Purcel, Colonel Nicholas Cusack, Sir Toby Butler, Colonel Garret Dillon, and Colonel John Brown; on the other Part:

IN the Behalf of the Irish inhabitants in the City and County of Limerick, the Counties of Clare, Kerry, Cork, Sligo, and Mayo.

IN consideration of the Surrender of the City of Limerick, and other Agreements made between the said Lieutenant General Ginckle, the Governour of the City of Limerick, and the Generals of the Irish army, bearing Date with these Presents, for the Surrender of the said City, and Submission of the said Army, it is agreed, That,

I. THE Roman catholics of this kingdom shall enjoy such privileges in the exercise of their religion, as are consistent with the laws of Ireland; or as they did enjoy in the reign of king Charles the Second: and their majesties, as soon as their affairs will permit them to summon a parliament in this kingdom, will endeavour to procure the said Roman catholics such farther security in that particular, as may preserve them from any disturbance upon the account of their said religion.

II. ALL the inhabitants or residents of Limerick, or any other garrison now in the possession of the Irish, and all officers and soldiers, now in arms, under any commission of king James, or those authorised by him, to grant the same in the several counties of Limerick, Clare, Kerry, Cork, and Mayo, or any of them; and all the commissioned officers in their majesties quarters, that belong to the Irish regiments, now in being, that are treated with, and who are not prisoners of war, or have taken protection, and who shall return and submit to their majesties obedience; and their and every of their heirs, shall hold, possess, and enjoy, all and every their estates of freehold and inheritance; and all the rights, titles and interests, privileges and immunities, which they, and every or any of them held, enjoyed, or were rightfully and lawfully entitled to, in the reign of king Charles II. or at any time since, by the laws and statutes that were in force in the said reign of king Charles II. and shall be put in possession, by order of the government, of such of them as are in the king's hands, or the hands of his tenants, without being put to any suit or trouble therein; and all such estates shall be freed and discharged from all arrears of crown-rents, quit-rents, and other public charges, incurred and become due since Michaelmas 1688, to the day of the date hereof: and all persons comprehended in this article, shall have, hold, and enjoy all their goods and chattles, real and personal, to them, or any of them belonging, and remaining either in their own hands, or the

hands

hands of any perfons whatfoever, in truft for, or for the ufe of them, or any of them: and all, and every the faid perfons, of what profeffion, trade, or calling foever they be, fhall and may ufe, exercife and practife their feveral and refpective profeffions, trades, and calling's, as freely as they did ufe, exercife, and enjoy the fame in the reign of king Charles II. provided that nothing in this article contained be conftrued to extend to, or reftore any forfeiting perfon now out of the kingdom, except what are hereafter comprifed: provided alfo, that no perfon whatfoever fhall have or enjoy the benefit of this article, that fhall neglect or refufe to take the oath of allegiance, made by act of parliament in England, in the firft year of the reign of their prefent majefties, when thereunto required.

III. ALL merchants, or reputed merchants of the city of Limerick, or of any other garrifon now poffeffed by the Irifh, or of any town or place in the counties of Clare or Kerry, who are abfent beyond the feas, that have not bore arms fince their majefties declaration in February 1688, fhall have the benefit of the fecond article, in the fame manner as if they were prefent; provided fuch merchants and reputed merchants, do repair into this kingdom within the fpace of eight months from the date hereof.

IV. THE following officers, viz. colonel Simon Lutterel, captain Rowland White, Maurice Euftace of Yermanftown, Chievers of Mayftown, commonly called Mount-Leinfter, now belonging to the regiments in the aforefaid garrifons and quarters of the Irifh army, who were beyond the feas, and fent thither upon affairs of their refpective regiments, or the army in general, shall have the benefit and advantage of the second article, provided they return hither within the space of eight months from the date of these presents, and submit to their majesties government, and take the above-mentioned oath.

V. THAT all and singular the said persons comprised in the second and third articles, shall have a general pardon of all attainders, outlawries, treasons, misprisions of treason, premuniers, felonies, trespasses, and other crimes and misdemeanours whatsoever, by them, or any of them, committed since the beginning of the reign of king James II. and if any of them are attainted by parliament, the lords justices, and general, will use their best endeavours to get the same repealed by parliament, and the outlawries to be reversed gratis, all but writing-clerks fees.

VI. AND whereas these present wars have drawn on great violences on both parts; and that if leave were given to the bringing all sorts of private actions, the animosities would probably continue, that have been too long on foot, and the public disturbances last; for the quieting and settling therefore of this kingdom, and avoiding those inconveniencies which would be the necessary consequence of the contrary, no person or persons whatsoever, comprised in the foregoing articles, shall be sued, molested, or impleaded at the suit of any party or parties whatsoever, for any trespasses by them committed, or for any arms, horses, money, goods, chattels, merchandizes, or provisions whatsoever, by them seized or taken during the time of the war. And no person or persons whatsoever, in the second or third articles comprised, prifed, fhall be fued, impleaded, or made accountable for the rents or mean rates of any lands, tenements, or houfes, by him or them received, or enjoyed in this kingdom, fince the beginning of the prefent war, to the day of the date hereof, nor for any wafte or trefpafs by him or them committed in any fuch lands, tenements or houfes: and it is alfo agreed, that this article fhall be mutual and reciprocal on both fides.

VII. EVERY nobleman and gentleman comprifed in the faid fecond and third article, fhall have liberty to ride with a fword, and cafe of piftols, if they think fit; and keep a gun in their houfes, for the defence of the fame, or for fowling.

VIII. THE inhabitants and refidents in the city of Limerick, and other garrifons, fhall be permitted to remove their goods, chattels, and provifions, out of the fame, without being viewed and fearched, or paying any manner of duties, and fhall not be compelled to leave the houfes or lodgings they now have, for the fpace of fix weeks next enfuing the date hereof.

IX. THE oath to be adminiftered to fuch Roman catholics as fubmit to their majefties government, fhall be the oath above faid, and no other.

X. No perfon or perfons who fhall at any time hereafter break thefe articles, or any of them, fhall thereby make, or caufe any other perfon or perfons to forfeit or lofe the benefit of the fame.

XI. THE lords juftices and general do promife to ufe their utmoft endeavours, that all the perfons comprehended

prehended in the above-mentioned articles, shall be protected and defended from all arrests and executions for debt or damage, for the space of eight months next ensuing the date hereof.

XII. LASTLY, the lords justices and general do undertake, that their majesties will ratify these articles within the space of eight months, or sooner, and use their utmost endeavours that the same shall be ratified and confirmed in parliament.

XIII. AND whereas colonel John Brown, stood indebted to several protestants by judgments of record, which appearing to the late government, the lord Tyrconnel, and lord Lucan, took away the effects the said John Brown had to answer the said debts, and promised to clear the said John Brown of the said debts; which effects were taken for the public use of the Irish, and their army: for freeing the said lord Lucan of his said engagement, past on their public account, for payment of the said protestants, and for preventing the ruin of the said John Brown, and for satisfaction of his creditors, at the instance of the lord Lucan, and the rest of the persons aforesaid, it is agreed, that the said lords justices, and the said baron De Ginckle, shall interceed with the king and parliament, to have the estates secured to Roman Catholics, by articles and capitulation in this kingdom, charged with, and equally liable to the payment of so much of the said debts, as the said lord Lucan, upon stating accompts with the said John Brown, shall certify under his hand, that the effects taken from the said Brown amount unto; which accompt is to be stated, and the balance certified by the said lord Lucan in one and twenty days after the date hereof;

FOR

For the true performance hereof, we have hereunto set our hands,

       Char. Porter,
Present,   Tho. Coningsby.
Scravenmore. Bar. De Ginckle.
H. Maccay.
T. Talmash.

A N D whereas the said city of Limerick hath been since, in pursuance of the said articles surrendered unto us. Now know ye, that we, having considered of the said articles, are graciously pleased hereby to declare, that we do for us, our heirs and successors, as far as in us lies, ratify and confirm the same, and every clause, matter and thing therein contained. And as to such parts thereof, for which an act of parliament shall be found to be necessary, we shall recommend the same to be made good by parliament, and shall give our royal assent to any bill or bills that shall be passed by our two houses of parliament to that purpose. And whereas it appears unto us, that it was agreed between the parties to the said Articles, that after the words, Limerick, Clare, Kerry, Cork, Mayo, or any of them, in the second of the said articles, the words following, viz. " And all such as are under their protection in the " said counties," should be inserted, and be part of the said articles ; which words having been casually omitted by the writer, the omission was not discovered till after the said articles were signed, but was taken notice of before the second town was surrendered: and that our said justices, and general, or one of them, did promise that the said clause should be made good, it being within the intention of the capi
             tulation,

tulation, and inserted in the foul draught thereof. Our further will and pleasure is, and we do hereby ratify and confirm the said omitted words, viz. " And all such as are under their protection in the " said counties," hereby for us, our heirs and successors, ordaining and declaring, that all and every person and persons therein concerned, shall and may have, receive, and enjoy the benefit thereof, in such and the same manner, as if the said words had been inserted in their proper place, in the said second article; any omission, defect, or mistake in the said second article, in any wise notwithstanding. Provided always, and our will and pleasure is, that these our letters patents shall be enrolled in our court of Chancery in our said kingdom of Ireland, within the space of one year next ensuing. In witness, &c. witness our self at Westminster, the twenty-fourth day of February, anno regni, regis & reginæ, Gulielmi & Mariæ, quarto per breve de privato sigillo. Nos autem tenorem premissor. predict. Ad requisitionem attornat. general. domini regis, & domini reginæ pro regno Hiberniæ. Duximus exemplificand. per presentes. In cujus rei testimonium has literas nostras fieri fecimus patentes. Testibus nobis ipsis apud Westmon. quinto die Aprilis, annoq. regni eorum quarto.

BRIDGES.

Examinat. { S. KECK.   } In Cancel.
per nos.   { LACON Wᴹ. CHILDE. } Magistros.

MILITARY

MILITARY ARTICLES agreed upon between the Baron De Ginckle, Lieutenant General, and Commander in Chief of the English Army on the one side.

AND the Lieutenant Generals de Usson and De Tesse, Commanders in Chief of the Irish Army, on the other; and the General Officers hereunto subscribing.

I. THAT all persons without any exceptions, of what quality or condition soever, that are willing to leave the kingdom of Ireland, shall have free liberty to go to any country beyond the seas (England and Scotland excepted) where they think fit, with their families, houshold-stuff, plate, and jewels.

II. THAT all general officers, colonels, and generally all other officers of horse, dragoons, and foot guards, troopers, dragooners, soldiers of all kinds that are in any garrison, place, or post, now in the hands of the Irish, or encamped in the counties of Cork, Clare, and Kerry, as also those called Rapparees, or volunteers, that are willing to go beyond seas as aforesaid, shall have free leave to embark themselves wherever the ships are that are appointed to transport them, and to come in whole bodies as they are now composed, or in parties, companies, or otherwise, without having any impediment directly or indirectly.

III. THAT all persons above-mentioned, that are willing to leave Ireland and go into France, shall have leave to declare it at the times and places hereafter mentioned, viz. the troops in Limerick, on Tuesday next in Limerick; the horse at their camp on Wednesday, and the other forces that are dispersed in the counties of Clare, Kerry, and Cork, on the 8th instant, and on none other, before monsieur Tameron, the French intendant, and colonel Withers; and after such declaration is made, the troops that will go into France must remain under the command and discipline of their officers that are to conduct them thither: and deserters of each side shall be given up, and punished accordingly.

IV. THAT all English and Scotch officers, that serve now in Ireland, shall be included in this capitulation, as well for the security of their estates and goods in England, Scotland, and Ireland, (if they are willing to remain here) as for passing freely into France, or any other country to serve

V. THAT all the general French officers, the intendant, the engineers, the commissaries at war, and of the artillery, the treasurer, and other French officers, strangers, and all others whatsoever, that are in Sligo, Ross, Clare, or in the army, or that do trade or commerce, or are otherwise employed in any kind of station or condition, shall have free leave to pass into France, or any other country, and shall have leave to ship themselves, with all their horses, equipage, plate, papers, and all their effects whatever; and that general Ginckle will order passports for them, convoys, and carriages by land and water, to carry them safe from Limerick to the ships where they shall be embarked, without paying any thing for the said carriages, or to those that are employed therein, with their horses, cars, boats, and shallops.

VI. THAT if any of the aforesaid equipages, merchandize, horses, money, plate, or other moveables, or houshold-stuff belonging to the said Irish troops, or to the French officers, or other particular persons whatsoever, be robbed, destroyed, or taken away by the troops of the said general, the said

general

general will order it to be restored, or payment to be made according to the value that is given in upon oath by the person so robbed or plundered: and the said Irish troops to be transported as aforesaid; and all other persons belonging to them, are to observe good order in their march and quarters, and shall restore whatever they shall take from the country, or make restitution for the same.

VII. THAT to facilitate the transporting the said troops, the general will furnish fifty ships, each ship's burthen two hundred tons; for which, the persons to be transported shall not be obliged to pay, and twenty more if there shall be occasion, without their paying for them; and if any of the said ships shall be of lesser burthen, he will furnish more in number to countervail; and also give two men of war to embark the principal officers, and serve for a convoy to the vessels of burthen.

VIII. THAT a commissary shall be immediately sent to Cork to visit the transport ships, and what condition they are in for sailing; and that, as soon as they are ready, the troops to be transported shall march with all convenient speed, the nearest way in order to embark there: and if there shall be any more men to be transported than can be carried off in the said fifty ships, the rest shall quit the English town of Limerick, and march to such quarters as shall be appointed for them, convenient for their transportation, where they shall remain till the other twenty ships be ready, which are to be in a month; and may embark on any French ship that may come in the mean time.

IX. THAT the said ships shall be furnished with forage for horse, and all necessary provisions to subsist the officers, troops, dragoons, and soldiers, and all other persons that are shipped to be transported into France

France; which provisions shall be paid for as soon as all are disembarked at Brest or Nants, upon the coast of Brittany, or any other port of France they can make.

X. AND to secure the return of the said ships, (the danger of the seas excepted) and payment for the said provisions, sufficient hostages shall be given.

XI. THAT the garrisons of Clare-castle, Ross, and all other foot that are in garrisons in the counties of Clare, Cork, and Kerry, shall have the advantage of this present capitulation; and such part of those garrisons as design to go beyond seas, shall march out with their arms, baggage, drums beating, ball in mouth, match lighted at both ends, and colours flying, with all the provisions, and half the ammunition that is in the said garrisons, and join the horse that march to be transported; or if then there is not shipping enough for the body of foot that is to be next transported after the horse, general Ginckle will order that they be furnished with carriages for that purpose, and what provisions they shall want in their march, they paying for the said provisions, or else that they may take it out of their own magazines.

XII. THAT all the troops of horse and dragoons that are in the counties of Cork, Kerry, and Clare, shall also have the benefit of this capitulation; and that such as will pass into France, shall have quarters given them in the counties of Clare and Kerry, apart from the troops that are commanded by general Ginckle, until they can be shipped; and within their quarters they shall pay for every thing, except forage and pasture for their horses, which shall be furnished gratis.

XIII. THOSE of the garrison of Sligo that are joined to the Irish army, shall have the benefit of this capitulation; and orders shall be sent to them

that

that are to convey them up, to bring them hither to Limerick the shortest way.

XIV. The Irish may have liberty to transport nine hundred horse, including horses for the officers, which shall be transported gratis: and as for the troopers that stay behind, they shall dispose of themselves as they shall think fit, giving up their horses and arms to such persons as the general shall appoint.

XV. It shall be permitted to those that are appointed to take care for the subsistence of the horse, that are willing to go into France, to buy hay and corn at the king's rates wherever they can find it, in the quarters that are assigned for them, without any let or molestation, and to carry all necessary provisions out of the city of Limerick; and for this purpose, the general will furnish convenient carriages for them to the places where they shall be embarked.

XVI. It shall be lawful to make use of the hay preserved in the stores of the county of Kerry, for the horses, that shall be embarked; and if there be not enough, it shall be lawful to buy hay and oats wherever it shall be found, at the king's rates.

XVII. That all prisoners of war, that were in Ireland the 28th of September, shall be set at liberty on both sides; and the general promises, to use his endeavours, that those that are in England and Flanders shall be set at liberty also.

XVIII. The general will cause provisions and medicines to be furnished to the sick and wounded officers, troopers, dragoons, and soldiers of the Irish army that cannot pass into France at the first embarkment; and, after they are cured, will order them ships to pass into France, if they are willing to go.

XIX. That at the signing hereof, the general will send a ship express to France; and that besides,

he

he will furnish two small ships of those that are now in the river of Limerick, to transport two persons into France that are to be sent to give notice of this treaty; and that the commanders of the said ships shall have orders to put ashore at the next port of France where they shall make.

XX. That all those of the said troops, officers, and others, of what character soever, that would pass into France, shall not be stopped upon the account of debt, or any other pretext.

XXI. If after signing this present treaty, and before the arrival of the fleet, a French packet-boat, or other transport ship, shall arrive from France in any other part of Ireland, the general will order a passport, not only for such as must go on board the said ships, but to the ships to come to the nearest port, to the place where the troops to be transported shall be quartered.

XXII. That after the arrival of the said fleet, there shall be free communication and passage between it and the quarters of the abovesaid troops, and especially for all those that have passes from the chief commanders of the said fleet, or from monsieur Tameron, the intendant.

XXIII. In consideration of the present capitulation, the two towns of Limerick shall be delivered and put into the hands of the general, or any other person he shall appoint, at the time and days hereafter specified, viz. the Irish town, except the magazines and hospital, on the day of signing of these present articles; and as for the English town, it shall remain, together with the island, and the free passage of Thomond-Bridge, in the hands of those of the Irish army that are now in the garrison, or that shall hereafter come from the counties of Cork, Clare, Kerry, Sligo, and other places above-mentioned,

tioned, until there shall be convenience found for their transportation.

XXIV. AND to prevent all disorders that may happen between the garrison that the general shall place in the Irish-town, which shall be delivered to him, and the Irish troopers that shall remain in the English-town and the island, which they may do, until the troops to be embarked on the first fifty ships shall be gone for France, and no longer; they shall intrench themselves on both sides, to hinder the communication of the said garrisons: and it shall be prohibited on both sides, to offer any thing that is offensive; and the parties offending shall be punished on either side.

XXV. THAT it shall be lawful for the said garrison to march out all at once, or at different times, as they can be embarked, with arms, baggage, drums beating, match lighted at both ends, bullet in mouth, colours flying, six brass guns, such as the besieged will chuse, two mortar-pieces, and half the ammunition that is now in the magazines of the said place: and for this purpose, an inventory of all the ammunition in the garrison shall be made in the presence of any person that the general shall appoint, the next day after these present articles shall be signed.

XXVI. ALL the magazines of provisions shall remain in the hands of those that are now employed to take care of the same, for the subsistance of those of the Irish army that will pass into France; and if there shall not be sufficient in the stores, for the support of the said troops, whilst they stay in this kingdom, and are crossing the seas, that, upon giving up an account of their numbers, the general will furnish them with sufficient provisions at the king's rates; and that there shall be a free market at Limerick,

merick, and other quarters, where the said troops shall be; and in case any provisions shall remain in the magazines of Limerick when the town shall be given up, it shall be valued, and the price deducted out of what is to be paid for the provisions to be furnished to the troops on ship-board.

XXVII. That there shall be a cessation of arms at land, as also at sea, with respect to the ships, whether English, Dutch, or French, designed for the transportation of the said troops, until they shall be returned to their respective harbours; and that, on both sides, they shall be furnished with sufficient passports both for ships and men: and if any sea commander, or captain of a ship, or any officer, trooper, dragoon, soldier, or any other person, shall act contrary to this cessation, the persons so acting shall be punished on either side, and satisfaction shall be made for the wrong that is done; and officers shall be sent to the mouth of the river of Limerick, to give notice to the commanders of the English and French fleets of the present conjuncture, that they may observe the cessation of arms accordingly.

XXVIII. That for the security of the execution of this present capitulation, and of each article therein contained, the besieged shall give the following hostages———And the general shall give———.

XXIX. If before this capitulation is fully executed, there happens any change in the government, or command of the army, which is now commanded by general Ginckle; all those, that shall be appointed to command the same, shall be obliged to observe and execute what is specified in these articles, or cause it to be executed punctually, and shall not act contrary on any account.

Octob. 19.   Baron De Ginckle.

INDEX.

INDEX.

N. B. The Numeral Letters refer to the Volumes, and the Figures to the Pages.

A

ABBEY of St. Mary's near Dublin, disputation there, ii. 239.
    Acts of power exercised by earl John, during the reign of Richard I. i. 181.
    Adair, Archibald, (a native of Scotland) tempted to conformity by the prospect of gain, iii. Is advanced to the bishoprick of Killala, ibid. His indecent behaviour, ibid.
    Adrian, pope, applied to by Henry II. i. 8. His motives for complying with the king's request, ibid. His bull, 9.
    Alan, archbishop, his miserable death, ii. 175.
    Alexander, pope, confirms the grant of Ireland made by Adrian, i. 103.
    Antrim, Randal Macdonnel, earl of, his character, iii. 53. Offers to levy and maintain a considerable army at his own expence, ibid. To make a descent upon the Scottish isles, ibid. His vanity and sincerity discovered, 58. Receives Robert Monroe hospitably at his castle, 203. Is made prisoner by him, ibid. His adventures and undertakings 253. His disappointment, 255. His regiment excluded from Londonderry, iv. 232.
    Armada, Spanish, part of it destroyed on the northern coast of Ireland, ii. 376. Effects of this incident, ibid.
    Armagh, synod convened there, i. 60.
    Armeric de St. Lawrence, intercepted by Cathal, i. 186. Killed with his men, ibid.
    Athunree, battle of, i. 321.

B.

BALE, John, appointed to the see of Ossory, ii. 242. His character and conduct, ibid. His treatment of the Irish, 243.
    Bagnall, sir Henry, exhibits his articles of treason against the earl of Tirone, ii. 400.
    Bellingham, his arrival in Ireland, ii. 228. His vigorous administration, 230. Summons the earl of Desmond to repair to Dublin, 231. Pierces into Munster, unexpectedly, and surprises him in his house, ibid. Converts him into a loyal subject by his behaviour, 232. Is removed from his government in consequence of the clamours and insinuations of his enemies, ibid.
    Barons, English, in Ireland, cause of their revolt, i. 206.
    Baronets, institution of the order of them, ii. 509.
    Bingham, sir Richard, his severity, ii. 365. His conduct disapproved of by sir John Perrot, 366. Gains a signal and decisive victory over the Scots, in the Irish province, 368.

INDEX.

Birmingham, William executed, i. 346.
Bishops, several protestant ones ejected from their sees, ii. 251.
Bulls, of Adrian and Alexander, promulgated, i. 135.
Burg, lord, appointed chief governor, ii. 416. Pursues the war in a vigorous manner, ibid. His sudden death, 418.
Black rent. ii. 10.
Blackwater, battle of, ii. 423. Its consequences, 424.
Braosa, Philip de, alarmed, i. 155.
Brereton, sir William, quells a new insurrection, after the execution of lord Grey, ii. 213.
Bruce, Edward, invited into Ireland, by the northern chieftains, i. 312. His barbarous progress, 314. Applies to Fedlim O'Connor, 316. Assumes the style and authority of king of Ireland, 319. Crowned at Dundalk, 320. Joined by his brother, ibid. Reduces Carrickfergus, ibid. Marches southward, ibid. Threatens the capital, 322. Spreads terror and consternation among the citizens, ibid. Retires to Ulster, 323. Is exceedingly distressed, 326. Acts with precipitation, 327. Is defeated and slain, ibid.
Benburb, battle of, between the Scots and Irish, iii. 334. Effects of it, 335.
Berkeley, lord, succeeds lord Roberts, as lord lieutenant of Ireland, iv. 164.
Butler, origin of the attachment of that house to the Lancastrian princes, ii. 34.
———, Pierce, kills sir James Ormond, and succeeds to his power and possessions, ii. 139.
Browne, archbishop of Dublin, zealous for the reformation, ii. 195. His representation to lord Cromwell, ibid. Supports the act of supremacy, 200.

C

CARRAGH, O'Connor, surprised by Cathal, and other invaders, i. 203. Falls bravely in the field, 204.
Carew, sir Peter, attacks sir Edmund Butler, ii. 302. And repels him, 303.
———, sir George, lord president of Munster, attends the earl of Ormond to a parley with O'More, ii. 449. Practises against the rebel leaders, 462. Descends to dishonourable proceedings, 464. Disappointed, but proceeds in his military operations, 465. Pierces into Kerry, and takes the castle of the lord Lixnaw, ibid. Gets the titular earl of Desmond into his hands, 472. Advises his confinement in the Tower of London, ibid. His precautions on a confirmation of the designs of Spain, 473. Proceeds to Cork, ibid. Attempts to intercept the Northerns in their march to the support of Don Juan D'Aquila, besieged in Kinsale, 476. But in vain, ibid. Assaults the castle of Dunboy, 485. Terminates the war in Munster, ibid. Appointed deputy to lord Mountjoy, 490. Advances reformation, ibid.
Cambrensis, his arrival in Ireland, i. 164. His altercations with the Irish ecclesiastics, 165.
Cashel, synod of, i. 88. Its constitutions, 89. Adulation of the clergy there, 90.

Castlehaven,

INDEX.

Castlehaven, earl of, makes a tender of his services to government, iii. 214. Reprimanded for his correspondence with the rebels, ibid. Indicted of high treason, ibid. Committed to close custody without being heard, ibid. Escapes from his confinement, ibid. Flies to Kilkenny, and unites with the confederates, ibid.

Cathal, surnamed the Bloody handed, gains the kingdom of Connaught, i. 184. Is joined by the princes of Thomond and Desmond, ibid. Intercepts De Courcey, and Armoric de St. Lawrence, 186. Elated with success, founds an abbey upon the field of action, 187. Marches into Munster, 189. Dethroned by William De Burgo, 201. Applies to him, 203. Artfully prevails on him to assist him in the recovery of his kingdom, ibid. Defeats and kills his rival, ibid. Is restored, 204. His ingratitude, ibid. Joins Meiler Fitz-Henry, ibid. Cedes two parts of his province, 205. Presents himself before king John, 220. Appeals to the English government, 228. Supported and defended by the king's interposition, 229.

Charles I. his accession, ii. 559. Augments his Irish forces, 560. A free gift is offered to him by the recusants, on condition of indulgence to the Romish worship, 562. He accepts of the free gift, 565. Eludes his royal promise of a parliamentary confirmation of the graces, with apparent insincerity, 570. Is supplied with money and soldiers by lord Wentworth. iii. 52. Favours the earl of Antrim's project, 53. Creates lord Wentworth, earl of Strafford, 56. Makes him captain-general of all the Irish forces, with power to lead them into Scotland, 66. Adopts unhappy measures, ibid. Concludes the Rippon treaty at London, ibid. Transmits orders for the disbanding the popish army in Ireland, ibid. Yields to the Irish agents, 74. Abandons the government to a couple of puritan lords justices, without abilities or character, ibid. Makes farther concessions, 75. Receives a remonstrance in form from the Irish agents, ibid. Makes new concessions to them, 86. Finds their demands increase, 87. Is in a very perplexing situation with regard to his Irish subjects, 220. Is disposed to an accommodation with the rebels, ibid. Issues a commission under the great seal of England, to several noblemen and gentlemen, to meet the principal recusants, to receive and to transmit their propositions, 222. His overture for peace is extremely provoking to the justices, ibid. His spirited behaviour upon the occasion, ibid. Orders the marquis of Ormond to treat about a temporary cessation of arms with the rebels, 233. Renews his orders and instructions for a cessation, 209. Creates the earl of Antrim a marquis, and grants him a commission for commanding such forces as he should raise, 252. Embarrassed by the Irish negotiators at Oxford, 268. His answer to the Irish agents, 270. His speech to them on their departure, ibid. Resolves to lay the whole burden and odium of treating with the Irish on the marquis of Ormond, 272. Commissions him to make a full peace with the catholic subjects of Ireland, ibid. Gradually favours the Irish catholics more and more, 277. Makes the marquis of Ormond, by his condescensions in their favour, very uneasy in his situation, 279. Refuses his offer to resign his government, ibid. Labours to conciliate both the popish and protestant party in Ireland, 281. Unhappily defeats his own purposes, 298. His private letters to the earl of Glamorgan, and the marquis of Ormond, 310. Disavows

the

INDEX.

the religious articles granted by the earl of Glamorgan, in his declaration to the English parliament, 314. Is beheaded, iv. 29.

Charles II. proclaimed in Ireland, by the marquis of Ormond, iv. 30. Purposes to repair to Ireland, 34. Pressed by the marquis of Ormond to repair to Ireland, 47. Listens to new counsels, 48. Proclaimed king in all the great towns in Ireland, 109. Publishes a declaration for the settlement of Ireland, 116. And instructions for the execution of it, 121. Gives a striking instance of his dissimulation, 162. Listens to his brother in favour of the papists in Ireland, 197. Removes the duke of Ormond from his government, ibid. Appoints the earl of Rochester lord lieutenant, 198. Dies, 200.

Chepstow, earl of. See *Strongbow*.

Chichester, sir Arthur, advances the work of reformation in Ireland, ii. 492. Proves himself a very useful agent and director, 505. Vested by the king, (James I.) with the territory of Innishowen, 515. Acts with temper in a troublesome situation, 526. His moderate conduct displeasing to the puritans, ibid. He is summoned to England, 530. Created baron of Belfast, and recalled, 540.

Clancarthy, earl of, surrenders himself to Gilbert, an English officer, ii. 305. Makes an humiliating submission before the council, surrenders his son as hostage for his fidelity, and obtains his pardon, ibid.

Clanricarde, earl of, defeats the Scottish invaders, ii. 264.

—————, Uliac, earl of, renders himself very serviceable in Connaught, iii. 158. Gives a striking proof of his unshaken loyalty, 213. Warmly recommends the propositions of the Irish insurgents to the state, 221. Commissioned, with the noblemen and gentlemen, to meet the principal recusants, 222. Attempts to recover Ulster from the parliamentarians, iv. 63. Pierces into the northern province, 94. Takes the castles of Ballyshannon and Donnegal, ibid. Is obliged to fly from the superior force of the enemy, ibid. Is extremely distressed, accepts conditions from the republicans, and retires from the kingdom, ibid.

Clarence, duke of, recalled from Ireland, i. 376. Sent over again, 377. Convenes a parliament at Kilkenny, ibid. Appoints sir Rowland Fitz-Eustace his deputy, ii. 50.

Clarendon, earl of, appointed lord lieutenant of Ireland, iv. 208. Expresses his satisfaction, in his speech to the privy council, at assuming the administration in such perfect peace and quietness, ibid. Empowered to restore some arms to those of the protestant militia who were fit to be entrusted with them, ibid. Is cautious in the exercise of his power, 210. His representations with regard to the admission of the Roman catholics into offices of trust and honour, ineffectual, 211. Is offended at lord Tyrconnel's conduct, and remonstrates against it, 214. Insulted by the earl's violence, 215. Remonstrates to the king against his heat and presumption, ibid. Is accused of male-administration in several instances, 216 Resigns the sword of state to Tyrconnel, 218. Embarks at Dublin, ibid. Is requested by some gentlemen of Ireland to present them to the prince of Orange, 236. Is received by the prince with coldness, ibid.

Clifford, sir Conyers, his defeat and death, ii. 434.

Cogan, Milo, invited by Murrough, son of Roderic O'Connor, to march into Connaught, i. 144. Accepts the invitation, ibid. Advances to Roscommon, ibid. Allowed a settlement by the Irish chiefs, 155. Massacred, 163.

Cole,

INDEX.

Cole, sir William, dispatches a full account of a conspiracy to the lords justices, iv. His letters to them either intercepted or suppressed, ibid.

Comyn, John, succeeds Laurence O'Toole, as prelate of Dublin, i. 162.

Connaught, its miserable situation described, i. 159. Gained by Cathal, surnamed the Bloody-handed, 184.

Coote, sir Charles, inflames the Irish rebels by his violent proceedings, and wanton cruelties, iii. 168. Takes Sligo, 307. Gains a victory over the archbishop of Tuam, and his forces who attempt to recover it, 308. Finds among other papers a complete and authentic copy of the earl of Glamorgan's private treaty, ibid. Relieved at Derry, by Owen O'Nial, iv. 38.

Cork, earl of, appointed one of the lords justices, iii. 6.

Corke, besieged, i. 190. Surrenders to the prince of Desmond, 191. Insolence of the citizens there, ii. 137.

Crofts, sir James, succeeds sir Anthony St. Leger, 238. Endeavours to gain the primate, ibid.

Cromer, archbishop of Armagh, his practices, ii. 194. He receives a commission from Rome, 207.

Crosby, sir Piers, ventures to oppose some measures of lord Wentworth's administration, iii. 39. Is sequestered from the council-board, ibid. Complains of this severity by petition, ibid. Removed entirely from the privy council, ibid.

Cromwell, Oliver, arrives at Dublin, iv. 44. Takes Drogheda by storm, 45. Orders the garrison to be put to the sword, ibid. Gains possession of Wexford by treachery, 49. Terrifies Ross into a surrender, 50. Obliges the marquis of Ormond to retire gradually to the city of Kilkenny, 51. Marches to invest Waterford, ibid. Surprises Carrick in his march, ibid. Surprises lord Broghill with a visit, 53. Is reinforced by the revolt of the Munster garrisons, 54. Alarms the county agents at Kilkenny by his approach, 58. Retires from that place disappointed, ibid. Returns to it and invests it, ibid. Proceeds, on the surrender of Kilkenny, to invest Clonmell, 59. Embarks for England, 60. Proclaimed protector of the commonwealth of England, Scotland, and Ireland, 98. Sends his son Henry to Ireland, ibid. Appoints Fleetwood lord deputy for three years, 100. Receives a petition from the officers of his own regiment, publicly avowing their dissatisfaction at his government, 102. Receives addresses from the army and the inhabitants of every county in Ireland, expressing their resolution to adhere to him, ibid.

————, Henry, sent to Ireland by his father, iii. 98. Succeeds general Fleetwood as lord deputy, 102. His character and conduct, ibid. He is created lord lieutenant on the accession of his brother Richard, 103. He resigns his office on the restoration of the rump parliament, ibid.

D

D'AQUILA, Don Juan, besieged in Kinsale, ii. 476. His bold answer to the summons of the lord deputy, 477. His romantic challenge to the vice-roy, to decide the quarrel in single combat, ibid. Urges the earl of Tyrone to an engagement with the besiegers, 479.

INDEX.

Full of rage, indignation, and resentment in consequence of the defeat and flight of O'Donnel and Tirone, he desires a parley with the lord deputy, 482. Treats with him, ibid. Fires at the *last* article of capitulation, and rejects it with disdain, 483. Behaves with great statelines, and treats the Irish with great contempt, 484.

De Burgo, William, surrenders to Meiler Fitz Henry, and returns to his allegiance, i. 205.

————, Richard, his ambition, i. 246. Opposed by Fedlim, prince of Connaught, ibid.

————, Walter, marches against the Mac-Arthys, slays their leader, ravages their country, and obliges them to give hostages for the performance of his severe conditions, i. 272. Makes extensive demands on the territories of Connaught, and bids defiance to all the rights and properties reserved by the native chiefs, 273. Receives a signal defeat from Æth O'Connor, ibid.

De Courcey, John, engaged in Ulster, i. 158. Defeated, 159. Yet retains his settlements, ibid. Appointed deputy on the assassination of Hugh de Lacy, 174. Proceeds to the business of war with indefatigable vigour, ibid. Makes an attempt upon the disordered province of Connaught, 176. Retreats speedily into Ulster, 177. Suppresses the commotions in Ulster and Argial, ibid. Unable to conceal his indignation on finding the merit of his services slighted, 184. Affects independence, 199. Is prevailed upon to support Cathal, the distressed prince of Connaught, 203. Defeated, with his allies, by De Burgo, ibid. His violent behaviour on the death of prince Arthur, 206. He treats king John's mandate to repair to his presence, and to do him homage, with contempt, ibid. Comes to an engagement with De Lacy at Down, and is forced to retire with disgrace, and no inconsiderable loss, 208. Is compelled by him to depart from Ulster, ibid. Receives the king's safe-conduct, ibid. Romantic detail of De Courcey's being betrayed into the hands of Hugh De Lacy, ibid. Of his interview with the French champion, 209. Of the surprising proof of his bodily strength, 210.

De Courtney, Philip, entrusted with the government of Ireland, i. 395. His violent and oppressive behaviour, ibid.

De Grey, John, bishop of Norwich, his administration, i. 226. Circumstances favourable to his government, ibid.

De Lacy, Hugh receives a considerable grant from Henry II. i. 101. Confers with O'Ruarc of Breffney, 106. Appointed chief governor, in the room of Fitz-Andelm, 150. His character, ibid. His conduct in the administration of his government, 155. He is recalled to England, 157. Restored to his government, ibid. His excellent administration, ibid. He is again recalled, 166. Assassinated, 174.

————, Hugh, son to the above, prevailed on to unite his forces in the cause of Cathal, prince of Connaught, i. 201. Is defeated by De Burgo, 202. Accuses John de Courcey to the king, 206. Is commissioned to subdue him, and to send him prisoner to the king, 207. Pierces into Ulster, and comes to an engagement with De Courcey at Down, 208. Forces him to retire with disgrace and no inconsiderable loss, ibid. Gains the earldom of Ulster, 213. Repairs to the king, 214.

De

INDEX.

De Londres, archbishop of Dublin, invested with the government of Ireland, i. 230. Acts as an English baron, ibid. Expresses his indignation at the enormous haughtiness of Pandulf, ibid. His transactions in the congress of Runningmede, 231. Sent into Ireland, 242. His conduct, ibid.

De Maurisco, Geoffery, receives a remarkable letter from Henry III. on his accession, i. 233. Continued in the administration, 242. Makes an expedition into Desmond, 251. Behaves insidiously, 253.

De Quiney, Robert, marries the daughter of Strongbow, i. 105. Is soon afterwards slain in battle, ibid.

De Valois, Hamo, appointed to succeed the earl Marshal in the administration of Ireland, i. 192. Invades the ecclesiastical possessions, ibid. Seizes several lands which had been granted to the see of Dublin, ibid. Feels compunctions for his offence, and makes atonement for it, 193. Removed from his government with disgrace, 199.

De Vesey, William, intrusted with the government of Ireland, i. 295. Fitted by his spirit and activity, vigour and inflexibility, for the management of a disordered state, ibid. Quarrels with the baron of Ophally, 296. Flies to France, ibid. Resigns his lands, ibid.

Dermod, king of Leinster, driven from his province, i. 20. Flies to England, ibid. Solicits aid from Henry II. ibid. Is in a hopeless situation, 21. Applies to the earl of Chepstow, 22. Engages Fitz-Stephen and Fitz-Gerald in his service, 24. Returns to Ireland, 25. His return discovered to Roderic O'Connor, ibid. His submissions and treaty, 26. Discovers his insincerity, by asserting, at the head of an army, the rights which he had solemnly relinquished, 27. Marches to Wexford, 28. Enters it in triumph, 30. Leads the British forces to Ferns, 31. Suspects the men of Wexford, ibid. Provokes Maurice de Pendergast, by his insolence and neglect, to renounce his service and to revolt to the prince of Ossory, 34. Is invaded by the Ossorians, ibid. Retires, with the Britons in his service, from Roderic and his confederates, 38. Receives the propositions of his enemies with the most insolent disdain, 41. Listens to second propositions from them with less arrogance, and greater temper, 42. Concludes a treaty with Roderic, ibid. Aspires to the monarchy of Ireland, 49. Encouraged by the British leaders, ibid. Again applies to the earl of Chepstow, ibid. Puts an end to the slaughter at Waterford, 55. Gives his daughter Eva in marriage to earl Richard, surnamed Strongbow, ibid. Dies, 63.

Derry, garrison of, an obstacle to John O'Nial's enterprizes, and mortifying to his pride, ii. 281.

Desmond, James, earl of, defeats a faction raised against the new king Edward IV. 57. Appointed lord deputy, in reward of his distinguished services, 58. Grows giddy with success and exaltation, ibid. Marches against the insurgents, ibid. Is taken prisoner, 59. Generously rescued by a son of O'Connor, of O'Fally, 60. Quarrels with the bishop of Meath, 61. Convenes a parliament at Wexford, 62. Repairs to England, with honourable testimonials of his good conduct, and is graciously received by the king, 63. Returns to his government in triumph, ibid. Ruined by the marriage of the king with Elizabeth Grey, 64. Disgraced, 65. Beheaded, 67.

Desmond, earl of, declares in favour of Perkin Warbeck, ii. 113. Openly supports him, 131. Pardoned, 134. His traiterous practices, 163. ———, Gerald,

INDEX.

——, Gerald, earl of, his character, ii. 288. A remarkable repartee of his, 289. Attends the queen, Elizabeth, with the earl of Ormond, ibid. Committed, with his brother, close prisoner to the Tower, 290. They are remitted to the chief governor of Dublin, there to reside as state prisoners, 310. They escape into their own country, are received with joy by their dependants, and breathe revenge for the injuries they have received, 311. The earl acts with duplicity, 327. Sends a dissembling letter to sir Nicholas Mally, 334. Demonstrates his hostile intentions by attempting to surprise the English camp, ibid. Proclaimed a traitor, 335. Sends an insolent message to sir William Pelham, 336. Has the consummate mortification to find his last overture rejected, 338. Is deprived of all remaining hope, 350. Is hunted from one wretched retreat to another, 351. Seized and murdered, ibid.

——, sir John, committed to the Tower of London, with the earl his brother, ii. 290. Returns to Ireland with him, and escapes to the south, 311. A striking instance of his barbarous disposition, 328. Keeps the royal army in continual alarm, 331. Is vested by a new bull from the pope, with the plenitude of his authority, 332. Is intercepted and slain, 350.

Digby, lord, directed to write to lord Muskerry, iii 291. Charges the earl of Glamorgan, before the privy-council, of a suspicion of high treason, 310. Arrives opportunely from the continent, 330. His declaration, in consequence of king Charles's captivity, 331. Attends the marquis of Ormond to Kilkenny, 338. Learns, on the point of going to France, the secret discontent of colonel Preston, 344. Forms a project to detach him from the nuncio, 347. Indefatigable against the parliamentarians, ibid.

Douglas, general, detached by king William to reduce Athlone, iii. 307. Proceeds in his expedition, ibid. Finds the enemy stronger than he expected, 308. Decamps at midnight, ibid.

Dowdal, John, primate, opposes the introduction of the liturgy, ii. 237.

Drogheda, invested, iii. 180. Its defence neglected by the state, ibid. Unsuccessful attempts to surprise the town, 182. The siege raised, 185.

Drury, sir William, appointed lord president of Munster, in the room of sir John Perrot, ii. 314. Administers justice impartially, ibid. His adventures in Tralee, 315. Succeeds sir Henry Sidney in the government of the kingdom, 326. His expedition against the southern enemy, 331.

Dublin, stormed in the midst of a treaty, i. 57. Invested by the confederates, 66. Settlement of it, 96. Almost destroyed by an accidental fire, 187. The magistrates and citizens appeal to the council on being excommunicated by the clergy, 279. Reduced to a composition, ridiculously abject and mortifying, ibid. Attempt to establish a seat of learning, 337. Rendered fruitless by being ill timed, ibid. A parliament convened, ii. 359. How composed, ibid. Irish chieftains admitted, ibid. Appear in the English garb, 360. An university founded, 387. The citizens in confusion, iii. 129. Alarmed by false rumours, ibid. Reduced to the most miserable extremities, 234. The city invested by the confederates, 342. Their demands, 343. Their dissensions, 344. Forces of the English parliament land there, 347. Its wretched

INDEX.

wretched state, 348. Encompassed on all sides, iv. 39. The blockade continued, ibid. Cromwell exercises new authority, 44. Plot for seizing the castle, 137. Objections of the commons to the act of explanation, 147. Quo Warranto against the charter of the city, 220. Attempts on the university, 221. Ridiculous triumph of the papists, 227. Confusion throughout the city, ibid. King James arrives there, 243. Returns, 259. His contest with the university, 267. James assembles the magistrates, 298. Confusion in the city, 302.

―――, archbishop of, a spirited reply of his, ii. 22.

Dunboy, fort of, surprized by Daniel O'Sullivan, ii. 484.

Duncannon, the siege of it raised, ii.

E

ECCLESIASTICAL AFFAIRS. The Irish clergy earnest to regulate their church i. 12. Synod convened at Armagh, 60. Zeal and vigour of archbishop Laurence, 66. Synod of Cashel, 88. An assembly of the Irish clergy convened at Waterford, 135. Bulls of Alexander and Adrian promulgated, ibid. Altercations of the English clergy with the Irish ecclesiastics, 165. Dispute about the succession to the see of Armagh, 214. Remonstrances of the Irish clergy against the admission of foreigners into their church, 275. Equally averse to the English as to the Italians, 276. Their remarkable ordinance against the English clergy, ibid. They endeavour to enlarge the jurisdiction of their courts, ibid. Demand, in a parliament held at Merton, that the common law should be reduced to a conformity with the canon, 277. Insolence of the Irish ecclesiastics, ibid. They excommunicate the magistrates and citizens of Dublin, 279. Irish clergy evade the demands of the pope, 333. Turbulence of the clergy, ii. 18. Schemes for extending the reformation of religion to Ireland, 189. A violent and insolent clamour raised among the clergy, by an attempt to circumscribe their privileges in one province, 191. Irregularities in the ecclesiastical constitution of Ireland, 192. Cromer, primate of Armagh, declares openly and boldly against the king's (Henry VIII.) supremacy, 194. Summons the suffragans and clergy of his province, and exhorts them to adhere inviolably to the apostolic chair, ibid. Enjoined by a private commission from Rome to persevere boldly in support of the papal authority, 207. Schemes of religious reformation, 232. Difficulties attending the reformation, 233, 234. The Liturgy introduced by proclamation, 236. Opposed by primate Dowdal, ibid. Prejudices against the Reformers, 237. A theological dispute at St. Mary's Abbey, 240. Protestant bishops ejected from their sees, 251. Scheme for re-establishing the Reformation, 271. Practices of popish ecclesiastics in Ulster, 485. The insolence of the popish clergy at the beginning of the reign of James I. 486. Effects of it, ibid. They denounce the vengeance of their spiritual authority on all those who attend on the established worship, 494. Proclamation against the recusant clergy, 495. Convocation at Dublin, 536. Articles of religion compiled by Usher, ibid. Protestant clergy alarmed, 562. Remonstrance of the Irish prelates, 563. Triumphant behaviour of the popish clergy, iii. 3. Their practices, 4. Proclamation against the popish hierarchy,

5. A

INDEX.

5. A convocation, 29. Circumstances of the clergy, ibid. They are supported by lord Wentworth, 30. Spirit and principles of Romish ecclesiastics, 103. Synods of the Romish clergy, 208. Their ordinances, 209. Supreme council and general assembly at Kilkenny, 210. Their order of government, and oath of association, 212. They chuse provincial generals, ibid. Send ambassadors to foreign courts to solicit succours, 213. Petition the king and queen, ibid. Temper and proceedings of the Irish clergy in convocation upon expectation of the arrival of Rinunccini the pope's nuncio, 289. Assembly of bishops, iv. 56. Their declaration, ibid. The factious and insidious conduct of the clergy with regard to the marquis of Ormond, 69. They traduce him, 72. Their assembly at James-Town, ibid. They require the marquis to depart from the kingdom, ibid. Their declaration against his government, ibid. They fulminate a solemn excommunication against all his adherents, 73. They suspend, but refuse to revoke their sentence of excommunication, 74. They are inflamed by the king's declaration from Scotland, ibid. Prelacy and the liturgy restored, 174. The popish clergy favoured on the accession of James II. 211.

Edward I. provoked by multiplied vexations arising from the disorders in Ireland, i. 285. Returns a favourable answer to the Irish petitioners, 286. Applies to the subjects of Ireland for subsidies, 295. Finds the clergy refractory, ibid. The laity complying, ibid. He repeats his application to the clergy for a subsidy, 303. His exactions in Ireland, ibid.

―――, III. has recourse to violent measures in consequence of the local feuds and insurrections in Ireland, i. 351. Publishes an ordinance, which gives great dissatisfaction, 353. Returns favourable answers to the Irish petitioners, 359.

―――, IV. marries Elizabeth Grey, and attaches himself closely to her family, ii. 64. Restores the earl of Kildare, 68. Invests him with the government of Ireland, ibid. His encomiums on the earl of Ormond, 73. His instructions for the administration of Ireland, 78.

Elizabeth, queen, full of fears and suspicions in consequence of the disturbances in Ireland, ii. 288. Gives ready ear to those ministers who recommend the maintenance of her prerogative, 320. Sends reprimanding letters to Sir Henry Sydney, and the Irish council, ibid. Alarmed by the designs of her foreign enemies on Ireland, 323. Mortifies sir John Perrot, 323. Impatiently endeavours to alleviate the charge of her Irish government, 371. Recalls some of her Irish forces from the Netherlands, ibid. Directs a conference with the rebellious northerns, 404. Her condescensions to the earl of Tirone, 415. The Irish rebels encouraged by her conduct, 421. Condemns the conduct of the earl of Ormond, 426. Mortified by the accommodation made by Essex with Tirone, 437. Alarmed at his behaviour, ibid. Shews great irresolution and distraction of mind, 488.

England, desperate state of the English government on the accession of Henry VI. ii. 20. Contests between the houses of York and Lancaster, 35. Duke of York defeated at Blore-heath, 48. Returns from Ireland on the victory of Northampton, 51. Is defeated and slain at Wakefield, 52. Discontents occasioned by the severe behaviour of

Henry

INDEX.

Henry VII. 85. Henry alarmed by them, 86. Lambert Simnel assumes the character of Richard duke of York, 89. Is commanded to personate the earl of Warwick, ibid. Real policy of this sudden change, ibid. Simnel is defeated at Stoke, 102. And taken prisoner, ibid. Plot of Perkin Warbeck, 110. Death of Wolsey, 290. Earl of Desmond and his brother committed to the Tower, 292. English ministry and parliament not well disposed to the civil reformation of Ireland, 355. Elizabeth impatient of the burthen of Ireland, 371. Earl of Tirone's submission to the English council, 383. James I. solicitous for the plantation of the escheated counties of Ulster, 504. City of London engaged in the plantation in Ireland, 509. Institution of the order of baronets, ibid. Treaty of Rippon, iii. 66. Irish agents in London, 71. The earl of Strafford impeached, 72. Act of attainder passed against him, 84. Resolutions of the English parliament in consequence of having received intelligence of the Irish rebellion, 152. Mode and spirit of their procedure, 153. Practices of the English parliament with the army of Ireland, 215. Declaration of the English parliament against the treaty of cessation signed by the marquis of Ormond, and the Irish commissioners, 243. Debates on Irish affairs at London, iv. 128. Spirited interposition of the English parliament, 175.

Esmond, lord, revolts to the parliament, and declares against the cessation, iii. 274.

Essex, Walter Devereux, earl of, tenders his services to queen Elizabeth for reducing a part of Ulster, and peopling it with English settlers, ii. 308. Is to be invested with a moiety of the country planted, ibid. Prepares for his expedition to Ireland, ibid. Meets with disappointments after his arrival, 310. Pathetically represents to the queen the distresses of his situation, ibid. Is commanded by the queen, (overpersuaded by his enemies) to remain in Ireland, 311. Pursues the earl of Desmond, the most dangerous of the insurgents, ibid. Returns to the prosecution of his schemes in Ulster, ibid. Obtains permission to return to England, after having been harrassed by his enemies, 312. Dies of vexation, 313.

―――, Robert Devereux, earl of, appointed lord lieutenant of Ireland, ii. 429. Arrives at Dublin with all the pomp of a military hero, 430. Commences his administration in such a manner as to offend the queen, ibid. Acts contrary to her directions, and in contempt of his instructions, ibid. Has the mortification of being considerably harrassed in his passage through Leinster, by O'More, the chieftain of Leix, 431. Opposed by the titular earl of Desmond, ibid. Wastes his forces in a fruitless pursuit of the rebels, ibid. Returns into Leinster with an enfeebled army, 432. Expresses his vexation in a cruel manner, ibid. Writes to the queen for an additional reinforcement, 433. Prepares with that reinforcement for his northern expedition, ibid. Confers with the earl of Tirone, 436. Agrees to a truce for six weeks, ibid. Incensed against the queen, ibid. Breaks out into the most extravagant menaces of revenge, 437. Departs precipitately from Ireland, and surprises the queen in her bed-chamber, 439.

FAULKLAND,

INDEX.

F

FAULKLAND, lord, appointed chief governor of Ireland. ii. 541. Urgently applies for an augmentation of the army, 555. Recalled, iii. 6.

Fedlim, prince of Connaught, opposes de Burgo, i. 246. Addresses himself to king Henry III. and receives an answer sufficient for his immediate purpose, 248. Is acknowledged as the king's liege-man, and has the royal commission to act against de Burgo, ibid. Suddenly appears at the court of England, 258. Repeats his application to the throne on having his territories invaded, ibid. Pleads his cause with success, ibid. Proves his gratitude by performing good services against prince David of Wales, 261.

Fitz-Andelm, William, appointed governour of Ireland by Henry II. i. 134. Lands at Wexford, 135. Begins his administration by a stately progress along the coast, ibid. Discovers no dispositions nor abilities suited to a government to be supported by a martial spirit, 136 The chief object of his administration, ibid. His government despised, 143. He is recalled, 150.

Fitz-Eustace, Sir Edward, appointed to the government of Ireland, ii. 44. Fitted for that government by his military accomplishments, ibid. Surprises O'Connor, the turbulent Irish chieftain of O'Fally, and puts his troops to the rout, 45. Removed from his government, 47.

―――― Sir Rowland, created baron of Portlester, 47. And entrusted with the administration of government, as deputy to the duke of Clarence, 56.

Fitz-Gerald, Maurice, consents, with some other adventurous knights of Wales, to take part in the Irish expedition, i. 24. Invested, jointly with Robert Fitz-Stephens, his maternal brother, with the lordship of the city of Wexford, and its domain, 30. Lands at Wexford, 35. Extricates Maurice de Pendergast from a dangerous situation, and secures his retreat by his valour and address, ibid. Attends Dermod, with his British forces, into the territories of Dublin, 44. Affected by the submission of the citizens, he becomes their intercessor with the prince of Leinster, ibid. Seized with a spirit of desperate valour, 70. Assailed furiously by O'Ruarc, with his battle-axe, 107. Rescues Hugh de Lacy, ibid. Marries his daughter to Hervey de Mountmorres, 125. Indulged with a new grant, ibid. His death, 136.

―――――― Maurice, appointed successor to Hubert, in return for the services of his noble family, i. 246. Receives a letter from king Henry III. 248. Is directed how to act in consequence of that letter, ibid. Dreading the king's resentment, thinks it expedient to repair to London, 257. Exculpates himself by oath from any part or concurrence in the death of earl Richard, 258. Is gained by de Burgo, ibid. Ordered by the king to take the speediest and most effectual measures for re-establishing Fedlim in full possession of his rights, 259. Removed from the Irish government, 262.

Fitz-

INDEX.

Fitz-Henry, Meiler, succeeds Hamo de Valois, i. 199. Marches to reduce William de Burgo, 204. Is joined by Cathal and O'Brien of Thomond, ibid. Receives hostages from them, 205. Is invested by the king with all the issues and profits of his pension to be expended on fortifying and improving Connaught, ibid.

Fitz Maurice, Maurice, marches against some insurgents, i. 282. Is seized and taken prisoner, ibid. Retires, when released from his confinement, to his own lands, to raise new commotions, 283. Unites with lord Theobald Butler, and makes private war upon the Irish of Munster, ibid.

————, James, threatens his country (Ireland) with an invasion, ii. 324. Retires to the continent with an unconquerable hatred of the queen (Elizab.) and an impatience of new disorders, ibid. His practices in Italy and Spain, 325. Procures a bull at Rome in his favour, ibid. Lands at Kerry with a troop of Spaniards, at a bay called Smerwick, 326. Is unable to suppress his vexation at the earl of Desmond's duplicity, 327. Falls in a skirmish with one of the sons of sir William de Burgo, 330.

Fitz-Stephen, Robert, arrives near the city of Wexford, i. 27. Marches to Wexford, 28. Leads up his forces to the walls, 29. Is obliged to retire, ibid. Leads his troops again to the assault, and is successful, ibid. Settles the terms of capitulation with the inhabitants, ibid. Receives deputies from Roderic O'Connor, 39. Sends them back without complying with their proposals, ibid. Dreading the instability of the men of Wexford, he determines to build a fort to keep them in perpetual awe, 43. He is besieged in the fort of Carig, ibid. Deceived, 72. Surrenders, ibid. Is cruelly treated by his enemies, ibid. Presented by the men of Wexford, as their prisoner, to the king, 82. Is sternly reprimanded by the king for his presumption, and ordered back to prison, ibid. Is released, 83. Has a considerable district in the neighbourhood of Dublin granted him, 100. Made one of Hugh de Lacy's coadjutors, 101. Settles in Desmond, 155. Obliged to take arms again, 163. Is relieved by Raymond le Gros, ibid. Is deprived of his reason, 164.

————Ralph, (son of Robert) assassinated, i. 163.

Fitz-Thomas, John, confiding in the pacific disposition of his rival, departs from the kingdom, and attends the service of king Edward I. in Flanders, i. 303. Attends the king's standard in Scotland, ibid.

————, Maurice, strictly enjoined on his allegiance, by the king, to pay due obedience and submission to his chief governour, the earl of Kildare, i. 340. Takes the field against John de la Poer, who had personally affronted him, ibid. Is invited by Darcy to his assistance, 343. Discovers a detestable propensity to oppression, ibid. Is honoured with the title of earl Desmond, and receives a confirmation of his royal liberties in the county of Kerry, 344. Is seized by the governour, sir Anthony Lucy, 346. Is discharged on great surety, after, a long confinement, and sent to England, ibid. Is summoned to attend a parliament in Dublin, 363. Slights the mandate, and summons an assembly of his own, ibid. Shocked at the intrepid severity of sir Ralph de Ufford, and conscious of his own irregular conduct, retires in

INDEX.

dismay, leaving his sureties to answer for his default, ibid. Again emboldened by the death of Ufford to appear and remonstrate against the wrongs he alledged to have received from him, 364. Is restored to favour, 365. Attends the king's service in France, ibid. Succeeds sir Thomas Rokeby as lord deputy, 369. Dies soon after his promotion, ibid.

Fitz-William, sir William, succeeds sir Henry Sidney in the government of Ireland, ii. 307. Remonstrates warmly against the commission granted to the earl of Essex, 309. Desires to be relieved from the burden of his Irish government, 313. Succeeds sir John Perrot in the government of Ireland, 378. Assumes the reins of government at a favourable period, ibid. Resolves to make his post as advantageous to him as possible, ibid. Marches into Ulster in pursuit of Spanish treasure, 380. Commits two gentlemen who had done services to the government to close durance in the castle of Dublin, 381. Inflames the disaffection of the northern chieftains by his cruelty, 384. Receives a singular answer from Mac-Guire, the chieftain of Fermanagh, 385. Behaves with great partiality with regard to the earl of Tirone, 399. Recalled, at his own solicitation, 403.

Fleetwood, general, appointed lord deputy of Ireland for three years, iv. 100. Succeeded by Henry Cromwell, 103.

Forbes, lord, arrives at Kinsale with twelve hundred men, iii. 200. His character, ibid. He disdains to unite with any not of the *Godly*, ibid. Reimbarks after some indiscriminating depredations, and proceeds to the bay of Galway, ibid. His intemperate and extravagant conduct, 201.

Francis I. king of France, determines to raise commotions in Ireland, ii. 163. Opens a negotiation with the earl of Desmond, ibid. His treaty rendered ineffectual by the earl's death, 165.

Furnival, lord, lands near Dublin, and assumes the reins of government, ii. 11. His successes. ibid. His administration odious, ibid. He departs from Ireland, with the execrations of all those clergy and laity alike who had been injured by the tyrannical exercise of his power, 15.

G

GAVEL-KIND, an old Irish custom, abolished, ii. 492.

Gaveston, Piers, appointed vicegerent in Ireland, i. 306. Popular and successful, 307. Envied and opposed by the earl of Ulster, ibid. Suddenly re-called, 309.

Ginckle, general, sends a detachment to the assistance of the earl of Marlborough, iii. 316. Thinks it not prudent to dispose his forces in winter-quarters, 319. Keeps them ready to oppose any sudden attempts, ibid. Encamps near Ballymore, 325. Reduces it, 328. Orders the breaches to be repaired, ibid. Advances to Athlone, to lay siege to it, ibid. Meets with great opposition, but is not disconcerted, 330. Convenes a council, 331. Makes himself master of Athlone, 334. Proclaims a pardon, 336. Marches from Athlone, 338. Comes to an engagement with Saint Ruth, 340. Leads his victorious troops to Galway, 343. Grants honourable conditions to the garrison of Galway,

INDEX.

way, 344. His cautious procedures, 345. Makes a succesful attempt to pass the Shannon, 347. Lays siege to Limerick, 349. Conceals his design, ibid. Publishes a declaration, 350. Is animated by the intelligence he receives of the reduction of Sligo, ibid. Gains an advantage over the enemy at Thomond bridge, 351. Rejects the demands of the capitulating Irish leaders, 353. Remonstrates against Sarsefield, called by both parties lord Lucan, ibid. *Glamorgan*, earl of, his character, iii. 286. Created generalissimo of the armies, English, Irish, and foreign, ibid. Arrives in Ireland, 292. Is received with particular satisfaction, ibid. Produces two commissions from king Charles I. to the confederates, 293. Enters into a private treaty with them, 296. Confers with Rinunccini, the pope's nuncio. 304. Makes concessions to him, ibid. His private treaty disclosed, ibid. He is seduced by lord Digby to Dublin, 309. Impeached by him, ibid. Imprisoned, 311. Examined before the council, ibid. His conference with the marquis of Ormond, ibid. His liberty demanded by the supreme council, 314. He is discharged, 315. And commissioned to treat with the confederates, ibid. His transactions disavowed by the king, ibid. Receives a private letter from the king, 317. Is disposed to comply with the nuncio's proposal, 321. Writes to the marquis of Ormond, ibid. His engagements and promises to the nuncio, ibid. His confident assurances to the king, 322. Infatuated by the behaviour of Rinunccini, 341. And transported with the favours he receives from him, ibid.

Glenvill, successor to Maurice Fitz-Maurice, defeated, i. 283.

Gormanston, lord, appointed lord deputy, ii. 114. Supported by the earl of Kildare and other lords, ibid. Convenes a parliament at Drogheda, ibid.

Grey, lord, constituted by king Edward IV. deputy to the duke of Clarence, ii. 75. Refused admittance into the castle of Dublin, ibid. Convenes his assembly, ibid. Appointed, by a new commission, deputy to prince George, the king's infant son, 76. Returns to England, 77.

H

HAMILTON, Richard, sent by the prince of Orange to the earl of Tyrconnel, iv. 237. His advice to him, ibid. He marches against the Northerns, 239. Obliges them to retreat, ibid.

Henry II. conceives a design, soon after he ascends the throne of England, to annex Ireland to his dominions, i. 4. His pretences, for the invasion of Ireland, 5. Applies to pope Adrian, 7. His design necessarily suspended, 12. Receives a supplicating visit from Dermod, king of Leinster, while he is engaged in Aquitaine, 20. Discourages the earl of Chepstow, 51. Treats his scheme of an adventure in Ireland with contempt and ridicule, ibid. Commands him passionately to be gone, ibid. Prepares for an expedition to Ireland, ibid. Alarmed at the progress of Strongbow, (the above-mentioned earl,) 61. Issues a royal edict, ibid. Summons the earl to appear instantly before him, 77. His resentment is allayed by the earl's submissions, ibid. Makes preparations for the intended invasion, ibid. Arrives at Waterford, 82. Orders the execution of an Ostman lord immediately on his landing, ibid.

INDEX.

ibid. Receives the Wexfordians in a gracious manner, ibid. Makes a short progress, 83. Returns to Wexford, 84. Marches to Dublin, 85. Receives the homage of several Irish lords, ibid. Attempts to reduce Roderic O'Connor, ibid. Feasts the Irish lords in Dublin, 87. Orders a synod of the clergy to be summoned, to enquire into the state of morality and religion, 88. Recalled to Normandy, 99. His dispositions and grants in Ireland, 100. Embarks at Wexford, 102. Treats with the legates, ibid. Threatens to return to Ireland, ibid. Is reconciled to pope Alexander, who confirms the grant of Ireland made by Adrian, 103. Establishes the several branches of his family, 109. Excites the jealousy and envy of his neighbours by that establishment, ibid. And finds the exaltation of his sons productive of a rebellion among them against himself, ibid. Surprised and alarmed at the behaviour of his eldest son, 110. Receives intelligence of new misfortunes, ibid. Withdraws several of his garrisons from Ireland, 111. Summons earl Strongbow to attend him at Rouen, 112. Permits him to employ Raymond in any service he shall deem necessary, 113. Alarmed by the marriage of Hervey de Mountmorres, with a daughter of Maurice Fitz Gerald, 125. Dispatches four commissioners to Dublin, to conduct Raymond to him, 127. Makes a generous observation on the burning of Limerick by the perfidy of O'Brien, 132. Makes a formal and solemn appointment of his son John to the lordship of Ireland, 151. Declines the pope's offer to crown him king of Ireland, 168. Sends him to his government with a considerable force and a magnificent retinue, but without any additional titles or ceremonial, ibid. Dies at Chinon in France, 178.

——— III. sends a remarkable letter to Geoffry de Maurisco, justiciary of Ireland, on his accession, in answer to a petition to the throne for new graces, 233. Makes grants, 244. Receives an application from Fedlim, prince of Connaught which surprises him, 247. Dreads the effects of Richard Marishal's dispositions, 249. Behaves with meanness on his death, 255. Receives a personal application from Fedlim, 258. Encourages him to expect a redress of all his wrongs, 259. Requires all the toparchs who had submitted, or were supposed to be well affected to him, to repair to his standard with their forces, in order to assist him against the king of Scotland, 260. Obliged repeatedly to enforce the observance of the English laws, 263. Vests his son, prince Edward, with the lordship of Ireland, 268. Makes the severest exactions, 273. *Henry* IV. the effect of his accession on Ireland, ii. 2. He receives the archbishops of Armagh and Dublin, deputed by an Irish parliament to repair to him, graciously, 3. Appoints his second son, Thomas, duke of Lancaster, vicegerent, ibid.

——— V. neglects Ireland on his accession, ii. 10.

——— VI. the disorders of Ireland increased on his accession, ii. 20. He orders, by a special mandate, the earl of Ormond to appear before him without delay, 30. Is petitioned to remove the earl from his government, 31. Complies with the petition, 32.

——— VII. finds his Irish subjects very much displeased with him on his accession, ii. 83. Alarmed with imperfect rumours of some plots secretly ripening to execution, 88. Apprehends some secret plots

INDEX.

in Ireland, ibid. Summons the earl of Kildare to repair to him, ibid. Engages the rebels headed by Lambert Simnel, near Stroke, in the county of Nottingham, 101. Defeats them, and takes Simnel prisoner, 102. Acts with apparent lenity and real policy, 104. Dismisses the earl of Kildare, and other lords who attended him at Greenwich, with marks of favour, 108. Receives archbishop Walter in a favourable manner, 114. Confers with him on the state of Ireland, ibid. Desires his opinion of a foreign ambassador's very florid harangue, 115. Returns a laconic answer to his uncourtly reply, ibid. Turns his thoughts to the regulation of his dominions, and to the establishment of the succession in his family, 116. Permits the earl of Kildare to confront his adversaries, before him, 132. Becomes acquainted with his real character, ibid. Directs him to prepare for his defence, 133. Finds the allegations against him dictated by private resentment and factious malignity, ibid. Surprises his accusers by a singular answer, 134.

———VIII. neglects Ireland on his accession, ii. 147. Courted by the two great rival monarchs, Francis I. and Charles V. 153. Receives a very extraordinary address from an Irish ambassador while he is going to chapel, 161. Is seduced by the emperor to declare war against France, 162. Is enraged against the earl of Desmond and his presumptuous treason, 163. Dispatches orders for the seizure of the earl, ibid. Exposes Ireland to all the evils of short-lived, feeble, and disorderly administrations, by being too attentive to the brilliant affairs of his reign, 164. Receives a strong petition for redress against the earl of Kildare's irregularities, 170. Orders the earl to repair to him without delay, 171. Becomes an instrument of Providence to introduce the first beginnings of the reformation in his kingdom, 188. Resolves to gain a reception for the new doctrines in Ireland, 189. His royal commission treated in Ireland with indifference and neglect, 195. Has the title of king of Ireland conferred on him by an Irish parliament, 215. Receives submissions from the Irish and degenerate English lords, 217. Flattered by the appearance of the most distinguished of his new Irish subjects at the court of England, 219. Dismisses them with striking marks of his favour, 220, 221. Takes measures to secure their attachment, ibid. Defects in his policy, and in his Irish administration, 222.

Hervey de Mountmorres, his character as a man and as a soldier, i. 112. He is inflamed with envy by the popularity of Raymond le Gross, ibid.

Hesculph, governour of Dublin, escapes from thence while it is stormed, i. 57. Appears at the head of a considerable force, consisting of troops collected in the northern islands, 64. Is defeated and taken prisoner, 65. Led to Dublin in triumph, ibid. Executed, ibid.

I

JAMES I. finds the popish party virulent in Ireland on his accession, ii. 486. Orders an act of oblivion and indemnity to be published by proclamation, 490. Constitutes Mountjoy lord lieutenant of Ireland, ibid. Issues a *commission of grace*, for securing the subjects of Ireland

against

INDEX.

against all claims of the crown, 492. Expresses a tenderness for the religious tenets of Rome, 495. But has a sincere abhorrence of those who taught the supreme authority of the pope, ibid. Commands the popish clergy of Ireland to depart within a limited time, ibid. His strong desire to reform Ireland by the introduction of English law and civility, favoured by the temerity of the Northerns, 499. Takes a speedy advantage of their precipitate flight from Ulster, ibid. Dispatches judges into the counties of Tirone and Tyrconnel, ibid. Issues a proclamation to justify his proceedings with regard to the earls of Tirone and Tyrconnel, against the clamours of the popish agents, ibid. Resolves to dispose of the lands in Ireland escheated to the crown in such a manner as to introduce all the happy consequences of peace and cultivation, 504. Proceeds deliberately with regard to the intended plantation in Munster, ibid. Finds the advice of sir Arthur Chichester upon that occasion the most serviceable, ibid. Institutes the order of baronets, 509. Makes provisions for the correction of some ecclesiastical abuses, 511. For the inferior clergy, and for the university, 512. Incorporates several of the towns in the northern counties, improved by plantation, 513. Highly pleased with the administration of sir Arthur Chichester, 514. Vests him with the territory of Innishowen, 515. Extremely disgusted at the petition of the lords of the Pale, 520. Receives the complaints of the Irish agents with temper and attention, 529. Admits the recusants to plead their cause before the council, 531. Finally pronounces their allegations groundless, ibid. Promotes doctor James Usher to the see of Meath, 537. Resolves to execute new plantation schemes, 538. Makes distributions of lands forfeited by rebellion, 539. Creates sir Arthur Chichester, baron of Belfast, 540. Recals him to England, ibid. Appoints sir Oliver St. John, his successor, ibid. Creates him, by way of amends for the mortifications he has received in the execution of his office, an Irish and an English peer, makes him lord high treasurer of Ireland, and privy counsellor of both kingdoms, 542. Gives a favourable reception to a project for the establishment of an extensive plantation in Connaught, 558. Resolves to augment the forces of Ireland, 559. Dies, ibid.

James II. ascends the throne, amidst the acclamations of a triumphant faction, iv. 202. Mistakes it for the universal joy of his subjects, ibid. Assures the earl of Granard, in a letter written with his own hand, that nothing shall be done in Ireland prejudicial to the protestant interest, 205. Declares his purpose of employing popish officers in England, 206. Cautions his parliament against the presumption of objecting to this exercise of prerogative, ibid. Appoints the earl of Clarendon, his brother-in-law, lord-lieutenant of Ireland, 208. Commands him to declare that he has no intention of altering the acts of settlement, ibid. Looks upon his representations about the admission of Roman catholics into office of trust, without taking the oaths of supremacy, as impertinent and uncourtly, 211. Cannot be persuaded to fill up the archbishoprick of Cashel, 212. Issues orders that the catholic clergy shall not be molested in the exercise of their functions, 213. Notifies his royal pleasure that their prelates should appear publicly in

the

INDEX.

the habit of their order, ibid. Prohibits the protestant clergy from treating of controversial points in the pulpit, ibid. His instructions to the earl of Tyrconnel, abused in the execution, ibid. Rejects an application from the citizens of Dublin, presented to him by their recorder, 220. Orders a quo warranto to be immediately issued, and judgment to be pronounced against this charter, ibid. Listens to the representations made to him of the state of Ireland, by Rice, chief baron of the exchequer, 224. Remits Tyrconnel to his government, ibid. Assures the university of Dublin, in a short answer, that he had no doubt of the loyalty of any of the church of England, ibid. Instructs Tyrconnel on his departure to dismiss almost all the protestant officers remaining in the army, ibid. Declares warmly against the iniquity of the acts of settlement, 226. Receives the intelligence of the prince of Orange's design against him with derision, 228. Is deserted by his subjects, on the landing of that prince, 229. Throws himself under the protection of the French king, 241. Effects of his embarkation for Ireland, 242. Sails from Brest with fourteen ships of war, six frigates, and three fire ships, ibid. Lands at Kinsale, ibid. Creates the earl of Tyrconnel a duke, 243. Arrives at the capital in a stately progress, ibid. Deems the reduction of the Northerns a peculiar object of attention, 244. Resolves to lead his forces to the walls, himself, at the siege of Derry, to encourage the besiegers, and to confound the stubborn insurgents, ibid. Advances towards the city, 246. Approaches with his advanced party to take possession of it, 247. Returns to Dublin, 259. Publishes a declaration, 260. Levies money by his prerogative, 264. His brass coinage, 265. Governs in a mean and cruel manner, 266. Contends with the university of Dublin, 267. Offers duke Schomberg battle, 276. Draws off his forces to Ardee, at the moment when an engagement seemed inevitable, ibid. Forms his magazines, and prepares for the campaign, 284. Finds his new auxiliaries refractory and disobedient, ibid. Is sensibly affected by the loss of Charlemont, ibid. Holds a council, 288. Resolves to defend the passage of the Boyne, 289. Is defeated, 296. Assembles the magistracy of Dublin, 297. makes an ungracious speech, 298. Flies to France, ibid.

James, son to the great rebel, earl of Desmond, sent by queen Elizabeth to Ireland, ii. 466. His adventure at Kilmallock, 467.

Inchiquin, lord, succeeds Sir Wiliam St. Leger, in the command at Ulster, iii. 199. Solicits the English parliament for supplies, 200. Struggles with difficulties at Cork, and is scarcely able to procure subsistance for his garrison, 201. Resolves to hazard an engagement with the rebels, ibid. Finds them advantageously posted, ibid. Defeats them, ibid. Claims the province of Munster, in which he had commanded, from the death of sir William St. Leger, without the title of lord president, as a reward for his zealous services, 273. Is mortified on applying to the king, at Oxford, by hearing of its having already been granted to the earl of Portland, ibid. Retires to Munster, fired with resentment, and enters into a secret negociation with the English parliament, ibid. Neglected by the English parliament, he is soon obliged, for the preservation of his forces and the protestants of Munster, to make a cessation with the Irish, ibid. Acts with vigour

against

INDEX.

against the Irish, iv. 5. Over-runs some counties, tak
opens a way for his famished troops to range freely
county of Tipperary, 6. Advances against the city
his victorious army, ibid. Takes it by storm, ibid
the inactivity of lord Taafe, ibid. Encounters him a
7. Gains a compleat victory, ibid. Gives some sign
to the parliament, 14. Remonstrates boldly against
his forces, ibid. Holds a secret correspondence with
Ormond, ibid. Obliged publicly to avow his revolt,
a crafty proposal from O'Nial, 20. Endeavours to for
gagement, but all his attempts are eluded by the wary
Quiets the commotions of the mutineers in his army, b
ance, and the assistance of the marquis of Ormond, 26.
Drogheda, and obliges the city to surrender, 37. At
horse and foot, employed to escort some ammunition,
parliamentarians, to Owen O'Nial, with success, ibid
dalk, and forces it to surrender, ibid. Reduces some
garrisons, and returns triumphantly to the camp at
Resolves to intercept a body of men on their march to
well's army, 50. Fails, and is defeated in the attemp

Innocent III. pope, begins a controvesy with king Jo
i. 214. Gains an advantage over him, 216.

John, king, by seizing the throne, in prejudice to t
thur, of Bretagne, son to his eldest brother, has all the
usurpation to encounter, i. 198. Enters into a controv
Innocent III. concerning a successor to the see of Arm
censed at the contempt of his authority, 215. Still more
Finds his violence softned by an acceptable present,
upon to invest Eugene, whom the pope had support
rights of the contested see, 216. Soon experiences the
quences of the pope's superiority, 217. Undertakes a
Ireland, 219. Arrives at Dublin, ibid. Grants his
charter of laws, 223. Makes a new division of counties
from Ireland 226. Interposes in favour of Cathal, king
228. Endeavours to gain the Irish princes by affability

Jones, Michael, colonel, appointed governor of Dub
liament of England, and commander of their forces ir
Finds it necessary to connive at the outrages of hi
Repelled by Preston in two skirmishes, 4. Comes to
with him, and gains a compleat victory, 5. Returns to
being able to improve his advantage, ibid. Receiv
accommodation from Owen O'Nial, 19. Cannot ventu
self of the distractions of the Irish, ibid. Consents to
tion from O'Nial, ibid. Applied to by the earl of Antr
to support him, ibid. Practised with, by the marquis
Surrounded with difficulties and distresses, 36. Gain
and provisions from England, by the negligence of prin
Finds resources in Ireland by his own industry and
Practises with the officers who served under Preston,
them and him to make an attempt upon the marquis o
ibid. Detaches most part of his horse to Drogheda, 3

INDEX.

marquis, 41. Returns a laconic answer to his letter about the prisoners he had taken, 42. Raises the siege of Drogheda with precipitation on the marquis's advancing, and retires to Dublin, ibid. Attempts to intercept him retiring with the remains of his army, but without success, 49. Made prisoner in the castle of Dublin, 106.

Jones, sir Theophilus, takes the field with ten thousand men, iv. 44. Joins with several other men of weight and consequence, in forming a bold design to seize the castle of Dublin, and to secure the persons of the commissioners, 106. Rides through the streets of Dublin exclaiming for a free parliament, 108.

―――, John, a zealous republican, one of the commissioners of parliament, under the direction of general Fleetwood, iv. 98.

Ireland, state of Ireland, favourable to an invasion in the eleventh and twelfth centuries, i. 2. State of the neighbouring kingdoms, 3. Scheme of invading Ireland, formed by Henry II. 4. Pretences for this invasion, 5. Application to pope Adrian, 7. His motives for complying with the request of Henry, 8. His bull, 9. Henry's design necessarily suspended, 12. Review of the state of Ireland at this period, 13. Factions and quarrels of its chieftains, 13, 14. First British colony in Ireland, 30. Horrid instance of revenge, 31. Success of the first British adventurers, nothing wonderful or extraordinary, 46. Cruel execution of the Leinster hostages, 59. Deputation of the Wexfordians, 79. Artfully received by Henry, 80. Submissions of the chieftain of Desmond, the first who acknowledged the king's sovereignty, 83. Meaning of a submission to Henry and his heirs, 94. Laws of England, how far established in Ireland, 95. Not as a model for a new polity, ibid. Rights of the English adventurers secured, 96. Settlement of Dublin, 97. Grant to the Ostmen of Waterford, ibid. Counties, sheriffs, and officers of state established in Ireland, 98. Provision in case of the death of a chief governour, 99. Grant of the sovereignty of Ireland, confirmed by pope Alexander, 103. Dispositions of the Irish chieftains, 105. Rebellion of Henry's sons, and general insurrections against the king, 110, 111. Revolt of the Irish lords, ibid. Mutual jealousies between Hervey de Mountmorres, and Raymond le Grofs, 112. Expedition to Munster, 116. Defeat of the Ostmen, 117. Insurrection and massacre at Waterford, 119. Desolation of Meath, by Roderic O'Connor, 120. Character of earl Strongbow, by the Irish annalists, and by Giraldus, 133. Bulls of Adrian and Alexander promulged, 135. Divisions of the Irish chieftains, 146. Miserable condition of the whole island, ibid. Grants by king Henry, in Thomond, Desmond, and Connaught, which explain the nature of his cession to prince John, 152. Miserable situation of Connaught, 159. Massacre of Milo de Logan, and Ralph Fitz-Stephen, 163. A general spirit of insurrection raised through Ireland, 170. Insurrection of the Irish natives, 171. Several of the prince's barons surprised and slain, 172. Distressful state of the country, 173. Fatal effects of rebellion in the family of Roderic O'Connor, 177. Acts of power exercised by earl John, during the reign of Richard, 181. Insurrection of the Irish, 184. Burning of Dublin, and disorders of the neighbouring country, 187. English defeated by Daniel O'Brien, 188. Cruel-

INDEX.

188. Cruelties exercised on his family after his death, 189. English driven out of Limerick, 190. Corke threatened with a siege, ibid. State of government in Ireland, at the accession of king John, 198. Grants to Philip de Braosa, and William de Burgo, 200. Cause of the revolt of the English barons in Ireland, 206. Romantic details concerning John de Courcey, and Hugh de Lacy, 208, 209, 210, 211. Remarks on those details, 212. Aid for the recovery of Normandy demanded of the Irish clergy, 214. State of Ireland at the time of king John's expedition to it, 218. Cause of John's displeasure against the Lacies, 219. And against William de Braosa, ibid. The Lacies fly from Ireland at the king's arrival, ibid. The wife and family of William de Braosa imprisoned, 224. The Lacies distressed in France, 225. Are restored to favour, and reinstated in their possessions, ibid. Circumstances favourable to the government of John de Grey, 226. Petitions to Henry III. on his accession, from his barons in Ireland, for new graces, 232. The Great Charter granted by king John to his Irish subjects renewed, 236. State of Ireland during the first years of the reign of Henry III. 240. Contest between the earl of Pembroke's successor, and the Lacies, 243. Grants made by Henry, 244. Commotions in Connaught, 245. Commotions in Ireland, on the death of Richard, earl Marishal, 255. Complicated disorders of Ireland, 261. The benefits of the English laws sued for by some particulars, 265. But denied to the Irish in general, ibid. True cause of this exclusion, 266. Grant of the lordship of Ireland to prince Edward, 269. This kingdom deprived of the advantage of his abilities, ibid. Commotions in the North, 270. In Desmond, 271. The Geraldines depressed, ibid. Recover their power, 272. Quarrels with Walter de Burgo, ibid. Exactions of the king, 273. Those of the pope still more oppressive, 274. Statute of Merton, 278. Ulster infested by the Scots, in the reign of Edward I. 283. Contest between the Geraldines, and the O'Brien's, ibid. Distress of the Geraldines, 284. Irish petition to be admitted to the benefits of English law, 286. The petition defeated, 288. Second application equally unsuccessful, 289. Insurrections, 291. Feuds of the English lords, 293. Expectations from the administration of William de Vesey, 295. Parliament of sir John Wogan, 297. The acts of this assembly, 298. Feuds of the English lords composed, 302. Effects of the absence of the baron of Ophally, and the earl of Ulster from Ireland, 304. Reconciliation of the great lords, in the reign of Edward II. 310. Origin of the Scottish invasion, 311. Lords of the English race summoned to a parliament in England, 313. Landing of the Scots, 314. Irish and degenerate English crowd to Edward Bruce, 320. General famine, ibid. Association of the English Lords, 321. Battle of Athunree, ibid. Consternation of the citizens of Dublin, threatened by Bruce, 324. English interest revives, 324. Horrible distresses of the Scots, 326. Miserable consequences of the Scottish war, 328. Petition for annual parliaments, 329. Degeneracy of English families, 330. Subsidy demanded, 331. Present disorders of Ireland, similar to those of England, 335. Attempts to establish a seat of learning in Dublin, 337. Disorders from malice and superstition, 339. State of Ireland at the accession of

Edward

INDEX.

Edward III. ibid. Pride and contention of the English families, 340. Irish of Leinster petition for a general denization, 342. But without effect, ibid. They rise under the leading of O'Brien, ibid. Their progress and cruelty, ibid. Repelled by the citizens of Wexford, 343. Pernicious grants of palatinates, 344. Fatal consequences of the assassination of the earl of Ulster, 349. Irruptions of O'Nial, ibid. Of Mac-William, 350. Loyalty and zeal of the Geraldines, ibid. Rigorous measures pursued by the king, 351. All of Irish birth disqualified to hold offices, 355. Irish subjects dangerously incensed, ibid. Convention of Kilkenny, 356. Spirited remonstrance and petition to the throne favourably received, 359. Irish parliament grants a subsidy, 365. Arrogance and sedition of an archbishop of Cashel, ibid. Ordinances for the regulation of the state of Ireland, 370. Provisions against the odious distinctions between the subjects of this land, against the growing dissentions of the English, 371. Subjects divided, 372. The country harrassed by O'Nial, and O'Brien, ibid. Consequences of lord Lionel's forbidding all the old English, or any of the king's subjects of Irish birth, to approach his camp, 374. A subsidy granted for his support, 376. Discipline of his troops, ibid. Factions inflamed by his conduct, 377. Statute of Kilkenny, 378. Influence of this ordinance, 379. Measures taken by the Irish enemy, 382. Their dangerous progress, 383. Instances of the abhorrence conceived of Ireland, 384. Misdemeanour alledged against sir William Windsore, ibid. Pensions paid to the Irish, 386. Representatives from the land of Ireland summoned to Westminster, ibid. Answer to the king's writs, ibid. Gradual declension of the English interest, ibid. Distresses of Ireland on the accession of Richard II. 392. Measures advised to relieve him, 394. Edmund and Roger Mortimer lord deputies, ibid. Ireland invested by the French and Scots, ibid. Stanly and Ormond chief governours, 399. Maintenance of the English power burdensome, 400. Terror and submission of the Irish chieftains, 404. Their homage, ibid. Their stipulations, 405. Four Irish princes entertained in Dublin at the king's table, in robes of state, 407. Truce granted to the degenerate English, ibid. No real advantages derived from the king's expedition to Ireland, 410. Insurrection of the Irish in Leinster, ibid. Distresses and dejection of the royal army, 415. The effect of Henry IV's accession on Ireland, ii. 2. Inroads of the Scots, 3. Measures for opposing them, ibid. Weakness of English government, 4. Effects of the duke of Lancaster's devices, ibid. Inconveniences and relaxation of the statutes of Kilkenny, 8. Instance of affected sovereignty over the old natives, 9. Their real power, ibid. Black-rent, 10. Ireland neglected by Henry V. ibid. Desperate state of the English government, ibid. Mortifying situation of subjects of the English race, 12. Their provocations, ibid. The chancellor refuses to affix a seal to a petition of parliament, 14. The petition renewed and transmitted, 16. Factions and dissentions, 19. Situation and dispositions of the Irish enemy, ibid. No general confederacy formed against the English, 20. Disorders of Ireland increased by the accession of Henry VI. ibid. Proceedings of an Irish parliament, 21. A bishop of Meath deputed by the earl of March, to govern

INDEX.

in his abfence, 22. Irifh enemy reduced, 24. Pathetic reprefentations to England of the weaknefs of Irifh government, 27. Complaints of the firft fubjects, ibid. Remarkable indulgences granted to the earl of Defmond, 28. Addreffes to the king to remove the earl of Ormond, 31. Origin of the attachment of the houfe of Butler to the Lancaftrian princes, 34. Contefts between the houfes of York and Lancafter, 35. Infurrections, 45. Generous conteft between O'Connor and his fon, ibid. Zeal of the fubjects and parliament of Ireland, in the fupport of the duke of York, 49. Effects of his death on the native Irifh, 52. Real influence of the war of York and Lancafter in Ireland, ibid. Intelligence received of the depofition of king Henry VI. 50. Act of attainder againft the Geraldines, 67. Obfequious compliances of Irifh parliaments, 68. Inftitution of the fraternity of St. George, 72. Revival of the houfe of Ormond, 73. Public confufion, 74. Rival parliaments and councils, 76. The influence of the earl of Kildare after his reftoration, during the reign of Edward V. and Richard III. 80. Acceffion of Henry VII. difpleafing to the Irifh fubjects, 83. The Yorkifts ftill employed in Ireland, ibid. Motives for this conduct, 84. Secret plots in Ireland apprehended by the king, 88. Lambert Simnel oppofed by the Butlers, and the city of Waterford, 92. An Irifh parliament fummoned, and the government adminiftered in his name, 96, 97. Valour and flaughter of the Irifh forces, at the battle of Stoke, in England, 101. Submiffion of Simnel's Irifh adherents to the king, 104. Laconic letters of two Irifh chieftains, 111. Houfe of Butler reftored to power, ibid. Dangerous feuds, ibid. Adminiftration of archbifhop Walter, ibid. Clamours againft the government of lord Gormanfton, 114. Inftances of archbifhop Walter's fimplicity, 115. Objects of fir Edward Poyning's adminiftration, 121. Infurrection of an Irifh chieftain, ibid. Irifh fubjects reconciled to the king, 134. Device for reftraining the Irifh enemies, 135. Dangerous confequence of the alliance between the earl of Kildare and Ulic of Clanricarde, 140. Battle of Knocktow, ibid. Its confequences, 141. Revival and increafe of the Englifh power in Ireland, 142. Ireland neglected on the acceffion of Henry VIII. 148. Whimfical embaffy from Ireland to the king, 161. Public Diforders, 165. Charles V. and Francis I. labour to raife infurrections in Ireland, ibid. The petition of the earl of Kildare's enemies to the throne, 169. Rumours of his condemnation and death, 172. Hoftilities againft the earl of Ormond, 176. Siege of Dublin, 177. Succours arrive from England, 179. Siege of Maynooth, 180. Effects of the furrender of this caftle, 181. Cruelty of William Skeffington, ibid. Five uncles of lord Thomas treacheroufly feized, 185. Execution of the Geraldines, ibid. A brother of lord Thomas preferved from the vengeance of the king, 186. Reformation of religion, 187. Its firft beginning in England, 188. Schemes for extending it to Ireland, 189. Circumftances of this country unfavourable to the defign, 190, 191. Particular prejudice in favour of the pope, 193. Practices of Cromer, archbifhop of Armagh, 194. Browne, archbifhop of Dublin, zealous for the reformation, 195. Irifh parliament convened, 196. Its ftatutes, 197, 198, 199. Oppofition of the partifans of Rome, 200. Meafures for paffing of the act of fupremacy, ibid. Subtilty of the

popifh

INDEX.

popish party defeated, 202. Necessity of vigour in the field, ibid. Factions formed against lord Grey, 205. Turbulence of the popish party, 206. Commissions from Rome to Cromer and his associates, 207. New insurrections repelled, 213. General despondency of the disaffected, ibid. The title of king of Ireland confirmed on Henry, 215. Submissions of the Irish and degenerate English lords, 217. Ordinances for the government of Connaught and Munster, 218. Measures taken by the king to secure the attachment of his great Irish subjects, 221. Defection in the policy of the king and his Irish administration, 223. Their consequences, ibid. Reformation of the state of Ireland, how far advanced, ibid. Dispositions in the state of Ireland, on the accession of Edward VI. 227. Arrival of Bellingham and his forces, 228. Insurrections of O'More and O'Connor, ibid. Distress of these chieftains, 229. New settlements in Leix and O'Fally, ibid. Secret practises of Rome, 230. Difficulties attending the reformation in Ireland, 232, 233, 234. Prejudices against the reformers, 237. The civil government necessarily vigilant, 244. Factions in the west, 245. Disorders in the family of O'Nial, 246. Queen Mary's graces to her Irish subjects, 249. Insurrections in Leix and O'Fally, 252. Incursions of the Scots, ibid. Bull and cardinal Pole received by the Irish parliament, 253. Acts for the re-establishment of popery, 255. Acts for the civil government, ibid. Explanation of Poynings' law, 256. Private act relative to archbishop Brown, 258. War between O'Nial and O'Donnel, described by the Irish annalists, 261, 262, 263. Scots defeated by the earl of Clanricarde, 264. State of Ireland on queen Elizabeth's accession to the throne, 266. Conference between sir Henry Sydney and John O'Nial, 269. Scheme for re-establishing the Reformation, 271. Irish parliament of the second year of queen Elizabeth, ibid. Temper of this assembly, ibid. Its Laws, 272. How received by the people, 274. Alarming spirit of the Romish party, 275. New excesses of John O'Nial, 276. Accommodation between him and the earl of Sussex, 277. Garrison of Derry offensive to O'Nial, 282. Wise measures of Sydney for reducing him, 284. Sydney's regulations of Tyrowen, 287. Elizabeth's fears and suspicions, 290. Disorders occasioned by the absence of Sydney, 291. Temper of the house of commons, 292. Clamours and discontents, 294. Act of this assembly, ibid. Progress of the civil reformation in Ireland, imperfect, 299. Causes retarding it, 300. Insurrections, 301, 302. Submissions of Sydney's brothers, 304. The earls of Clancarthy and Thomond terrified from their intentions to rebel, 305. Scheme of plantation in Ireland formed by sir Thomas Smith, 307. Assassination of his son, 308. Project of Walter earl of Essex, ibid. Secret practices of the earl of Leicester, 309. Return of the earl of Desmond and his brother, 310. Letter of the pope to encourage insurrections intercepted, 311. Insurgents repressed and quieted, ibid. Leicester suspected of causing Essex to be poisoned, 312. Complaints against Sydney's design, 317. How received by the queen, 320. Irish petitioners treated with severity, ibid. The designs of Elizabeth's foreign enemies on Ireland, 323. Preparations against invasions, 325. Duplicity of the earl of Desmond, ibid.

Miseries

INDEX.

Miseries of his dependants, 337. Severities of the royal army, ibid. Fatal action at Glandalagh, 340. Troops arrive from Spain, 341. Surrender and execution of their garrison, 343. Insurrections, 344. Conspiracy against lord Grey, 345. Rigour of the queen's officers, 347. English ministry and parliament not well disposed to the reformation of Ireland, 355. A general extension and execution of the English laws the principal object of sir John Perrot's administration, 356. Parliament at Dublin, how composed, 357. Irish chieftains admitted, ibid. Appear in the English garb, 360. Scheme for the suspension of Poyning's law violently opposed by the commons, ibid. Temper of the house, 361. Speedy prorogation, ibid. New appearances of danger in the North, ibid. Defeat of the Scots, 362. Answer of a Scottish chieftain to the insult of an Englishman, 363. Base machinations to irritate the queen against Perrot, 364. Reformation of Connaught, 365. Earl of Desmond and his associates attainted in parliament, 366. Scheme for the plantation of Munster, ibid. Defect and abuses of this scheme, 367, 368. New disorders in Connaught, ibid. Repeated insurrections of the De Burghos, ibid. Some of the less reformed Irish solicit to engage in the service of the Netherlands, 371. Others enlist in the army of Spain, ibid. Execution of English law rendered odious in Ulster, ibid. Practices of popish ecclesiastics in this province, 372. Part of the Spanish armada driven by storm on the northern coasts of Ireland, 379. Effects of this incident, 380. Disaffection of the northern chieftains enflamed by the cruelty of Fitz-William, 384. Practices and preparations for insurrection in the northern province, 385. Composition established in every province of Ireland, 387. Interval of apparent tranquillity, ibid. Foundation of the university of Dublin, ibid. Success and cruelties of the Irish in Ulster and Connaught, 404. The Northerns condescend to a short truce, 408. Spirit of rebellion extended to Leinster and Munster, ibid. Fruitless expedition against the Northerns, 410. They repent of their treaty, ibid. Are encouraged by Spain, 412. Irish rebels encouraged by the queen's conduct, 421. Hostilities renewed, 422. Battle of Blackwater, ibid. Consequences of this action, 424. Insolence of the disaffected, and distress of the royalists, 425, 426. A truce granted to the Northerns, 437. Irish insurgents elevated, 439. Assisted by Spain, 440. Encouraged by the pope, ibid. His present to the earl of Tirone, ibid. The truce broken by this earl, ibid. Applications to Rome, 444. A bull in favour of the Irish insurgents, ibid. Their power, 445. The weakness of government, ibid. Rebels elated by the seizure of the earl of Ormond, 450. Jealousies and suspicions of the friends of government, ibid. Terms proposed for the enlargement of Ormond, 451. Rejected by Mountjoy, ibid. Rebels of Leinster harrassed and distressed, 453. Ulster desolated, ibid. The rebels deprived of foreign supplies by new coinage, 457. The queen's soldiers impoverished, ibid. Causes of discontent and rebellion in Munster, 458. Leaders and preparations of the rebels, 461, 462, 463. Distresses of the rebels, 466. James, son of the rebel earl of Desmond, sent to Ireland, ibid. His adventure at Kilmallock, 467. Munster rebels submit in great numbers, 468. Rumours of a Spanish invasion, 471. Its effects, ibid. The design of

Spain

INDEX.

Spain confirmed, 472. Spanish fleet in the harbour of Kinsale, 473. The time of a Spanish descent unfavourable, 475. The place inconvenient, ibid. The Spaniards separated, ibid. The Northerns march to the support of Don Juan D'Aquila, ibid. Royalists reinforced, 477. Progress of the siege of Kinsale, ibid. Six Spanish ships arrive at Castlehaven, 478. Which produce a general revolt of the Irish, ibid. Distresses of the besiegers, 479. Defeat of the Irish confederates, 480. Flight of O'Donnel and Tirone, 481. The Spanish posts surrendered, 484. Desperate efforts of the governor of the castle of Dunboy in his expiring moments, 485. War revived in Munster with rancour and cruelty, 486. Hideous calamity of the rebellious Northerns, 487. Insurrections in the reign of Elizabeth, not influenced by religious motives, 485. Popish party of this reign, 486. Their principles and practices, ibid. Sentence of the Spanish universities, ibid. Effects of popish virulence on the accession of James, ibid. Insolence of the citizens of Cork and Waterford, 487. Southern cities intimidated, 489. Act of oblivion and indemnity, 490. Favour shewn to Tirone and O'Donnel, ibid. Progress of reformation by Carew and Chichester, 491. Tainistry and Gavelkind abolished, 492. Commission of grace, ibid. Cautiously executed, 493. Practices of popish ecclesiastics, 494. Proclamations against the recusant clergy, 495. Execution of penal laws, ibid. Its effects, 496. Trial of Lalor, ibid. Conspiracy and flight of the earl of Tirone and Tyrconnel, 497. Favourable to the designs of James, 499. Rebellion of O'Dogherty, 502. Escheated counties of Ulster, 504. Scheme of the Northern plantation, ibid. Errors of Elizabeth's plantations corrected, 506. Distribution of lands, 507. City of London engaged in the plantation, 509. Institution of the order of baronets, ibid. Execution of the scheme for the provision of the clergy and university not entirely conformable to the original idea, 512. Causes of discontent in Ireland, 515. From discoverers, 516. From penal statutes, 517. Temper of the recusants and puritans, 518, 519. Design of holding an Irish parliament, ibid. Alarming to the recusants, ibid. Petition of the lords of the pale, ibid. Management of elections, 522. The recusant party elevated and turbulent, 523. Contests on the opening of the parliament, 524. Agents of the recusant party, and their petition to the king, 528. Session of the Irish parliament, 532. Mutual good temper of the recusants and the administration, 533. Laws, 534. Subsidies favourably received, 535. A conspiracy immediately detected and suppressed, 538. Scheme for the plantation of several counties in Leinster, ibid. Commissioners sent from London to enquire into the state of Ireland, 541. Review of complaints and discontents during the late Irish administrations, 544. Grievances and abuses from plantations, 546. From enquiries into defective titles, 547. Infamous practices of discoverers and crown agents, 549. Inferior grievances, 550. Miserable state of the Irish army, 552. No advantage taken of the weakness of government, ibid. and why, 553. Difficulties arising from the deficiency of the revenue, 556. Project for supplying the deficiency, ibid. Scheme against the corporations rejected as dangerous, ibid. Scheme for a plantation of Connaught, 558. Suspended by a treaty

with

INDEX.

with the inhabitants, 558. And by the death of James, ibid. Turbulence of the Irish recusants on the accession of Charles, 560. Irish army augmented, and irregularly maintained, ibid. Affected loyalty of the recusants, 561. A free gift offered to the king, on condition of indulgence to the Romish worship, 562. Free gift of the Irish accepted, 565. The graces transmitted to the lord deputy, ibid. Summary of the graces, 566, 567, 568. The royal promise of a parliamentary confirmation of them eluded with apparent insincerity, 570. The graces, however, highly satisfactory to the Irish subjects, 571. Effects of the royal graces, iii. 3. Temper of the recusants, ibid. Their practices, ibid. Proclamation against their hierarchy, 5. Insolence of the Romish party, 8. Debates in council on the bill of subsidy, 18, 19, 20. English articles and canons established, 32. High commission court erected, ibid. Introduction of a linen manufacture, 34. Project of a western plantation revived, 35. Progress of the inquisitions in the western provinces, 36. Clamour against the proceedings, 37. Insurrection of Scotland, 49. Zeal and liberality of the Irish commons, 59. New army levied, 60. Sudden change of disposition in the Irish parliament, 61. Causes of this change, ibid. Remonstrance of the commons against the clergy, 63. Their new regulations of subsidies, 64. Orders for disbanding the Irish army, 66. Increasing spirit of opposition in the Irish parliament, 67. Injudicious complaints, ibid. Orders for the assessment of subsidies, 68. Torn from the commons' Journal by the king's command, ibid. Remonstrance of grievances voted hastily by the commons, 69. Transmitted to England, ibid. Irish agents in London, 71. They present the remonstrance to the throne, 75. Answer of sir George Ratcliffe, ibid. The agents decline a particular reply, ibid. New session of the Irish parliament, ibid. Demands the commons, 76. They protest against the preamble of the first subsidy bill, ibid. Lords prepare a petition of grievances, 77. Motion of the bishop of Meath, 78. Lords jealous of their privilege, 79. Queries presented by the commons to the upper house, for the opinion of the judges, 81. Transmitted to the parliament in England, 82. Impeachments in Ireland, 83. A prorogation, 84. Effects of the act of attainder passed against the earl of Strafford in Ireland, ibid. Concessions of the king to the Irish agents, 86. Their farther demands, 87. Important questions arising from the impeachments of the commons, 88. Undecided 89. Arbitrary proceedings of the commons, ibid. Against the clergy, ibid. Against the university, 90. Queries resumed, 91. Answer of the judges unsatisfactory to the commons, ibid. Their decisions on the several queries, 92. They recede from the impeachments, 93. They oppose the sending the disbanded army into foreign service, ibid. Suspicious attempts to examine the king's stores, 96. Return of the Irish agents, 97. Peace of Ireland fatally interrupted, 99. Causes and occasions of rebellion, 100. Temper of the mere Irish and old English, ibid. Influence of religion, 103. Spirit and principles of Romish ecclesiastics, ibid. Schemes of insurrection discovered by Herber Mac-Mahon, 105. Influence of the Scottish insurrection, 106. Proposal for seizing the castle of Dublin, 116. Scheme of proceeding

in

INDEX.

in Dublin, 118. And in the country, 119. Fantaſtical projects of ſome conſpirators, ibid. Aſſembly at Multifernam, 122. Conſpirators repair to Dublin, 123. Their conſultation, ibid. Supineneſs of government, 124. Council aſſembled at the houſe of Sir John Borlace, 128. Confuſion in Dublin, ibid. Falſe rumours, 129. Meaſures for the public defence, 131. Lords of the Pale apply for arms, 132. Anſwer of the juſtices and council, ibid. The proclamation of government offenſive to the lords of the Pale, 133. Second proclamation, ibid. Diſpatches to the king and to the earl of Leiceſter, ibid. Succeſſes of the rebels in Ulſter, 134. Proceedings in Cavan and Longford, 135. Errors of the Engliſh, 136. Their calamities, 137. Rancorous ſpirit of the rebels, 138. Their pretended commiſſion from the king, ibid. Their ſubſequent manifeſto, 141. Remonſtrance from Longford, 142. Oppoſition given to the rebels, 144. Diſpatches and ſupplies from the king, 145. Defeat of the rebels at Liſburn, 146. Horrid cruelties of the rebels, 147. Maſſacre in Iſland Magee, 148. Conduct of the lords juſtices, 151. Flame of rebellion extended, 157. State of Munſter, 158. The lords juſtices recall the arms they had diſtributed, 159. Repeat their proclamation againſt any reſort to Dublin, 160. Their inſidious manner of offering pardon to the rebels, ibid. They oppoſe the meeting of a parliament, 161. Allow the ſeſſion of *one* day, 163. Tranſactions of the parliament, 163, 164. Agents ſent to the king, 165. Private repreſentations of the lords juſtices, ibid. The agents and their papers ſeized, 166. Rebels elated, ibid. Reject overtures of accommodation, 167. Frame their oath of aſſociation, ibid. Provoked by the cruelties of ſir Charles Coote, 168. March to inveſt Drogheda, ibid. Animated by their victory at Julian's-Town Bridge, 169. Meeting and interview at the hill of Croſty, 172. Seven noblemen, their adherents of the Pale, declare for war, ibid. Lords of the Pale ſummoned by the ſtate, ibid. Their anſwer, 173. Addreſſes of the lords to the king and queen, 174. They concert their operations, 175. Proclamations ſigned by the king, 176. Inſurrections in Munſter, 177. The leaders, their procedure, ſucceſs and diſſenſion, 178, 179. Drogheda inveſted, 180. Defence of it neglected by the ſtate, ibid. Unſucceſsful attempts to ſurpriſe the town, ibid. Skirmiſh at Swords, 182. Siege of Drogheda raiſed, 185. General diſpoſition of the Pale to be reconciled to government, 186. Diſpleaſing to the lords juſtices, 188. Their priſoners racked, 189. Motives and conſequences of this procedure, 189, 190. Inſurgents of the Pale driven to deſperation, 191. Battle of Kilruſh, 193. Diſtreſs of the kingdom, 195. State of Leinſter, ibid. Of Connaught, 197. Of Munſter, 199. Battle of Liſcarrol, 201. Cruelty and conſternation of the rebels, 203. The Iriſh chieftains prepare to fly to foreign countries, 205. Prevented, ibid. Practices of the Engliſh parliament with the army of Ireland, 215. Practices of the lords juſtices, 216. Of Reynolds and Goodwin, 217. Diſcontent of the military officers, 218. Their complaints conveyed to the king, 219. The Iriſh confederates become tractable, 226. Meeting at Trim, ibid. Progreſs of the treaty diſpleaſing to the lords juſtices, ibid. They project an expedition, 227. Battle of Roſs, 229. Diſtreſs of Dublin, ibid. In-

INDEX.

terview at Trim, ibid. Complaints and demands of the Irish, ibid. Their remonstrance transmitted to the king, 230. Opposed by the lords justices, 231. Their violences, ibid. Circumstances of the kingdom justify the king's orders for a treaty of cessation, 233. Expedient of the new justices for the support of the army, 234. Progress of the treaty with the Irish, 235. The old Irish averse to any treaty, 240. The more moderate of the confederacy prevail, 241. Treaty of cessation injoined, 243. Odious to many in England and in Ireland, ibid. Forces sent from Ireland to the assistance of the king, 248. Their ill success, 249. Affairs of Ulster, 255. The covenant eagerly taken by the British forces, of this province, 256. Irish alarmed, 260. Offer the command of their forces to the marquis of Ormond, ibid. Demand that he should proclaim the Scots and their adherents rebels, ibid. Irish treaty at Oxford, 262. Insolence of the popish agents, ibid. Their final demands, 264. Extravagant requisitions of some protestant agents, 266. Propositions offered by those of the Irish privy-council, 268. Practices of the confederates in foreign courts, 281. Their military operations, 282. Duncannon taken by the Irish, ibid. New demands of the confederates, 284. Sligo taken, 307. Attempt to recover it, 308. Battle of Benburb, 335. Effects of this action, ibid. Proclamation of the peace proposed in several cities, ibid. The adherents of the peace excommunicated, ibid. The confederates invest Dublin, 344. Their demands, 345. Their dissentions, 346. Sudden retreat of the confederates, ibid. Treaty between Clanricarde and Preston, 347. A new general assembly declares against the peace, 352. The parliamentarians masters of Dublin, 357. State of Ireland on the departure of the marquis of Ormond, iv. 3. Battle of Knocknoness. 7. General assembly at Kilkenny, 8. Agents chosen for Rome and France, ibid. Their instructions, 9. Answers of the queen and prince to the Irish agents, 12. Irish treat about a cessation with lord Inchiquin, 13. Excommunication pronounced against those who should support the cessation, 16. Return of the agents from France, 21. Appointment of commissionaries of trust, 28. Various parties and interests in Ireland, in consequence of the execution of the king, 30. Alarming intelligence, 38. Battle of Rathmines, 40. Storm and massacre of Drogheda, 45. Progress of the parliamentarians in Ulster, 46. Wexford strengthened, 49. Siege of Duncannon raised, 50. Perverseness of the citizens of Waterford, 52. Consequences of the revolt of the Munster garrison to Cromwell, 54. Obstinacy and insolence of the citizens of Waterford, ibid. County-agents at Kilkenny, 57. Alarmed at the approach of Cromwell, 58. Attempts to relieve Clonmel, 60. Defeated, ibid. Clonmel surrendered, ibid. State of Ireland on the departure of Cromwell, 60. Attempt to recover Ulster from the parliamentarians, 63. Limerick refuses to receive a garrison from the marquis of Ormond, 64. The citizens of Limerick relent, 68. Progress of the parliamentarians, 73. New General assembly, 76. Attempt on Limerick defeated, 80. Betrayed by the burghers, 90. Severe executions, 91. General consternation, 93. Galway surrendered, ibid. Acts for distribution of lands in Ireland, 95. Trials of Irish rebels, 96. Dispositions of the forfeited lands, 97. Designs and proceedings of the royalists, 104. Their

INDEX.

104. Their leaders, 106. Their success, 107. Convention of estates, 109. Temper of different parties in Ireland at the restoration 111. Irish catholics odious, 112. Severe ordinances against them strictly executed, ibid. Petition in favour of dissenters suppressed, 114. Declaration for the settlement of Ireland, 116. Instructions for the execution of it, 120. Temper and proceedings of the Irish parliament, 124, 125. Debates on the act of settlement in Ireland, 126. Indiscretion of the Irish agents, 128. Dismissed with disgrace, 130. Thirty thousand pounds granted by parliament to the duke of Ormond, 134. Act of settlement passed, 135. Court of wards abolished, ibid. Objections to the act of settlement, ibid. Court of claims, 136. New interest alarmed and provoked, 137. Plot for seizing the castle of Dublin, ibid. Address of the house of commons, 138. Scheme of a general insurrection detected and defeated, 139 Plan for an act of explanation, 141. The act debated, ibid. Dissatisfaction of the Irish, 145, 146, 147. Objections of the commons of Dublin, 147. Proceedings of the Irish parliament, 148. Act of explanation passed, ibid. Perplexities in the execution of it, 149. Bill for prohibiting the importation of Irish cattle into England, 150. Its effects on Ireland, 151. Motion for a perpetual prohibition, 153. Violence of the two English houses, 154. Their bill receives the royal assent, 155. The duke of Ormond endeavours to alleviate the distresses of Ireland, arising from the prohibition bill, ibid. Scheme for suppressing the popish interest in Ireland, 165. History of the Irish remonstrance, 167. Terror of protestants, 173. Attempts to rescind the acts of settlement, ibid. Spirited interposition of the English parliament 175. The popish plot, 183. Evidences of a popish plot encouraged, 190. Accused persons conveyed to London, 191. Designs of the king and duke of York, 197. The influence of James II.'s accession on the catholics and protestants, of Ireland, 202. New lords justices appointed, 204. Their conduct, 205. Effects of the duke of Monmouth's rebellion, 205, 206. Militia disarmed, 207. The nation, in a ferment, 209. Protestant party harrassed and plundered, ibid. Attempts to invalidate the acts of settlement, 210. New lord chancellor, 211. Popish judges and privy councellors, ibid. Favours to the popish clergy, 212. More changes in the courts of law, 219. Quo warranto against the charter of Dublin, 220 Other charters resigned or seized, ibid. New corporations, ibid. Attempts on the university of Dublin, 221. General distress, ibid. Attempts to remove Tyrconnel, 225. Birth of a Prince, 227. Ridiculous triumph of the papists in Dublin, ibid. Enterprise of the prince of Orange, 228. Its effects in Ireland, ibid. Rumours of a popish massacre, 229. Confusion in Dublin, 230. And in the other parts of Ireland, 231. Conduct and proceedings of the garrison of Londonderry, 233. Association of northern protestants, 235. They retreat from general Hamilton, 239. They assemble at Coleraine, 240. They fly to Derry, ibid. Bravery of the garrison, 241. Provoked, 246. Declare for a brave defence, 247. Appoint their governors, ibid. Regulate their operations, ibid. Their resolution, 249. Still obstinate, 251. Extremely distressed, 253. Relieved in their extremity, 254. The siege raised, ibid. Conduct and success of the Enniskilliners,

INDEX.

Enniskilliners, 254, 255. Battle of Newtown-Butler, 256. Bill for repealing the acts of settlement, 262. Cruel act of attainder, ibid. Passed, ibid. Concealed, discovered, 263. Other acts of parliament, ibid. Sufferings of the university of Dublin, 267. And of the protestant clergy, 268. Insolence of the popish clergy, 269. Bigotry of James, 270. Levies raised for the service of Ireland, 271. Carrickfergus surrendered, 272. Newry and Carlingford burnt, 274. Irish retreat to Drogheda, ibid. Conspiracy discovered, 277. Excursions and success of the Enniskilliners, ibid. Misery of the English camp, ibid. The English commons enquire into the conduct of the war in Ireland, 281. Action at Cavan, 283. Action in the bay of Dublin, 284. Charlemont surrendered, 285. Battle of the Boyne, 295. Dublin in confusion, 302. Conduct of Fitzgerald, 303. Address of the protestant clergy, ibid. King William's declaration, and commission of forfeitures, 304, 305 Irish prepare to renew the war, 305. Waterford and Duncannon reduced, 306. Vigorous defence of the garrison of Limerick, 311. English artillery surprised, 312. Siege of Limerick, still continued, 313. A breach, 314. A storm, ibid. English repulsed, ibid. Enterprize of the earl of Marlborough, 317. Cork and Kingsale reduced, 320. English forces retire to winter quarters, ibid. General disorder and distress, ibid. Rapparees, 321. Civil administration at Dublin, 322. Attempt on the English frontier, 325. Action at the Moat of Grenoge, ibid. Arrival of Saint Ruth, 327. Ballymore reduced, 328. March to Athlone, ibid. The English town forced, 329. Efforts to gain the Irish town, ibid. Resolution of the besieged, 330. Athlone taken, 333. Proclamation of pardon, 336. Final defeat of the Irish, 342. Galway besieged, and surrendered upon honourable conditions, 344. Situation of the Irish in Limerick, 345. Preparations for the siege, 346. Attack at Thomond-Bridge, 348. The garrison discontented, 351. A parley, ibid. English prisoners released, 352. Their distresses, ibid. Terms of capitulation proposed by the garrison, ibid. Rejected, 353. Treaty renewed, ibid. Articles of capitulation settled and signed, 355. War of Ireland finally concluded, ibid.

Ireton, general, prepares for the siege of Limerick, iv. 88, 89. Commences the siege in form, 89. Executes, when master of the city, the severest vengeance on those who had been the most inveterate opposers of the English government, 91. Catches the fatal infection which wasted several parts of Ireland, and dies at Limerick, 92.

K.

KELLY, Ralph, bishop of Cashel, his arrogant and seditious behaviour, i. 366.

Kildare, earl of, (in the reign of Edward III.) attacked by sir Ralph Ufford, as a disaffected and rebellious lord, i. 364. Reduced, taken, and imprisoned, ibid. Released, ibid. Furnishes men at arms for the king's service in France, 365. Attends the king to France, ibid. Distinguishes himself by his valour at the siege of Calais, ibid.

―――, Thomas, earl of, chosen lord chief justice of Ireland, in the reign of Henry VI. ii. 50. Summons a parliament at Dublin, ibid.

Confirmed

INDEX.

Confirmed in his station by the new king, ibid. The acts of his former administration afterwards confirmed and ratified by the Irish parliament, 57. His commission superseded by the appointment of George duke of Clarence, to the lieutenancy of Ireland for life, ibid. Attainted of treason, 66. Imprisoned, ibid. Afterwards released, ibid. Escapes to England, and repairs to the king, ibid. Constituted lord deputy, 68. Continued in that post on the restoration of Henry VI. 70. Devises a scheme for resisting and subduing the Irish enemies, and preventing the extortion and oppression of the English rebels, 71. Removed from his government by the unwearied assiduities of his enemies, 72. Dies, 74.

────, Gerald, earl of, appointed lord justice by the king, ii. 75. Refuses to obey the king's letters of dismissal, authenticated only by the privy signet, ibid. Summoned to England by the king, 77. Again entrusted with the government as deputy to Richard duke of York, ibid. His interest and power increases, 79. He is continued lord deputy on the accession of Henry VII. 83. His unrivalled power, 84. Summoned by the king to attend him, 88. Evades the mandate, ibid. Receives Lambert Simnel with every expression of respect and affection, 91. Averts the storm gathering against him by submissions to the king, and by promising to attone for his late error, by his future conduct, 104. Is continued in the government, 107. Resumes it with full power and consequence, 109. Removed from the administration, 110. Disgusted at his abrupt removal, 111. His transactions, during the insurrection of Simnel, invidiously recalled to view, and condemned with great severity, 112. Receives a letter from Perkin Warbeck, ibid. Unites with the new deputy, lord Gormanston, and concurs in support of him, 114. Dreads the effects of the archbishop of Dublin's representations, 115. Repairs to the court of England, 116. Finds Henry strongly prejudiced against him, ibid. Vigourously opposes an Irish chieftain, 120. Arrested and confined, 121. An act of attainder passed against him for treason and rebellion, 128. He is sent prisoner to Henry, to answer for his supposed offences before the throne, 131. Admitted to confront his accusers in the king's presence, 132. Triumphs over them, and is restored to his estate and honours, 134. Invested with the office of chief governour of Ireland, 136. Discovers a want of refined policy, 139. Takes the field, 140. Gains a complete victory. 141. Has the garter conferred on him, ibid. Continued in his government on the accession of Henry VIII, 147. Dies, 149.

Kildare, Gerald, earl of (son of the foregoing earl) elected lord deputy, by the council and nobles, on his father's death, ii. 149. He routs the insurgents, and pursues them with considerable execution, ibid. Repairs to England to confer with the king, and to receive directions for his future conduct, ibid. Convenes a parliament at his return, ibid. The honours, privileges, and possessions of his ancestors are confirmed to him, 150. He is called out to the field, ibid. Summoned to England to answer the charges brought against him by his enemies, 152. Is pronounced clear of every imputation, and regains his liberty, 154. Recommends himself to the royal favour, by attending the king to Calais, ibid. Supplants the earl of Ormond, 162.

Is

INDEX

Is appointed his fucceffor, ibid. His partiality to his kinfman, 163. Again fummoned to anfwer to the accufations of his enemies, 164. Acquitted and difmiffed, ibid. Reftored to favour, ibid. Appointed chief governour, 166. His extravagance and infolence, 167. Intrigues of his enemies, 168. He is commanded to attend the king, 171. Vengeance denounced by Henry againft the whole lineage of Kildare, 186.

──────, reftoration of that noble family, in the reign of queen Mary, ii. 249.

──────, earl of, (in the reign of king Charles I.) provoked at the neglect of lord Wentworth, the lord deputy, iii. 22. Impatient of his infolence to him, he hurries to the court of England, ibid. Meets with a mortifying reception from Charles, ibid.

Kilkenny, inconveniences and relaxation of its ftatutes, ii. 8. Supreme council, and general affembly there, iii. 210.

Kinfale, Spanifh fleet in the harbour, ii. 473. Progrefs of the fiege, 476.

Kirk, col. arrives in Lake Foyle, with thirty fhips, iv. 250. Retires, ibid. Makes an hazardous attempt to relieve the garrifon of Derry, which he had abandoned, 253.

Knocknonefs, battle of, iv. 7.

Knocktow, battle of, ii. 140. Its confequences, 141.

L.

LALOR, a popifh ecclefiaftic, feized, in confequence of a royal proclamation, ii. 496. Brought to trial, 497. Condemned, ibid.

Lancafter, duke of, appointed chief governour of Ireland, ii. 3. His arrival there, 4. His devices, ibid.

Laurence, archbifhop, his zeal and vigour, i. 66.

Le Grofs, Raymond arrives in Ireland, i. 52. His victory and cruel execution of his prifoners, ibid. Sent by earl Strongbow to king Henry, II. 61. Jealous of Hervey de Mountmorres, 112. Appointed general by earl Strongbow, ibid. His fucceffes, 115, 116. He retires in difcontent, ibid. Recalled, 118. Marries the fifter of earl Strongbow, 120. Commanded to attend the king, 127. Prepares for his departure, 128. Prevailed on to march againft O'Brien, of Thomond, ibid. His fucceffes in Thomond and Defmond, 129, 130, 131. Joint-chief governour with Fitz-Andelm, 134. Reinforces the garrifon of Cork, and obliges the men of Defmond to raife the fiege, 163.

Leicefter, earl of, his infidious practices, to involve the earl of Effex, in a feries of perplexities, ii. 312. Sufpected of having caufed that unhappy nobleman to be poifoned, ii. 313.

Leinfter, irifh of, petition for a general denization, i. 342. But without effect, ibid. They rife in arms under the leading of O'Brien, ibid. Their progrefs and cruelty, ibid. Repelled by the citizens of Wexford, 343.

Leix, Englifh fettlement there, ii. 229. Infurrection there, 252. Denominated the queen's county, 256.

Leven, earl of, his peremptory mandate to the royalifts of Ulfter, iii. 204. His

INDEX.

204. His arrival with a reinforcement, 206. Returns in a dishonourable manner to Scotland, ibid.

Leviston, sir Richard, arrives at Cork with ten ships of war, ii. 477. Is by contrary winds exposed to a battery against his ship, 478. Returns to Kinsale in a shattered state, 479.

Lionel, lord, (second son to Edward III.) made chief governour of Ireland, i. 373. His forces and attendants, ibid. His arrival in Ireland, 374. His prejudices, ibid. He forbids the old English to approach his camp, ibid. Consequences of this prohibition, 375.

Loftus, Adam, lord chancellor, appointed one of the lords justices, on lord Faulkland's being recalled, iii. 6. Controuled in his attempt, in conjunction with his colleague, for the suppression of popery, 8. Refuses obedience to the order of council, 45. Commanded to deliver the great seal into the hands of the lord deputy, and committed to prison, ibid. Accuses lord Wentworth as the real author of his disgrace, ibid. Purchases his liberty, and his former station in a mortifying manner, 46.

London, engaged in the plantation of Ulster, ii. 509.

Lucy, sir Anthony, enters upon his administration, with a determined purpose to support the interest of his royal master, Edward III. i. 245. Summons a parliament to meet at Dublin, ibid.

Ludlow, general, on the death of Ireton, exerts himself with vigour, to complete the reduction of the Irish, iv. 92. Occasions a universal dismay among the whole Irish party, 93. Receives an offer of submission from the earl of Clanricarde, ibid. Refuses to give up the commission he had received from parliament, 101. Appointed to command the forces of the commonwealth in Ireland, 103. Impeached by sir Charles Coote of high treason, 105. Arrives in the port of Dublin, 108. Recalled to England, ibid.

Lundy, governour of Derry, his character, iv. 240. Suspected of retaining a regard to king James and his service, ibid. Trusted and employed by the prince of Orange, 241. Refuses to take the oaths to the new king, ibid. Announces his resolution of marching to engage the enemy, ibid. Abandons his post, 246. Hides himself within the walls of Derry, 247. Resigns all care of the city, and conceals himself in his own house, ibid. Escapes to the ships in a disguise suited to his meanness, ibid.

M.

MACARTHY, of Desmond, prevailed upon to raise the siege of Cork, i. 191.

Mac-Guire, chieftain of Fermanagh, a spirited answer of his to sir William Fitz-William, ii. 385.

Mac-Mahon, Heber, a Roman ecclesiastic, informs lord Strafford of a general insurrection intended in Ireland, iii. 105.

Magaghagan, governor of Dunboy, makes a desperate effort in his expiring moments, ii. 485.

Malby, sir Nicholas, marches to attack sir John Desmond, ii. 333. Receives a dissembling letter from the earl of Desmond, 334. Answers it by a severe expostulation, ibid. Prepares to reduce his castles, after

having

INDEX.

having first endeavoured to reclaim him in a gentle expostulating way, ibid. Is prevented by the ceasing of his authority with the death of sir William Drury, ibid. Retires to his government of Connaught, ibid.

Marlborough, earl of, arrives in Cork road, iv. 316. Drives the enemy from a battery, and lands without opposition, ibid. Has a dispute with the prince of Wirtemberg, about priority, 317. His polite behaviour upon the occasion, ibid. Effects of his brave purpose 319.

Marshal, earl, appointed to succeed Hugh de Lacy, i. 188. Succeeded by Hamo de Valois, 192.

Marishal, Richard, on the death of earl William, (son to the protector) alarms king John by his bold and independent spirit, i. 249. Repairs to Ireland, ibid. Is invested by the king with all his rights, ib. Opposes the administration of the bishop of Winchester, 250. Retires to Wales, ibid. Confederates with Lewellyn, ibid. Fruitless attempts to reduce him, ibid. The minister projects a scheme to destroy him, ibid. Letters under the king's seal, to the lords of Ireland, concerning him, 251. Deceived by Geoffrey de Maurisco, 253. Collects forces and commences hostilities, ibid. Is betrayed, ibid. His tragical death, 254.

Mary, queen, her graces to her Irish subjects on her accession, ii. 249. Restores young lord Gerald to the honours of his ancestry, ibid.

Matilda, Wife of William de Braosa, and her family imprisoned in the castle of Bristol, i. 224.

Maynooth, castle of, invested by sir William Brereton, ii. 180. An insolent defiance returned by the garrison, ibid. The castle gained by bribery, ibid.

Meath, bishop of, appointed deputy to the earl, of Marche, ii. 22. Violently opposed, ibid. Scandalously accused of having taken a chalice from one of the churches of his diocese, 23. Pleads his innocence with dignity, ibid.

Merton, statute of, transmitted to Ireland for the direction of the king's subjects, i. 278.

Metz, bishop of, sends an inflammatory letter to Con. O'Nial, ii. 208.

Monroe, Robert, lands at Carricfergus with his Scottish troops, iii. 202. Is joined by some of the provincial forces, ibid. Advances to Newry, ibid. Reduces the castle speedily on the flight of the rebels, ibid. Returns to Carricfergus, 203. Makes an incursion into the county of Antrim, ibid. Visits the earl of Antrim at his castle of Dunluce, with an appearance of amity and respect, ibid. Makes him prisoner, seizes his castle, and commits all his houses to the custody of the Scottish forces, ibid.

Moore, Roger, his character, iii. 107. He attaches himself to the son of the rebel earl of Tirone, 108. Vows to make one brave effort for the restoration of his brethren, ibid. Practises with Richard Plunket, and Connor Macguire, 109, 110. Engages with the Northerns, 110. Beholds with secret pleasure the progress of the conflagration lighted up by him, 116. Undertakes a very bold enterprize, 118. Is particularly elevated at the prospect of a general discontent and clamour, 166. Receives the deputation of parliament, addressed to him and his associates, with disdain, 167. His advice to the rebels, ibid. Dignifies

INDEX.

his followers by the name of the *catholic army*, ibid. His practices in the Pale at length successful, 172. His discontent and death, ibid.

Mountjoy, lord, appointed by queen Elizabeth, lord deputy of Ireland, ii. 448. Despised by the Irish, ibid. Attempts to surround Tirone, 449. Rejects the terms proposed for the enlargement of the earl of Ormond, 451. His opperations and success in Ulster, 452. Their influence, ibid. His progress interrupted by intelligence from England, 454. His fears dissipated, 455. His manner of conducting the war, ibid. He divides the Northerns, 456. Deprives the rebels of subsistence, ibid. Receives the queen's approbation of his services, 458. Proceeds to Cork, 473. Prosecutes the Northerns, 487. Embarrassed by the diversity of the queen's instructions, 488. Concludes the treaty with Tirone, 481. Marches into Munster, 488. His spirited conduct, 489. Intimidates some of the southern cities, 490.

Mortimer, Roger, arrives at Youghall, to take upon him the administration of government, i. 323. Marches to join the main body, ibid. Dismisses his army and repairs to Dublin, 324. Proceeds to Meath, ibid. Occasions a revival of the English interest by his spirited and well-supported government, 324.

Muskerry, lord, marches to the relief of Limerick, iv. 90. Is defeated by lord Broghill, and obliged to retire with considerable loss, ibid. Charged with the assassination of several Englishmen, but honourably acquitted on his trial, and permitted to embark for Spain, 96.

N

NORRIS, sir John, ordered to repair to Ireland, ii. 405. Entrusted, in the absence of the deputy, with the absolute command of all military affairs, ibid. Produces skirmishes by his attempts to relieve the castle of Monaghan, 406. Marches to the borders of Tirone, 409. Receives pathetic addresses from the earl of Tirone, 410. Conceives pity for him, ibid. Marches into Connaught, 412. Demands some additional forces from the lord deputy, ibid. Marches again to the northern borders, 414. Abruptly ordered to his government of Munster, 416. Dies within two months after his disgrace, apparently in consequence of the anguish occasioned by it, 418.

O

O'BRIEN, of Thomond, conceives the design of cutting off a body of Ostmen in the service of the English, in their march to the main army, i. 117. Suffers them to encamp in a state of careless security, ibid. Falls suddenly upon them, and wreaks his fury on them, ibid. Lays siege to Limerick, 127. Proposes an interview with the English general, 129. Makes submissions and renews his engagements to the king of England, ibid. Behaves in the most perfidious manner, 132.

————, Daniel, levies a considerable force, and declares hostilities against the English borderers, i. 188. His troops are victorious, ibid. His

INDEX.

ibid. His territories ravaged, ibid. Charged by the Irish leaders with perfidy, in secretly favouring and assisting the common enemy, 189. A bloody contest between the provincial chiefs prevented by his death, 190.

O'Connor, Roderic, prince of Connaught, leads a numerous army to Dublin to strike his enemies with terror, i. 18. Is solemnly inaugurated there, ibid. Over-runs the province of Leinster with an irresistible force, 19. Pierces into Munster, and regulates that province at his pleasure, ibid. Returns to Meath, and holds a magnificent convention of the states, ibid. Is informed of the return of Dermod, 25. Receives solemn professions of the most abject submissions from him, 26. Accepts his insidious submission, 27. Remits the small portion of territory in Leinster requested by him, ibid. Hastens to make the necessary dispositions in other provinces, ibid. Is busily engaged in measures for supporting the dignity of his station, 35. Summons the estates of the nation, ibid. Revives ancient institutions, ibid. Ordains new laws, and by every popular proceeding, studies to gain the respect and command the obedience of his vassals, 36. Marches against Dermod and his followers, ibid. Dismisses his northern forces, dreading their insincerity, 37. Enters the territories of Dermod, and commences hostilities, ibid. Attempts to prevail on the British forces to detach themselves from Dermod, 39. His timid policy, 42. He listens to the suggestions of his clergy, and rather than hazard an engagement, consents to treat with a prince whose perfidy he had already experienced, ibid. Draws off his army, leaving the prince of Leinster with his Britons, at full liberty to extend their conquests unmolested, 43. Endeavours to reduce Donald O'Brien, 45. Alarmed at the intelligence of a reinforcement for Dermod, ibid. Finds it necessary to retire, ibid. Takes the field again, 50. Marches to Clandathan, as if determined to give battle to the confederates of Leinster, ibid. Obliged to retire into his own province, 57. His flight throws the citizens of Dublin into the utmost consternation, ibid. Marches into Meath, 58. Sends an embassy to Dermod, ibid. A striking instance of his brutal cruelty, 59. He encamps with his troops at Castleknock, 67. Receives overtures towards a treaty from earl Strongbow, 68. Completely mortified by the desertion of his old and intimate associate O'Ruarc of Breffney, 85. Confounded, harrassed, and afflicted, but unwilling to resign his title to the monarchy of Ireland, ibid. Collects his provincial troops, and entrenches himself on the banks of the Shannon, 86. Despairing of success by any longer contentions, determines to save his own province at least from the depredations of an incensed and victorious enemy, by a submission, 122. Determines to treat immediately with the king of England, ibid. Sends three deputies to him at Windsor, 123. The treaty between them ratified in a grand council, 124. His death, 196.

————, Fedlim, joins the earl of Ulster with his provincial troops, i. 315. His character, 316. Is considered by Edward Bruce as a proper object for his artifice, ibid. Receives an application from him, ibid. Listens to his overtures, 317. Enters into a negotiation with him, ibid. Returns to Connaught, 318. Enabled by a select

body

INDEX.

body of English forces, under the command of sir John Birmingham, to meet his rival in the field, 319. Is reinstated in his possessions and dignity, ibid. Is slain at the battle of Athunree, 321.

O'Connolly, Owen, a servant of sir John Clotworthy, pitched upon by Mac-Mahon as a person fit to be entrusted with the design of the conspiracy, iii. 125. Endeavours to convince Mac-Mahon of his perilous situation, 126. Affects compliance, ibid. Repairs to sir William Parsons, and gives a clear and particular information against the conspirators, ibid.

O'Donnel, the chieftain of Tirconnel, bids defiance to the English government, and absolutely refuses to admit a sheriff into his district, ii. 376.

————, Hugh, son of the foregoing, made prisoner by stratagem, ii. 377. Confined in the castle of Dublin, ibid. Contrives an escape, 384. Flies for immediate shelter to some of the Irish septs in the nighbourhood of the capital, ibid. Regains his country after many severe sufferings, with an implacable detestation of the English power, ibid. Is invested soon after, on the resignation of his father to the chieftainry of Tirconnel, ibid. Marries a daughter of the earl of Tirone, 386.

O'Dogherty, sir Cahir, determines to assert his independency, and to bid defiance to the English government, ii. 502. His duplicity, ibid. His cruelty, ibid. His death, 503.

O'Hanlon, an Irish chieftain, remarkably turbulent, ii. 121. Vigorously opposed by the earl of Kildare, ibid. Grows formidable, ibid.

O'Moore, the principal rebel of Leinster, sends insolent proposals to lord Mountjoy, for the releasement of the earl of Ormond, ii. 449. Receives a spirited rejection of them, 451. Is killed, 453.

O'Nial, Hugh-boy, his irruptions, i. 349.

————, Con, chieftain of his sept, and distinguished by the title of Boccagh, or the Limper, takes arms and invades Meath, ii. 154. Retires towards the North, ibid. Makes submissions which are favourably received, ibid. Is presented, in the name of king Henry VIII. with a collar of gold, 155. Attends on the government in Dublin, bearing the sword of state, 162. Sends assurances of support to lord Thomas, 174. Prepares to make his peace, 183. Makes new submissions, ibid. Receives a letter from the bishop of Metz, exciting him to draw the sword against the heretical opposers of the pope, 208. Makes his peace by the fullest renunciation of the papal authority, 217.

————, John, his character, ii. 247. He is provoked, ibid. Takes arms, ibid. His progress, 248. His war with O'Donnel, described by the Irish annalists, 260. His turbulence and arrogance provoke sir Henry Sydney to march northwards, in order to terrify him, 268. His brutality, ibid. His policy, 269. Requests Sydney to honour him with a visit, ibid. Confers with him, ibid. Defends his conduct, with acuteness, ibid. New excesses committed by him, 275. His insolence and caprice, 276. Comes to an accommodation with the earl of Sussex, ibid. Swears allegiance, 277. Attends the lord-deputy to Dublin, swears allegiance, and promises to repair to the queen, to renew

INDEX.

renew his dutiful submissions to the throne, ibid. His appearance and retinue, 278. He is reconciled to the queen, ibid. Affects an extraordinary zeal for her service, ibid. His conduct still suspicious, 279. Offended at the garrison of Derry, 281. His observation on the promotion of Mac-Arthy, the Irish lord of Desmond, ibid. He provokes the hostilities of the English, ibid. Proposes a conference with the lord-deputy, 282. Refuses to attend, ibid. His open rupture with English government, 283. And the reason of it, ibid. His irruptions, ibid. His practices in Ireland and foreign countries, 283, 284. He endeavours to amuse the lord deputy, ibid. His distresses, ibid. He is disappointed, and deserted, 285. Resolves to submit, ibid. Is dissuaded, ibid. Applies to the Scots, ibid. His tragical death, 286.

O'Nial, Owen, by his arrival in the county of Donnegal, after a tedious voyage from Dunkirk, prevents the dispersed rebels from abandoning Ireland, iii. 205. His character, ibid. He is unanimously declared, by the northern Irish, head and leader of their confederacy, ibid. Receives a letter from the earl of Leven, 206. His reply to it, ibid. Is chosen provincial governor for Ulster, 212. Obliges Monroe, who attempted to suprise him in his quarters, to retire with some loss, 235. Advances to West-Meath, 240. Called by the Nuncio into Leinster, to oppose the peace, 335. Instantly marches at the head of ten thousand barbarous ravagers, ibid. Rejects the offers made to detach him from the nuncio, 339. Lays with his whole army in the neighbourhood of Kilkenny, ready to execute the nuncio's orders, 340. His forces make violent and indiscriminate ravages, 344. His character opposed to Preston's, 346. Affects to dread an insidious designs against him and his forces, ibid. Calls off his men from their posts, and decamps in the night, 347. Is refractory, 354. Grows every day more terrible, 357. Is recalled to the defence of Leinster, iv. 5. Conjured by the nuncio to march without delay against the betrayers of the church, 16. Contrives to make a truce with the Ulster Scots, in order to be more at leisure to prosecute his operations, 18. His consequence is increased, 20. He continues his depredations, ibid. Consents to serve under Jones, 21. Resumes the command rashly conferred upon him, ibid. Declares in favour of the nuncio's measures, and bids defiance to the royal party, 31. Consents to a treaty on the marquis of Ormond's application to him, ibid. Commences a treaty with the parliamentarian leaders, 36. Engaged by lord Digby to march to his relief, 38. Grows disgusted with his new friends, the independents, 42. Concludes an accommodation with the marquis of Ormond, 51. His death, ibid.

———, sir Phelim, his character, iii. 116. Confers with Roger Moore, 118. Engages to head the northern insurrection, ibid. Appointed to seize Londonderry, 119. Surprises the castle of Charlemont, 134. Seizes the fort of Dungannon, 135. Is tempted on his trial, and at his death, to confess that he acted by authority of king Charles, and to produce the proof of his commission, 139.

O'Ruare, of Breffney, makes a vigorous effort against the garrison of Dublin, i. 78. Is defeated, ibid. His defeat embittered by the loss of his son, in the field of battle, ibid.

O'Sullivan,

INDEX.

O'Sullivan, Daniel, seizes Dunboy, ii. 485. Threatens to rekindle the flames of war in Munster, ibid. Put to flight, ibid.

O'Toole, Lawrence, the prelate of Dublin, his death, and character, i. 160.

Ormond, earl of, an acceptable governor, ii. 15. Finds his influence every day declining, and his opponents enabled to insult him with impunity, 30. His magnanimous behaviour, 31. Accused of high treason, 34. The king interposes, and stops the prosecution, ibid. His execution on the accession of Edward IV. 57.

――――, sir John de, (brother to the above earl) flies to Munster from the fury of his enemies, in England, ii. 57. Commences hostilities, ibid. Is defeated by the earl of Desmond, 58.

――――, sir James, killed by Piers Butler, ii. 139.

――――, earl of, in the reign of queen Elizabeth, involved in litigations with the earl of Desmond, ii. 288. Collects his followers, and repels his outrages, 289. Defeats him, and makes him a prisoner, ibid. Consents to refer the controversy to the queen, ibid. Lays his grievances before the queen, 290. Accuses Sydney of partiality to his rival, ibid. Quiets the queen's apprehensions, 304. Offers his services to restore the tranquillity of Munster, ibid. Is sent to Ireland for that purpose, ibid. Assists Sydney in the pacification of Munster, ibid. Prevails on his brothers to resign themselves to justice, ibid. Entrusted with the military command in Ireland, with the title of lord lieutenant of the army, 418. His conference with the earl of Tirone, 419. Comes to an accommodation with him, ibid. Proceeds, being again appointed lord-lieutenant of the army, to make head against the Northerns, 440. Parleys with the earl of Tirone, ibid. And agrees to renew the cessation for a month, ibid. Marches into Munster, on the expiration of the truce, and by his activity gains some advantage over the earl of Tirone and his confederates, 445. Parleys with O'Moore, 449. Is seized by the rebels, 450.

――――, earl of, (in the reign of Charles I.) refuses to deliver up his sword to the usher of the black-rod, iii. 21. Summoned by the lord-deputy to answer for his disobedience before the council, ibid. Appears a particular favourite at the Irish court, 22. Marches to Naas, 182. His spirited reply to lord Gormanstown, 183. Commissioned to march to the Boyne, 184. Forbidden to pursue the rebels, 185. Receives addresses from the insurgents of the Pale, 186. Desires instructions in what manner he was to treat with those who surrendered, ibid. Directed to make no distinction between noblemen and other rebels, 188. Detached into the county of Kildare, 192. Engages the rebels, 193. Gains a victory over them, ibid. Defeats the practices of the English parliament, with the army of Ireland, 215. Is created a marquis, 216. Declines the post of lord-lieutenant, 223. His first treaty with the confederate Irish, 224. They become more tractable, 226. A meeting appointed at Trim, ibid. Progress of the marquis's treaty, displeasing to the lords justices, ibid. Takes the command of an expedition proposed by them, ibid. Drives the rebels from several of the places they had occupied, 227.

Forms

INDEX.

Forms the siege of Rofs, ibid. Obliged to retreat, ibid. On the point of failing by the neglect or treachery of the juftices, he is happily refcued from deftruction, 288. Seizes the advantage given him, ibid. Gains a complete victory, ibid. Tranfmits a remonftrance to the king, 231. Ordered by the king to treat about a temporary ceffation of arms with the rebels, 233. Proceeds to a treaty with the confederate Irifh, 235. His cautious behaviour, 237. He is difgufted with the pride of the Irifh agents, 238. Sufpends his negociations, ibid. Endeavours to bring Prefton to an engagement, but in vain, ibid. Created lord-lieutenant, 249. Embarraffed by the Scotch, and by the Irifh, 250. Attempts to break the Irifh confederates, 255. Privately folicited by the Irifh confederates at Kilkenny, to accept the fupreme command of all their forces, 260. Required by them at the fame time, to proclaim the Scots rebels, in confequence of their outrageous infringement of the ceffation, ibid. He finds a way to amufe them, 261. Embarraffed by a commiffion he receives from the king, 272. Commences his treaty with the confederates, 274. Cautioufly determines to lay the propofitions made, and the anfwers returned, before the king. 276. Grows impatient at his fituation, 279. Petitions to be removed from his government, ibid. Renews the treaty with the Irifh confederates, 283. Privately directed to fufpend the execution of any fentence againft the earl of Glamorgan, 317. Concludes a treaty with the Irifh confederates, 323. His cautious and fpirited fpeech to lord Mufkerry, 326. Receives intelligence of the king's having refigned himfelf to the Scottifh army, 329. Concludes a peace with the confederates, 331. Is invited to Kilkenny, by them, 338. Is received there with joy, ibid. Is informed that O'Nial and Prefton are on their march to cut off his retreat, 339. He regains the capital, 340. Makes preparations againft the fiege of Dublin, 342. Treats with the Englifh parliament, 343. His negociations with the parliament broken off, 349. He involves himfelf reluctantly in the engagements of the earl of Clanricarde, ibid. Sufpects Prefton, and defpifes him, 350. Renews his treaty with the parliament, 354. Engages to deliver up Dublin, and all the king's garrifons, &c. &c. 356. Leaves the regalia to be delivered to the commiffioners appointed by the parliament, and embarks for England, 359. Prefents himfelf before the king at Hampton-court, iv. 11. Advifes the queen and prince to return a general and gracious anfwer to the Irifh agents, 12. Arrives at Cork, 22. Treats with the general affembly at Kilkenny, 23. Oppofed by the clergy, 24. His treaty interrupted, 25. Concluded, 26. Makes application to O'Nial, Coote, and Jones, 31. His diftreffes and difappointments, ibid. Takes the field, 34. Advances againft Dublin, 37. Urges the king, (Charles II.) to repair to Ireland, 47. Makes preparations to oppofe Cromwell, 50. Is obliged to retire gradually to the city of Kilkenny, 51. His troops refufed admittance by feveral cities, 54. He is unable to perfuade the magiftrates of Waterford to grant his troops a free paffage through their city, ibid. Obliged to difmifs his forces, ibid. His conduct, 55. Provoked at the ingratitude which he meets with, he defires the king's permiffion to retire from Ireland, 57. Attempts to relieve Clonmel, 60. Per-

INDEX.

So. Permits the northern catholics to elect a general in the place of Owen O'Nial, 63. Tries, but in vain, to prevail on the citizens of Limerick to receive a garrison, 64. He applies to the clergy, ibid. Finds them factious and infidious, 66. Threatens to withdraw himself from Ireland, 67. Pressed by the alarmed nobility not to carry his design into execution, 68. Encouraged by some promising appearances, he suspends his purpose of embarking, ibid. Is invited by the magistrates of Limerick to honour them with a visit, and to regulate the garrison, ibid. Is excluded by a tumult, 69. Traduced by the clergy, 70. Required by them to leave the kingdom, 71. Makes propositions to the commissioners of trust, 76. Retires to France, 77. Appointed lord lieutenant of Ireland, 131. Receives from the Irish parliament the sum of thirty thousand pounds, 134. Gives the royal assent to the bill of settlement, with some others, ibid. Called to England, 142. His prudent behaviour, 156. Encourages manufactures, 157. Is undermined by his enemies, in England, 159. Repairs to the English court, 161. Enjoys the utmost degree of popularity, notwithstanding his disgrace, 179. Is suddenly restored to favour, 181. And to the government of Ireland, ibid. His administration, 182. His measures for the security of his government, 183. He is censured by lord Shaftesbury in the house of lords, 189. His removal attempted, ibid. He is recalled to England, 194. Suddenly removed, 198.

Ossory, earl of, (in the reign of Henry VIII.) hostilities against him, ii. 176.

Oxford, an important scene of Irish negociation, iii. 262. A bill brought in for a perpetual prohibition of importing all cattle from Ireland, in the parliament held there, iv. 150. Its effects on Ireland, 151.

————, earl of, created marquis of Dublin, i. 396. Invested with the dominion of Ireland, ibid. Supplied with money and forces, 396, 397. Marches in a stately progress to take possession of his Irish sovereignty, 397. Returns to London, ibid. Is created duke of Ireland, ibid. His disgrace, defeat, and flight, 398. His lordship of Ireland resumed, ibid.

P

PARSONS, sir William, receives information of a conspiracy, from Owen O'Connolly, iii. 126. Prejudiced against his appearance, ibid. Removed from his government, 233. Imprisoned, 239.

Pelham, sir William, chose by the council at Dublin, chief governour, ii. 334. Makes provisions for a vigorous renewal of the war in Munster, ibid. Receives an insolent message from the earl of Desmond, 236.

Pembroke, earl of, Ireland deprived of an useful and powerful patron, by his death, i. 243.

Pendergast, Maurice, revolts to the Ossorians, i. 34. His dangerous escape, 35.

Perrot, sir John, appointed lord-deputy, ii. 356. Principal object of his administration, ibid. His success in Connaught, ibid. His

progress

INDEX.

progress to the South interrupted, 357. His successful practices with the Irish, in Ulster, 358. His extensive schemes for the improvement of Ireland, 359. Regulates the province of Ulster, 362. Attacked by secret enemies, 363. His indiscretion, ibid. He is mortified by the queen, 365. He solicits to be recalled, ibid. Continues to administer his government with fidelity and success, ibid. Disapproves of sir Richard Bingham's conduct, 369. Marches into the West contrary to his instructions, 370. Resigns his government, 378.

Pole, cardinal, his bull received by the Irish parliament, ii. 255.

Poynings, sir Edward, arrives in Ireland, to assume the office of vicegerent, ii. 119. Objects of his administration, 120. Takes the field, 121. Prepossessed against the earl of Kildare, ibid. Alarmed, 122. Summons a parliament, ibid. His law, 141.

Plunket, Oliver, (the popish bishop of Armagh) tried, condemned, and executed, iv. 193.

Preston, colonel Thomas, arrives at Wexford, with his forces, iii. 207. Cautiously retires before the marquis of Ormond, to avoid an engagement, 238. Yields to the instances of Rinuncini, 304. Professes to be devoted to his service, ibid. Executes his order, ibid. Resents his partiality to Owen O'Nial, 344. Commences a private treaty with lord Digby, ibid. His demand, 345. Behaves with indiscreet violence, 346. Negotiates with the earl of Clanricarde, 347. Receives a letter from the marquis or Ormond, 350. Consents to become the earl of Clanricarde's major-general, 351. Consults with the marquis of Ormond on the operations of war, ibid. Begins his march, 352. Terrified by the Nuncio's sentence of excommunication, ibid. Recalled from his petty expeditions into Leinster, to oppose the progress of lord Inchiquin, 354. Advances towards Dublin, by a forced march, iv. 4. Defeated at Dungan-Hill, ibid. Flies to Carlow with his horse, 5. Receives a mortifying order from the supreme council, ibid. Binds himself by a solemn oath to support the king's rights, and to obey his lord-lieutenant, 14. Takes vigorous measures to oppose Owen O'Nial, 17. Besieges Athlone, and reduces it, 18.

R

RANELAGH, lord, quits his government in vexation and despair, iii. 218. Hastens to Dublin, with a resolution to lay before the king, a full account of the distresses of his province, and the pernicious conduct of the justices, ibid. His design defeated, ibid. Accused as author of all the extremities which the troops had experienced in Connaught, ibid.

Rathmines, battle of, iv. 40.

Rinunccini, directed to hasten to Ireland, iii. 300. Arrives as nuncio, at Kilkenny, 303. His reception by the supreme council, ibid. His conferences with the earl of Glamorgan, 304. His objections to the treaty of peace, 305. He practises with the popish bishops, 306. He obtains new concessions from Glamorgan, ibid. His zeal and artifice in opposition to the peace, 317. Opposes the peace after its ratification and proclamation, 332. Excommunicates the adherents

of

INDEX.

of the peace, 336. His entrance into Kilkenny, 340. He imprisons the members of the supreme council, ibid. He appoints a new council, ibid. His vain expectations, 341. His intemperate behaviour in the general assembly summoned to Kilkenny, iv. 9. Opposes the cessation which he had himself recommended, 15. Thunders his sentence of excommunication against all those who contrived or favoured it, 16. Declares war (with O'Nial) against the supreme council, 18. Is driven to Galway, ibid. Admonished to depart from the kingdom, 22. His consternation and flight, 88.

Roberts, lord, appointed lord lieutenant of Ireland, iv. 162. His character and conduct, 163.

Rochester, earl of, appointed lord lieutenant of Ireland, iv. 198.

Rokeby, sir Thomas, assumes the reins of government in Ireland, with an equity and integrity unknown to many of his predecessors, i. 368. Removed, 369. Restored, ibid.

Rosen, mareschal, his barbarity at the siege of Derry, iv. 251. His speech to king James, 277.

Ross, surrendered to Cromwell, iii. 50.

Russel, sir William, appointed lord deputy, in the room of sir William Fitzwilliam, ii. 403. Amused by Tyrone, ibid.

S

ST. JOHN, Oliver, his administration odious, ii. 540. Recalled and rewarded, 542.

St. Leger, sir Anthony, appointed lord deputy, and sent to Ireland, ii. 232. Suddenly removed, 238. Again entrusted with the government of Ireland, 251.

St. Ruth, lands as chief commander of the French forces, iv. 327. Resolves on a defensive war, ibid. Takes his station behind Athlone, ibid. Betrays a carelessness and confidence unworthy of a commander, 333. Retires in vexation, 334. Resolves to wait the approach of the English army, 337. Draws his main army in front of his camp, 338. Is killed by a cannon ball, 341.

Saunders, a celebrated English ecclesiastic, for his zeal against queen Elizabeth, invested with the dignity of legate, ii. 324.

Schomberg, duke of, lands at Bangor, in the county of Downe, iv. 272. Lays siege to Carricfergus, ibid. Takes it, ibid. Advances, ibid. Encamps at Dundalk, 275. His distresses, 276. Declines a battle with James, ibid. Conspiracy in his camp, 277. He is reinforced, 279. Decamps, removes his sick, and retires to winter-quarters, 279. Furnishes his frontier garrisons with stores, 285. Endeavours to dissuade the prince of Orange from passing the Boyne, 292. In vain, ibid. Retires in disgust, ibid. Is slain by his own men, 296.

Shaftesbury, lord, censures the duke of Ormond, in the house of lords, iv. 189. Disappointed, 190.

Shrewsbury, earl of, sent into Ireland to take the administration of government, ii. 32. An account of his administration, 33, 34.

Simnel, Lambert, assumes the title of duke of York, ii. 89. Is commanded to personate the earl of Warwick, ibid. Arrives at Dublin,

INDEX.

lin, 91. Is received by the lord deputy, and favoured by all the Yorkists, ibid. Is acknowledged and proclaimed king, 92. Is opposed by the Butlers, and the city of Waterford, ibid. Assisted by the duchess of Burgundy, 94. Animated by the arrival of troops from Flanders, 96. Crowned, 97. Convenes a parliament, ibid. With difficulty contrives to maintain his household, 99. Finds it necessary to change the scene, ibid. Is attended into England by a great number of partizans, 100. Comes to an engagement with king Henry, at Stoke, 101. Is bravely supported by the valour of the Irish forces, ibid. Taken prisoner, 102. Consigned by the king to the menial offices of his kitchen, ibid.

Skeffington, sir William, appointed deputy to the duke of Richmond, ii. 165. His instructions, ibid. Made lord deputy, 179. His inactivity, 180. His cruelty, 181. His death, 184.

Sorleboy, an old Scottish chieftain, his answer to the insult of an Englishman on the death of his son, ii. 363.

Strongbow, Richard, earl of Chepstow, generally called so for his extraordinary feats of archery, enters into a covenant with Dermod king of Leinster, to assist him with a considerable force, i. 23. Receives a new application from him, 50. Discovered by Henry, he prepares for an expedition into Ireland, 51. Lands at Waterford, 54. Marries Eva the daughter of Dermod, 55. Marches to Dublin, ibid. Invested with the lordship of that city, 58. Alarms the king by his progress, 62. Is reduced to the utmost difficulties, 68. Summons a council of war, ibid. Enters into a treaty with Roderic O'Connor, ibid. Marches to Wexford, 72. Is attacked at Hidrone, 73. Desists from his attempt to relieve Fitz-Stephen, 74. Goes to Waterford, ibid. Meditates an invasion of Ossory, 75. Exercises a royal sovereignty in Leinster, 65. Is summoned to appear before king Henry, 77. Obeys the mandate, ibid. Meets the king near Gloucester, ibid. Restored to favour, ibid. Recalled from Ireland, 111. Appointed chief governour of Ireland, 112. Appoints Raymond le Gross general, 114. Gives his sister Basilia, in marriage to him, 120. Is in a distressful situation, 127. Dies in Dublin after a tedious indisposition, 130.

Stukely, Thomas, an adventurer, contrives to insinuate himself into the affections of sir Henry Sydney, ii. 323. Reviles the queen, Elizabeth, and flies to the continent, ibid. Arrives at Rome, and is caressed by the Irish catholics, ibid. Embarks with a body of eight hundred Italians, (to be paid by Philip king of Spain) for Ireland, 324. Arrives in Portugal, 325. Is killed there in battle, 326.

Surrey, Thomas, earl of, created lord lieutenant of Ireland, ii. 153. His conduct and success, 154. His advice to the king, 157. Expresses his desire to be recalled, 158. Appointed to command the forces destined to invade France, ibid. Returns to England, with the prayers and acclamations of all the Irish subjects, ibid.

Sussex, Fitz-Walter, earl of, succeeds Saint Leger as lord deputy, ii. 252. Obliged to march against the insurgents, 253. Defeats them, ibid. Recalled, 263. Marches into Thomond, on his return, to repress the violences of Daniel O'Brien, 264. Considered by

INDEX.

queen Elizabeth, on her accession, as a meritorious governor, 266. Marches against John O'Nial, 276. Concludes a treaty with him, 277. Defends the Pale against him, 280.

Sydney, sir Henry, marches northward, as chief governour in the absence of the earl of Sussex, to terrify John O'Nial, ii. 276. Has a conference with him, ibid. Made chief governour, 280. Attends at Dundalk, agreeably to the desire of O'Nial, for a conference, 282. Again obeys his invitation, 283. Marches into Tirowen, 287. Reprimanded by the queen for neglecting to controul the insolence of the earl of Desmond, 290. Seizes him by surprize, and conveys him prisoner to Dublin, ibid. Makes a progress through the southern and western provinces, 305. Permitted to return to England, 307. Returns to his goverment, 313. His regulations, 314. A shade of popular odium cast on his administration, 316. Occasions a general discontent by a bold act of government, 317. Again reprimanded by the queen, 320. Grows weary of his situation, 322. Earnestly solicits to be recalled, ibid. Permitted to resign the government of Ireland, 326.

T

TALBOT, colonel Richard, chosen by the Irish catholics their advocate, iv. 129. Employed to expostulate with the duke of Ormond, to whom they imputed the king's intentions against them, 131. Expostulates indecently and intemperately with him, ibid. Is committed to the Tower, and released only on a humble submission, ibid.

————, Peter, brother to Richard, his insolent behaviour, iv. 171. Proposes to celebrate mass in Dublin with extraordinary splendor, ibid. Seized for being engaged in the popish plot, 184. Removed from his brother's seat in the neighbourhood of Dublin into the Castle, ibid.

Temple, sir John, his stratagem for supplying Dublin with provisions, iii. 131.

Tirlough, Lynnogh, an old Irish chieftain, expresses his uneasiness at his new habiliments, ii. 375.

Tirone, earl of, suspected of having entered into a treaty with the Spaniards, ii. 379. Repairs to England, and, with an affectation of loyalty, renews his assurances of attachment and fidelity to queen Elizabeth, 381. Gives one of his daughters in marriage to the young chieftain of Tirconnel, 386. Condemns Hugh Ne Gavelock, to die by the hand of the executioner, ibid. His artful behaviour, his conduct suspicious, 399. Accused by sir Henry Bagnal, 400. His affected loyalty, 401. He provokes his countrymen, 402. Assumes the title of the O'Nial, ibid. Amuses sir William Russel, 403. His hostilities, 405. His danger and address, 406. His affected submission, 410. Renews his professions of submission, 411. His insolence, 413. Confers with the earl of Ormond, 419. Comes to an accommodation, 420. Renews hostilities, 422. Gains a victory over sir Henry Bagnal, 423. Desires a parley with the earl of Essex, 435. Has a conference with him, 436. Agrees to a truce, 437. Receives

a

INDEX.

a present from the pope, 440. Breaks the truce, ibid. Foiled in Munster by the earl of Ormond, 445. Escapes from lord Mountjoy, 449. And gains the northern quarters, ibid. Harrassed, distressed, and deserted, 454. His scheme for completely reducing the besiegers of Kinsale, 479. Urged by Don Juan to an engagement, ibid. Advances reluctantly against the English camp, 481. Is discomfited, ibid. Flies, with the wretched remains of his followers, and conceals himself in his own territory, ibid. Sues for mercy, 482. His overtures are accepted, ibid. Concludes a treaty with lord Mountjoy, 481. Makes the most humiliating submissions to him, 488. Renews his submission to king James on his accession, ibid. Confirmed in his honours and possessions, 490. His conspiracy and flight, 497.

Tuam, the popish archbishop of, defeated in his attempt to expel the British garrison from Sligo, iii. 308. His forces vigorously attacked and routed, ibid. He is slain in the action, ibid.

Tyrconnel, Talbot, earl of, arrives in Ireland, iv. 213. Models the army, ibid. His insolence and meanness, 214. His schemes, 215. Assisted by Nagle, an able and acute lawyer, 216. Appointed successor to lord Clarendon, 217. His character, ibid. His removal attempted, 224. He meets the king at Chester, ibid. His design against the act of settlement, 226. His agents insulted in London, ibid. His terror and artifice, 235. Is practised with secretly by the prince of Orange, 237. Created a duke by king James, 243.

U

UFFORD, sir Ralph, his administration, i. 362. His rigorous treatment of the great factious lords, 363. Summons the earl of Desmond to attend a parliament in Dublin, ibid. Marches into Munster, and possesses himself of the earl's lands, ibid. Dies suddenly. 364.

Vivian, the pope's legate, his arrival in Ireland, i. 134.

Ulster, Richard, earl of, envies and opposes Gaveston the chief governour, i. 308. Receives an honourable mark of king Edward's confidence, 309. Quarrels with the Giraldines, 310. Is defeated and made prisoner, ibid. Obliged to submit to such terms as the conquerors imposed, ibid. Is summoned to parliament in England, 313. Undertakes the war against the Scots, 315. Is joined by Fedlim O'Connor, ibid. Retires before the Scots, 318. Retires to the walls of Dublin, 322. Is seized and imprisoned, ibid. Released from his confinement, 324.

Usher, doctor James, entrusted with the compilation of articles of religion, ii. 537. His profession adopted by the convocation, and ratified by the lord deputy, ibid. He is promoted to the see of Meath ib. He exasperates the recusants by his unpopular doctrine, 538.

W

WALKER, George, a clergyman of Yorkshire, zealous and indefatigable in the defence of law, liberty, and religion, iv. 244. Chosen one of the new governours by the garrison of Derry, 247. A remarkable

INDEX.

able and spirited speech of his, 248. He is killed in the battle of the Boyne, 295.

Waller, sir Hardress, a dangerous opponent to the convention, iv. 108. A determined enemy to monarchy, ibid. Averse to every thing tending to a restoration, ibid. Mixes with the council of officers at Dublin, ibid. His artful behaviour, ibid. He is disappointed, ibid. Reduced and sent prisoner, to England, 109.

Waller, archbishop of Dublin substituted in the room of the earl of Kildare, as deputy to the duke of Bedford, ii. 110. Convenes his parliament, 111. Attends on the king, and is received with favour, 114. A striking instance of his simplicity, 115.

Wandesford, lord deputy, perplexed and intimidated, iii. 71. His sudden death, 72.

Warbeck, Perkin, arrives at Cork, ii. 112. Is supported by the earl of Desmond, 113. Is suddenly called into France, ibid. Makes a second attempt on Ireland, 131. Is supported openly by the earl of Desmond, ibid. Besieges Waterford, ibid. Retires to the king of Scots, ibid.

Wentworth, Thomas, lord viscount, appointed chief governour of Ireland, iii. 9. His address in procuring a voluntary subsidy from the Irish, 10. His arrival in Ireland, ibid. His dispositions and principles, 13, 14. He disgusts the privy council, ibid. Gains a continuance of the voluntary subsidy, 16. Undertakes to manage the parliament, 17. His object and measures, ibid. His protest, 24. He refuses to confirm the graces, 26. Supports the clergy, 31. His care of the university, ibid. His scheme for improving the revenue, 33. His administration odious, 38. His insolence and rigour, 39. Repairs to England, 43. His administration approved by the king, 44. Returns to Ireland, ibid. Is still odious and arbitrary, 45. His contest with lord chancellor Loftus, ibid. Merits of his administration, 46. Alarmed by the insurrections of Scotland, 51. He imposes an engagement on the Ulster Scots, ibid. Supplies the king with money and soldiers, 52. Defeats the attempts of the earl of Argyle, ibid. Disapproves the earl of Antrim's project, 55. Recalled to England, 56. Created earl of Strafford, ibid. And knight of the garter, ibid. Returns to Dublin, 57. Meets a parliament, ibid. Returns to England, 60. Makes preparation for his return to Ireland, 66. He is impeached, 72. Act of attainder past against him, 84.

William, prince of Orange, his enterprize, iv. 228. His concise and phlegmatic reply to a formal address of the protestant subjects of Ireland, 237. Sends Richard Hamilton, a popish general, to practise with the earl of Tyrconnel, ibid. Resolves to undertake the Irish war, 281. Lands at Carricfergus, 286. Advances southward, 287. Encamps near the river Boyne, 290. Is wounded, 291. Resolves to pass the river, 292. Defeats James's army, 298. Advances towards the capital, 299. Encamps at Finglass, near Dublin, 303. Publishes a declaration, calculated to detach the lower order of subjects from their leaders, 304. Reduces Waterford and Duncannon, 306. His anxieties, ibid. Resolving to depart he returns to Chapel-Izod, ibid. He is diverted from his intentions, and joins the army, 307. Besieges Limerick,

INDEX.

Limerick, 310. Meets with a vigorous resistance from the garrison, 311. Raises the siege, 314, and embarks for England, 316.

Willoughby, sir Francis, governour of the fort of Galway, arrives at Dublin at a critical juncture, iii. 127. His advice, 128. It is obeyed, ibid. He is appointed to the custody both of the castle and the city, ibid.

Wogan, sir John, his parliament, i. 297. Its statutes, 298.

Wolsey, cardinal, displeased with the earl of Kildare, ii. 152. His advice for the administration of Irish government, 154.

Worcester, Tiptoft, earl of, made lord deputy of Ireland, ii. 64. With the most honourable and extensive powers, ibid. Provoked and alarmed, 65.

Y

York, duke of, defeated at Bloreheath, ii. 48. Flies into Ireland, ibid. Finds the subjects and parliament of Ireland zealous for his support, 49. Returns to England on the victory of Northampton, 51. Is attended by the Methians, and others in Ireland, ibid. Is defeated and slain at Wakefield, 52.

FINIS.

www.ingramcontent.com/pod-product-compliance
Lightning Source LLC
Chambersburg PA
CBHW030545300426
44111CB00009B/867